The Education of Nations

The Education
of Nations

How the Political Organization of the Poor, Not
Democracy, Led Governments to Invest
in Mass Education

STEPHEN KOSACK

OXFORD
UNIVERSITY PRESS

OXFORD
UNIVERSITY PRESS

Oxford University Press is a department of the University of Oxford.
It furthers the University's objective of excellence in research,
scholarship, and education by publishing worldwide.

Oxford   New York
Auckland   Cape Town   Dar es Salaam   Hong Kong   Karachi
Kuala Lumpur   Madrid   Melbourne   Mexico City   Nairobi
New Delhi   Shanghai   Taipei   Toronto

With offices in
Argentina   Austria   Brazil   Chile   Czech Republic   France   Greece
Guatemala   Hungary   Italy   Japan   Poland   Portugal   Singapore
South Korea   Switzerland   Thailand   Turkey   Ukraine   Vietnam

Published in the United States of America by Oxford University Press
198 Madison Avenue, New York, NY 10016

www.oup.com

Oxford is a registered trade mark of Oxford University Press in the UK and certain other countries.

Library of Congress Cataloging-in-Publication Data
Kosack, Stephen, 1978–
The education of nations : how the political organization of the poor, not democracy,
led governments to invest in mass education / Stephen Kosack.
     p.   cm.
Includes bibliographical references and index.
ISBN 978-0-19-984165-3 (cloth)—ISBN 978-0-19-984167-7 (pbk.)
1. Education and state—Developing countries—Cross-cultural studies.
2. Education—Economic aspects—Developing countries—Cross-cultural studies.
3. Poor—Education—Developing
countries—Cross-cultural studies. I. Title.
LC98.K67   2012
370.9172'4—dc23   2011040212

9 8 7 6 5 4 3 2 1

Printed in the United States of America
on acid-free paper

TABLE OF CONTENTS

PREFACE: MASS EDUCATION THAT SHOULD NOT BE

This is not the book I expected to write. Several years ago, when I started to research its central question—when will a government serve poor citizens, in particular by investing in their education?—I was confident that I already had an important part of the answer: leaders have the incentive to serve the poor when they are democratically elected. For my generation of political scientists studying policymaking in the developing world, it has been an article of faith that democracies outperform autocracies in serving poor citizens. No wonder: although leaders come to office with many motivations, in order to *stay* in office they must first satisfy those citizens who, if unsatisfied, could remove them from office. Democratic institutions give this power to the whole citizenry, or at least those with the franchise. Because poor voters always outnumber rich, democratically elected leaders should reliably be relatively more inclined than autocratic leaders to serve poor citizens. There also appeared to be good empirical evidence of this inclination. Few studies had directly traced changes in regime type to changes in education policymaking, and those that did looked only at single cases.[1] But several studies had found a convincing cross-national correlation between regime type and various measures of pro-poor education.[2]

Thus I had little doubt that if I looked over long periods in diverse settings, I would see that education policy would turn systematically more pro-poor when the government turned from autocratic to democratic, and systematically more elitist when it turned from democratic to autocratic. That is not what I found. In this book I examine a half-century of government action in education in Ghana, Taiwan, and Brazil, three countries I chose because they vary widely on dimensions often thought to affect education policymaking—culture, geography, level of economic development—and, most important, have all been through transitions between democracy and autocracy. These transitions mattered little. That is, if mass education depended on democratic incentives, most of the expansion of mass education in these three countries would not have happened.

A telling example is early Ghana. In 1951, Ghana was still the British Gold Coast. But in that year the British, who were slowly warming to the idea of Gold

Coast independence, ceded control over education policymaking to a new government of Ghanaians. At the time, out of the approximately 1.3 million children in the Gold Coast aged 5 to 14, just 140,000 were in primary school. Only 4 percent of Gold Coast residents had ever attended school. The new Ghanaian government set out to change this. It built almost 5,000 primary schools, particularly in rural areas, and abolished tuition fees at primary school. It opened dozens of training centers and consciously paid teachers *more* than they could earn in professions demanding similar qualifications. In January 1952, more than 110,000 children began primary school—more than twice as many as in the previous year. After Ghana gained its independence in 1957, the government accelerated its efforts, and by 1966 it was providing quality primary education to more than 1.1 million students—an increase of almost 800 percent in just 15 years. In these years the government put, on average, almost half its education budget into primary schools, a relative commitment it would not reach again until the 1990s. The reward was remarkable student achievement even as enrollment soared. Only in 2002 did average Ghanaian math scores return to their 1960 level; English scores have never rebounded.[3]

Why did Ghana's government expand mass education with such zeal? As I wrestled with this question, familiar explanations were not much help. It was not Ghana's colonial inheritance; as mentioned, the British invested little in Ghanaian education. It was not that Ghana's economy needed huge numbers of skilled workers. On the contrary, throughout this era, Ghana's economic policymakers struggled in vain to provide jobs for all the new graduates the education system was generating, not the other way around. It was not that Ghanaian culture had a traditional reverence for education; in fact, just a few decades prior to its independence many Ghanaians saw formal schooling as a foreign import of little practical use. In 1876, commenting on missionary efforts to educate Ghanaians, the Asantehene, the king of the Asantes, Ghana's dominant ethnic group, remarked, "Ashantee children have better work to do than to sit down all day idly to learn hoy. They have to fan their parents, and do other work which is better."[4]

And it was not that Ghana was democratic. It was not. Almost as soon as Ghana gained independence, the ruling Convention People's Party (CPP) banned its opponents' political parties. In 1958, the party gave itself the power to detain anyone of Prime Minister Kwame Nkrumah's choosing for up to five years without trial, and subsequently locked up its political opponents by the hundreds, if not thousands—no one is sure of the exact figure. In 1960, the CPP declared Ghana a Republic, itself the sole political organization in the state, and Kwame Nkrumah president-for-life. No cross-national measures of regime type, such as the widely-used Polity measure or the measures by Adam Przeworski and his colleagues, classify Ghana as a democracy during this period. Yet despite lacking democratic incentives, Ghana's government went to extraordinary lengths to expand quality mass education.

In fact, the more I examined education policymaking across Ghana, Taiwan, and Brazil, the less it seemed that democratic incentives had anything to do with government efforts to expand mass education. In all three, the first indigenous governments to expand mass education were autocratic. In Brazil, the initial expansion continued through a transition to democracy, but in Ghana, later democratic governments systematically made education more elitist. In Brazil, education policy changed in only minor ways through a transition to democracy in the 1980s; in Ghana it took another autocratic government before Ghanaian education became systematically pro-poor again. Taiwan remained autocratic into the 1990s; during that time, education policy turned elitist, and then pro-poor again a decade before Taiwan became democratic.

Something else was clearly driving mass education. The puzzle drove me back to a more fundamental question of political economy: what makes poor citizens important to a government's survival? In this book, I offer the start of an answer—one that can explain the expansion of mass education over long periods in three very different developing countries, and may be of help in understanding policymaking variation in other developing countries and in other policy areas. Rather than focusing on whether the country is democratic, I offer evidence that the important dynamic is mass organization aided by political leadership. In brief, a government serves the poor—including providing them the opportunity to become educated—when a political leader creates organizational structures that help the poor to act collectively, to support a government that is acting in their interest or to oppose one that is not. In other words, democracy is no substitute for the hard work of political organizing that leverages numbers into political power and makes poor citizens a force to be reckoned with—either a capable supporter of a pro-poor government or a credible threat to an elitist government.

In one sense, this is not a surprising contention. Organizational dynamics are the centerpiece of much of the scholarship about policymaking in developed democracies. A scholar of American or European politics could not make a credible case that policymaking variation stemmed from variation in formal political institutions without first showing that collective action was either irrelevant or was fundamentally conditioned by formal institutions. Yet when Western scholars turn their attention to policymaking in the developing world—where regime type and its associated rules for selecting leaders are, if anything, weaker and more fluid than they are in the developed world—they have usually devoted their attention almost exclusively to regime type. (I am explicitly distinguishing work on *policymaking* from work on politics more broadly in the developing world, such as work on social movements, revolutions, and political development; in these works, collective action has long played a central role.) There are exceptions, such as Bates (1981), Rogowski (1989), and Waldner (1999)—and, not coincidentally, these works are also among the more successful at explaining policymaking variation in developing countries. But recently, the most influential scholarship on policymaking in developing countries has focused on formal regime institutions with surprisingly conscious intensity. This is true both of notable works such as Acemoglu and Robinson (2005) and Bueno de Mesquita et al. (2003), which examine distributive policymaking in general, as well as of the growing body of scholarship specifically about education policymaking in developing countries. This scholarly focus persists despite new evidence that cross-national correlations between regime type and distributive policymaking may be largely spurious.[5] And it feeds a sense among scholars, not to mention the general public, that poor citizens wishing for a government that is responsive to their material needs should seek democracy, and that once they have it, they can relax, secure in the knowledge that the institutions of democracy will keep government largesse flowing their way.

I hope that the evidence I offer here casts some doubt on the usefulness of regime type as a reliable guide to policymaking in the developing world. It is impossible to deny that democracy, among its many qualities, does create incentives for leaders to serve the poor. The logic with which I opened this preface is not wrong; rather, the problem is that it is myopic. Those incentives are weaker than the incentives of leaders of all governments—autocratic and democratic, of developed and developing countries—to serve those who are organized. In this book I show that the latter incentive was far more powerful in Ghana, Taiwan, and Brazil.

I also hope this scholarly critique serves a more positive purpose: the notion that variation in distributive policymaking, and particularly in education policymaking, *can* be understood, with relative parsimony, as driven by systematic, observable phenomena. This is not how education policymaking is generally considered outside of political science; instead, both inside and outside the academy, discussions of education policy tend to be normative. The focus is on what education policy *should* be: what policy would most increase economic growth, help children reach their potential, advance the progress of human civilization, or meet some other normative goal. When that goal is not met, those advocating it turn their attention naturally to politics. But because the discussions began in a normative frame, the subsequent political analysis is often normative as well: either it assumes away underperformance[6] or blames it on insufficient "political will," the ignorance of policymakers, or the poor state of the knowledge on which policymakers rely. Writers as diverse as Sun Yat-Sen, Adam Smith, Karl Marx, John Stuart Mill, and Isaiah Berlin have written compellingly of the government's moral duty in education; the obvious corollary is that political leaders who make inadequate education policies are failing on a moral dimension. Scholars, particularly of education and economics, generally respond by devoting themselves to providing policymakers with an ever-expanding set of aspirational analyses of what policies policymakers should choose, and urging them to listen. The implication is that education policy would be better if only leaders *got it*, had stronger wills, or were better people.

While there is value in improving education policy options and communicating them to policymakers, it is not helpful to think that policymakers choose suboptimal education policies when they do not want or know about better options. The normative view attributes too much agency to political leaders. If leaders were free to pursue policies of their choosing, then, perhaps, their policy choices could be explained by differences of political will, knowledge, or morality. But leaders are not free to choose what policies to pursue. They rule at the pleasure of a particular set of citizens—selected voting blocs or certain business elites, landowners, workers, or other economic, social, religious, or ethnic communities. There are some citizens and groups whose support a leader needs to stay in power, and some whose support he or she can govern without. Leaders must serve the former when making policy, or they soon will find themselves looking for other work. This is as true of education as any other policy arena with distributive consequences. Indeed, one of the reasons that education is generally examined with a normative lens is that its distributive consequences are substantial—among other things, an individual's education helps determine her earning power and potential for upward social mobility. These distributive consequences constrain a political leader. They mean that she cannot choose any education policy she wants; instead, she is generally free to select from among only those education policies whose main beneficiaries are those whose support she needs to continue governing. If those policies also serve goals like growth or social harmony, that is a happy coincidence.

Thus to understand education policy decisions requires answering two questions: Whose support do political leaders need to stay in power? And what sort of education do those citizens want? This book develops a framework for answering these two questions. Re-conceptualizing education policy decisions with this framework is my second goal for this book. I hope the framework is a useful guide to the systemic circumstances that lead governments to make the education policies they do.

I have incurred many debts in the long process of writing this book. The first task of field work is getting the money to do it. My first debts are therefore to the National Science Foundation, which supported me for three years with a Graduate Research Fellowship, and to Yale's MacMillan Center for International and Area Studies and Leitner Program in International and Comparative Political Economy, both of which provided generous grants to fund my field-work expenses. Once I completed the field work, a Leylan Dissertation-Writing Fellowship from Yale and a Research Fellowship from the Brookings Institution gave me two years to devote to writing what follows.

Often a researcher begins a project like this one already knowing a great deal about the areas to be studied. I chose instead to let the data select the countries for me. This helped me to select three countries well-suited to examining the strength of my framework relative to other common explanations. But it also meant that I was a stranger to each country and highly dependent on the generosity of Taiwanese, Ghanaians, and Brazilians, as well as on the constant support of my advisors at Yale, to tow me up a steep learning curve.

I began my field work, arbitrarily, with Taiwan. The generosity of Huang Min-hsiung gave me an institutional home in Taipei at the Institute for European and American Studies at Academia Sinica, whose scholars made me a part of their community. Frederick F. Chien helped me begin my interviewing by contacting on my behalf, and even setting up interviews for me with, former ministers, "manpower planning" officials, and several other important members of the Kuomintang. I am still overwhelmed by the generosity showed me by those I interviewed; often they spent two hours or more with me, tolerating my detailed questions as I built my understanding of the politics behind the education system's development. I'm particularly grateful to Chang Pei-chi, Chen Peiying, Ching-hsi Chang, Chiu Yu-bin, Fan Sun-lu, Hsu Li-the, Hsu Shui-the, Huang Yushi, Kuo Wei-fan, Lee Chung-Chi, Liou Ching-Tien, Mao Kao-wen, Shih Ying, and Wu Jin. Lin Jih-Wen, Chi Huang, and Chu Yun-han helped me understand Taiwan's politics, and Fan Yun arranged for me to present my preliminary work at National Taiwan University and even invited me to spend the Chinese New Year with her family. Chuing Prudence Chou spent hours discussing my findings with me. Emma Lee and Claire Wang provided me with excellent research assistance and help translating during interviews. And finally, Weitseng Chen helped me with the otherwise daunting task of find a short-term apartment in Taipei.

In Brazil, I spent my days at the Fundação Getúlio Vargas in São Paulo, where George Avelino gave me an institutional base and graduate students Marcelo Tyszler and Henrique Heidtmann were always willing to discuss ideas over the best coffee I've ever had. Early meetings with Paulo Renato de Souza, Eunice Ribeiro Durham, Maria Helena Guimarães de Castro, and Denisard Alves helped me begin to understand the complex world of Brazilian educational politics and economics and opened the doors to dozens more vital interviews with officials and academics who, as in Taiwan, overwhelmed me with the generosity with which they shared their abundant knowledge and scarce time. In São Paulo, I am especially grateful to Ladislau Dowbor, Moacir Gadotti, Bernadette Gatti, Guimar Namo de Mello, Rose Neubauer, Romualdo Portela de Oliveira, and José Marcelino Pinto; in Rio de Janeiro, my thanks go to Ricardo Barros Argelina Figueiredo, Creso Franco, Ruben Klein, Yvonne Maggie, Alberto de Mello e Souza, and Violeta Monteiro; and in Brasília, I am indebted to Jorge Abrahão, Isaura Belloni, Paulo Corbucci, Anamélia Lima Rocha Fernandes, Reynaldo Fernandez, Linda Goulart, Alberto Rodriguez, Antônio Carlos da Ressurreição Xavier, Sergei Soares, José Amaral Sobrinho, and Zuleide Araújo Teixeira. In Brasília I also had the good fortune to meet Bob Verhine, who later helped me arrange a trip to Salvador, where he shared his own immense store of knowledge of Brazilian education, let me use his office as a base, and helped me pack my schedule with invaluable meetings with Edivaldo Boaventura, Maurício Campos, Edilson Freire, Katia Siqueira de Freitas, Renata Procerpio, Alexandre Paupério, Celina Souza, Jansen Teixeira, and

Eraldo Tinoco—each of whom gave me several hours in which to pick their brains about Bahian education. Also in Salvador, Paulo A. Meyer M. Nascimento saved me from relying on my pitiful Portuguese by translating for free; on a day when Paulo couldn't make it, Eraldo Tinoco, the vice governor of Bahia, patiently endured my bungling. Finally, José Rodrigo Lima, Sabrina Cruz, Tatiana Tsuruta, and my São Paulo roommate Thiago Abreu made being in Brazil a joy.

In the last country, Ghana, my greatest debt is to one family: the Bostios. Kojo and Patricia Botsio offered me a room in their home in Legon, and they, Kojo's mother Ruth, and their son Ziko shared with me insights into Ghanaian politics and valuable memories of Kojo Botsio, Mr. Botsio's father and Ghana's first Minister of Education; later, Mrs. Botsio introduced me to many of the key figures whom I interviewed, and when I caught typhoid fever toward the end of my stay, she saw that I got excellent medical care and sat up nights with me to make sure my fever did not get too high. To this day I feel that I have a second family in the Botsios and a lifelong friend in Ziko—who I believe will one day be Ghana's president. As in Brazil and Taiwan, Ghanaians amazed me with their willingness to share their time and knowledge; I am especially grateful to Ivan Addae-Mensah, William Kofi Ahadzie, the late F. K. Buah, John Budu-Smith, Eunice Dapaah, Peter Darvas, J. S. Djangmah, Paul Effah, James K. Glover, Nancy Keteku, Nikoi Kotei, Henrietta Mensah-Bonsu, Judith Sawyer, and Anthony Yaw Baah for offering their experiences and knowledge of the development of Ghana's education system. Kwesi Jonah spent hours with me helping me to understand the power bases of Ghanaian governments, and at the University of Ghana, Ernest Aryeetey, Evans Aggrey-Darkoh, William Baah-Boateng, and A. Baah-Nuarkoh offered their expertise on Ghana's political economy. Officials at the Padmore Library in Accra, at the Ministry of Education, and especially at the library of the Ministry of Finance helped me over many days to track down and copy data and other official records on Ghanaian education. Finally, the Banful family in Legon took me in during a preliminary trip I took to Ghana, and welcomed me back to their home periodically for enjoyable visits throughout my stay.

Once I returned to the United States, my thinking was refined and enriched by conversations with a wide range of colleagues, many of whom spent some of their scarce free time reading earlier drafts. I am particularly grateful for the insights and thoughtful feedback I got from Dan Galvin, Katie Glassmyer, Lloyd Gruber, Jacob Hacker, Archon Fung, Tarek Masoud, Tom Pepinsky, Ken Shadlen, Richard Snyder, Avi Spiegel, and Jennifer Tobin, as well as seminar participants at Yale, Brown, Harvard, the Brookings Institution, and the London School of Economics. I would also like to thank my supportive editor at Oxford University Press, David McBride, and his assistant Caelyn Cobb.

My last and most important debt is to my advisors at Yale, where I began this project as a graduate student: Susan Rose-Ackerman, Gustav Ranis, and Frances Rosenbluth. Many advisors would at least be skeptical of a project of the geographic scope of this one; most would be too busy to offer the level of support I eventually needed once I realized what I had gotten myself into. Susan, Gus, and Frances took the opposite approach: they were behind me at every stage. They met with me constantly as I developed my theory and began to plan the field work, sharing their knowledge of the countries I selected and opening their rolodexes to help me make contacts. After I began the field work, they tolerated lengthy memos from me every few weeks on my progress, often commenting just days later on how my thinking was evolving and on what else I needed to do. And after I returned to the United States, they read through dozens of drafts of chapters, offering detailed comments and pushing me to clarify my thinking and condense the overwhelming amount of information I gathered. I am forever thankful for their support.

The Education of Nations

CHAPTER 1

The Two Roots of Mass Education

Mass education is one of sustainable development's most important ingredients. Education helps citizens raise their wages and productivity, allowing them to make use of new technologies and better manage their farms and businesses.[1] In turn, the entire economy benefits. There are few economic success stories in which mass education has not played a starring role, and the information age has only increased its importance. There is compelling evidence that when a developing country invests in its human development—education and health—it prepares itself for a virtuous cycle of growth as well as further human development, while those counties that seek growth without human development generally find themselves before long in a vicious cycle of low growth and low human development.[2]

But when will a government invest in mass education? In this book I argue that it is possible to answer this question, and even, to some extent, to predict such investments. The answer, furthermore, is uncomplicated: with just two systemic factors, it is possible to forecast whether a government will choose to focus its resources and effort on expanding quality mass education. These two factors are accurate predictors because they determine if investing in mass education is in leaders' self-interest: whether such investments will help the government stay in power or whether leaders are better off steering educational resources to more limited, elite-oriented education. Both factors are exogenous to education. And each is a sufficient condition: when it appears, the government can be expected shortly thereafter to shift its focus from elite to mass education.

But the key factors are not those that social scientists or the public typically look to when trying to understand government policymaking decisions. The government cannot be expected to invest in mass education when the economy needs it. Nor when the culture values it. Nor when its leaders or civil servants are particularly clever or civic-minded. Nor, most surprising for a political scientist, when its leaders are democratically elected. These factors are not irrelevant, but none is sufficient to induce a government to invest in mass education.

The first factor that *is* sufficient is a tight but flexible skilled labor market—employers facing a skilled labor crunch that they cannot alleviate with foreign skilled labor, and a flexible labor market, where skilled wages fall when the supply of skilled labor increases. The second factor that is sufficient is government engagement in "political entrepreneurship of the poor": subsidizing the otherwise prohibitive collective action costs that poor citizens face in becoming politically powerful, so that government leaders can rely on their support to stay in power. When either factor is present, it is in the government's self-interest to invest in mass education; when both are absent, it is not in the government's self-interest to invest in mass education. Governments can, of course, choose to ignore their self-interest and serve other goals, like economic growth, or can serve citizens whose support the government does not need to stay in power. But ignoring self-interest is risky, and governments that do are as common as corporations that ignore profit. In the three countries I examine in this book, when either factor was present, the government began shortly thereafter to invest heavily in mass education.

Why are political entrepreneurship of the poor and a tight but flexible labor market sufficient to make expanding mass education in the government's self-interest? This chapter outlines the reasons; the rest of the book develops them and shows that, over long periods, they have affected education policy similarly in Ghana, Taiwan, and Brazil, three countries that have little else in common.

First, however, I defend my contention that other plausible factors are insufficient to make mass education important to a government's survival.

1. Mass Education and the Market

Because education (human capital in this context) is a factor in production, economic models often assume that it operates on market principles. The most influential models in this tradition (e.g., Schultz 1961, 1963; Becker 1964; Findlay and Kierzkowski 1983) treat the economy's level of education as the aggregate of individual decisions: of employers to offer skilled workers higher wages, and of individuals to respond by investing in privately-held education capital.

There is ample microeconomic evidence that people view education to a great extent as an investment in their future earnings—as Shultz (1961, 2) put it, "people invest in themselves." But individual decisions are a poor guide to aggregate levels of education.[3] At root, the problem is constrained credit. As early as 1962, Milton Friedman recognized that education had too little value as collateral for banks to offer educational loans without a government guarantee (Friedman 1962). Thus even when a person can reasonably expect higher earnings tomorrow if he or she has an education, it is difficult for someone to borrow against those future earnings in order to buy education today. As a result, the only people who can invest in education are those with the current assets either to buy education or to use as collateral against an educational loan, and an economy in which only some people can afford education will generally find itself with an undersupply of skilled labor.

The way around this problem is government subsidy of education. The government can intervene to make up for what the private sector, because of constrained credit, lacks the incentive to provide. This rationale is a primary reason that education is typically a public charge. It is governments, not the private sector, that build most of the schools, hire most of the teachers, set most of the fees, and provide most of the aid or loans to offset the fees. Even education provided by the private sector, not the government, is provided only with the government's blessing, under the government's regulations, and often with substantial amounts of government money.

In theory, this government subsidy might exactly compensate for constrained credit markets for educational loans, enabling individuals to purchase education up to the point at which the present value of the wage premium for skilled labor is equal to the combined public and private resources needed to educate a worker (Findlay and Kierzkowski 1983). Indeed, early models assumed that a government would have the incentive to do exactly this. Because an undersupply of skilled labor would lead to high skilled-wage premia that would in turn threaten profits, businesses would pressure the government to step in and subsidize individual investments in education. In Arthur Lewis's classic dual-economy model (1954), he predicted:

> There may at any time be a shortage of skilled workers in any grade. . . . Skilled labour, however, is only a very temporary bottleneck in the sense that if capital is available for development, the capitalists or their government will soon provide the facilities for training more skilled people. (145)

There is truth in this: the skilled-labor needs of businesses are highly motivating to a government concerned with staying in power. But I provide evidence in later chapters that there are only limited conditions under which businesses will pressure the government to invest in mass education; in particular, skilled wages must be elastic to supply, and businesses must be facing a skilled labor crunch that they cannot alleviate with foreign skilled labor. Where these conditions are not present, governments will still provide limited and specific worker training to help businesses meet their skilled-labor needs, but not mass education—no matter how high the economic return to mass education.

Thus although governments are usually motivated by the skilled-labor demands of businesses, it does not follow that government interventions in education are economically optimal. In fact, government investments in education tend to go against economic logic. Consider, for example, educational enrollments and spending for the 1990s, which I present in Tables 1.1–1.3. While there is disagreement among economists on the specifics of an economically optimal investment

Table 1.1 **Education budget priorities, by region, for the 1990s**

		Proportion of the education budget that goes to:		
	GDP per capita	*Primary*	*Secondary*	*Tertiary*
South Asia	$528	53%	27%	21%
Sub-Saharan Africa	$879	49%	29%	22%
Eastern Europe and Central Asia	$2,640	43%	38%	19%
Latin America and Caribbean	$4,039	46%	31%	23%
East Asia and Pacific	$5,536	45%	36%	19%
Middle East and North Africa	$5,756	39%	44%	16%
OECD	$26,020	30%	45%	25%

Notes: Source: *World Development Indicators*. My calculations. GDP per capita is in constant 1995 US dollars.

in education, there is general agreement that the poorer a country is, the more it should focus its attention on primary education, where the economic returns are thought to be higher, and the less it should invest in higher education.[4] In the 1990s, this consensus was particularly widespread. Table 1.1 presents the average proportion of education budgets devoted to each level of education, by region, in the 1990s. Variation in primary and secondary spending is small, but it is in the right directions—primary is lower in wealthier regions, while secondary is higher. By contrast, there is almost no variation in the proportion of the budget devoted to tertiary education. This is the case even though tertiary enrollments vary enormously across the regions (Table 1.2): gross tertiary enrollment in OECD countries is almost 50 percent, while in South Asia it is barely five percent, and less than three percent in Sub-Saharan Africa.

This means that governments' *relative* commitments to their tertiary students vary enormously in exactly the opposite direction recommended by economic optimality. Table 1.3 again arranges regions by wealth, and shows for each the ratio of per-student spending at each level to the sum of per-student spending at each of the three levels.[5] This is equivalent to picking three average students out of the population—one primary student, one secondary, and one tertiary—and then taking one dollar out of the education budget and asking how much of that dollar is spent on each student's education. In South Asia in the 1990s, the tertiary student got more than 10 times more of that dollar than the primary student. Compare that to the OECD, where the budget values tertiary students less than twice as highly as primary students. Certainly it does cost a great deal more to educate a tertiary student than a primary student. This, however, makes the choice even more paradoxical: if the cost of providing a single student in a poor country with a university education is enough to teach many students to read and

Table 1.2   **Gross enrollment ratios, by region, for the 1990s**

	GDP per capita	Primary	Secondary	Tertiary
South Asia	$528	101%	43%	5%
Sub-Saharan Africa	$879	80%	25%	3%
Eastern Europe and Central Asia	$2,640	97%	84%	27%
Latin America and Caribbean	$4,039	105%	58%	19%
East Asia and Pacific	$5,536	106%	56%	15%
Middle East and North Africa	$5,756	92%	64%	16%
OECD	$26,020	103%	109%	47%

Notes: Source: *World Development Indicators.* My calculations. GDP per capita is in constant 1995 US dollars.

Table 1.3   **Relative Per-Student Spending, by Region, for the 1990s**

Region	GDP per capita	Proportion of one education dollar that goes to:		
		a Primary Student	a Secondary Student	a Tertiary Student
South Asia	$528.36	7.7%	10.4%	81.9%
Sub-Saharan Africa	$878.73	4.1%	10.0%	85.9%
Eastern Europe and Central Asia	$2,639.91	31.0%	22.4%	46.6%
Latin America and Caribbean	$4,039.14	15.3%	21.6%	63.0%
East Asia and Pacific	$5,535.80	17.6%	20.3%	62.1%
Middle East and North Africa	$5,755.99	17.4%	26.5%	56.0%
OECD	$26,019.55	24.3%	29.8%	45.9%

Notes: Source: *World Development Indicators.* My calculations. GDP per capita is in constant 1995 US dollars. Proportions are based on net enrollment for the primary and secondary levels and gross enrollment for the tertiary level. "Gross" enrollment is the ratio of total enrollment, regardless of age, to the population of the age group that officially corresponds to the level of education; "net" enrollment is the ratio of enrollment of only those in the age group that officially corresponds to the level of education to the population in that age group.

write, with far more benefits for the economy, why is more of the available money not spent on primary education?

The problem is that a government's motivation to provide businesses with the skilled labor they need is only one of its motivations in designing its education policy. Even in Taiwan, a country widely thought to have designed its education

system with an economic rationale, I provide evidence that educational investments have never followed government perceptions of what the economy needed.
The economy's needs are only a limited and contingent motivation for a government's educational investments.

2. Education and Culture

Thus a full accounting of government education policy must take account of the
government's other motivations. What are these? One potential motivation is
culture. Societies with high levels of education often come to regard education as
an integral part of their culture. Scholars of East Asia's spectacular recent development, in which high levels of education figured prominently, often credit the
spread of Confucian culture, which values learning, to China's neighbors over the
thousands of years preceding Asia's integration with the world economy (e.g., Dai
1989; Rozman 1991).[6] In the West, deferring gratification to become educated is
a part of Max Weber's Protestant Ethic (Weber 1952 [1904]). Then there are Mediterranean, Latin American, and African societies where there has traditionally
been less education—and thus, by this line of reasoning, have cultures that place
less value on education.[7]

Implicitly underpinning these cultural explanations is a political analysis: that
cultures in which education is highly valued have governments that invest in
education commensurately. In other words, Confucian and Protestant cultures
may have bequeathed Asian and Northern European politicians with the motivation to provide good education, while Mediterranean, African, and Latin American leaders lack that will because their cultures fail to value education as highly.
But this cultural analysis is not of much help in explaining patterns of educational investment. It is not the case that governments of cultures that allegedly
place higher value on education provide more resources to education than cultures that allegedly place less value on education. Two of the countries in this
book illustrate the point: the government of Ghana, a country in a region sup-
posedly low on cultural reverence for education, has spent less of its budget on
education than Taiwan, a country with strong Confucian traditions, in only four
years in the latter half of the twentieth century. Culture is also an unhelpful explanation for most of the features of education investment and policy: since culture changes slowly, over many generations, it is impossible to use culture to
explain the timing of educational commitments or anything about their nature.
Knowing that a culture values education also sheds no light on how a government decides to allocate the educational opportunity that it is creating: why it
decides to build schools of certain types in certain areas, how many resources it
chooses to offer them, or how much it decides to charge for access to them. Thus
it cannot explain why governments sometimes expand mass education and
sometimes restrict it.

3. Democracy

Another source of government motivation may be the demands of citizens. Since skilled workers generally earn more than unskilled, parents can be expected to want their children to become educated and to pressure the government for assistance.

In determining how citizen demands for education will incentivize a government, the key question is which citizens a government has incentives to serve. These will be the citizens whose demands for education subsidies the government has the most incentive to realize. The obvious place to begin looking for an answer is regime type, which *should* be a good predictor of which citizens a government will need to serve. Democratically elected governments should be more accountable than autocratic governments to poorer citizens because a democratically elected government needs the votes of a significant proportion of poor citizens to stay in office. In any country with the usual right-skewed distribution of income, the median voter's income will be less than the mean[8]; to win over that voter, government policy should be progressive and redistributive. By contrast, an autocratic ruler is not institutionally accountable to the poor, and can safely ignore their demands.

This logic is the source of a near-dominant contention in political science about policymaking in developing countries: that democracies will do more to raise the quality of life of poor citizens than autocracies. The theory behind this contention is developed in recent seminal works like Acemoglu and Robinson (2005) and Bueno de Mesquita et al. (2003; 2002)[9] and backed up by a growing empirical literature that finds positive cross-national correlations between democracy and various measures of pro-poor policymaking, such as social spending (e.g., Brown and Hunter 1999), health policy (Zweifel and Navia 2000), and labor-friendly wage policy (Rodrik 1999).[10] Education is a policy area where the connection with regime type has seemed to be especially robust: a large number of studies have found a positive correlation between democracy and overall government investments in education (e.g., Brown 1999; Brown and Hunter 1999; Brown 2002; Sylwester 2000; Lake and Baum 2001; Baum and Lake 2003; Stasavage 2005; Ansell 2010) and between democracy and educational investments specifically targeted at the poor (e.g., Brown 1995; Brown 2002; Stasavage 2005; Ansell 2010).

In this book, I argue that this contention is incorrect, at least for education. Empirically, the regime type of governments in Ghana, Taiwan, and Brazil seems largely irrelevant to whether they invested in mass education. Figure 1.1 shows years when governments at the national level[11] were investing in mass education, in the sense of decreasing the cost and increasing the quality and availability of the education accessible to poor citizens. (I go into more detail on what constitutes a mass education policy below and in Part I of the book.) The figure also shows when the countries had democratic governments. Of the 173 country-years I analyze in this book, regime type correctly predicts education policy in fewer than half. Democratic governments were in power in 60 country-years, but

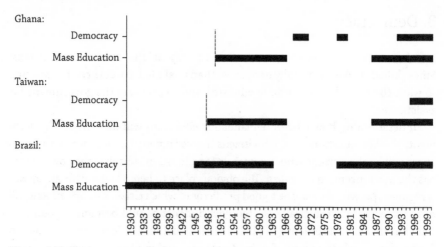

Figure 1.1   Regime type and education policymaking in Ghana, Taiwan, and Brazil

invested in mass education in only 33 of these, while autocratic governments made elitist education policy in only 51 of the 113 country-years they were in power. Furthermore, every democratic government that invested in mass education (Ghana from 1992 to 2000; Taiwan from 1996 to 2000; Brazil from 1946 to 1964) was simply continuing a policy begun under a previous autocratic government. In the three countries, only one regime-type transition precedes the expected change in education policy: the 1964 shift in Brazil from democracy to autocracy, which was followed closely by an obvious shift from a mass education policy to an elitist policy. But Brazil's other regime-type transitions do not coincide with changes in education policy: regime type cannot explain investment in mass education in the autocratic period prior to 1945 or the continuing elitism of education policy after a return to democracy in 1985. In Ghana, two democratic periods—from 1969 to 1971, and from 1979 to 1981—fail entirely to coincide with investment in mass education, which occurred much earlier while Ghana was autocratic; another democratic period, starting in 1992, came six years after the government began to invest in mass education again, during a period when the country was not democratizing. And Taiwan was autocratic when the government expanded mass education in the 1950s and 60s, and still autocratic when it began expanding mass education again the 1980s—it did not become democratic for another decade.

What explains this disconnect? Undoubtedly, democratic institutions do create incentives for a government to serve the poor. The issue is the strength of these incentives. To a democratic government concerned with survival, the needs of voters are only one concern, and probably not the primary concern. There is good reason to think that leaders in developing countries perceive less of a threat to their power from voters than from organized interest groups, such as the business community, large landholders, or the military. Organized interest groups can directly threaten a leader; they can also influence the electorate, through emotional appeals, careful selection of wedge issues about which some poor citizens care more than they care about their material welfare, vote-buying, and spreading information that might damage the government's support among its voting base. Classic works across several subfields of political science provide evidence that the incentive to serve those who are organized outweighs the incentive to serve the median voter, at least in developing societies. In developed democracies, some of the most important work on policymaking credits the organization of particular groups with policies targeted at those groups.[12] Second, in developing countries, regime type, like formal institutions in general, is well-known to be more fluid than in developed countries.[13] Third, a number of compelling studies explain policy-making patterns in developing countries with variation in collective action—differences in elite mobilization (e.g., Waldner 1999) and differences in the inherent abilities of certain interest groups to mobilize themselves (e.g., Bates 1981, Rogowski 1989, Rudra 2002, 2008). Finally, the cross-national large-N literature that finds a connection between democracy and pro-poor policymaking, while large and influential, is not conclusive, and some recent scholarship finds that democracy has at best a tenuous connection to pro-poor policymaking (e.g., Mulligan, Gil, and Sala-i-Martin 2004; Ross 2006).[14]

If collective action is more important for government incentives than regime type, poor citizens are at a substantial disadvantage, whether they can vote or not. If votes were the only consideration, democratically elected governments might reliably court poor citizens. Governments that become more democratic would consistently become more pro-poor in their policymaking as a consequence. But in a contest of organization, numbers are a well-known disadvantage, because they increase the temptation to free ride (Olson 1965). In a contest of organization, leaders who decided to make policy for poor citizens would need to be able to count on poor citizens to turn out to support them if their rule was ever threatened. But each individual poor citizen has an incentive to stay home, because his or her individual contribution to the survival of a government is negligible and the cost of participation is high: poor citizens are short on spare resources and generally lack free time and easy means of communication and interaction, especially when they are scattered across large rural areas. Thus in a contest of organization, a government that ignores organized, resourceful elites and courts the disorganized median voter does so at its peril.

If political power has more to do with collective action than the right to vote, regime type is at best an indirect and unreliable guide to a government's policy-making incentives.[15] Rather, given a constant degree of organization among poor citizens, policymaking should not change perceptibly if the government changes from democratic to autocratic. But given a constant regime type, policymaking will become systematically more responsive to poor citizens when poor citizens become more organized and supportive of a government's survival. Whether poor citizens can vote is not unimportant, because organizing to vote a government out is easier than organizing to overthrow a dictator. In this sense, democratic institutions might contribute *indirectly* to policymaking incentives. But democratic institutions are not a substitute for organization. To be politically important, poor citizens have to organize, no matter what type of regime they live in.

But how do poor citizens become organized? How do they leverage their numbers into political strength, given that those numbers mean that each individual poor citizen has the incentive to stay home and let others attend meetings or demonstrations? In this book I argue that the key is "political entrepreneurship" of the poor: helping poor citizens to organize and realize their latent political power. Political entrepreneurs subsidize the otherwise insurmountable collective action costs of poor citizens. With this organizational help, poor citizens can often realize the latent political power that comes from their vast numerical advantage to credibly support governments that serve them or threaten governments that do not. Political entrepreneurship is a concept about which political scientists and economists have theorized a great deal but done little empirical research. The evidence in this book suggests that the concept is a promising explanation for government actions that appear puzzling from other perspectives.

4. This Book's Framework

To understand the patterns of educational investment in the world, it is necessary to ask two questions: 1) whose support does a government need to stay in power? and 2) what sort of education policy do those citizens want? The answers to these two questions underpin this book's framework for understanding government action in education. They not only provide a guide to the government's general goals for its educational investments, but also provide the basis for detailed predictions of the mechanisms through which the government will try to realize these goals. That is, the framework explains both the government's ideal education system and how it will try to create that system.

THE GOALS

Whose support does a government need to stay in power—and when, specifically, will a government need the poor's support to stay in power? In Chapter 2, I argue that the key to political power, at least in the developing countries I consider here, is organization. Where poor citizens are disorganized, it does not make sense for leaders to make policy in their interest, because doing so means diverting resources that could potentially go to groups that are more organized and hence more threatening. But because poor citizens cannot organize on their own, the key to a government that needs their support is "political entrepreneurship."

A political entrepreneur is a political agent who sees profit—typically political power and whatever rewards that power brings—in helping a disorganized group organize around its common interests. For simplicity, we can think of a political entrepreneur as a single would-be political leader, though in fact it may be a group of individuals desiring a range of types and positions of political authority. The concept of political entrepreneurship was developed by scholars of American politics, who sought to explain how large groups were able to organize despite Olson's (1965) insights about free-riding.[16] Jones (1978, 499) offers a useful definition: "A political entrepreneur is someone who recognizes that a group of individuals share a desire for the provision of a collective good or common goal, and who believes there to be a profit to himself in undertaking the costs of providing an organization which will furnish such a goal."

I adapt the concept of political entrepreneurship to explain variation in the political power of poor citizens in the developing world. Poor citizens share common interests but face burdens that preclude them from organizing themselves. Political entrepreneurship can lessen these burdens, allowing poor citizens to realize their latent political power. Poor citizens are short on spare resources and the free time to identify and organize around areas of common interest; they may also be spread over large areas, making interaction and information-sharing difficult. To lessen these burdens, a political entrepreneur can identify disorganized poor citizens with common interests; create organizational structures and information-sharing mechanisms that facilitate recognition of these common interests with a minimum of effort; help aggregate these interests and transform them into policy options that can be demanded of a government in exchange for the group's support; and police free-riding, create norms of group action, and engineer selective incentives so that individual poor citizens are motivated to act collectively. In this way, political entrepreneurship allows poor citizens to become an organized, durable political force—one that can credibly and reliably support a government that is acting in their interests or threaten a government that is not. The organizational structures created in this process often have democratic features, like elections of local leaders and extensive deliberation. But these structures should not be conflated with democracy as a regime type. Their focus is not on voting, political competition, or alternations of power. And their ultimate goal is not a democratic regime. Rather, the goal of political entrepreneurship is a mutually dependent relationship between the political entrepreneur and the organized poor, whereby the political entrepreneur attains political power and the poor attain pro-poor policies.

Thus the answer I offer to the question I posed earlier—when will a government need the poor's support to stay in power?—is: when they have been organized by a political entrepreneur who has then acquired political authority. Political entrepreneurship allows the poor to be among the citizens on whom the government depends for power. I call this group of politically indispensible citizens the government's "vital constituency." Where political leaders are not engaged in political entrepreneurship of the poor, the vital constituency is elites. Where they are engaged in political entrepreneurship, it is a signal that the poor are in the vital constituency, either alone, where political entrepreneurship is anti-elite, or in a cross-class alliance with some elites. I detail these three vital constituencies—elite, poor, and cross-class—in Chapter 2. They are the citizens whose demands the government will try to meet when it designs its education policy.

What sort of education will the vital constituency demand? In answering this question, it becomes clear why it is important to know whether the vital constituency includes the poor. A vital constituency that includes the poor not only incentivizes the government to provide education to more of the population; it also changes the sort of education the government will provide, because individual poor families will want fundamentally different education systems than individual wealthy families. Because education credit markets are constrained, a poor family in a developing country is not likely to be able to afford any education without assistance. Simply out of necessity, the poor demand *Bottom-Up* education: a system that allows them easy access to education, starting from grade one and continuing up as far as the government's education budget allows. By contrast, a system that concentrates on the lower levels is wasteful from the perspective of wealthier families, who do have the current assets to afford primary and perhaps secondary-level education. For wealthy families, it is the upper levels—the most valuable, but also the most expensive without a subsidy—that are the most difficult to afford. Wealthy families therefore demand *Top-down* education.

Thus political entrepreneurship is key to understanding a government's educational incentives. Political entrepreneurship determines whether the poor are in the vital constituency—whether the vital constituency is elite, poor, or a cross-class alliance. In turn, this vital constituency determines whether the government's incentives are to build an education system that is Top-Down, Bottom-Up, or balances the demands of both elite and poor: an *All Levels* system. We will see these systems in practice in Ghana, Taiwan, and Brazil. Brazil and Ghana provide examples of all three systems. Taiwan's government produces only Top-Down and All Levels systems; its vital constituency is never exclusively poor, so its government never tries to produce a Bottom-Up system. The terms Top-Down, Bottom-Up, and All Levels describe education systems in only the most general sense, but later I argue they are the first step to more detailed predictions about how governments will fashion most aspects of the education system. Many of the key features of education follow directly from the government's general goal, among them whether the government invests in universities or primary schools, who is able to attend, whether teachers are paid well or poorly, whether schools charge fees, whether the government offers scholarships to help offset the fees, and the involvement of the private sector in education.

The demands of the families in the vital constituency explain much of a government's educational motivations. But to complete the picture it is also necessary to integrate the demands of employers, who, provided they are inside the vital constituency, will also make demands on the education system. Naturally employers will only want the government to train their workers if they employ skilled labor, so employer demands will be low or non-existent in the least developed countries and will grow as the economy becomes more sophisticated. But even employers of substantial numbers of skilled workers may not want the government to train their workers. Worker training takes time, and a firm facing a shortage of skilled workers will probably prefer either to import skilled workers trained at another government's expense, or to ship production abroad to a location that already has skilled workers. Only if these two options are closed to them will employers demand worker training from the government.

These employer demands take one of two types, depending on the supply elasticity of skilled wages. If skilled wages are inelastic to supply, as they are in most developing countries where skilled workers are generally unionized or publicly employed, skilled wages will not fall even with a substantial increase in the number of skilled workers. In these circumstances, employers facing a skilled labor shortage will demand *Selective Worker Training*—a system that trains just the number of workers needed to a high level of competence, to justify the high wages that the inelasticity of the market forces employers to pay. Because the wages awaiting graduates of this training are high, it will be attractive to families in the vital constituency. Thus a government facing demand for Selective Worker Training from employers in its vital constituency will simply need to integrate such training into the education system it is providing the families in its vital constituency.

If, however, skilled wages are flexible, employers facing a skilled labor shortage, and the rising skilled wages that shortage will cause, will want the government to design a system that tries to lower skilled wages by increasing the supply of skilled workers as much as possible. This entails *Broad Worker Training*—a worker training system that educates as many workers as possible with the minimum skills the employer requires. Unlike Selective Worker Training, Broad Worker Training is not going to be attractive to families in the vital constituency, since the graduates of this system are not well-remunerated—the objective of the system is to lower skilled wages as much as possible. Thus a government facing a demand for Broad Worker Training will need to provide it *alongside* whatever education it is providing to families in its vital constituency. The upside of this is that a demand for Broad Worker Training gives the government the incentive to direct educational opportunity to families outside the vital constituency. And because most employers of skilled labor will need workers with basic skills such as reading and writing that are part of primary school, a Broad Worker Training system will involve mass education. Thus an employer demand for Broad Worker Training is the second source, along with political entrepreneurship, of government motivation to invest in mass education.

Employer demands are the second dimension of the book's framework for determining government motivations in education. In the three countries I examine in this book, employers are sometimes outside the vital constituency, and sometimes do not demand worker training. But among the three are long periods in which employers demand worker training. Taiwanese employers demand Broad Worker Training for a substantial part of the country's modern history; and Ghanaian and Brazilian employers frequently present the government with demands for Selective Worker Training.

The character of families and employers in the vital constituency allows a full picture of the kind of system a government will try to create. Ghana, Taiwan, and Brazil show the two dimensions working in combination to produce remarkably similar government action in widely different contexts. Indeed, it seems not to matter much which country we examine: if the vital constituency is of a certain type, the government's educational goals seem to develop as a matter of course.

Table 1.4 summarizes the key predictions of the framework for a government's educational motivations. The shaded boxes are circumstances where the government has the motivation to produce mass education.

THE MEANS

This similarity of government motivations, even in widely varied contexts, becomes apparent when we examine the means governments use to realize their general goals for education. From the framework in Table 1.4, it is possible to derive detailed predictions for *how* a government will act to realize its educational goals. I develop these predictions in Chapter 3. Detailed predictions for implementation are unusual among political-economic studies of education and of policy more generally, which generally concentrate on how a government decides on its ideal policy and then assume that the government can implement it. But implementation should be at the heart of any framework for analyzing policymaking, both because a government does not have unlimited powers of implementation, and because the particulars of implementation offer valuable evidence for or against abstract policymaking predictions.

I conceive of the government's options for implementing its education policy as a toolkit. The toolkit consists of most of what we associate with an education system: schools, teachers, books and equipment, curricula, exams, and financial aid, to name a few. But it also includes things that are not so concrete, like tracking, which puts together other tools like curricula, exams, and financial aid to give a student at one level of a track a greater likelihood of proceeding to the next level of the track. (American schools, for example, often have a "gifted and talented" track, in which students take more advanced classes to prepare them for still more advanced classes the following year.) And the toolkit includes things that are often not thought of as parts of public schooling at all, like outsourcing education

Table 1.4 **The Vital Constituency and the government's educational goals**

Employers	Families in the Vital Constituency		
	Elites (no political entrepreneurship)	Elites and the Poor (cross-class political entrepreneurship)	Poor (anti-elite political entrepreneurship)
Need skilled workers in a flexible skilled-labor market	*Education System* Top-Down *Worker Training* Broad	*Education System* All-Levels *Worker Training* Broad	*Education System* Bottom-Up *Worker Training* Broad
Need skilled workers in an inflexible skilled-labor market	*Education System* Top-Down *Worker Training* Selective	*Education System* All-Levels *Worker Training* Selective	*Education System* Bottom-Up *Worker Training* Selective
Do not need skilled workers or are outside the vital constituency	*Education System* Top-Down *Worker Training* None	*Education System* All-Levels *Worker Training* None	*Education System* Bottom-Up *Worker Training* None

Notes: Shaded boxes are circumstances where the government has the motivation to produce mass education.

to companies or non-profit institutions in the private sector. But once we understand a government's goals for education, it becomes clear that outsourcing is a way for the government to provide education without directly producing it—and potentially without paying for it.

The toolkit is large and the tools varied. But for my purpose each tool has two potential effects: it raises or lowers the price and/or the quality of the education available to those inside and outside the vital constituency. Consider a college entrance exam. By controlling access to college, the exam can increase the price of entering college. The exam may cost time and money to take, and more time and money to prepare for. If a student must attend a cram school to have a realistic chance of passing the exam, that is a high price; if the student must attend an expensive or exclusive preparatory high school to have a realistic chance of passing, that is a higher price. The same exam may also improve the quality of college, if it restricts access and thereby frees more of colleges' resources for educating each remaining student. Each of the government's other policies functions similarly.

But the government naturally faces limitations. They are of several types. First, the toolkit is imprecise: although it allows the government to direct opportunity to certain families, it does not usually allow the government to individually select families from inside the vital constituency and exclude those outside. Nor might the government want to, for another limitation is that the government must preserve social stability, the lack of which is threatening both to its power and to its support from the vital constituency. Third, the government faces capacity constraints: its budget is limited, and it may have limited technical capacity, especially if it is at a low level of development. And fourth, few governments will be able to build an education system from scratch exactly as they would want: after the first government to build the country's modern education system, every government will inherit an education system from its predecessor and will have to mold it as best it can. Each of these limitations bears on predictions of the framework for government action; these are detailed in Chapter 3. In some circumstances governments are able to alleviate their limitations. For example, a government with a severe budget constraint may be able to turn to foreign aid. Indeed, in two of the cases—Brazil and Ghana—foreign aid provided substantial new resources for education. Chapter 3 outlines the rationale with which a government accepts such aid; this rationale and the case chapters shed light on why the aid to Ghana was widely judged to be well-spent, while aid to Brazil is usually considered wasted.[17]

Despite some limitations, altogether the tools in the government's educational toolkit provide it with powerful means of manipulating the education system to serve its vital constituency. Thus the way the government uses the tools in the toolkit allows testing of the predictive power of the framework in Table 1.4 on a number of dimensions. To take one example, a government that should, based on its vital constituency, be pursuing a Top-Down education policy should not be putting highly qualified teachers in all its primary schools. In similar ways, I judge the accuracy of the framework by comparing the predicted to actual government actions for each element of the government's education toolkit. In each of the three countries, there are a few minor inconsistencies, where governments use their toolkits in ways contrary to the framework's prediction. But in the vast majority of instances the government wields its toolkit in harmony with the framework's predictions.

I selected Taiwan, Ghana, and Brazil to give the framework a difficult test. Together these three cases provide nearly the maximum variation available in the world on most dimensions, including the three I introduced earlier that should, according to existing theories, be explanatory: regime type, culture, and the level of development. Taiwan, Ghana, and Brazil have each been through at least one, and often more than one, regime transition over the last fifty years, and together the three cover virtually all the variation available in the developing world in culture and development: Taiwan is near the top of developing countries, Ghana is near the bottom, and Brazil is in the middle. The three also vary in the degree to which their policymakers are believed to have been making education policy according to the economy's needs: for proponents of economic optimality in policymaking, Taiwan is often held up as a model of a government listening to the signals the economy was sending and responding appropriately, while Ghana's and

Brazil's governments are typically believed to have made education policy inappropriately from an economic perspective.[18] Lastly, the three vary widely in culture and colonial history, and in inequality: Taiwan is one of the most equal countries in the world; Brazil is one of the most unequal; and Ghana is in the middle.

Despite this variation, the two roots of education I introduce here—political entrepreneurship and the labor conditions faced by employers who need skilled laborers—explain education policymaking in all three. Successive governments in each country adjusted their education systems predictably and similarly, in line with this framework and contrary to existing explanations. Of course, a framework that explains government action in three countries, no matter how different, may fail at explaining the other two hundred. But evidence over long periods in three such different contexts is suggestive of its general accuracy and applicability.

This book is an attempt to answer a question of development that existing theories do not: how, and in whose interests, do governments produce education— and in particular, when do they invest in mass education? In the following chapters, I hope to show that governments provide mass or elitist education based on the success of political entrepreneurs at organizing the poor politically, and on the flexibility of the wage market for employers who face a shortage of skilled workers. Knowing these factors is enough to predict the goals of a government's education policy; given them, governments act systematically, wielding their education toolkits to shape their education systems in very similar ways.

This finding has implications for our understanding of one of the pillars of sustainable development. Education's role in development is widely recognized. Yet despite this value—and despite the pleadings of economists and public servants, despite the spread of democracy, despite the enticement of billions in aid, and despite leaders' own promises to their peoples—education underperforms and is inequitable nearly everywhere. The reason is that common sense, democracy, research, pleadings, monetary enticements, and promises do not make education policy. Instead, education policy is made in the interest of the vital constituency, whose constitution, in turn, depends on the interaction of political entrepreneurs and skilled labor markets. From these two factors, it is possible to build a framework for understanding education policymaking of consistent accuracy and broad generality. Developing and testing this framework is the task of the remainder of the book.

THE FRAMEWORK

CHAPTER 2

The Government's Educational Goals

This chapter is devoted to the goals and means of government education policy: how the government will want the education system to look, and why. Governments face demands from their citizens for education and possess a set of budgetary and policy tools with which to meet those demands. A government will use the tools at its disposal to design an education system, or alter the existing system, to satisfy as closely as possible the education demands of the particular group of citizens on whom its power depends.

This chapter lays out the educational demands different governments will face from their citizens, and how each government will want its education system to look, given the particular demands of its *vital constituency*—the particular citizens whose support it needs to stay in power. The analysis is the basis for a framework for understanding the educational goals of a particular government. The framework is based on an extension of the collective-action model of politics to include political entrepreneurs, who seek political power by subsidizing the poor's collective action costs. The framework is independent of regime type, in the sense that whether the government is autocratic or democratic has no independent effect on which groups are in the vital constituency. Instead, political entrepreneurship determines whether the poor are in the government's vital constituency. Depending on the wealth of the vital constituency, and depending on its demand for skilled workers, the government's goal will be to create an education system that is Top-Down (favors higher education over primary), Bottom-Up, or All-Levels, and which includes no worker training, or worker training that is either Broad (trains as many workers as possible) or Selective. These options—three for the education system, three for worker training—lead to a nine-celled typology of how a government will want the education system to look when different groups are politically powerful. The chapter's argument is that, given the groups on whom the government depends for power, this typology describes the goals of any government, no matter its regime type or its geography, history, or culture. And although the inequality of a country's wealth and the level of its economic development will alter some of the relative allocations which the government will try to effect—for example, more developed countries will likely have more investment in higher education—these factors operate through the demand of politically powerful groups; they do not independently influence government policy.

The chapter proceeds as follows. In Section 1, I define "education," as I use the term, and outline its key features. Then in Section 2, I derive demands for education policy along two separate dimensions, one for families, who demand education for their children, and one for employers, who demand education for their workers. For each dimension, there are three ideal types, which I use later in the chapter to make detailed predictions for how different governments will try to provide education. In Section 3, I consider the interest-group politics through which a government will come to depend on certain groups of families and employers for its power. These are the government's *vital constituency*, and it is their educational demands that the government will try to meet. Section 4 defines the broad goals of government education policy by identifying three ideal types each of families and employers to create a nine-celled matrix of vital constituencies, each of which prefers a different type of education system. The argument is that when the vital constituency takes one of the nine forms in the matrix, the government's goal is to create the type of education system in that cell of the matrix. Section 5 concludes the chapter.

1. Education

This is a framework for understanding how governments decide to provide education. But "education" has many definitions, and it is important to be clear about what I mean by the word. *Education* is formal skills training in preparation for employment or another calling, or for personal edification. This definition includes the development in students of knowledge or technical, problem-solving, or critical-thinking ability or other skills. It excludes most informal on-the-job training, informal mentoring, learning-by-doing, or self-study. The key distinctions are between formality and informality, and standardization and idiosyncrasy: education is provided formally and by a standardized method. It is provided through educational institutions: schools.[1]

Education is often described as a public good, like clean air or national defense. It is not. Education is neither non-rival nor non-excludable, the two criteria of public goods. When one student sits at a school desk, that desk is usually unavailable to others. And as we shall see repeatedly in the pages that follow, it is quite possible to exclude groups of people from access to education.[2] Education is rightly lauded for its spillover benefits to the economy and society. But the primary beneficiary of education is the student, not society. When a person goes to school, that person acquires knowledge, status, and the promise of higher wages later. Nobody else gets anything.[3]

A number of features of education are important for understanding the distribution of demands for it across a citizenry. First, education is progressive—a student cannot attend secondary school without first graduating from primary school—and progressively costly to produce: a year of secondary education is more costly than a year of primary education of similar quality, and a year of tertiary is more costly than a year of secondary. It is also progressively rewarding: in the vast majority of countries, all levels of education have a positive private return in the form of increased wages after graduation. The higher pay reflects the higher ability and hence productivity of more educated employees. In most cases this investment value of education is the primary reason students attend school, and in many cases it is the only reason. This is because education is expensive. Students bear costs in three areas: direct costs—whatever fees schools charge, the cost of required books and uniforms, and the cost of transportation to and from school; the cost of living while in school; and the opportunity costs—the wages students forgo by going to school instead of working. Only a person with access to substantial assets and an abnormally high discount rate on future earnings will have the luxury of not considering education primarily for its investment value. That person may still choose to go to school, for education has a second benefit: its consumption value. For many people, education is itself enriching, and this value generates a willingness in many to pay for it. Yet even if many people find education enriching, there will still be few for whom its consumption value equals or exceeds its high cost, and who have the means to afford that cost. For most, education will be firstly an investment, and only secondarily an activity they enjoy.[4] Thus throughout the following analysis I consider education as an investment in future earnings, and only make passing reference to its value as a normal consumption good.

The future earnings with which the job market rewards education vary with demand and supply, as in any market. When demand is high for the skills and knowledge education imparts, education has higher value as an investment. Likewise, education is a better investment when fewer people have those skills and knowledge. At the macroeconomic level, demand is generally a function of economic development. Less advanced economies demand fewer tertiary graduates and more primary graduates; as an economy develops, the demand for higher-skilled workers increases commensurately, as, all else being equal, will the wage-premia tertiary graduates earn relative to graduates of lower levels.[5]

The value of education as an investment also rises with its quality, which is at least partly a function of resources. There is a lively debate about the effect of resources on quality. More resources certainly do not guarantee better education. In the United States, for example, test scores have not risen since the 1960s despite average annual increases in per-student spending of more than 3 percent (e.g., Hanushek 2003; Coleman 1966). But resources can help to improve educational quality. In cross-country regressions of upper-middle and high-income countries, higher per-student spending explains about half the variance in test scores (OECD

2003), and there is considerable evidence for a link between educational resources and wages (for a discussion, see Card and Krueger 1996a, 1996b).

Given the above, it is possible to conceive of education's investment value as a function of three conditions: the education's quality and scarcity, and the economy's level of development.

Consumers of education receive its return—higher wages—in the future, but they must bear its costs immediately. Most consumers of education therefore afford it only with the help of a subsidy. Absent government assistance, consumers will hardly ever be able to borrow to pay for education.[6] Education is simply bad collateral.[7] If a car buyer defaults on her car loan, she can turn over the car, which the bank can sell to repay the loan. But a bank cannot take a student's education if he defaults on his education loan. The bank can go after his wages or other assets, but this takes time and requires a level of enforcement commitment and capacity that only a few governments—mostly in the developed world—possess. Education loans are therefore risky for banks, and an interest rate high enough to compensate for that risk is also likely to be higher than students' return on that education, which is rarely more than 20 percent and is more likely to be in the neighborhood of 10 to 15 percent.[8] Hence most educational lending is either by governments, or by banks assisted by government subsidies.

The absence of well-functioning private education credit markets leaves many consumers unable to afford education without a subsidy. In developing countries, where citizens are poorer, the problem is all the more acute. This is where the government comes in. Modern education is dominated by governments. Governments build most of the world's schools, hire most of the teachers, set most of the fees, and provide most of the aid or loans to offset the fees. What the private sector, not the government, provides, it does so only with the government's blessing, under the government's regulations, and often with substantial amounts of government money. It is not an exaggeration to say that in every country in the world the education system is primarily a public creation, even that portion that is run by the private sector.

The education system the government produces will only coincidentally be that which the economy would design for itself. Governments are not like markets: they are not after profit. A market might invest in education according to its return. It might observe the wages being paid in the economy—high for those with certain skills, low for those with others—and build the education system to take advantage, and in the process reduce, those differences. It might build schools to teach the skills most in demand, and therefore promising the highest wages, in the economy, and direct credit to students willing to learn those skills. A market after profit might balance the demand and supply of skill in an economy.[9] But a government's goal is not profit; it is power. Governments want power out of simple necessity. No leader, whether selfish or altruistic, can govern if she does not win and maintain the support of those who choose who can govern. Would-be leaders may of course want power not for itself but for what it allows them to achieve: wealth or status, for example, or the chance to make life better for fellow citizens. Yet those goals are of necessity secondary, for none of them can be realized if the would-be leader is not able to attain and maintain power. Thus political power must be a leader's first goal.[10]

To stay in power, a government must produce education not to maximize education's investment returns, but to satisfy the groups on whom its power depends, so that they will continue to support it. To determine what this means for education requires answering the two general questions I posed in the first chapter. What type of education system will each citizen want? And which citizens will belong to groups whose support the government needs? The following section takes up the first question; Section 3 considers the second.

2. The Two Dimensions of Demand for Education

To understand what kinds of education systems different citizens prefer, I begin with a simple utility function: I assume that citizens prefer more income to less and therefore try to maximize their income. With this formulation, the following section develops an understanding of the kind of education system different citizens want from the government. The answer is straightforward: each citizen prefers that the government produce an education system that minimizes the price she pays for education and maximizes the return she gets from it. But the system that does this is different for different citizens.

To understand variation in citizens' demands, it helps to think of citizens as falling into two overlapping groups: families and employers. Both wish to maximize their income: families by selling their members' labor in the job market; employers by hiring families' members' labor in the job market. But here, of course, the similarity ends, because families' income is maximized when the wages their members can earn are highest, while employers' income is maximized when the wages they have to pay for workers with the skills they need are lowest. Thus determining demand requires considering families and employers separately.

WHAT FAMILIES WANT

First consider families. A family has resources—current wages and other assets—which it can use to invest in the education of its children. The quantity of these resources differs across families. Since families cannot borrow against future earnings to fund current education, they must possess sufficient resources either to fund their education or to offer as collateral against which to borrow. Thus whether education is an affordable investment is a function of a family's current resources.

Determining whether education is a good, as opposed to affordable, investment is a different matter. Whether education is a good investment depends on
its price relative to its return. Properly, it depends on whether the gross lifetime
earnings of an educated worker equal or exceed education's total cost in the three
areas mentioned above: the fees that a child has to pay to the education system to
become educated; the opportunity cost of the forgone earnings the child could
have earned if she was not going to school; and the forgone earnings the child
could have earned as a worker without education after graduating from the education system until the end of her working life.[11]

The earnings of the educated worker depend on the factors already mentioned—
economic development, and the education's quality and rarity—but it will depend
on one other factor not already mentioned: ability. Students differ in their ability
to absorb education. Yet despite the very real variation in ability among students,
I assume from here on that education appears to be an equally profitable investment even to two families whose children differ in ability. This is a strong, potentially controversial assumption. A wide literature in education demonstrates that a
student's ability to absorb education is affected systematically by numerous factors, among them socio-economic status, IQ, and a student's home environment.
But in determining the demand of a particular family for education, the assumption is justified because the existence of systematic differences in ability does not
mean that parents can know beforehand whether educating their child is a good
investment. Research in behavioral genetics has demonstrated that parents cannot
accurately assess their child's ability unless the family is at the top of the socio-
economic ladder (Turkheimer et al. 2003; Turkheimer and Waldron 2000; Jensen
1981). All other parents face tremendous difficulties: it is difficult to know how
and when to judge whether a student has potential (children bloom at different
times at different things); even if a child's potential can be accurately judged, it is
hard to think that a parent is able to discern it without bias; and even a lack of
ability can be overcome by greater investments in education—extra classes,
tutors—which, as long as the wages of an educated worker are high enough, can
make education a good investment even in a child with little ability. Empirical
work shows that the rich tend to have a much lower price elasticity of demand for
education than the poor, indicating that a family's ability to pay is a more important driver of education spending patterns than a child's ability to learn.[12] Lastly,
what matters to the decision to acquire education is *relative*, not absolute, ability:
even if parents could accurately judge ability in their child, to know whether education is a good investment they would have to know the distribution of ability in
the population and where their child's ability fits in that distribution. Because a
family cannot judge *a priori* the ability of their child to acquire education relative to
other children, it does not make sense to think of families' demand for education
varying systematically with the ability of their children. Thus in the analysis that
follows, I assume that all families want education equally and differ only in their
capacity to afford that education.

Differences in capacity to pay affect whether children enter school, but also how far they progress through school. As discussed earlier, education is progressively more costly, at least to produce, at successive levels. If its price rises with its production cost, the percentage of families who can afford each additional year of school will decline. But the problem is not simply the price; it is also the opportunity cost. If education is a good investment, then each additional year of schooling raises the wages a student could earn if he went to work. By staying in school, the student is forgoing an exponentially increasing quantity of wages. As the direct and opportunity costs of education rise, so will the resources families will have to possess in order to afford the education.

To see how ability to pay affects demand for education, consider two families, one poor and one rich, in a hypothetical developing country that is generic in every way except that the government completely ignores education. The rich family probably has the resources to afford excellent primary and secondary school. They may also be able to send their children to a good tertiary institution, even one of the best ones abroad—though the fees of a world-class institution, not to mention the quality of primary and secondary instruction necessary for their child to pass the entrance exam of one of these institutions, may tax the resources of even the wealthiest family in a developing country.

Now let the government become involved in education. What sort of education system would the rich family want the government to produce? Ideally, every family would like the government to create an education system that gives a world-class education to its children and its children alone, for free, leaving everyone else to fend for themselves. This ideal is important to establish, but it is useful only in theory: the government cannot meet this demand. Below I consider a government's response to citizens' demands; suffice it for now to say that a government will need the support of more than one family to stay in power, and it faces other constraints, among them a limited budget.

Barring the ideal, a family's next-best education system will still lower the price of and raise the return on its children's education. The rich family can probably afford good-quality primary, secondary, and even tertiary education on their own. But for them the most expensive and valuable level is tertiary. The rich family thus is helped most by a government system that lowers the price and raises the quality and rarity of its children's tertiary education. The most obvious solution is to lower the fees, but lowered fees would also allow more families to afford to send their children to tertiary education, probably undermining its quality and certainly increasing the number of tertiary graduates competing for jobs. A complete solution therefore involves lowering fees and simultaneously restricting access. Any efforts to restrict access to the wealthy child's tertiary institution—while still ensuring that the wealthy child can attend, of course—raises the quality of the child's tertiary education and means less competition in the job market when the child graduates, both of which raise the wages the child can expect after graduating and thereby the return on the education. If the government has money left in the education budget after sufficiently raising the quality of tertiary education and eliminating its fees, the wealthy family may then wish the government to tackle education at the next-most-expensive level, secondary, followed by primary. Because it concentrates efforts at the highest levels of education, I call this kind of system *Top-Down*.

Now consider a poor family. This family may only be able to afford a few years of meager-quality primary education for their child before the costs become too onerous.[13] If the family is in extreme poverty—living at or near subsistence—they may not be able to afford any education, because the opportunity cost of the lost labor of the child would put the family below the subsistence line. Certainly, all else being equal, they can afford far fewer years of education, and/or education of much lower quality, than the rich family.

Thus the poor family would be helped most by an education system that begins at the primary level and works up the progression, lowering or eliminating its cost (and perhaps compensating families for the opportunity cost of the lost labor) and raising its quality, up to the limit of the education budget. I call this sort of system *Bottom-Up*. The poor family shares with the wealthy family a preference for education that is as restricted as possible; however, in any country with the typical right-skewed distribution of income, there will be far more poor families than wealthy families, and thus a policy that serves poor families entails increased access to education at all levels.

Table 2.1 shows education policy demands for the two families, given a limited education budget.

These two families illustrate extremes of demand that actually exist along the income continuum. Families in between the two extremes demand education analogously to the two families in Table 2.1: the richer the family, the higher the level it will be able to afford on its own, and thus the higher the level on which the

Table 2.1   **Education-policy demands of a rich and a poor family in a typical developing country**

	Family's resources	
	Poor	*Rich*
Education acquired from own resources	Incomplete, poor-quality primary	High-quality primary and secondary, and mediocre tertiary
Most-valuable education policy	*Bottom-Up* High per-student spending on primary; High enrollments	*Top-Down* High per-student spending on tertiary; Low enrollments

family will want the government to concentrate its resources. Families at very low levels of income will want the government to devote resources just to the primary level. Further up the income scale, families will find it valuable for the government to devote less of its budget to primary education—some of which they can afford on their own—and put the remaining resources into secondary education. Still further up the income scale, families will prefer that the government put no resources into primary education and instead devote its budget to secondary education and tertiary education. And at the limit, the wealthiest families will prefer that the government put all its resources into tertiary education. Figure 2.1 graphs the distribution of the education budget a family might want, depending on that family's position on the income scale.

Figure 2.1 is drawn to hold some important features of demand constant, in particular the level of economic development, and inequality and per-capita wealth. It describes family preferences more or less in a typical developing country, one where the mean and variance of family wealth are in the mid-range of developing countries and where the economy is developed enough to make use of, and pay for, the skills of a tertiary graduate. But economic development, inequality, and family wealth will all alter Figure 2.1—economic development because it will alter the investment return on education, and inequality and average wealth and because they will alter families' ability to afford education.

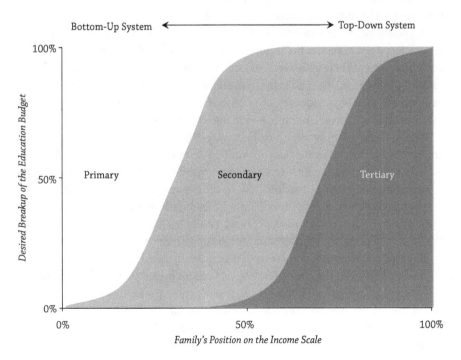

Figure 2.1 Education-policy demands along the income scale in a typical developing country

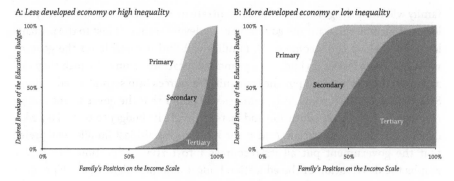

Figure 2.2   Education policy demands, at high and low levels of inequality and economic
development

First consider economic development. In a developed economy, activities requiring skills account for a higher proportion of economic output. All else being
equal, less developed economies will have little or even no demand for tertiary
graduates, lowering the investment return on tertiary education. Therefore in less
developed economies the lines on the figure would be condensed to the right, as
in panel A of Figure 2.2. In a more developed economy, the economy will demand
increasing numbers of tertiary graduates, and the lines on the figure would be
stretched to the left, as in panel B of Figure 2.2.

Inequality has analogous effects on Figure 2.1. As inequality increases, so does the
proportion of poor families in the population, and thereby the proportion who would
prefer investments in primary education. In a country with high inequality, then, the
lines on the figure will be condensed to the right, as in panel A of Figure 2.2. Likewise
in a country with low inequality, the proportion of poor families will be lower, and
the lines on the graph will be stretched to the left, as in panel B of Figure 2.2.

Lastly, average family wealth will also alter Figure 2.1, because it will alter the
amount of education families can afford. To a certain extent, the cost of education
will rise with average family wealth, as economic development drives up the price
of educational inputs like teachers' salaries. But even after adjusting for price inflation in education, the poorest family in Denmark will be able to afford a lot
more primary education than the poorest family in Chad. This dynamic will shift
the lines in the figure to the left as average family wealth rises.

This analysis leads to a simple way of determining the education-policy demands
of families in developing countries. Poorer families prefer that more of the education budget go into primary education; richer families prefer that more of the education budget go into tertiary education. Economic development and the mean
and variance of family wealth all change family demands, because they alter either
the investment return on education or a given family's ability to pay for education.
But they do not change the relative preference of the poor for investments in primary education and the rich for investments in tertiary education.

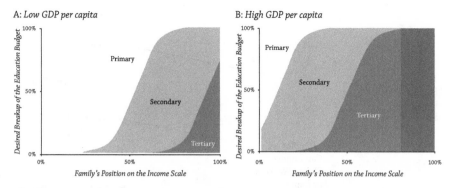

Figure 2.3   Education policy demands, at high and low GDP per capita

WHAT EMPLOYERS WANT

So far I have examined only the demands of families who rent out their labor in the job market. But some citizens are not simply members of families; they are also employers. And employers may place entirely different demands on education policy.

Employers, like families, are income-maximizing. But all else equal, a family's income is maximized when the wages its members can earn are highest, while an employer's income is maximized when the wages it must pay its workers are lowest. An employer's labor costs depend in part on the availability of the kind of workers she employs: the fewer there are, the more pay each will be able to demand for his services. This availability, and the government's ability to alter it, will determine what kind of education policy the employer favors. This section analyzes the circumstances under which she will want government assistance in educating workers and the form she will want this assistance to take. To distinguish education with the purpose of serving employers from education with the purpose of serving families, I label the former *Worker Training*.

Not every employer will demand worker training from the government. Determining an employer's demand involves a decision tree, as in Figure 2.4.

In the first place, an employer of no or few skilled workers will not need worker training (Figure 2.4, question 1), nor will an employer whose desired skills are already abundant in the workforce. These employers are satisfied with no government assistance with worker training.

It is when employers have difficulty finding workers with the skills they need that they may demand worker training. But even such a shortage may not induce the demand. First, an employer must be able to wait for the workers to be trained, a process that could take years. Schools take time to build or retool, teachers take time to train or retrain, curricula take time to design, and students take time to learn. If an employer is facing wages higher than it can profitably pay, it may be bankrupt long before the first new graduate is available for work.

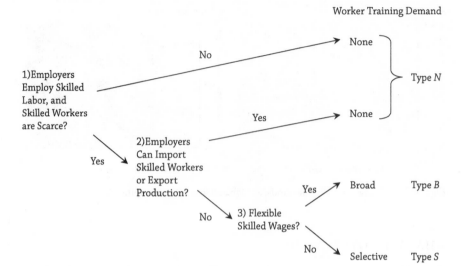

Figure 2.4 Employer demands for worker training

Notes: Type *N* employers do not need worker training. Type *S* employers want *Selective Worker Training*. Type *B* employers want *Broad Worker Training*.

Second, short of demanding worker training from the government, an employer of skilled labor may have two easier, quicker options (Figure 2.4, question 2). First, she might be able to import skilled workers from abroad. If a skilled worker trained at another government's expense is earning wages lower than what the employer is willing to pay, that worker may be lured into emigrating. Second, she might be able to move production abroad. If another country contains a pocket of skilled workers available at wages lower than what the employer is currently paying, it may be cheaper simply to move operations there, rather than tempting the workers all to emigrate. Both these options depend to some extent on open borders. Importing workers requires an immigration policy that allows skilled workers to immigrate.[14] And to the extent that the employer produces for the domestic market, producing abroad requires a trade policy that will not close the domestic market to an employer who chooses to produce abroad. If the United States put high enough tariffs on Chinese imports, it would not be profitable for a U.S. employer who produced for U.S. consumers to produce in China, no matter how low Chinese wages are.

Thus in Figure 2.4, the employers who do not demand worker training are: employers who do not need skilled workers, either because they do not employ skilled workers or because skilled workers are abundant; and employers who need skilled workers but can import them or move their production abroad to a location with them. I label these employers type *N*.

But for employers who need skilled workers and are able to wait for them to be trained, and who are not able to import skilled workers or export production, worker training could be valuable. There are two basic types of worker training, which I call *Broad* and *Selective*. The two types differ in their relative emphasis on the quantity and quality of the training. Since an employer's profits are highest when the wages she has to pay are lowest, the ideal worker training policy will lower wages for the skills she needs. Worker training has the potential to lower an employer's wage bill, by training as many workers as possible in the skills the employer needs. The more workers there are with those skills, the lower the wages the employer will have to pay to hire one of those workers. A system that tries to lower wages is Broad Worker Training. Broad Worker Training emphasizes quantity. Resources are finite, and the point of the worker training is to lower skilled wages. It is therefore important that a graduate be educated in the skills the employer demands, but equally important that he not be overeducated. A worker with extra skills may demand higher wages, or may become attractive to a competitor, or an employer in another industry or another country. Any resources spent on overtraining workers are not just wasted; they work against the goal of lowering the wage rate. Broad Worker Training should educate the maximum number of workers in the minimum skills the employer demands. I call employers who demand broad worker training type *B*.

Yet there are situations in which a Broad Worker Training system will not lower wages, no matter how many skilled workers it trains. The most important requirement is skilled wage flexibility (Figure 2.4, question 3).[15] If skilled wages are elastic to the supply of labor, an increase in the supply of skilled labor will lower skilled wages. But often skilled wages are inflexible. Unions, in particular, protect wages, thereby lowering the elasticity of wages to the supply of workers. There is also the "brain drain" problem: if a skilled worker is free to migrate, he may take his skills to another country where they are better remunerated. The brain drain can prevent wages from falling much below whatever wage rate prevails in the world, by siphoning off workers who would have to work for wages too far below that rate.[16]

If skilled wages are inflexible, there is no point to training as many workers as possible: skilled wages will not fall. Employers may still demand worker training from the government, because training workers is expensive. But the training will be *Selective* targeted assistance for worker training. Selective Worker Training can take the form of specialized training centers, or grants or tax breaks to allow employers to train their own workers. The emphasis of Selective Worker Training is on quality, not quantity. Training more workers than necessary is a waste, because those workers will be unemployed. Instead, a Selective Worker Training system is engineered to provide workers with precisely the skills the employer wants, or allows the employer to train the workers themselves to their exact needs. I label employers who demand Selective Worker Training type *S*.[17]

We now have an answer to the first question that I posed at the end of the previous section: What type of education system will different citizens want? For families, demand varies with wealth, with richer families preferring greater investments in tertiary education. For employers, demand depends on whether the employer needs skilled workers and can access skilled workers abroad, and on the flexibility of skilled wages. The second question is: whose demands will the government try to meet?

1. The Vital Constituency

Which families and employers will the government try to serve? This section analyzes who they will be: in particular, whether the families in it will be primarily elites, the poor, or a cross-class alliance, and whether it will include employers who need skilled workers in a labor market with flexible skilled wages. The nature of this constituency will determine whether the government will try to provide Bottom-Up, Top-Down, or All-Levels education, and whether it will provide Broad or Selective Worker Training.

To stay in power, political leaders depend on the support of certain groups of citizens. These are the groups any of which, if it withdrew its support, would cause the leaders to lose control of the government they run. I label them the leaders' *vital constituency*, or "VC."[18] The idea of the vital constituency is similar to the re-election coalition in a democracy or the "winning coalition" of Bueno de Mesquita et al. (2003).[19] All political leaders and, by extension, all the "governments" (in the European sense) they lead, have vital constituencies.[20] For the vast majority of governments, the power of the VC stems from the leaders' desire to govern, and to govern for as long as possible. Some leaders do not wish to retain power indefinitely, but such leaders cannot govern even for a limited period without the acquiescence of all citizens and groups who possess the ability to oust them from power. Thus all leaders govern only while their vital constituency supports them.

While the vital constituency is similar to existing concepts, I give it a new label to highlight the different mechanism that determines which citizens are inside it. My argument is that the vital constituency depends on collective action, not regime type. A citizen can be inside the vital constituency even if they cannot vote or outside it even if they can. Rather, the vital constituency is a combination of interest groups, formed of citizens who are organized into loci of political power.

The reason for looking to a different mechanism is that regime type is not a reliable guide to the distribution of political power, at least in the developing world.[21] There is no doubt that, all else being equal, it is easier for the poor to be politically powerful in a democracy. Democratic institutions offer poor citizens an easy way of influencing the selection of the government, one that requires very little effort and no organizing to use. It is far more difficult for poor citizens to have such influence in an autocracy. But the regime-type perspective on political power is too narrow to be useful in considering a government's incentives. For regime type to be a reliable guide to the distribution of political power, the distribution of political power would have to be at least partly determined, not just influenced, by regime type, and there is good reason to think that it is not. Though it is harder for poor citizens to influence the selection of the government in an autocracy, it is far from impossible, and though it is easier for poor citizens to influence the selection of the government in a democracy, their influence is far from guaranteed. A democratically elected government, particularly in the developing world, generally has far more to fear from organized interest groups, such as the business community, large landholders, or the military. These interest groups can use the resources they can mobilize to influence the government directly. They can also affect the government indirectly by influencing the electorate: through emotional appeals, careful promotion of wedge issues about which some voters care more than they care about their material welfare, vote-buying, and empty or misleading promises and claims. A large and growing body of research about developed democracies points to the overwhelming political influence of the organized relative to the disorganized.[22] A democratically elected government that ignores organized, resourceful interest groups and courts the disorganized median voter is not likely to govern for long. On the other hand, where poor citizens are organized, their numbers often allow them to imperil a government even when it is a dictatorship, as mass revolutions have long shown.[23]

Empirical analyses of policymaking tend to look either at democracies or autocracies. But if we step back and consider the two literatures together, they suggest that the bases for government support vary to such a degree under both democratic and autocratic regimes that the categories begin to lose their meaning.[24] The response in both literatures has been to create additional regime-type categories, including hybrid or intermediate regimes.[25] But insofar as the object is to explain policymaking, the problem is not likely to be misclassification or misspecification of regime types, but rather that a regime's formal institutions are not sufficiently important to the distribution of political power to influence a government's policymaking motivations. In Ghana, Taiwan, and Brazil, formal regime institutions either do not affect the distribution of political power or already reflect this distribution; where formal institutions would allot political power to those not in the vital constituency, they are circumvented or quickly changed. Thus there is no reasonable way of judging the distribution of political power in a country by examining its regime type.

Instead, to understand the distribution of political power, and therefore the government's policymaking incentives, an analyst must consider collective action directly. Though the literature on policymaking in developing countries is heavily influenced by the institutional perspective, there are notable works that do explain policymaking variation with collective action. Bates (1981) does so for agricultural policymaking in Africa, as does Rogowski (1989) for trade policy. This book considers educational policymaking similarly.

To determine the sort of education system a government will have incentives to build—Bottom-Up, Top-Down, or All-Levels—we need first to understand when poor citizens are inside the vital constituency and hence indispensible to the government's survival. If groups must organize to be politically powerful—if they cannot simply have their power handed to them by the franchise—the next question is: when are the poor able to organize? Since Olson (1965), we have understood that the larger a group is, the more difficulty it has acting collectively. The incentive to free-ride gives the advantage to smaller and more concentrated groups, in which individuals have more incentive to contribute to the collective effort, and to wealthier groups, which have more resources to police their ranks and selectively incentivize members to participate. Thus while the poor's numbers are a source of tremendous political power, they are at a disadvantage in realizing this political power, since numbers make collective action difficult. Olson's insight suggests that in the developing world, elites, not the poor, have the advantage. Absent other factors, elites—the military, the bureaucracy, and the business and agrarian elite—are the groups with the easiest time acting collectively. They are therefore in an advantageous position to become the government's vital constituency: their collective-action advantages give them a political advantage, and absent another source of countervailing power, the government will probably need their support to survive.[26] On the other hand, the vast poor citizenry in a typical developing country are scattered and short on time and money. Their collective action disadvantages preclude them from organizing themselves. Thus it is not surprising that most studies of policymaking that directly examine collective action predict that policy will be biased against the poor, and that this bias will lessen only as the poor's collective-action disadvantages lessen.[27]

Yet the poor's case is not hopeless. The poor's sheer numbers give them the possibility of political power that might rival elites'. The problem is that this power is latent. But while poor citizens are unlikely to be able to organize on their own, they can with help. A source of this help is a "political entrepreneur" of the poor. A political entrepreneur is a political actor who recognizes the latent power of a disorganized group and sees it to his or her advantage to subsidize or arrange for a subsidy of the collective action costs of that group. When a political entrepreneur recognizes such potential in the poor, he or she can help them to organize despite their collective action disadvantages, enabling them to realize their latent political power. Throughout this book I offer evidence that it is political entrepreneurship of the poor, not a country's institutions, that allows poor citizens to become a political force capable of supporting a government that makes policy in their interest or threatening a government that does not.

POLITICAL ENTREPRENEURSHIP OF THE POOR

The concept of "political entrepreneurship" is broader than simply an agent who organizes the poor. It was developed by scholars of American politics as a way of explaining the existence of the political organization of any large group despite free-riding incentives.[28] Like economic entrepreneurs, political entrepreneurs are motivated by personal gain, either material or something immaterial of value to them. The specific political entrepreneurs explored in this book realize those gains by subsidizing the collective-action costs of one or more groups of poor citizens with common interests, helping them to realize their latent political power, which they then rely on to attain and retain political office.[29] They realize the latent power of poor citizens by lessening the burdens that preclude poor citizens from organizing themselves.[30] Chief among these burdens is their numbers. To lower this barrier, the political entrepreneur can create structures that create norms of group action, police free-riding, and engineer selective incentives so that individual poor citizens are motivated to participate in the common effort. Additionally, poor citizens are short on spare resources and may lack the free time to identify and organize around areas of common interest; they may also be spread over large areas, making interaction and information-sharing difficult. A political entrepreneur can help poor citizens with each of these by:

- identifying one or more groups or subgroups of poor citizens with common interests;
- creating local organizational structures and information-sharing mechanisms that facilitate discussions among these citizens about their common interests with a minimum of effort;
- helping to translate these discussions into policy options that aggregate their common interests and can be demanded of a government in exchange for the groups' support; and
- linking these local structures together into regional or national coalitions.

I noted in Chapter 1, and repeat here, that while the organizational structures created in this process often have democratic features, like elections of local leaders and extensive deliberation, they are quite different from a democratic regime type. A regime that is affiliated with a political entrepreneur of the poor may be, and often is, highly undemocratic. In a regime affiliated with a political entrepreneur, holders of high government office, or the political party into which they are organized, may rarely change. Elections, if they are held at all, may be highly rigged. A democratic regime type is not the goal of political entrepreneurship; rather the goal is a mutually dependent relationship between the political entrepreneur and the poor. So long as poor citizens remain organized, politically active, and supportive of the political entrepreneur's political ambitions, democracy is irrelevant to a political entrepreneur. In fact, to the extent that democracy threatens this mutually dependent relationship, there are incentives for a political entrepreneur to seek an undemocratic regime type, through which she might solidify the political control that allows her to provide the collective goods and selective incentives that keep members politically active.[31]

What does political entrepreneurship look like? Political entrepreneurs organize poor citizens through organizations like unions, political parties, farmers or peasant associations, or religious institutions. To the extent that poor citizens are homogenous, a political entrepreneur may work only with one sort of organization. But in a country with economic and social cleavages that divide the poor,[32] they may organize sub-groups of poor citizens into several types of organizations— unions to organize urban workers, farmers' associations to organize rural farmers, etc. In some cases, organizations may already exist and all the political entrepreneur may need to do is associate herself with them and attempt to translate their demands into policy. But most of the time, the political entrepreneur must create the necessary organizations from scratch. The form these organizations will take varies widely: this book describes methods of organizing poor citizens in Brazil, Taiwan, and Ghana that are remarkable in their diversity. Their similarity is their common goal: to mobilize poor citizens and create the mutually dependent relationship between them and the political entrepreneur that allows the political entrepreneur to count on their political support.

By allowing poor citizens to realize their latent political power, the entrepreneur creates a source of countervailing political power to elites—a challenge to the elite vital constituency that is otherwise the default. Where we see a government affiliated with a political entrepreneur, the vital constituency is no longer only the elites; instead, it will involve the poor. Hence, it will make pro-poor education policy.

Whether this pro-poor education policy will be Bottom-Up or All-Levels depends on whether the poor constitute the vital constituency on their own or join elites inside the vital constituency (a cross-class alliance). This depends on the political entrepreneur and her strategy. A political entrepreneur can organize the poor on only their behalf; we can think of Fidel Castro or Mao. This type of entrepreneur is anti-elite. He seeks a government supported by a vital constituency of the poor only. A second type of political entrepreneur seeks a cross-class alliance. He may arise from a split among elites[33]: one faction may wish to challenge another, and organize the poor to increase its relative power. Or he may arise in response to an anti-elite political entrepreneur and the resulting political competition—if elites can compete for the poor, they may defeat the challenge.

For political scientists, this discussion of political entrepreneurship begs several questions. What conditions make affiliated political entrepreneurship more or less likely? When are entrepreneurs prone to being cross-class or anti-elite? As this book is primarily about government policymaking in education, I leave these questions to the side. I use political entrepreneurs as an identification strategy: the success of political entrepreneurs helps to determine the vital constituency,[34] and, in turn, education policy. I only speculate, in the concluding chapter, on questions of when political entrepreneurs of the poor arise and when governments affiliate with them.

The addition of the two types of political entrepreneurs leads to a three-part typology of vital constituencies: elites; the poor; and a cross-class alliance. Absent political competition, the vital constituency is elites. The vital constituency changes when a political entrepreneur creates political competition. If the political entrepreneur is anti-elite, the new vital constituency is the poor. If the political

Table 2.2 **Vital Constituencies, With and Without Political Entrepreneurs**

Affiliation with Political Entrepreneur

None	*Cross-Class*	*Anti-Elite*
The Default: Elites (Military; Bureaucracy; and/or Agrarian; and/or Industrial Elites)	Elites and the Poor (Cross-Class Alliance)	Poor

Notes: "Political Entrepreneurs" are of the poor only; elites, facing fewer collective action costs, do not need an entrepreneur's collective-action subsidy to organize.

entrepreneur is cross-class, it is a cross-class alliance. The new vital constituency lasts only as long as the political entrepreneur maintains a collective-action subsidy to the poor. With the withdrawal of this subsidy, the power of the poor returns to its dormancy, and the vital constituency returns to its default, the elites. Table 2.2 describes the typology.

Table 2.2 describes vital constituencies entirely independent of the government's regime type, for the reasons detailed above. Just as important, it describes the vital constituency independently of the *policies* the government is making. Because the connection between political entrepreneurship of the poor and pro-poor policymaking is tight in each of the countries I examine in this book, the reader may be concerned that the framework is a tautology: that pro-poor education signals political entrepreneurship of the poor. But the connection between political entrepreneurship of the poor and pro-poor policymaking is a hypothesis. Political entrepreneurship itself is not about policymaking; it is about organization. It is possible for a government to be engaged in political entrepreneurship and not offer pro-poor policies, or for a government unaffiliated with a political entrepreneur to offer pro-poor policies. Identifying political entrepreneurship is a matter of observing whether the government is assisting the collective action of poor citizens.

As long as the state of political competition is constant, a government stays in power while it maintains the support of its vital constituency. How? Earlier I introduced a simple utility function in which all citizens prefer more income to less. Thus every member of the VC will want the government to do whatever it can to increase the member's income. When the government concentrates its policy and resources on meeting this demand, each member of the VC will be happiest and most likely to continue supporting the government. Governments buy the loyalty of their vital constituency by acceding to their demands over its largesse. In other words, it is the educational demands of the vital constituency—and no one else's—that the government will try to meet.

As with families, whose demands I illustrated with two archetypical families even though they exist along a continuum, this typology of three vital constituencies is only illustrative. In reality, vital constituencies can take many forms other than the three in Table 2.2. Families' wealth is along a continuum. In particular, some families will be middle class. In predicting education policy, wealth is by far the most important dimension, for it not only determines ability to pay for education but is instrumental in the operation of most of the tools of education policy, which I discuss below. As noted earlier, other cleavages may demarcate sub-groups of the poor. For education policy, two cleavages are particularly relevant: geography and ethnicity. A vital constituency may include or exclude groups of a particular ethnicity, or those who reside in a particular region. These dimensions are important because, as I describe below, the tools the government uses to allocate education across the population allow it to distinguish families not just by wealth, but also by ethnicity and region. However, these additional dimensions will affect educational demand only marginally: a poor family of one ethnicity may, for example, prefer that education have a different cultural content than a poor family of another ethnicity, but both will prefer that the government concentrate on primary education. Thus the importance of these two cleavages is in delineating *whose* educational demands the government will try to meet.

But aside from divisions along the key dimension of wealth and the peripheral dimensions of geography and ethnicity, I assume, for the purpose of predicting a government's education policy, that the vital constituency is impermeable. That is, the vital constituency is constituted from groups along these three dimensions, not sub-groups or individual families. Put another way: the government serves a vital constituency that is a collection of groups, not individual families, and a political entrepreneur organizes families below a certain income, and perhaps of a certain region or ethnicity. Sub-groups or individual families cannot be peeled off the vital constituency in the course of political competition through selective targeting of education.[35] In some policy analyses, this would be a controversial assumption; but it is in the nature of education policy. Targeting sub-groups or individual families with education policy is normally impossible—the education-policy toolkit available to a government is simply too imprecise; its accuracy is based on the three dimensions of wealth, geography, and ethnicity, and with minimal exceptions it cannot target smaller groupings. Once a government decides that poor citizens of a certain ethnicity in a certain region are inside its vital constituency, it delivers educational opportunity to them as a group, not as individuals.

EMPLOYERS IN THE VITAL CONSTITUENCY

In considering educational demands, the second important category of citizen is employers. Determining whether employers are inside the vital constituency is not generally a challenge: the vast majority of political leaders depend on the support employers, for the structural reason that citizens' income depends on the jobs they provide.[36] Across Taiwan, Ghana, and Brazil, for example, there were only two governments that did not need the support of at least some employers, and they were ephemeral. Instead, the key is the labor market conditions I introduced above (Figure 2.4): whether employers are facing a domestic shortage of skilled workers; whether they have access to foreign skilled workers to meet that shortage; and the flexibility of skilled wages. These determine employers' type (B, S, or N) and hence their demand for worker training.

The first of these conditions—a skilled labor shortage—is easy to measure: it is signaled by a sharp rise in skilled-wage premia. Defining the latter two is more complex. A closed border can be literal—laws and troops at the border preventing people, goods, or both, from crossing—or metaphorical: an economic or cultural aversion to using foreign workers or producing in foreign countries. An economic aversion stems from a lack of mechanisms that can reduce the transaction costs involved in producing elsewhere or using foreign workers in domestic production: a language barrier; a large distance lacking cheap transportation; unstable macroeconomic conditions; onerous government regulation. A cultural aversion can flow from inter-ethnic distrust or sharp differences in working customs: e.g., differences in respect for hierarchy. Often a closed border can have both literal and metaphorical elements: a subset of countries and foreign workers is closed to a firm through cultural or economic barriers, and the remainder is closed by laws and soldiers. Where firms gain or lose access to foreign skilled workers, the proximate cause is somewhat secondary. It can be a change in any aspect of a border closing. In identifying a change in the access of employers to foreign skilled labor, the primary thing to look for is the opening or closing of an overseas location that can be either a site for production or a source of skilled workers.

The third factor, skilled-wage flexibility, is also affected by border policy, specifically emigration policy: wages are more elastic to labor supply when workers have no other choice but to look for work in the domestic job market. But the more common source of skilled-wage inflexibility is the strength of unions of skilled workers, whose very existence is largely to ensure that skilled wages are inelastic to labor supply.[37]

Thus to identify employer type, I look to three indicators: whether unions of skilled workers are strong; whether skilled wages are rising; and whether employers are able to access a source of lower-cost foreign skilled labor. These three indicators determine whether employers are type N, S, or B. Thus they determine whether employers will demand worker training and, if they do, whether they will want it to be Broad or Selective.

FAMILIES OUTSIDE THE VITAL CONSTITUENCY

What of those outside the vital constituency? What influence, if any, do they have on the government's education policy? Since the government does not need their support to continue governing, in normal circumstances it may safely ignore their demands. They have one means of influence over the government, but it is a costly one: revolt.[38] Revolt influences the government because it causes instability, and instability is threatening, both to the government's hold on power, and to the vital constituency's income. A government can deal with a revolt as doctors deal with a disease: either prevent it, or cure it. To prevent a revolt, the government can meet the minimum demands of those outside the VC; I call this *placating*. To "cure" a revolt, the government can forcibly stop it, through repression. With revolts, as with disease, preventing is usually cheaper than curing—both to the government and to the vital constituency. It is in the interest of governments, and their vital constituencies, to allow as much largesse to flow to those outside the VC as is minimally necessary to keep them from revolting, unless the value of the largesse is deemed higher than the cost of repressing the revolt.

From the idea of the vital constituency's support as the basis for a government's power, we can derive two factors that would weaken a government's grip on power or cause it to fall. The first is a lack of ability. Leaders must be able to put together and implement a policy package that satisfies their entire vital constituency. That is, the government must be able to implement policies that are at least close to the Pareto set of its members.[39] If it instead makes some members happy by making other members unhappy, the aggrieved citizens are likely to stop supporting the government, tipping the balance of power away from the government. The second is a mistake of choice. Leaders are not omniscient, and the society they govern is made up of groups of continuously shifting relative power. They have some control over the distribution of this power—that is the idea behind political entrepreneurship. But leaders may easily underestimate the power of a group to bring it down, and wrongly conclude that they can govern with a vital constituency that does not include that group.

These two problems—a lack of ability and a mistake of choice—lead to an important feature of the vital constituency: except for any placating minimum given to the rest of the citizenry, it gets all the government can offer. While the distribution of political power among societal groups is constant, the vital constituency's support is necessary and sufficient for the government to rule. Therefore the groups inside the vital constituency do not have to tolerate diversions of the government's largesse away from themselves. But even if the government was able to deliver some largesse to those outside the VC without threatening their support, it would not want to, for resources are empowering—they help groups pay their collective action costs—and shifting the power balance away from the vital constituency also threatens the government's rule.[40]

The preceding discussion developed a method for identifying a government's vital constituency, the groups of families and employers on whose support the government's power depends, independently both of regime type and of the policies the government is making. In a typical developing country where the government is not affiliated with a political entrepreneur of the poor, the vital constituency will be elites—which, in most developing countries, means the bureaucracy, the military, large landowners, and the captains of industry. Where the government is affiliated with a political entrepreneur, the poor will be in the vital constituency. Where that political entrepreneur is cross-class, the poor will join elites in a cross-class alliance; where the entrepreneur is anti-elite, the poor will constitute the vital constituency on their own. The government will try to meet the demands for education of any groups inside its vital constituency. The rest of the citizens are either repressed or will receive only a bare minimum of educational opportunity from the government to keep them from revolting.

4. The Goals of Education Policy

I have now offered answers to the two questions I posed at the start: what is the distribution of educational demands among the citizenry, and whose demands will the government try to meet. Using these two, I defined the broad goals of a government's education policy, given its vital constituency. To review, recall that vital constituencies can take three types—elites, a cross-class alliance, or the poor—and that each type may include employers, who can also take three types— N, B, or S. Thus there are nine possible education-demanding vital constituencies. Table 2.3 shows the matrix. The columns of Table 2.3 (boxes 1–3, 4–6, and 7–9) show the three types of vital constituencies, based on political entrepreneurship of the poor, as in Section 3 and Table 2.2 above: if the government is not affiliated with a political entrepreneur of the poor, the vital constituency is the elites; if it is affiliated with a cross-class political entrepreneur, the VC is a cross-class alliance; and, finally, if it is affiliated with an anti-elite political entrepreneur, the VC is the poor alone. The rows of Table 2.3 (boxes 1, 4, and 6; 2, 5, and 7; and 3, 6, and 9) show employer types in the vital constituency: Type B employers need skilled workers and operate in a flexible labor market; type S employers also need skilled workers but operate in an inflexible labor market; and type N employers do not need skilled workers. Since type N employers do not need skilled workers, they are equivalent to a vital constituency that does not include employers, and I put both in the same row: boxes 3, 6 and 9.

Boxes 4 and 7 in the table are shaded because they are unlikely. Although it is theoretically possible for a vital constituency of the poor or a cross-class alliance to have a flexible labor market (the United States is an example), in practice, where the poor are part of the vital constituency, the government is likely to allow unions and take other steps to protect the poor's wages. Usually, then, a vital constituency that includes the poor will not have a flexible labor market.

We saw in Section 2 that the demand of families for education will vary with their wealth and the demand of employers for education will vary with their need for skilled labor and the kind of labor market they face.[41] These demands will determine the sort of education system demanded by each of the nine types of vital constituencies in Table 2.3. Table 2.4 shows these demands. Poorer families prefer that the government concentrate on the lower education levels, so vital

Table 2.3 **The Education-Demanding Vital Constituency**

Employers	Political Entrepreneurship of the Poor		
	None	Cross-Class	Anti-Elite
Type B (Need skilled workers in a flexible skilled-labor market)	1 Elites and Type B Employers	4 Elites and the Poor (Cross-Class Alliance), and Type B Employers	7 Poor and Type B Employers
Type S (Need skilled workers in an inflexible skilled-labor market)	2 Elites and Type S Employers	5 Elites and the Poor (Cross-Class Alliance), and Type S Employers	8 Poor and Type S Employers
Type N (Do not need skilled workers) or outside the Vital Constituency	3 Elites	6 Elites and the Poor (Cross-Class Alliance)	9 Poor

Notes: "Elites" includes the military, the bureaucracy, and/or agrarian, and/or industrial elites. "Political Entrepreneurs" are of the poor only; elites, facing fewer collective action costs, do not need an entrepreneur's collective-action subsidy to organize. Shaded areas are unlikely, because in such a broad VC wages will not fall as the number of skilled workers increases. Types B, S, and N denote employers with different demands for worker training, as in Figure 2.4.

constituencies of the poor (boxes 7–9 in Table 2.4) will demand a Bottom-Up system. Wealthier families prefer that the government concentrate on the upper education levels, so the default vital constituency of elites (boxes 1–3) will demand a Top-Down system. In between these two columns is a cross-class alliance: a vital constituency that contains both poor and wealthy families. Such a vital constituency will present the government with both sorts of demands—Bottom-Up and Top-Down. A government of a cross-class alliance will therefore need to provide All Levels of education (boxes 4–6).

In the rows of Table 2.4 are employer types. If employers need skilled workers— if they are facing a skilled-worker shortage, and cannot access skilled workers abroad—they may demand Broad or Selective Worker Training, depending on the flexibility of the labor market. In a flexible labor market, type B employers demand Broad Worker Training, which seeks to lower skilled wages (boxes 1, 4, and 7). As in Table 2.3, boxes 4 and 7 in Table 2.4 are shaded: when the vital constituency includes the poor, the labor market is likely to be inflexible, meaning employers will be type S, not type B. In an inflexible labor market, type S employers demand Selective Worker Training, which seeks to provide employers with only the

Table 2.4 **Demands for education policy by different Vital Constituencies**

Employers	Families inside the Vital Constituency		
	Elites (no political entrepreneurship)	Elites and the Poor (cross-class political entrepreneurship)	Poor (anti-elite political entrepreneurship)
Type B (Need skilled workers in a flexible skilled-labor market)	1 *Education System* Top-Down *Worker Training* Broad	4 *Education System* All-Levels *Worker Training* Broad	7 *Education System* Bottom-Up *Worker Training* Broad
Type S (Need skilled workers in an inflexible skilled-labor market)	2 *Education System* Top-Down *Worker Training* Selective	5 *Education System* All-Levels *Worker Training* Selective	8 *Education System* Bottom-Up *Worker Training* Selective
Type N (Do not need skilled workers) or outside the Vital Constituency	3 *Education System* Top-Down *Worker Training* None	6 *Education System* All-Levels *Worker Training* None	9 *Education System* Bottom-Up *Worker Training* None

Notes: A "Top-Down" education system concentrates its resources at the highest level and takes on a lower level only insofar as the government has extra resources after making sufficient improvements to the level above it. A "Bottom-Up" education system concentrates its resources on the lowest level and takes on a higher level only insofar as the government has extra resources after making sufficient improvements to the level below it. "Selective" worker training provides employers with targeted assistance for worker training—usually specialized training, grants, or tax breaks—engineered to provide them with enough, and only enough, of the skilled workers they need. "Broad" worker training uses the education system to lower the wages of workers with the skills the employer needs by educating as many workers as possible in those skills. Shaded areas are unlikely, because when the vital constituency includes the poor, wages will not be elastic to the supply of skilled workers.

number of skilled workers they need, but with exactly the skills they need (boxes 2, 5, and 8). Type *N* employers do not need skilled labor: either they are not facing a skilled-worker shortage, or they can access skilled workers abroad by importing them or moving their production abroad. Thus type *N* employers do not demand worker training, and to a government are equivalent to a vital constituency that does not include employers.

Tables 2.3 and 2.4, like the typologies on which they are based, are obviously simplifications. A vital constituency may include employers of several types: one skilled sector of the economy may have a flexible labor market (type *B*), while another may be heavily unionized (type *S*), and a third might employ mostly non-skilled workers (type *N*). And the three-part typology of vital constituencies does not include the middle class: a vital constituency may, for example, include elites and the middle class, and exclude the poor, or include the middle class and the poor and exclude elites. The typology of vital constituencies also does not include the role of inequality, economic advancement, and per capita income, all of which will adjust the demands of families away from the ideal-types of Bottom-Up and Top-Down education systems. Here I leave out these possibilities for simplicity, though for each of the case studies I define the vital constituency with greater precision. But predictions for these possibilities follow the same logic, combining the predicted demands of families in Figure 2.3, and of employers in Figure 2.4. For example: if only some employers employ skilled labor in a flexible wage environment, only those employers would demand broad worker training, while the rest would not have a demand for worker training. Likewise a vital constituency with elites and the middle class would demand both improvements at the primary and secondary levels, and increased access and improvements to the tertiary level.

We now have a framework for understanding the broad goals of government education policy. Vital constituencies fit into a nine-part typology, each of which is associated with a different ideal education system. For each type, the government will build an education system, or adjust the existing education system, so that it comes as close as possible to the ideal education system of its vital constituency. The next question is: how will the government do this?

CHAPTER 3

Building the Education System

Goals are only half the story. If governments were omnipotent, knowing their goals for education would be enough. But government power is limited. Furthermore, these limits vary: governments differ not just in their educational goals, but in the resources they can devote to education and the success with which they can translate resources into education. Thus when a framework like the one in the previous chapter confines itself to goals, its accuracy is difficult to assess. A true picture of a government's intent for education comes from observing what the government does with the resources and tools it has: its relative investment in universities, secondary schools, and primary schools; where it builds schools; how well or poorly it trains, pays, and supervises the teachers in these schools; the fees schools charge and the scholarships and financial aid they offer; and the degree to which the government allows, regulates, and subsidizes education in the private sector.

This chapter analyzes these limits and uses them to develop specific predictions about how the government will use its resources and tools; these predictions allow testing of the framework in Ghana, Taiwan, and Brazil. The chapter's objective is to consider, myopically, how a government would shape every particular aspect of the education system if its only goal was to serve its vital constituency.[1] Then in later chapters I examine how closely actual governments in Taiwan, Ghana, and Brazil came to adjusting each aspect of their education systems as they would have if their singular purpose was to serve their vital constituencies.

The goals of education policy are in Table 3.1, which reproduces Table 2.4. They deal with the availability and price of various levels and types of education. In the previous chapter I argued that citizens in the vital constituency are happiest when the level and type of education most valuable to them is available to them, and only them, at minimum cost. To create a system that tries to meet that demand, the government has a wide range of tools at its disposal. A typical education system includes schools, teachers, access restrictions (such as exams), financial aid, tracking, and some degree of outsourcing to the private sector. These things have the primary purpose of educating. But they are also "tools" through which the government can channel educational opportunity to certain groups of citizens and away from others, creating for the vital constituency a system that is so constituted and priced as to meet the vital constituency's educational demands as closely as possible. Used together, the tools in the education toolkit allow the government to create one of the nine types of systems, one for each type of vital constituency. They permit one government to make good primary education widely available (a Bottom-Up system) and another to put the bulk of its resources into higher education and close that system off to the poor (a Top-Down system).

Table 3.1 **The Framework**

Employers	Families inside the Vital Constituency		
	Elites (no political entrepreneurship)	Elites and the Poor (cross-class political entrepreneurship)	Poor (anti-elite political entrepreneurship)
Type B (Need skilled workers in a flexible skilled-labor market)	1 *Education System* Top-Down *Worker Training* Broad	4 *Education System* All-Levels *Worker Training* Broad	7 *Education System* Bottom-Up *Worker Training* Broad
Type S (Need skilled workers in an inflexible skilled-labor market)	2 *Education System* Top-Down *Worker Training* Selective	5 *Education System* All-Levels *Worker Training* Selective	8 *Education System* Bottom-Up *Worker Training* Selective
Type N (Do not need skilled workers) or outside the Vital Constituency	3 *Education System* Top-Down *Worker Training* None	6 *Education System* All-Levels *Worker Training* None	9 *Education System* Bottom-Up *Worker Training* None

Notes: A "Top-Down" education system concentrates its resources at the highest level and takes on a lower level only insofar as the government has extra resources after making sufficient improvements to the level above it. A "Bottom-Up" education system concentrates its resources on the lowest level and takes on a higher level only insofar as the government has extra resources after making sufficient improvements to the level below it. "Selective" worker training provides employers with targeted assistance for worker training—usually specialized training, grants, or tax breaks—engineered to provide them with enough, and only enough, of the skilled workers they need. "Broad" worker training uses the education system to lower the wages of workers with the skills the employer needs by educating as many workers as possible in those skills. Shaded areas are unlikely, because when the vital constituency includes the poor, wages will not be elastic to the supply of skilled workers.

They allow a government to create Broad or Selective Worker Training. And they allow a new government to alter the system it inherits from the previous government, molding it into the system the new vital constituency wants.

The education toolkit is powerful. It can channel educational opportunity using important criteria, such as wealth, ethnicity, and geography. Often the vital constituency can be distinguished using these same criteria. Farmers, for example, may have similar incomes and locations, as may workers or soldiers. But the toolkit is not omnipotent. Sometimes groups in the vital constituency share similar finances, or mix geographically or ethnically, with those outside it. To the extent that the vital constituency cannot be distinguished along lines of wealth, geography, or ethnicity, the toolkit is imprecise. And this imprecision is only one of several constraints on the government. Building, staffing, and funding an education system take substantial technical and financial capacity, and no government has unlimited supplies of either. Then there is the inflexibility of an education system: once built, it is hard to change. Lastly, there are limits to how blatantly the government will be able to close off educational opportunity to those outside the vital constituency. The high value of education sows discontent among those denied it, and the more obvious and unfair the denial, the less they may be inclined to keep quiet. Certain tools in the toolkit—those based on ethnicity, for example—carry this risk, and may be too dangerous for many governments to use. A government must preserve social stability, both for its own sake and for the vital constituency's.

I begin in Section 1 with the tools and then consider their limits in Section 2. Section 3 lays out predictions for how governments will use the toolkit, incorporating path dependence. The first government to create a modern education system—the government I call the *pioneer*—has more freedom in serving its vital constituencies than later governments, which are left to mold the existing system.

1. The Government's Education Toolkit

A modern education system customarily consists of a number of elements. Education occurs in school buildings, operated by the government or private entities. Inside these, teachers use books and other classroom materials to implant skill and knowledge in students. Their success is often evaluated by exams, which may also determine whether a student is eligible to acquire further education. Schools may charge fees to cover the part of their cost that is not funded from other sources. The government or private entities may help some students to offset these fees with financial aid, which they can allocate according to some assessment of a student's need, merit, or another criteria. All these aspects of an education system allow it to do its primary job: educating students.

But these same elements serve a second purpose. Schools, teachers, and classroom materials are always in limited supply, as are the financial resources to pay for them. Questions of distribution are thus an inevitable part of the design of any education system. The distribution has consequences for each student's education. A change in the distribution changes the price and quality of the education available to each student, and thereby the return on that education. Because price and quality are the key criteria through which families choose to invest in the education of their children, the government must design its education system so that price and quality meet the demand of the vital constituency.

The elements of the education system allow the government to do this. The building of schools, the training and paying of teachers, the providing of books and other materials, the content and consequence of exams, the price of education, the availability of financial aid to offset the price, and the freedom of private entities to provide education—each of these inevitably involves a decision about the price and quality of every student's education. Thus I begin with the prediction that every government will design each element of its education system to meet one of two goals: either to lower the price and maximize the quality of the education of its vital constituency; or to provide suitably priced education to those outside the vital constituency to induce them to become skilled workers for employers inside the vital constituency.

I divide the "education toolkit" into five categories: schools; fees; academic restrictions and discriminatory pricing; tracking; and outsourcing. Table 3.2 summarizes the toolkit. The remainder of this section considers how each tool adjusts the price and quality of a student's education. Along the way, I note the limits of each tool in targeting the vital constituency with precision.

TOOL 1 : SCHOOLS

The government's most important set of tools is schools themselves. The government needs to decide how many of the three levels—primary, secondary, and tertiary—to build, where to build them, and the resources to devote to each. Resources are both physical—buildings, books, chalk, desks—and human: teachers. Physical resources are straightforward production inputs, produced by the government itself or purchased from an outside supplier. Teachers are a more complex sort of resource; they cast the government in the role of an employer. The government must decide whether to staff its classrooms with teachers who are trained or untrained. Teachers need not be trained: the government has the option of simply hiring people off the street to staff classrooms. But if they are trained, the education they offer will usually be of higher quality. If the government decides to use trained teachers, it has the same options as any employer who wishes to hire skilled workers: it can import teachers trained elsewhere, or use teachers trained in the education system. Because the government is also the producer of education, the latter decision entails

Table 3.2 **The government's education-policy toolkit**

Schools	Fees	Access restrictions and discriminatory pricing	Tracking	Outsourcing
Teachers (trained or untrained)	Enrollment	Quotas	Quality	To:
	Books and other equipment	Exams	Curricula (academic or vocational)	Firms
		Financial aid		Non-profit organiza-tions
Physical resources	Uniforms	*Types:*		
	Activities	Scholarships	[Tracking uses:	
Location	School improvements	Grants	schools (of differing quality and/or teaching differ-ent criteria); exams; and financial aid]	*Types:*
		Subsidized loans		High-quality (directed to VC)
		Tax breaks		
		Opportunity-cost payouts		Low-quality (directed outside VC)
		Criteria:		
		Need		
		Merit		Foreign
		Ethnicity		Domestic

devoting one part of the education system to the training of teachers for the other parts of the system.

Adjustments in schools have straightforward effects on education's price and quality. Building a school closer to a family will lower the transportation costs of schooling available to that family; increasing the quantity or quality of the re-sources—physical and human—devoted to that school will increase the quality of the education available to that family. But these price reductions and quality im-provements precisely target the vital constituency only to the extent that the vital constituency clusters geographically. If members of the vital constituency live in the same area as non-members, a school built in the area lowers the price of educa-tion to both members and non-members. The same is true of efforts to raise the quality of the education at a school, whether with more resources or better teachers.

TOOL 2 : FEES

Transportation costs are just one segment of education's price. A government must also decide what to charge students to attend each type of school. This price is the sum of school fees, which come in many forms: there are enrollment fees, fees for books and other equipment, fees for uniforms, fees for special activities, fees for school improvements, and myriad others. If a government charges lower fees, more students will be able to afford them. This lowers the price of education, but also the quality: not only does every student contribute less to the production cost of their education, but, if the government spends more producing education than it collects in fees, whatever resources the government commits to the education in addition to the fees must be spread over more students. Obviously the opposite is true for higher fees: they mean fewer students can afford to go, and those who can must pay more. But higher fees also mean higher quality.

In the same way that schools precisely target the vital constituency only when it clusters geographically, fees precisely target the vital constituency only when it is distinguishable by wealth. A fee decrease will lower the fees for everyone at a school, not just members of the vital constituency; to the extent that members of the vital constituency have the same level of financial resources as non-members, a fee decrease will equally benefit both.

TOOL 3 : ACCESS RESTRICTIONS AND DISCRIMINATORY PRICING

A fee decrease will ordinarily allow more students to attend. But the government can limit the number of new students, preserving or increasing the quality of the education for the remaining students even as they pay less. The most obvious method is quotas, by which a government can allow only certain students access. Quotas can be based on anything the government can discern in applicants; two options are wealth and ethnicity (for example, affirmative action). A second access restriction is an entrance exam. A fee decrease at the tertiary level might allow more secondary graduates to afford to attend the university; with quotas or an entrance exam, the government can limit the number of new university students despite the fee decrease.

These access restrictions are only as accurate as their distributive criteria. They can direct access to the vital constituency to the extent that the vital constituency is distinguishable along the dimension on which they are based: need, merit, ethnicity, or something else. Quotas are one of the most accurate tools, since they can be linked to almost any criteria; but they bring other problems, discussed below. Exams are far less accurate: anyone can prepare independently for one, and the aptitude measured may not be wholly possessed by students in the vital constituency, no matter what other advantages they have. In most countries there are stories of students "pulling themselves up by their bootstraps"—succeeding against the odds.

The government can also limit a flood of new students by giving a fee decrease only to a certain number of students. Scholarships, subsidized loans, tax breaks on personal education expenditures, and other financial aid are all selective fee decreases. Scholarships, grants, and tax breaks directly subsidize the price students pay to attend school. Subsidized loans correct the failure of the education-credit market to provide loans against future earnings; the government can provide loans itself, or guarantee private banks a certain return on them to mitigate their riskiness. Financial aid can be given to all students attending a certain type of school, but it can also be given on numerous criteria, thereby determining more selectively whose education will be cheaper. Financial aid given by wealth criteria—or on the basis of "need"—will restrict the price decrease to applicants from poorer families. Financial aid given on ethnic background will restrict the price decrease to applicants of a certain ethnicity. And merit-based financial aid can lower the price for applicants who have demonstrated ability.

Like quotas, financial aid can be based on almost any distributive criteria, and is therefore one of the more accurate tools in the toolkit. It is also one of the most versatile: within the limits of the budget, it can be set to make up for some or all of the price of education, including its opportunity cost. Need-based financial aid, for example, can be in the form of payouts to poor families who send their children to primary schools to make up for the lost labor of those children. Another example is merit-based financial aid, which can be given as stipends to graduate students to make up for the earnings they lose by not working.

Need and ethnicity are measured straightforwardly. But merit is harder to discern, and therefore the effect of merit-based aid needs more attention. In a system where every school is the same, and an exam tests all graduates on the knowledge and ability learned in school, merit aid might be given on the basis of performance on that exam. A government might thereby restrict access to higher levels to students who had shown higher ability at lower levels. Financial aid given to those students would lower the price of education to students of high ability. But the government does not have to create every school equal, and in a system with differences between schools, merit becomes harder to discern. This difficulty brings us to another tool at the government's disposal: tracking.

TOOL 4 : TRACKING

Tracking is differentiated education with cumulative advantage: each level of a track builds on the advantages acquired in the previous level. Tracking is not actually its own tool, but rather a selective combination of several tools already mentioned: schools, tests, and financial aid.

Until now, I have written of a school system in which schools within each level—primary, secondary, or tertiary—are homogeneous. But they need not be: the government can build some schools within a level that are different than the others. One possibility is to make some better—to give them more and better resources. Students in these schools will receive better education, which increases the value of that education and enables them to perform better in higher levels. They will also, all else being equal, perform better on an exam than those who have had inferior education. Another possibility is to give different tracks different curricula. The possibilities for curricula differences are infinite, but two particular types of difference deserve mention. The first is a difference in the relevance of the curricula to an exam. A graduate from a school whose curriculum is designed around an exam will, all else being equal, do better on that exam than a student from a school whose curriculum is irrelevant to the exam.

The second type of difference is between academic and vocational curricula. Vocational education is distinguished from academic by its applied content. It teaches a curriculum designed to impart a practical skill in preparation for a specific, generally blue-collar, vocation. Academic education, by contrast, generally prepares a student for further study or for white-collar work. Schools can concentrate on one or the other, or within a single school there may be two tracks—one teaching vocational skills and one academic—each preparing students for two different types of work or study: vocational graduates for blue-collar work or further training in a specialized trade school, and academic graduates for white-collar work or more academic education.

A track builds from such differences. It is constituted by combining differentiated schools, curricula, and/or entrance exams designed to test the knowledge and ability learned in those schools. The key feature of a track is that it compounds initial differences. At the extreme, an elite track might begin with primary schools that are better than others, and which teach a different curriculum. It may follow those with entrance exams that test the sort of knowledge and ability taught in those primary schools and which determine access to an elite group of secondary schools teaching a different curriculum from the other secondary schools in the system. And it may follow those with an entrance exam to a university that tests the knowledge and ability in the curriculum of the elite secondary schools. A student in this track, simply by going to a better primary school teaching a different curriculum, has a much better chance of going to the university than one who is not in the track. In general a track gives a student from a certain school, or from a certain class within a school, a good chance of gaining admission to higher levels. In a system with tracks, passage from one level to the next ceases, to some extent, to be based on ability, and instead becomes a function of a student's track.

Tracking also carries an important implication for merit-based financial aid. In a system with tracks, exams cannot accurately measure ability, because students are taught different curricula in classrooms of varying quality. Thus in a system with tracks, financial aid allotted to students who perform well on an exam will lower the price of education for students whose track prepares them for that exam.

Tracking is an excellent tool for targeting access to the vital constituency, particularly when the government cannot completely refashion an existing education system into one that is ideal for its vital constituency. (Path-dependence in education systems is extremely common; I examine it below.) Because tracking combines several tools—schools, exams, and financial aid—it can be fashioned to be more accurate than any one of those tools individually. For example, an exam can more accurately target the vital constituency if it tests knowledge or skills that students from the vital constituency are particularly likely to possess, because they have greater access to schools that teach it. Naturally, the downside is that the cumulative advantage offered by a track could just as easily propel a student from outside the vital constituency, if he is able at some point to gain entrance to the track.

TOOL 5 : OUTSOURCING

Readers may note that I have so far neglected one important aspect of almost all actual education systems in the world today: parts of them are private. To meet the vital constituency's demand for education, the government can directly produce education. Directly producing education has important benefits: it gives the government direct control over the system, which is especially helpful if the government wishes to use education to encourage obedience or national pride.[2] But like any producer, the government also has the option of outsourcing. Doing so has a singular advantage: it makes education available at little or no cost to the government. Yet it also has a singular disadvantage: it subordinates the government's motives in providing education to the motives of the market, with which it can only interfere within the limits of its powers of regulation.

There are several reasons why a government may accept market motivations in order to free up resources. The first is to provide education to those outside the vital constituency without using the education budget. The following section considers circumstances in which the government may want to provide some education to those outside the vital constituency—for instance, to offer employers Broad Worker Training or to preserve social stability. The government needs a way to provide this education without threatening the flow of government resources to the education of those inside the vital constituency. Outsourcing is one option: the government has regulatory power that it can use to ensure that the education provided in the private sector is of a low enough quality and/or high enough price to be unthreatening to the education provided to the vital constituency. Imagine a country with one excellent public university, whose graduates are very highly remunerated because demand for university graduates in the job market is high. With its other tools, the government might ensure that these graduates are normally children of the vital constituency. Because of the job-market demand for university education, parents of non-VC children who did not make it into the government's university might be willing and able to pay for university education, even of a lesser quality. Thus the private sector might find it profitable to open such alternative universities. If the government opened the door to private universities, and simultaneously regulated the price to some high minimum and/or the quality to some low maximum, it could both control the proportion of non-VC children able to attend, and ensure that the education those children received was uncompetitive with the education provided in the public university.

The second reason the government might choose to outsource is to provide private education to those *inside* the vital constituency, allowing them to acquire more education and/or education of a greater quality than the government's budget would otherwise allow. In the same country as in the example above, the government might not be able to provide both a high-quality public university and high-quality primary and secondary schools. If the vital constituency is wealthy enough, it will prefer that the government put its money into the university and allow the private sector to provide high-quality primary and secondary schools that feed into the university. As in the example above, the government can use its regulatory power to ensure that the price and the quality are high enough to make those private schools good preparers of future university students, and inaccessible to those outside the vital constituency.

Yet whether outsourcing is intended to provide education to those inside or outside the vital constituency, outsourcing always entails the same disadvantage: private producers have their own reasons for producing education, and the government must ensure that the private producers' goals are met to a sufficient extent to motivate them. This disadvantage makes outsourcing among the least accurate tools in the government's toolkit for targeting education to the vital constituency. A private producer's motivations will probably never fully parallel the government's, and in outsourcing to that producer the government is accepting the private actor's motivations, including to whom that actor wishes to provide education, of what kind, and at what price.

Private producers fall into two categories: firms and non-profit organizations. Firms will be motivated by profit, and outsourcing to them means accepting their profit motive. Non-profit organizations may be motivated by various factors: altruism, membership, or the goals of those persons or governments that provide their funding. I consider firms and non-profit producers in turn.

A firm producing education will try to maximize profit. If the government allows it to consider producing education, a firm will observe the willingness and ability of families in the population to pay for education, determine whether providing that education at the price families are willing and able to pay is profitable, and, if it is, produce that education. Unlike the government, a firm will not create an education system that loses money: it will only produce education the price of which generates more revenue than its costs. Wherever there is unmet demand for education by families with the resources to afford education at the price the private sector would charge, there is room for the government to allow the private sector to produce education. Absent any other aid, these families are the potential beneficiaries of a government decision to allow private production. At the extreme, the government may benefit all these families by granting complete freedom to the private sector to produce education. Or it may be more selective. It may, for example, grant the private sector the right to produce education of only a certain level. Or it may limit the number of firms licensed to produce or the number of students they are allowed to educate.

Because firms are motivated by profit, they can be counted on to produce any sort and quality of education for which there is unmet demand by families with resources. It is this aspect of outsourcing to firms that allows outsourcing to be both a way of providing poor quality education to those outside the vital constituency, and an alternate way of providing high quality education to those inside the vital constituency. If unmet demand exists for better education than the government is providing, a firm will be willing to provide better education, just as it will be willing to provide poorer quality education if there are families willing to pay for education of a lower quality than what the government is offering.

Because firms require profit, education produced by firms may be expensive. This reality is a feature of any government decision to allow the private sector to produce education. The government has the option of limiting the profits that firms are permitted, but in the process it will discourage firms from entering the education market. The government also has the option of using another of its tools—financial aid—to subsidize the private-sector price. It can give scholarships to students attending private schools. Or it can allow students in private schools access to subsidized loans. But these subsidies partly offset the savings the government can realize by using the private sector.

The government can avoid the problem of providing firms with profit if it can outsource to the second type of producer, non-profit organizations, which by definition lack the profit motive. Some non-profits may even be willing to offer education at a money-losing price. Non-governmental organizations (NGOs) often use donations to subsidize schooling. Religions for centuries have subsidized schools from their collection baskets.

But non-profits replace profit with a host of other motives. These are not a mystery: most non-profits are very clear about to whom they wish to provide education of what kind and at what price. And to some extent they may be flexible: an NGO or a religious organization may wish to build a primary school in a poor village but may allow the government to tell it in which village it can build. But non-profits probably cannot be pressed into providing just the type of education the government would have. Thus who will benefit from outsourcing to a non-profit will depend partly on what kind of education the non-profit wishes to provide. In allowing a non-profit to provide education, the government is to some extent accepting the goals of the non-profit providing it.

Most outsourcing will be domestic. But the government also has the option of outsourcing to foreign firms or non-profits. A certain amount of foreign outsourcing is a feature of any country with an open border: a family with wherewithal can consider sending their children abroad to any school in any country that will accept them and for which it can pay the requisite fees and other expenses. But this is an expensive way to educate a child, open to relatively few families in even the richest country. In an effort to direct access to foreign education, the government can use its other tools and/or its regulatory power. For example, the government has the option of lowering the price of studying abroad by subsidizing it, thereby opening it to more families. On the other hand, the government can raise the price of studying abroad—for example, by requiring that students pass a difficult exam before they are given an exit visa. With a combination of targeted access restrictions and financial aid, the government can open or close studying abroad as an option to almost any group of citizens it wishes. But studying abroad is expensive enough that those taking advantage of it will likely be a small group; it will be a rare government that will prefer subsidizing the education of a large group of students in foreign countries to providing that education domestically.

In sum, outsourcing can free the government from the cost of providing education itself. But private education is guided by the motives of the actor providing it: for a firm, profit; for a non-profit, myriad goals, from doing good to following the dictates of a funder. The government has some room to manipulate these goals and allow them to be selectively pursued through its regulatory power. It can also restrict access to, and subsidize the price of, private education, just as it does public education. But these countervailing tools have limits, and a government decision to allow the private sector to produce education is ultimately at least a partial acceptance by the government of the goals of private-sector providers, of who will benefit from their pursuit, and of who will not.

Thus far this section has described five categories of tools in a government's education toolkit. Manipulation of schools, fees, access restrictions and discriminatory pricing, tracking, and outsourcing all raise or lower the price and quality of education available to various citizens. If the book's framework is accurate, these manipulations should consistently favor the vital constituency, raising the quality and/or lowering the price of the education available to them, and raising the price and/or lowering the quality of education available to those outside the vital constituency. In the case chapters we will see that with rare exceptions governments use their toolkit in exactly this way.

Yet I have also noted that each tool is imprecise in its ability to target the vital constituency. Much of the imprecision stems from a common cause: reliance on a family's financial resources and location to delineate whether or not its children will benefit from education. A few tools—those using merit or ethnicity—can make use of other criteria. But in general the tools make use of pricing differences—direct, opportunity, and transportation—and are therefore most accurate when they can be used to direct educational opportunity to those in a locality who can afford to spend a particular amount on their children's schooling. Reliance on pricing means that the government can rarely design its education system to serve *only* its vital constituency. Most important, although pricing is a good way to direct education to the rich, it is not a good way to direct it to the poor. It is easy to use pricing to make education available only to rich people: you simply set the price high enough that poor people cannot afford it. But it is impossible to use pricing alone to make education available only to poor people, because whatever the poor can afford, the rich can afford too. A government that wishes to include the poor and exclude the rich must therefore rely on other tools. We will return to this problem below in considering how governments with various vital constituencies are likely to construct their education systems: those with wealthy vital constituencies can construct education systems that are unavailable to the poor, but those with poor vital constituencies may have to settle for systems that are preferred by the poor but are still available to the rich.

Naturally, the toolkit's imprecision will be compounded by any imprecision in the government's identification of its vital constituency, particularly when the government cannot identify the vital constituency along the key dimensions of wealth, geography, and ethnicity. The government's vital constituency is a collection of groups. These groups may share similar finances—if they are farmers, or entrepreneurs—and may share an ethnicity and a location—an urban center, or a particular rural region. But they may not, or may not to a sufficient extent to delineate them on those dimensions from other groups outside the vital constituency.

The imprecision of the toolkit is one constraint on the government as it tries to orient the distribution of the education system to serve its vital constituency. Alongside this imprecision are other important constraints that limit the government's ability to wield its toolkit freely. These constraints are the subject of the next section.

2. Constraints

While imprecise, the government's toolkit is powerful, and, in the absence of other constraints, the government might be able to use it to design an education system very close to the vital constituency's ideal. But the imprecision of the toolkit is not the government's only constraint. In this section, I explore three other constraints: governments have limited capacity, education systems are inflexible and path dependent, and governments must preserve social stability even as they try to meet the educational demands of their vital constituencies.

CAPACITY LIMITS

The first set of limits with which the government must deal in building its education system is its capacity. Capacity limits are of two types: financial and technical.

Ideally, the vital constituency would want the government to fully meet its demand for education. But in reality, no government has unlimited funds with which to meet this demand. For example, families in the vital constituency may ideally want the government to fund fully their education all the way from kindergarten through medical or law school. But doing so might bankrupt even the richest government. In addition, the education ministry will be only one of many clamoring for resources. Before resources reach schools, the financing of education goes through at least two levels of budgeting: the government must decide how much of its total budget to spend on education, and how much of its education budget to spend on each part of the education system.

This book has very little to say about the first of these two levels; in general I treat the overall education budget as largely exogenous. My focus, rather, is on how the government chooses to spend its education budget, not on the contribution it makes to the education budget relative to its health budget or defense budget.

There are two reasons for this. First, while the vital constituency has views about the proportion of its taxes that should go to education, in large part these views have nothing to do with education. Instead they depend on myriad other factors that are outside the scope of this framework. For instance, an agrarian country may need to weigh its education spending against agricultural development and support, while an industrialized country may need to weigh education against subsidies to industry. The range of such options is almost infinite, and no two governments will have the same set of policies and spending against which to weigh education. It might be possible, with a large sample of countries, to control for other uses of government money, and therefore discern one government's relative commitment to education over another's. Many existing studies on education policy in political economy rely on large samples to do precisely this.[3] But as this book relies on a small sample of detailed case studies, it is ill suited to the question of the relative size of the education budget. Thus while I do not ignore the size of the education budget when I turn to the cases, I also do not try to predict it.

The second reason for focusing on the allocation of the education budget rather than its size is that comparatively little of the variation in education spending is in the size of the budget. An example from the case studies is illustrative: in Taiwan over the 1990s, the proportion of the government's budget spent on education rose less than 2 percentage points, from 17.5 to 19.2 percent of total spending. But over the same period, per-student spending on primary students nearly tripled, even after adjusting for inflation (Republic of China 2005b). The magnitudes differ similarly in Ghana and Brazil. In addition, an individual's demand for the overall level of education spending (as distinct from the distribution of that spending) does not rise or fall much with his or her income: even in a country with extensive private options for education, like the United States, empirical work generally shows that individual income has at most a miniscule impact on the desired level of public education spending.[4] The rigidity of education budgets makes it reasonable to conceive of them as a constraint on the government. This rigidity is not complete, and in certain circumstances the government will be able to increase its relative contribution to the education ministry. But the constraint exists, forcing much of the government's choices onto the distribution of the budget.

There is one notable source of funds that I do not assume to be exogenous: foreign aid. A government cannot usually cause a donor to give it more foreign aid; in this sense, foreign aid is as exogenous as the rest of the education budget. But governments can choose whether or not to *accept* foreign aid. In this sense, foreign aid is not exogenous, and this book's framework can shed some light on a government's decision to accept it. Indeed, in two of the countries, Ghana and Brazil, aid interacts with the education policymaking predicted by the framework.

In these countries, the government's decision about whether to accept foreign aid is similar to its decisions about whether to outsource. Donors of foreign aid, like private providers of education, have their own goals in mind when they give aid. Governments accept aid when these goals coincide with the government's, and in these instances the donor will see its aid used effectively. For example, a government trying to provide education for a poorer vital constituency will find it advantageous to accept help from an external donor that wants to improve access to basic education; a government with a wealthier vital constituency may find help from donors interested in funding institutions of higher education or improving international cross-cultural or academic relations.

But if a donor's goals are at odds with the government's, the government will only accept the aid if it believes it can manipulate its use or siphon it off to other uses. The government serves its vital constituency, and it will not allow any aid it receives to do otherwise. Governments are assisted in this by the fundamental fungibility of aid: developing-country governments have a good track record of adjusting their budgets so that the marginal effect of any aid is to increase spending on what the government, not the donor, wants.[5] Thus where the government's goals differ from the donor's, the government may still accept foreign aid; the difference is that, where the government's goals are different than the donor's, the donor will likely watch unhappily as its aid is either misused or wasted.

The education budget is the government's first major capacity limitation. Its second is its technical capacity. Education is a complex product to produce. First, it takes time. Schools and universities take time to build, teachers take time to train or retrain, and students must devote years to study before reaping education's intellectual and pecuniary rewards.

Education is also demanding of capital, expertise, and administrative competence. To build and staff a school of reasonable quality, a government needs to provide the materials and engineering know-how to build the school; a system to hire and handle the employment of teachers, and probably a system to train them; a distribution system capable of getting materials and equipment to schools; and a general administrative structure to keep control of the operation of education day-to-day. If a government decides to use access restrictions, discriminatory pricing, or tracking, it will need the extra capacity to provide and administer exams, quotas, and/or financial aid. This level of technical capacity is easily found in most developed countries, but for many developing countries it is taxing.

Of the requirements of quality education, the provision of qualified teachers is among the most taxing. If qualified teachers are not essential to quality education, they are generally accepted to be one of the most important contributors. They are also a potential headache for a government: attracting competent candidates in the job market can be expensive, and training them takes time and costs still more money. Once they are hired they may be very difficult to fire or retrain when the government needs their services elsewhere. Thus a government that makes an effort to provide them is making a costly investment in the education of the students the new teachers will teach. (I return to the quality of teachers below. The costliness of this investment makes the quality of teachers a signal of the quality of education the government is trying to provide.)

Like its budgetary constraints, the government can relieve its technical constraints with outside assistance. Donors of foreign aid can, for example, also be a source of technical capacity: the World Bank and most donor agencies regularly provide expertise in education-system planning and teacher-training to developing countries. These can be of great help to a government lacking these capacities. The logic of accepting them is the same as for financial capacity: only if they will either serve the vital constituency or can be put to other uses.

INHERITANCE AND THE INFLEXIBILITY OF EDUCATION SYSTEMS

The second limit on the government is the inflexible nature of education. In most existing analyses of education in political science, education is often treated simply as another form of redistribution.[6] The implication of this treatment is that the government can mold an education system as it wishes. But education systems are not like pensions or tax policy. Just as education is complex to produce and takes time to consume, it is complex and time-consuming to adjust.[7] While this characteristic of education often insulates it from the variability that can plague other areas of government policy, it also means that the education system will respond slowly to the government's efforts to change it, often to the dissatisfaction of members of the vital constituency for whom rapid change would be more desirable.

The first government to build a modern education system has considerable freedom to design one in the interest of its vital constituency.[8] But future governments are left to adjust as best they can the system the previous government left them. These governments inherit a system of schools and their students, teachers and administrators, financing, curricula, any exams, quotas, or financial aid the previous government used to regulate access and pricing to different levels, and some degree of outsourcing. A new government with substantially different goals for education than its predecessor will not find this system easy to change. Administrators and teachers are entrenched in their positions, and may have specialized expertise. The previous government may have attempted to lock in some aspects of the distribution of educational resources, by using dedicated taxes or particular divisions of responsibility between regions or levels of government.[9] Curricula, exams, quotas, and financial aid are easier to adjust, but they still may require substantial evaluation to determine which the government needs to change or implement in order to direct opportunity to the vital constituency. Finally, the government may inherit a system that makes some use of outsourcing in providing education, and where the motivations of private-sector providers are out of step with the new government's, the new government will need to reorient them. The constraints imposed on a government by the education system it inherits are idiosyncratic to the country and to time. The point is simply that no government, after the first one to create a modern education system, has the freedom to start from scratch. In reorienting the education system to serve the new vital constituency, it must do what it can with what it has.

PRESERVING STABILITY

The government's third and final limitation is its need to preserve social stability. The vital constituency cares about its income, and this depends on a certain amount of domestic tranquility.[10] Stability is not always contingent on educational opportunity, but it can be. In situations where groups perceive the government to be practicing gross favoritism in the distribution of educational resources, those who feel cut off from those resources may not accept it quietly. This is more likely the more glaring the differences between the opportunity available to those outside and those inside the vital constituency.

Two situations in particular may lead to unrest. First, following a major shift in the vital constituency, if the government completely cuts off newly disempowered groups from educational opportunities they previously enjoyed, these groups may be inclined to destabilizing dissatisfaction. Imagine a group of families in a country where university education was highly subsidized and a university degree was well-rewarded by the job market. If these families had believed that their children would be able to attend the universities, they may have consequently invested in primary and secondary education; if suddenly university education was cut off to their children by a new government with different priorities, they might find their previous investments worth much less than they expected, and their disappointment might lead them to protest.

Even in a country with a stable vital constituency, gradually increasing inequality in educational opportunity might foment unrest. Imagine the same country as in the previous example. If for many years universities continued to accept the same number of students, even while the demand for university students in the job market was increasing, university graduates would be able to demand ever-larger salaries. Parents of students outside the vital constituency, whose children face extreme difficulty in attending university, might, on observing the growing returns to a university education, find their children's exclusion more and more difficult to take, and might eventually decide not to take it.

Faced with unrest stemming from a lack of educational opportunity available to those outside the vital constituency, the government can repress the aggrieved, or placate them. Repression is costly, and may add to instability, so placating is usually preferable. In placating, the government's goal is to deliver as little largess to those outside the vital constituency as possible, both because that largess is costly to its ability to serve its vital constituency, and because largess can empower groups outside the vital constituency and thereby tip the balance of power away from the VC, threatening the government's hold on power. The latter is a particular concern with educational opportunity, because more educated citizens tend to present governments with heightened demands, and there is a strong connection in developing countries between education and political instability.[11]

Short of repression, the government has two options: delay or deliver. Delay entails a period of stalling or reassessment. The government may, for example, appoint a commission to study the subject of the dissatisfaction. Delay has two advantages over immediately delivering some increased educational opportunity to restive non-VC groups. First, it allows a period during which the government may be able to diffuse tensions but still avoid giving those groups what they want. Second, it allows the government to acquaint itself more fully with what, exactly, the restive groups want. Since the government will try to placate them with as little education using as few resources as possible, full information on their demands is vital.

Delay may not be an option if a government faces a threat from particularly demanding groups. In both this case, and after the delay proves no longer satisfying to restive groups, the government will need to find some way of delivering some minimal educational opportunity to them. In delivering, the government must be guided by two goals: it must give to the offended groups as little educational opportunity as possible to get them to return to stable participation in the life of the country; and it must preserve as much as possible the educational opportunity it was delivering to its vital constituency.

These goals are partly helped by the imprecision of the government's education policy tools, because this imprecision can dampen perceptions of the inequality in educational opportunity. The reality that an occasional gifted student who works extra hard might succeed even if she is not a member of the vital constituency in part reflects the failure of the government's toolkit to exclude her, but it may also keep her parents and those who observe her success from thinking that educational opportunity is skewed enough that they need to protest its distribution. Likewise the precision of the more discerning tools, such as quotas, is, from the perspective of stability, a liability: quotas blatantly give preference to one group over another, and thereby make inequality in educational opportunity easy to identify.

In this section I have described three limitations on the government's use of its toolkit. The first is its capacity. Capacity limits are both financial—the government faces a limited and inflexible budget—and technical—education is a complex product to deliver, and the necessary personnel, expertise, and other resources may tax a developing-country government. The second limit is the system the government inherits from its predecessor. Education systems are not easy to alter. The first government to build a modern education system will have substantial freedom to create a system to serve its vital constituency, but future governments will have to mold the existing system as best they can. Finally, the government will need to preserve social stability. Where it cannot repress agitating groups, the government may need to provide just enough educational opportunity to keep these groups from threatening social stability, and do so in such a way as not to downgrade the education it is providing to the vital constituency.

Thus far in this chapter I have explored the education toolkit and the limitations on its use. The purpose is to explore, myopically, how a government would shape the various features of its education system if its sole purpose is to serve its vital constituency. From this analysis, I can now translate this book's framework into detailed predictions for how the actual governments in Taiwan, Ghana, and Brazil should have made education policy.

3. Predictions

To realize the educational demands of its vital constituency, I have argued that the government will need to create one of nine types of education systems. To do so, the government has a powerful education toolkit, consisting of schools, fees, access restrictions and discriminatory pricing, tracking, and outsourcing. Subject to three limitations—its capacity, including its budget; the education system it inherits from the previous government; and its need to preserve social stability— the government will use its toolkit to create the education system that the vital constituency wants.

How will the government create the system its vital constituency wants? There are two distinct scenarios to consider. The first is a government without the inheritance limit: one building the education system from scratch.

STARTING FRESH

I label the first government to produce a modern education system the *pioneer*. It does so at, or shortly after, a particular moment: the birth of the modern sector of the economy (Lewis 1954). This is the point at which education ceases to have value only as a consumption good; it also becomes an investment. In a country whose economy is dominated by unmechanized agriculture, the vast majority of the populace is engaged in activity for which modern skill is unnecessary; in this country, education will not generally determine wages and will therefore be primarily a consumption good. With the birth of the modern sector, skills become valuable and wages differentiated between the skilled and non-skilled, and education becomes an investment.

At that point, employers will begin to demand skilled workers, and employers' and families' demands for education will take the forms I have outlined in this chapter. The existence of these demands does not mean that the government will produce a modern education system automatically; for that, employers and families who wish to invest in education must be part of the vital constituency. The *pioneer* is the first government to have such families and employers inside its vital constituency.

The remainder of this section deals with how the pioneer government builds its education system. I first consider how that system will serve families and then employers.

Education for Families

When families who want skilled jobs in the burgeoning modern sector become part of the vital constituency, the government will begin to use its education toolkit to meet their demands for modern education. The pioneer government has a singular advantage over those that follow. It has the freedom to produce an education system that only serves its vital constituency: it does not have to take away education from those who were previously receiving it, or deal in any other way with the limitation of inheritance.

This advantage has a number of implications. First, schools will go where the vital constituency lives, and will be well-resourced with supplies and trained teachers. The pioneer government can restrict access from the start of education, keeping out non-VC children (subject to the limited precision of the government's tools). Because those schools thereafter are overwhelmingly inside the vital constituency, passage from one year to the next, or one level to the next, will be relatively easy, up as far as the system goes; there will be no tracking. Table 3.3 shows the way in which the pioneer government will use the various tools in its toolkit to serve its vital constituency. In the three case studies, I look to whether the pioneer wielded its toolkit in the ways outlined in Table 3.3 for evidence that it was serving its vital constituency.

Not every government will make use of every one of the tools in Table 3.3. The government's toolkit is like a menu, from which it may pick and choose. The prediction is simply that, when a government chooses to use one of the tools, it will do so in the way described by Table 3.3. Yet while there are differences in the tools different governments will use, we will see in the case chapters that governments—at least those in Taiwan, Ghana, and Brazil—are remarkably similar in their use of the toolkit. Particularly striking is the similarity with which governments invest in quality teachers in order to provide quality education—a particularly costly investment, as I noted in Section 2 above. Indeed the quality of teachers—in particular, how well they are trained and paid—is a prime indicator of whether the government is trying to provide quality education. The definition of a well-paid teacher is one who earns at least as much as an employee of similar qualifications can earn in another profession. The definition of a well-trained teacher is one who has education at, or preferably above, the level he is teaching: it is a rare teacher who can effectively teach a level of education of which he is not a graduate.

Table 3.3 **Use of the education toolkit by the pioneer government**

Tool	Characteristics
1. Schools	High-quality
Teachers	Well-trained and well-paid
Physical resources	High
Location	Close to the vital constituency
2. Fees[†]	Low
3. Access restrictions and discriminatory pricing	Gives advantages to the vital constituency; ensures easy passage for VC students from one grade or level to the next
Quotas	Distinguishes between the VC and non-VC children on the key dimensions of wealth, geography, or ethnicity
Exams	Gives advantages to VC children by testing material they are more likely to know
Financial aid	Reduces the price of education for VC children by offering scholarships, grants, or subsidized loans If VC is poor: criteria using need or ethnicity If VC is wealthy: criteria using merit or ethnicity
[4. Tracking][††]	[Not used by the pioneer]
5. Outsourcing (domestic or foreign; to firms or non-profits)	Used if the VC is wealthy, to provide any level below which the Top-Down public system does not go (e.g., the primary level if the government provides secondary and tertiary); all private schools are regulated to be very high quality

Notes: [†] Fees are for enrollment, books and other equipment, uniforms, activities, school improvements, etc. [††] Tracking is not used by the pioneer government because the system serves just the vital constituency.

The framework in Chapter 2 predicts that, depending on whether the vital constituency is elites, poor, or a cross-class alliance, the pioneer government will create one of three types of education systems: Top-Down, All-Levels, or Bottom-Up. The detailed predictions in Table 3.3 provide a picture of what each of these systems will look like in terms of access and resources. Figure 3.1 shows the three systems graphically, for a hypothetical case in which elites constitute around a

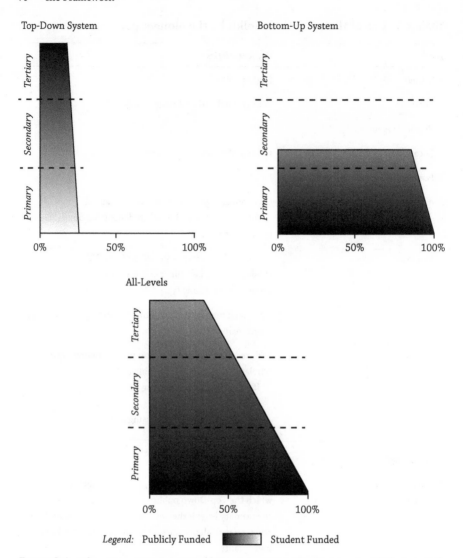

Figure 3.1 Education systems created by a pioneer government serving different vital constituencies

quarter of the population and no access discrimination is possible by geography or ethnicity. Access simply reflects the proportion of the population that is inside the vital constituency: children of these families are the only ones who will have access to the system (except where there is Broad Worker Training, which I consider shortly).

The Top-Down system in Figure 3.1 serves only elites (a quarter of the population in this example), while the Bottom-Up system serves the entire population, including elites, because, without access discrimination along lines of ethnicity or geography, whatever the poor can afford the wealthy can also afford. In both systems, passage from one year or level to the next is easy: most graduates of one grade will be admitted to the next grade. Passage from one year or level to the next is harder under the cross-class alliance, in which the government provides an All-Levels system: simple resource limitations will probably prevent the government from offering all levels to everybody. As a result, even though there will be no engineered access restrictions under an All-Levels system, the children of elites, who possess inherent advantages in educating their children,[12] will be more likely to find their way to the upper levels of the system and will therefore constitute a greater proportion of tertiary students than of primary students.

The second difference predicted by the framework is the relative proportion of public (or non-profit) resources at each level. The Bottom-Up system puts all the resources into the lower levels. Although there may be slightly more room for students to fund part of their education at higher grades—to the extent that some of the poor are less poor than others, and can afford to pay small fees—the education will be free or highly subsidized in every grade. The government will not create or allow student-funded education above those grades, since this education would be available only to elites, who are not part of the vital constituency.

A system with All Levels will similarly have mostly public funding at all levels: at the lower levels, which serve the poor, the proportion of public funding will be at or close to 100 percent. At the higher levels, which are intended to serve the demands of elite families, there will still be public resources available, but also more room for student funding, with which elite families may supplement public resources in order to increase the quality of the higher levels. This is the second reason for the lower access from one grade or level to the next under the All-Levels system.

Finally, in the Top-Down system public funding is concentrated in the upper levels, while student funding is extensive in the lower levels, approaching 100 percent in the first grade of primary. This keeps poorer children from gaining access to the system and frees public resources to be spent on the more-costly upper levels, where they are of more benefit to elite families.

The particulars of the systems in Figure 3.1 will depend on the vital constituency, which, as noted in Chapter 2, will evolve over time. In Chapter 2, I argued that three factors in particular alter demand: economic development, average income, and income inequality. Economic advancement will alter the relative value of tertiary over primary education, upping tertiary's value as an investment. Growing inequality—which is likely in a country entering the early stages of economic development[13]—will likewise increase the relative preference of wealthier citizens for tertiary education. With rising per-capita incomes, all citizens, rich and poor, will tend to value tertiary education more highly.

The pioneer will need to deal with each of these changes as it arises. For example, consider a government with an elite vital constituency and an economy in the very early stages of economic development. That economy may not have much use for education over the secondary level, and the pioneer will therefore build an education system that concentrates on secondary education, not the tertiary level as in the Top-Down system pictured in Figure 3.1, since secondary is the highest level with a positive economic return. As the economy develops, however, it will increasingly have use for higher levels of skill, which will raise the return to higher levels of education and the vital constituency's demand for those higher levels. The pioneer will build these higher levels as the its vital constituency demands them.

Education for Employers

Table 3.3 and Figure 3.1 describe the education system a government will create if it is meeting only the demands of families. If employers inside the vital constituency are type N (they do not demand worker training), educating the vital constituency's children is the government's only educational job. But if a vital constituency contains employers of types S—who demand skilled workers in a labor market where skilled wages are inflexible—or B—who also demand skilled workers but face a labor market where skilled wages are flexible—the government will have one of two additional jobs. For type S employers, the government will also need to lower the price of worker training to the point where a *sufficient* number of families decide to invest in worker training for their children. If these employers are type B, the government will need to lower the price of worker training to the point where a *large* number of families decide to invest in worker training for their children—enough to flood the job market with skilled workers and thereby lower skilled wages.

The basic difference between serving type S and type B employers is in who will be targeted by the worker training. Specific Worker Training will target children from inside the vital constituency; Broad Worker Training will target children from outside. This is because of the different labor market conditions faced by type S and B employers. If employers are type S, the government is not trying to lower skilled wages, because wages are inelastic to labor supply. With good wages awaiting graduates of worker training, the government can draw students to worker training from inside the vital constituency. But because Broad Worker Training seeks to lower skilled wages, the demands of type B employers are directly in conflict with the demands of families, of which type B employers are also members. Herein is a contradiction. As families, employers prefer that the government concentrate its resources on providing their children with the best education at the cheapest price possible, while educating as few other children as possible. As employers, though, they prefer that the government concentrate its resources on educating as many children as possible in the skills they need in their workers. Broad Worker Training thus draws from outside the vital constituency. This allows the government to separately provide higher quality education for families in the vital constituency.

Figure 3.2 shows how the government will integrate the demands of families and employers, depending on whether employers are type *B* or *S*. The figure is drawn for the same hypothetical case as in Figure 3.1, where elites are a quarter of the population, and assumes that elites are the vital constituency. The key difference is that Broad Worker Training draws students from outside the vital constituency, while Selective Worker Training draws students from inside the vital constituency.

In sum, the main prediction of this book's framework is that the pioneer government, which has the freedom to build its education system largely from scratch, will provide quality education to its vital constituency and only its vital constituency. The pioneer's system will have quality teaching in its schools and easy progression from one level to the next, up as far as the system goes. If the system is Top-Down, the system will provide education all the way up to higher education, which will be fully funded, while lower levels will have increasing amounts of student funding and other access restrictions that keep out poorer children. If the system is Bottom-Up, the system will provide broad access to the lowest levels,

An Example Elite Vital Constituency

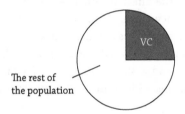

Access to Education and Worker Training

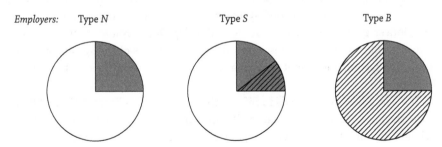

Figure 3.2 Access to education and worker training with different employer types for an example elite vital constituency

Notes: Shaded areas (■) denote education provided to families in the vital constituency. Striped areas (▨) denote worker training (education to serve employers). Type *N* employers do not need worker training. Type *S* employers want Selective Worker Training. Type *B* employers want Broad Worker Training.

where public funding will be full; upper levels may allow some limited student funding, but these fees will never be too high to prevent a VC family from affording them. A Bottom-Up system will extend up only so far as the budget allows: the government will not allow higher levels, which will only serve those outside the vital constituency. In an All-Levels system, there will be public funding throughout, but it will be concentrated at the lower levels in order to increase access. Lastly, worker training will vary with employers' demands. Type N employers demand no worker training. Where type S employers demand Selective Worker Training, the system will draw into worker training students from *inside* the vital constituency, while in Broad Worker Training (type N employers), the students will come from outside the vital constituency.

THE GOVERNMENTS THAT FOLLOW

What happens when the vital constituency changes? In each of three countries I consider in this book, only the first government can build the system from scratch to meet just the demand of its vital constituency. Subsequent governments must do what they can with the system they inherit. Thus the predictions for subsequent governments are different than those for the pioneer. This section develops those predictions. To show the effect of inheritance on an education system, I consider two vital constituency shifts: from elite to poor and vice versa. I then deal briefly with a shift to a cross-class alliance and shifts in the demands of employers, and with the changes to the education system that will likely follow threats to social stability. I end a short discussion of vital constituency shifts along the other two dimensions aside from wealth: geography and ethnicity.

From the Elites to the Poor

Governments that serve elites are ever vulnerable to takeover by the disgruntled masses, mobilized with the help of a political entrepreneur. When this happens, how can we expect the education system to change? If the framework is accurate, the pioneer government will leave behind a Top-Down system that serves the elites. It will concentrate its resources at the upper levels of the system; at lower levels, the system is excellent but expensive, available only to those with substantial wealth.

The new government needs to reform this system into a Bottom-Up system to serve the poor. Its reform package will need a number of elements. It must bring primary schools close to where the poor live, since for a poor family, transportation costs are onerous. It must eliminate or minimize fees, and if poor families are living at subsistence, it may need to make payments to families to cover the opportunity costs of education. And it must ensure the quality of the lower levels: it must provide materials and trained teachers.

Those are the minimal requirements. To meet them will require a radical reorientation of the education budget. Resources must be shifted from the upper to the lower levels. But this shift highlights the first implication of inheritance: the newly empowered poor may want access to the levels previously closed off to them. Thus it is unlikely that the new government will eliminate the upper-level tertiary and secondary institutions; instead, it will open up these levels to the poor even as they are starved of resources. The result will be increasing access to the upper levels but a precipitous decline in their quality.

Because the poor outnumber the wealthy, the government's reorientation of the system will also need to make primary schooling available to more of the population. And if the government cannot distinguish elites along the other dimensions of geography or ethnicity, it will not be able to exclude elite children from primary education—whatever the poor can afford, the elites can also afford. But this will be the only education the children of the elites can expect under the new government: they will receive neither financial nor regulatory help. The wealthy may find their only recourse in the face of declining educational quality is to send their children abroad.

Figure 3.3 shows at the most basic level how the new government will transform the Top-Down system it inherits into a Bottom-Up system to serve the poor. The figure shows both the change in public funding—from the upper levels to the lower levels—and the increase in access at all levels.

From the Poor to the Elites
A shift from a poor to an elite vital constituency entails the reverse: reforms that transform a Bottom-Up system that served the poor into a Top-Down system that serves the rich. This means developing upper levels with resources transferred

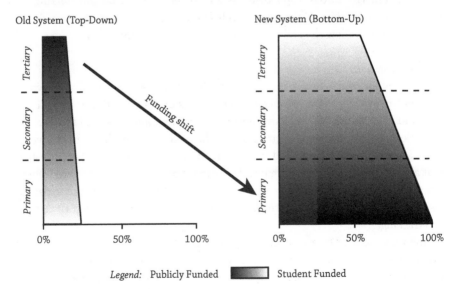

Figure 3.3 Changes to the education system after a vital constituency shift from elite to poor

from the lower levels, reforming the lower levels so they provide quality education only to the rich, and erecting access controls to the upper levels.

Inheritance plays a role in the particular reforms to expect. The new government will probably not completely eliminate the schools of the old Bottom-Up system. First, the teachers in those schools will want to maintain their jobs, and might be part of the elite, and thus a part of the new vital constituency. Second, eliminating schools might arouse the poor and threaten social stability—a possibility I consider in more depth below. But even if it cannot completely eliminate the old schools, the government can reduce its contribution to the point where it is doing little more than paying salaries. It can further reduce the quality of the education available to the poor—and thus the competitiveness of their education relative to elites'—by removing oversight or performance incentives.

Instead of completely eliminating the lower levels, the government can be expected to make use of its tracking tool to develop an elite track through them. Elite schools or classes in this track should be excellent—to prepare the children for higher levels—and relatively expensive—to keep the poor out and free the government's resources for use in the higher levels. The government can provide this track itself if it recovers its costs in fees, or outsource it to the private sector. Entry from these schools into the restricted upper levels should be easy, perhaps via a test that is geared toward the education received in the elite track. While the lower levels of the elite track will rely mostly on student funding, the track might also offer merit-based aid along the way to ease the financial burden on elite families.

Figure 3.4 shows how the new government will transform the old Bottom-Up system it inherits into a Top-Down system to serve elites, by transferring resources from the lower to the upper levels and constructing a track through the lower levels that allow the children of elites entry to the upper levels.

Toolkit Predictions

To effect either of the two systemic changes just considered—from Top-Down to Bottom-Up and vice versa—the government relies on its education toolkit (Table 3.2). Table 3.4 shows how the government will use its toolkit to mold the existing education system. The main differences from the predictions for the pioneer government are the use of tracking and the treatment of any elements of the old system that are not used in the new system and yet cannot be completely eliminated. These remnants can expect poor resources and teachers, and their students can expect to be cut off from the new system through access restrictions, discriminatory pricing, and tracking.

The remainder of this section notes a few additional changes that we should expect to see when the vital constituency shifts from elites or the poor to a cross-class alliance or when employers in the vital constituency change types. The section will finish with a short discussion of the role of ethnicity and geography in the construction of education systems.

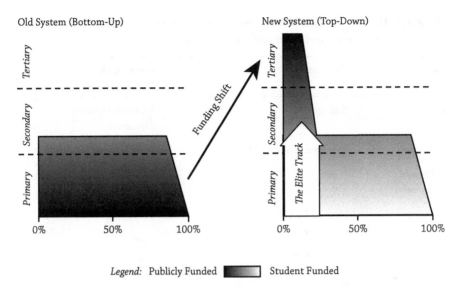

Figure 3.4 Changes to the education system after a vital constituency shift from poor to elite

To a Cross-Class Alliance

In most respects, a change of the vital constituency from either elite or poor to a cross-class alliance has similar implications to vital constituency changes from elite to poor and vice versa. But one additional consideration is important when a vital constituency changes to a cross-class alliance: the difficulty of serving the new groups even as it continues to serve the old. The government following a vital-constituency shift from poor to elites or elites to poor faces a task that is difficult—it must completely reorient the education system—but it has the advantage of being able to take away educational opportunity from one group in order to expand educational opportunity for another. The government that faces a VC shift from poor or elites to a cross-class alliance may not be able to take educational opportunity away from anyone. In the most difficult case, a shift to a cross-class alliance may require the government to provide educational opportunity to nearly the whole citizenry.

Transforming a Top-Down or a Bottom-Up system into one that provides All Levels is a recipe for dissatisfaction all around. At a minimum, the new system will put a strain on the education budget. In the best case, the government will have commensurate additional capacity—financial, technical, or both—to meet the enlarged demands on the education system. But if not, resources previously devoted to the levels on which the old system concentrated must be tapped to develop the new parts of the system. A Pareto-improvement is impossible; the old system will suffer. This difficulty carries a number of implications for how governments can be expected to behave.

Table 3.4 **Use of the education toolkit to change an education system between Top-Down and Bottom-Up**

Tool	New System	Lingering Elements of Old System
1. Schools	High-quality	Eliminated or left to deteriorate
Teachers	Well-trained and well-paid	Poorly-trained and/or -paid
Physical resources	High	Low
Location	Close to the vital constituency	
2. Fees[†]	If VC is poor: Low If VC is wealthy: Low for high levels, high for low levels	High
3. Access restrictions and discriminatory pricing	Gives advantages to the vital constituency; ensures easy passage for VC students from one grade or level to the next	Keeps those from outside the vital constituency in the abandoned areas of the system or from entering the system altogether
Quotas	Distinguishes between the VC and non-VC children on the key dimensions of wealth, geography, or ethnicity	Same
Exams	Gives advantages to VC children by testing material they are more likely to know	Same
Financial aid	Reduces the price of education for VC children, by offering scholarships, grants, or subsidized loans. If VC is poor: criteria using need or ethnicity If VC is wealthy: criteria using merit or ethnicity	Same
4. Tracking	Allows a path for the VC through any lingering elements of the old system	Keeps those outside the VC from the VC track.

(continued)

Table 3.4 (continued)

Tool	New System	Lingering Elements of Old System
5. Outsourcing (domestic or foreign; to firms or non-profits)	Used if the VC is wealthy, to provide any level below which the Top-Down public system does not go (e.g., the primary level if the government provides secondary and tertiary); all private schools are regulated to be very high quality	Same

Notes: † Fees are for enrollment, books and other equipment, uniforms, activities, school improvements, etc.

If the old system was a Top-Down system, the government must increase access at the upper levels while trying as much as possible to maintain their quality. Under the previous system, exams or other access restrictions at the upper levels favored children of the old elite vital constituency. In the new system, these will no longer give elite children preference. If poorer students are seemingly less prepared or qualified to enter the upper levels, the government will simply need to adjust the access restrictions—by, for example, "affirmative action" policies based on ethnicity or wealth. Even if the government is able to maintain its spending on the upper levels, this increase in access will mean that the upper levels must educate more students with same resources. But the government is not likely to be able to maintain its spending on the upper levels, because its second job is to increase the lower levels' access and quality. Thus resources will likely decline at the upper levels. Professors' salaries may decline even as they are asked to teach more students. Students may have less equipment or less comfortable accommodations. Fees may rise. With time, the strains on the system will only get worse: more poor children will graduate from primary school and want to enter secondary school, to which the government will not want to deny them access. A few years later, these secondary graduates will try to enter the tertiary level, which children of the elites previously dominated. And on entering the job market, they will compete with elites for jobs, lowering the return on education.

Resource shortages mean that a government trying to move from a Bottom-Up to an All-Levels system is likely to rely heavily on its outsourcing tool. Outsourcing is an obvious way to minimize the decline in quality of the education available to the wealthy. Some outsourcing at the lower levels was likely a feature of the old system—the private preparatory schools and the rest of the apparatus that prepared the wealthy to enter the elite upper levels. This outsourcing can remain, but the government must increase access to the upper levels by enough that some poor students gain access; the advantages imparted by the superior education elites can buy must not prevent poorer students from entering the upper levels. At the upper levels too, outsourcing may be attractive: if education has a high enough return to make it a good investment even after paying the full, profit-making cost of it, the private sector may find that educating the children of the wealthy, even at very high standards, is profitable. For poorer students, another kind of outsourcing may help the government cope with its new demands: out-sourcing to non-profits. Non-profits share a government's lack of a profit motive, and may also share the new government's desire to provide education to the pre-viously uneducated poor.

The challenge of transforming a Bottom-Up system into an All-Levels system is analogous. Again, the government can make use of some combination of direct provision and outsourcing. But there is little doubt that, barring a huge increase in the education budget, some resources that previously went to the lower levels will have to be transferred to the upper levels, making a Pareto-improvement in the education system nearly impossible.

In short, a shift to All-Levels from either a Top-Down or a Bottom-Up system will likely sow dissatisfaction. When introducing the concept of the vital constit-uency in Chapter 2, I noted that it is the government's job to satisfy whatever vital constituency it depends on for power. A government producing education for everyone, absent a job market with a voracious appetite for skilled workers, will not be able to satisfy its vital constituency; it will have made a mistake of ability. A mistake of ability can be fatal to a government. A government that has a diffi-cult time satisfying its vital constituency's demand for education will probably have a difficult time satisfying its demand in other areas. If so, the government will probably fall. Even if education is the only area of discontent, and if the gov-ernment holds on in spite of this discontent, education will be its constant threat: citizens in the vital constituency will complain and protest; elections will be fought about it; a crisis atmosphere will surround it. The government will enter a process I call "churning." It will endlessly examine its unsolvable problem, search-ing for a way to convince its vital constituency that things will soon improve. Government commissions will investigate it; new proposals and plans will be developed and implemented with abandon; the education ministry will become a hot potato, led by a procession of ministers, each of whom has blame for the sys-tem's most recent failure waiting for them at the end of their short tenure. The government will search for a cure that does not exist. The churning process only ends when an unlikely confluence of exogenous factors—for example, a large increase in the education budget coupled with a commensurate rise in the appe-tite of the job market for skilled workers—allows the government suddenly to meet its vital constituency's demands, or, much more likely, when the govern-ment changes its vital constituency or falls to a new government with a new vital constituency.

Changing Employer Types

Thus far I have considered the effect only of changes in the families in the vital constituency. But governments may also face changing demands for worker training when employers in the vital constituency change types. In these situations, the government will find itself needing either to add worker training to the education system, or remove worker training.

How will it respond? First consider a situation in which employers start or stop demanding Broad Worker Training. Broad Worker Training draws its students from outside the vital constituency (Figure 3.2). Broad Worker Training is thus another instance when the government is likely to make use of its powerful tracking tool. If the government has sufficient resources, it can develop an entirely new network of schools, with their own curricula, to provide the new worker training, and use exams or quotas to ensure that those who attend the new system are from outside the vital constituency. But without an exogenous increase in the government's resources, the provision of a new track in the education system will divert resources from the old track. There is a way to minimize this diversion: wherever possible, the government can unite the two tracks in facilities that draw on the same resources. This is easiest when the government was previously providing lower-level schools: the government can teach both curricula in the same schools to students drawn from different populations, and then channel them into specialized schools at higher levels.

Employers' demands for Broad Worker Training will only last as long as employers continue to face a skilled-worker shortage, cannot access skilled workers abroad, and face a flexible wage market. When any of these conditions is not met, their demands will end, and the government will try to end Broad Worker Training. As with the other changes to the system considered so far, the government may not want to completely do away with Broad Worker Training: doing so might leave members of the vital constituency out of work and might arouse the anger of those outside the vital constituency who were enrolling their children in it. But at the very least the government will reduce its contributions until the training system is but a shell of its previous self, providing education that is close to worthless. In some cases, the end of the demand for Broad Worker Training will be caused by a change in the vital constituency to include the families of students in the Broad Worker Training: for example, if the vital constituency shifts to include workers, the government may move to protect their wages. In this case the government may try to merge the Broad Worker Training into the general (VC-oriented) education system, raising its quality and resources and removing distinctions and barriers between it and the rest of the education system.

Now consider a situation in which employers start or stop demanding Selective Worker Training. Since Selective Worker Training draws its students from inside the vital constituency, it is much less of a challenge for the government to provide than Broad Worker Training. Selective Worker Training promises good wages. Thus as an investment it is little different from any other sort of education the vital constituency will want—aside from any non-wage-based social stigma attached to blue collar work. All the government need do is ensure either that the education system itself provides the proper curricula and other resources to train workers, or that businesses have assistance to do the training themselves. That is, as with the rest of the education it provides, the government may produce Selective Worker Training itself, or outsource it. In the latter case, the government may offer tax breaks, grants, or other assistance to businesses to ensure that, although the government is not directly producing the training, it is meeting the costs.

A Threat to Stability

The systems just described are built to serve the families and employers, and only the families and employers, inside the vital constituency. The exceptions are accidental: the government's tools are imprecise, and in the process of directing education as the vital constituency wants it may inadvertently provide education to others. But there is one circumstance in which the government will deliberately educate those outside the vital constituency: to preserve social stability. In Section 3, in outlining the government's responsibility to the vital constituency, I noted that instability is dissatisfying to the vital constituency. Preserving stability means keeping groups outside the vital constituency from revolting. This does not require giving them largesse: the government can repress them. But repression is expensive, and if the government cannot or chooses not to repress disgruntled groups, it must deliver to them enough largesse to keep them from taking their anger to the streets.

The stability limitation has very specific implications for how a government will provide educational opportunity to those outside the vital constituency. First, the lack of educational opportunity must be obviously threatening to the government's stability: non-VC families must be actively protesting. For non-VC parents to take to the streets, parents must perceive that the government is denying their children educational opportunity and must be angry enough about the lack of opportunity to threaten stability. I make no claims about the threshold at which anger turns to protest.[14] But once parents do turn to protest, the government will need to stop them.

As I discussed in Section 3, a government facing such instability has two choices: repress or placate. If the government chooses to repress, the education system will not change. But if it chooses to placate, it can do so by either delaying or delivering. I have already discussed delaying, in considering the difficulties a government faces when the vital constituency expands into a cross-class alliance. In that circumstance, as in this one, delay has a number of advantages: it better acquaints the government with the nature of the protesters' dissatisfaction and allows additional time during which the government can avoid delivering even as it appears to be taking the protesters' grievances seriously. In theory the government may be able to stall indefinitely.

In the end it may need to deliver. Once it decides to deliver, the government's responsibilities in placating a non-VC group are to stop the protests and to preserve the flow of educational opportunity to the vital constituency. To preserve the flow of opportunity to the vital constituency, the government must choose a method of providing education that is a minimal draw on the government's capacity and of a quality low enough that its graduates are not much competition for graduates of the superior education the vital constituency receives. This education will be more successful at stopping the protests if it can shift the responsibility for education in the eyes of the protesters away from the government.

Such incentives point to one solution: outsourcing. Absent financial aid, outsourcing is costless to the government. And, particularly when the outsourcing is to profit-making firms, regulating the new education such that its quality is very poor is easy. Where demand is high enough to lead to street protests, private firms will have no trouble finding students who want education not provided by the government system. Absent government controls to ensure quality, these private firms are unlikely to provide quality education on their own: quality education is expensive, and poor quality is not usually obvious until after the student has graduated, by which time the firm has already made its money. (I know of no private school in the world that refunds its tuition if the graduate does not find a job.) All the government need do is unleash the private sector to ensure a flood of poor-quality education is available to the protesting families at no cost to the government. If the government is able to engineer the private sector's offerings so that they are available to business entrepreneurs from inside the vital constituency, so much the better: in addition to stopping the protests, the government will have been able to transfer wealth into the vital constituency and away from protesting group, thereby reducing its influence.

BEYOND DIFFERENCES IN WEALTH: ETHNICITY AND GEOGRAPHY

This section has focused mostly on the vital constituency as a distinct income group. But I have noted that the government may distinguish its vital constituency along two other dimensions: ethnicity and geography. Ethnicity is the simpler of the two, because several of the tools in the government's toolkit can be wielded strictly on ethnic criteria. For example, to open a school only to those from a certain ethnic group, the government can simply implement ethnic selection mechanisms—e.g., quotas, or affirmative action—to preference the new ethnic group. Ethnicity is a risky selection tool, however: it is more blatant and obvious than wealth-based criteria and thus threatens the illusion of equality in educational opportunity on which social stability often rests.

Geography is slightly more complex than ethnicity, because it usually interacts with wealth. The government can, of course, implement strictly geographic criteria: for example, it can require that a certain proportion of students be from a certain region or state. Yet the geography of the vital constituency also determines where schools go, and this geography has much more of an impact on the poor than on the wealthy. An elite vital constituency will be served by a Top-Down education system, which concentrates on a few schools at the upper levels. These elites can afford higher transportation costs and are more interested in the quality of the schooling than its proximity. But a poor vital constituency cares much more about where schools are, because transportation costs are more burdensome for poor families. Thus where the vital constituency includes poor people who are geographically concentrated in a certain region, building schools in that region may be an effective way to provide educational opportunity only to the poor people inside the vital constituency.

The differential effects of school location on the wealthy and the poor also affect how substantially the location of schools will change when the vital constituency shifts. Where the vital constituency shifts to include the elites, the location of schools might not change much. But where the vital constituency shifts to include the poor, or shifts from a poor group in one location to a poor group in another, the government will shift the location of the system. In the former case, it will build schools close to the poor, and in the latter it will build schools in the location of the new group, and starve or eliminate the schools in the location of the old group.

This section has used the framework of Chapter 2 to derive specific predictions for how governments will produce education depending on the type of their vital constituencies. I showed how systems will differ depending on whose demands they are built to serve—families or employers—and how economic changes—changes in income, inequality, and economic advancement—will feed into the education system through changes in the vital constituency's demands. Finally, I defined how a government will use its education toolkit to build an education system; how a system built from scratch will differ from one that was adjusted to serve a new vital constituency; how a government will be handicapped by, and will deal with, limitations of capacity, and how it will seek to preserve social stability in the face of public unrest over education.

4. A Note on Policymakers and Their Motives

The wide range of predictions in the previous sections will form the basis for testing this book's framework in Taiwan, Ghana, and Brazil. But no matter the accuracy of these predictions, a reader may still find the framework implausible if it cannot plausibly account for the behavior of those making the predicted education policies.[15] Thus before concluding this chapter, I briefly consider how the policies predicted above are conceived and implemented by rational, capable, and well-meaning policymakers. In turn, this discussion will lead to two additional predictions.

At first glance it may be difficult to imagine that the theoretical government I have described here and in the previous chapter would be staffed by well-meaning policymakers. The theoretical government seems, in its actions, to be unconcerned with the public good. It does not care about students' well-being, national progress, or economic health. It devotes itself slavishly to its vital constituency. Yet in all three countries I examine in this book, the policymakers who implement educational reforms are almost always qualified, committed, and well-meaning. It is not their intention to make education policy that harms the country or any student's education. How is it that policymakers who seek to do good end up systematically making decisions as theorized in this chapter? The answer is in the interaction of two realities, one of politics, the other of education.

The political reality, already discussed at length, is the need to make policy so as to stay in power. Political scientists have long noted that because a policymaker can only make policy if she is in power, she must choose policies so as to preserve her power.[16] That is, no leader can wield power without compromising any belief or policy that would cause her to lose power. Thus while would-be leaders may want power not for itself but for what it allows them to achieve—wealth, status, the chance to make life better for fellow citizens—those goals are of necessity secondary. None of them can be realized if the would-be leader is not in power. Thus a leader's first goal must be to attain and retain power.

A reader might still argue that slavish devotion to the vital constituency is implausible, because the world is full of policymakers who want to do what is right, regardless of the political consequences. These policymakers may pursue the national good out of good-will and patriotism, even if it is politically suicidal in the end. Shouldn't the wide range of examples of such leaders mean that we cannot count on them to act in the myopic, power-obsessed way predicted here? This critique brings us to the second reality, of the nature of education.

The reality of education is that no one agrees what kind of education policy is best. There is widespread agreement that *education* has great value, but not whose or what kind of education has the most value. In fact, there are very few educational policies that are generally accepted to be good or bad: each can be "good" when viewed from one angle, "bad" when viewed from another. Because *education* has value, and it is not clear what education is best or worst, any argument for more or better education of any type can be compelling. I noted this in Chapter 1, when considering whether governments can be counted on to make education policy in the economy's interest. The government of the world's poorest nation can contend that its university is under-resourced by world standards and insist that the nation will not be able to develop if it does not have a stock of qualified scientists and engineers to staff its economy. This argument resonates even if the university already accounts for three-quarters of the government's education budget and most primary schools in the country lack textbooks. At the same time, the world's richest country can marshal persuasive evidence that its primary schools are unequal and its students unprepared for the modern world, even though the government is spending more on each of these students than a poor government spends on students in its university. One government can argue that the nation is best served by a meritocracy, while another can argue for improving the education of the under-privileged. Governments can generally make a reasonable case for more and better education of any type, for anybody.

Because arguments for more or better education are compelling, there will usually be good people who believe them, good people willing to push for them, and good people willing to implement them if given the chance. A policymaker who wants the poor government in the above paragraph to better its university does not have to be naïve or narrow-minded: he may perceive that university enhancements come at the expense of education for the poor, but may have determined, drawing on reasonable analysis, that the economic growth produced by better university graduates holds out more potential to help the poor than educating the poor. Such a rationale is not hypothetical; it is in widespread use.[17]

Thus we get nowhere by assuming that, just because two policymakers favor different policies, they therefore differ systematically in knowledge, competence, zeal, patriotism, or good intent. Generally those who make education policy do so with the public interest at heart. But in education, the public interest is a matter of debate, and honest people disagree. To put it in this chapter's terms: the operation of any tool in the government's toolbox can be easily rationalized. An exam may select children of the elite vital constituency into the upper levels of education: better schools and preparation and a targeted curriculum can give them advantages that few in the rest of the population can match. But a policymaker implementing an exam does not have to think of the exam as a selection tool: she may simply be trying to fill the scarce spaces in the upper levels with those who will best absorb the education. In fact their superior preparation may mean that applicants from the vital constituency *are* the students who can best absorb the education.

Putting the two realities together—politicians must make policy to stay in power, and most education investments can be seen as good—allows us to see how well-intentioned policymakers might implement education policy as predicted by this book's framework. Rather than thinking of leaders making education policy according to its normative value, we can instead think that leaders are unlikely to have the authority to make education policy unless their idea of what constitutes a "good education policy" coincides with service to the government's vital constituency. That is, the government will empower policymakers whose objectives are its vital constituency's objectives, and disempower those with competing objectives.

This discussion leads to two additional predictions from the framework. First, the most pressing problems that policymakers perceive in the education system will be problems with the way the education system serves the vital constituency, not those outside of it, and that the solutions policymakers will favor will be the solutions that improve the education system's service to the vital constituency. Second, any policymakers who perceive that the most pressing problems with the education system are with the system's service to those *outside* the vital constituency, or to any other goal (economic growth, for example), either will find their efforts at changing the system constantly frustrated or will be removed from power and thereby barred from making changes to the system.

Because they lend plausibility to the causal mechanism, these predictions about the motivations of policymakers are just as important to the validity of the framework as any data on the allocation of the government's education budget or the location of primary schools. The coming chapters show the two predictions repeatedly borne out. I cite interviews with dozens of policymakers who perceive the particular problems and favor the particular solutions that serve the vital constituency. Policymakers from governments with different vital constituencies will understand the same education system differently and will favor different reforms to improve it: a policymaker from a government with an elite vital constituency, for example, may note failings in the quality of the universities, while a policymaker from a government with a poor vital constituency will perceive a problem in the access of the poor to quality primary schools. Later chapters will also highlight a few examples of policymakers who pushed objectives at variance with the government's vital constituency, and, as a consequence, were continually frustrated, to the point where they had to either compromise or, more often, resign. This is not to say that policymakers' skill and ideas have no effect. Only the objectives are pre-determined, not the means. In implementation of these objectives, there is tremendous room for innovation, for talent and diligence to make their mark. But the result must serve the vital constituency.

5. Conclusion

This chapter has described the means of government education policy. In order to test the accuracy of the framework in Chapter 2, I have laid out specific predictions for how various governments will respond to different vital constituencies, circumstances, and constraints, in building and reforming their education systems.

Recall the basic argument of Chapter 2. That chapter argues that a government will build its education system, or mold the existing system, to serve the groups of citizens on whom its power depends, the groups I call the vital constituency. Depending on the nature and success of political entrepreneurs at organizing groups with collective-action disadvantages, the vital constituency takes one of three types: elites, poor, or a cross-class alliance. Because those with different resources benefit most from different levels of education—the rich most from higher levels, the poor most from lower levels—these three vital constituencies prefer different education systems: elites prefer a "Top-Down" system that concentrates on higher levels; the poor prefer a "Bottom-Up" system that concentrates on the lower levels; and a cross-class alliance prefers an "All-Levels" system that provides access to good education at both lower and upper levels. The vital constituency may also include employers who demand worker training. Employers' need for skilled workers, access to outside supplies of skilled labor, and the flexibility of wages will jointly determine their demand for worker training, which can take one of two forms: "Broad," which preferences quantity of worker skills over quality of skilled workers in an effort to lower skilled wages; and "Specific," which preferences quality over quantity and does not try to lower skilled wages.

In this chapter I have used the arguments of Chapter 2 to derive predictions for how the government will go about meeting the educational demands of its vital constituency. I have argued that the government has a powerful education toolkit consisting of tools in five categories: schools, teachers, access restrictions and discriminatory pricing, tracking, and outsourcing. These tools allow the government to target educational opportunity as demanded by the particular families and employers in its vital constituency. The toolkit is imprecise—its ability to target particular families is limited—and the government faces other limitations: limited capacity, including a limited and inflexible education budget; the inflexibility of education systems; and a need to preserve social stability. Yet subject to these limitations, the framework predicts that governments will wield their toolkits in ways that do direct educational opportunity as their vital constituencies demand, and that they will do so with great similarity. Governments that face elite vital constituencies will provide quality schools and teachers and easy progression from one level to the next, all the way up to higher education, which will be fully funded. The lower levels, by contrast, will have increasing amounts of student funding, along with other access restrictions keeping out poorer children. Governments facing poor vital constituencies will build systems that concentrate resources on the lower levels and provide broad access to them. Higher levels may draw on some limited student funding, but these fees will never be too high to prevent a VC family from affording them and the government will not allow levels higher than its budget can fund, since these levels will only serve those outside the vital constituency. A government facing a cross-class alliance will provide public funding throughout the system, but will concentrate that funding at the lower levels in order to increase access. Lastly, worker training will vary with employers' demands. Where type S employers demand Selective Worker Training, the worker training system will draw students from inside the vital constituency, while in Broad

Worker Training (type *N* employers), the students will come from outside the vital constituency.

This chapter also laid out how a new government will change the education system it inherits from the previous government. An elitist government that inherits a Bottom-Up education system will move funding from the lower levels to the upper levels and develop an elite track through the lower levels to ensure that elite children gain access to higher education. A government dependent on the poor that inherits a Top-Down system will do the opposite: it will shift resources to the lower levels, increasing their quality, and open access to the higher levels even as they lose funds. A government of a cross-class alliance that inherits a Top-Down or a Bottom-Up system faces the most challenging situation: unless it also can draw on new resources, it must, with the same resources, provide quality education in the previously neglected levels even as it maintains the existing system. This situation will often lead to "churning," as the government stalls for time and resources by making small, insufficient fixes to the education system while publicly searching for elusive silver bullets.

This chapter dealt with these predictions in some detail. The point of this is to produce testable predictions for how actual governments will act. Governments cannot do exactly as they want, so we will rarely see governments implementing education policies that conform perfectly to the goals defined in Chapter 2. Likewise, building an education system is not like adjusting an interest rate: in producing education, governments are not able to instantly create the system they want. Instead they will use their education toolkit to manipulate the system so that it comes as close as possible to the goals outlined in Chapter 2. The task of the next few chapters is to show that, over lengthy periods in three very different developing countries, governments do indeed wield their toolkits as predicted.

PART

EVIDENCE

Why Taiwan, Ghana, and Brazil?

Taiwan, Ghana, and Brazil have two advantages for testing the accuracy of the framework developed in Part I. First, they have little in common. The framework is meant to be general. Thus it should be able to describe education equally well in countries that are very different.

But Taiwan, Ghana, and Brazil are not just different; they differ in ways that allow testing of other plausible explanations of education. I selected them with four main criteria: each must have been through at least one regime-type transition; as a group, they needed to include both governments that are commonly thought to have made education policy according to the economy's needs and those that are thought to have ignored the economy's needs; the three needed to vary as widely as possible in inequality; and they had to vary widely in culture.[1] A detailed account of how these criteria led me to select Taiwan, Ghana, and Brazil is in Appendix A. Since 1950, each of the three countries has been through at least one regime-type transition. Taiwan shifted from autocracy to democracy once in 1996; Brazil shifted from democracy to autocracy in 1964 and back to democracy in 1979; and Ghana has flipped between democracy and autocracy no fewer than five times since 1950.[2] The three thus provide ample opportunity for testing whether regime type transitions precede changes in education. Second, they include one country, Taiwan, whose governments are widely thought to have made education in the economy's interest, as well as two, Ghana and Brazil, whose governments are not thought to have been economically motivated.[3] The three are also at different levels of economic development: using the World Bank's income categories, Taiwan is a currently a high-income country; Ghana, a low-income country; and Brazil, a lower-middle-income country. Third, their income distributions vary widely: in the 1980s, for example, Taiwan, with a Gini coefficient of .3, was one of the most equal countries in the world; Brazil, with a Gini of nearly .6, was one of the least equal; and Ghana, with a Gini of .48, was in between.[4] Finally, the three countries sit on different continents and vary widely in history and culture, economic development, and inequality. Taiwan was a Japanese colony; Ghana was British; and Brazil was Portuguese.

The task of the coming chapters is to demonstrate that none of these explanations can explain the education policies of these countries—even in the circumstances it seems best equipped to explain. No regime-type transition except one, Brazil's in 1964, produced the expected change in education. Even the government of Taiwan, an economically successful Asian Tiger, was demonstrably driven by politics, not economics, in making its education policies. The economic usefulness of Taiwan's education policy was instead an accident of its vital constituency: wherever the needs of Taiwan's economy differed from the demands of the vital constituency predicted by this book's framework, the government always favored the vital constituency, not the economy. Inequality does not independently influence education in any of the three countries; instead, its only effect on education is through the educational demands of the vital constituency as outlined in Chapter 2. Finally, governments in all three countries make education policy similarly to serve their vital constituencies regardless of their culture or colonial histories.

In the following chapters, the analysis of each country begins with the "pioneer" government—the first government to create a modern education system to serve its domestic vital constituency. For Taiwan and Ghana, the pioneer government is the government that throws off the colonial yoke: the first post-colonial government is the first that has the possibility of creating a modern education system to meet the demands of its domestic vital constituency. For Taiwan, that government takes the helm in 1949, when, after decades of Japanese colonial rule, the Chinese Nationalists (*Kuomintang*, or KMT) moved the government of the Republic of China to Taiwan. For Ghana, the key year is 1951, when the first Ghanaian leaders gained partial control of the government.[5] Taiwan and Ghana began their post-colonial existence already possessing, or destined shortly to possess, a modern economy in which education was a key determinant of wages, and with vital constituencies that included wage-earners and their employers; thus their first post-colonial governments were also their pioneer governments. Brazil, by contrast, gained its independence a century before it developed a modern economy in which education predicted wages. Its modern economy developed in the early twentieth century, and it was not until 1930 that Brazil had a government that needed the support of those whose wages were correlated with their education. In that year, the government of the agrarian oligarchs (for whom education was largely a gentleman's pastime) was overthrown and the modernizing government of Getúlio Vargas took control. Thus in Brazil, I begin my analysis in 1930. In each of the three countries, I stop the analysis in 2000, to avoid the uncertainty inherent in the effects of current policies.

I present evidence from these periods that shows both the correlation between the vital constituency and education and the process behind this correlation. To show the correlation, I first divide each country into periods based on the nine vital-constituency types I constructed in Chapter 2—that is, according to whether the government is affiliated with a political entrepreneur successful at organizing the poor; whether that political entrepreneur is cross-class or anti-elite; the ability of employers to find the skilled labor they need in domestic or foreign labor markets; and the flexibility of skilled wages. I present substantial detail on the political and economic analysis behind this periodization to reassure the reader that the vital constituency can be easily determined independently of education policy. Table II.1 shows the periodization of the vital constituencies. The table shows that the sample has both a lot of variation—every one of the seven possible boxes[6] has at least one country-period—as well as substantial overlap: four of the seven contain more than one country-period. The periodization is also different from the regime types in the cases, which are in Table II.2.[7] In only two instances does a change in regime type overlap with a change in the vital constituency: Ghana in 1972, and Brazil in 1964. In two other instances, Taiwan in the late 1980s and Brazil around 1990, democratization and the change in the vital constituency roughly coincide. In all remaining instances, a vital constituency change occurs without a corresponding change in regime type, or a change in regime type fails to change the vital constituency.

The primary prediction of this book is that the vital constituency will determine how the government will use its "education toolkit." To test the connection

Table II.1 **Education-demanding Vital Constituencies of Taiwan, Ghana, and Brazil**

Employers	**Families in the Vital Constituency**		
	Elites (no political entrepreneurship)	Elites and the Poor (cross-class political entrepreneurship)	Poor (anti-elite political entrepreneurship)
Type B (Need skilled workers in a flexible skilled-labor market)	1 Taiwan: ~1965 - late-1980s	2	3
Type S (Need skilled workers in an inflexible skilled-labor market)	4 Brazil: 1967–~1990 Ghana: 1966–1972	5 Brazil: 1930–1961; ~1990–2000 Ghana: 1951–1966	6 Ghana: 1981–2000
Type N (Do not need skilled workers) or outside the Vital Constituency	7 Ghana: 1972–1981 Brazil: 1964–1967	8 Taiwan: 1949–~1965; late-1980s–2000	9 Brazil: 1961–1964

Notes: "Elites" includes the military, the bureaucracy, and/or agrarian and/or industrial elites. "Political Entrepreneurs" are of the poor only; elites, facing fewer collective action costs, do not need an entrepreneur's collective-action subsidy to organize. Shaded areas are unlikely, because in such a broad VC wages will not fall as the number of skilled workers increases. Types *B*, *S*, and *N* denote employers with different demands for worker training, as in Table 2.4.

Table II.2 **Vital Constituencies and regime types in Taiwan, Ghana, and Brazil**

Employers	Families in the Vital Constituency		
	Elites (no political entrepreneurship)	Elites and the Poor (cross-class political entrepreneurship)	Elites (no political entrepreneurship)
Type B (Need skilled workers in a flexible skilled-labor market)	1 Taiwan: ~1965 – late-1980s *[Regime Type: Autocracy]*	2	3
Type S (Need skilled workers in an inflexible skilled-labor market)	4 Brazil: 1967 – ~1990 *[Regime Types: Autocracy to 1978, Democracy 1979 on]* Ghana: 1966–1972 *[Regime Types: Autocracy 1966–1968, Democracy 1969–1971]*	5 Brazil: 1930–1961 *[Regime Types: Autocracy 1934–1944, Democracy 1945 on];* ~1990–2000 *[Regime Type: Democracy]* Ghana: 1951–1966 *[Regime Type: Autocracy]*	6 Ghana: 1981–2000 *[Regime Types: Autocracy 1981–1992, Democracy 1993–2000]*
Type N (Do not need skilled workers) or outside the Vital Constituency	7 Ghana: 1972–1981 *[Regime Types: Autocracy 1972–1979, Democracy 1979–1980]* Brazil: 1964–1967 *[Regime Type: Autocracy]*	8 Taiwan: 1949– ~1965 *[Regime Type: Autocracy];* late-1980s–2000 *[Regime Types: Autocracy to 1996, Democracy 1996–2000]*	9 Brazil: 1961–1964 *[Regime Type: Democracy]*

Notes: Regime Types are from Przeworski et al. (2000), except Brazil prior to 1945, for which I use the Polity IV measure of democracy (Marshall and Jaggers 2000).

between the two, the analysis of each period's vital constituency is followed by an analysis of each element of the education toolkit, as well as an "evidence summary" table, which shows how well the vital constituency predicts the government's use of the education toolkit. An example is Table II.3. The "Characteristics" column of the table summarizes each indicator, drawing from the data[8] and analysis of that period about the nature and coverage of the education system, teacher pay and quality, school locations and fees, the incidence of tracking, and the prevalence of private education. The third column then reports whether those characteristics are as predicted by the framework: a solid box indicates that the characteristics are as predicted; a semi-open box indicates that they are partly as predicted; and an open box indicates that they are not as predicted.

In addition to the correlational evidence, I also process-trace in each period from the vital constituency to education policy. The process-tracing relies on secondary analyses, legislative debates, and, most important, interviews. Interviews are the most important evidence because, as I noted in Chapter 3, the framework more plausibly describes government action if it also describes the *perceptions* of policymakers. In each period, I tried to interview the minister of education and other key officials in order to observe whether the particular problems they perceived with the education system were the specific problems that were keeping the system from realizing the demands of the vital constituency, and whether the solutions they favored were solutions that would help the education system to better realize the demands of the vital constituency. Where policymakers did not express such perceptions, I looked for whether they also expressed frustration

Table II.3 **Sample evidence summary table**

Indicator	Characteristics	Conforms to Framework?
A. Enrollment	. . .	■/◪/□
B. Per-student spending	. . .	■/◪/□
C. The toolkit	. . .	
1. Schools	. . .	■/◪/□
Teachers	. . .	■/◪/□
Physical resources	. . .	■/◪/□
Location	. . .	■/◪/□
2. Fees[†]	. . .	■/◪/□
3. Access restrictions and discriminatory pricing	. . .	
Quotas	. . .	
Exams	. . .	■/◪/□
Financial aid	. . .	■/◪/□
4. Tracking	. . .	■/◪/□
5. Outsourcing (domestic or foreign; to firms or non-profits)	. . .	■/◪/□

Notes: ■: fully conforms to the framework; ◪: partly conforms to the framework; □: does not support the framework.

[†] Fees are for enrollment, books and other equipment, uniforms, activities, school improvements, etc.

that they could not make progress in fixing the education system as they wished. I also interviewed leaders in civil society: business associations (for a sense of the satisfaction of the businesses with the outputs of the education system); labor (for their perceptions of the quality of the education system and the job prospects of skilled graduates); education advocacy groups (for a sense of the nature and level of any public dissatisfaction with the education system); and international organizations (for a sense of the interaction of the education system and education policy with outside resources and influences). Finally, I interviewed academics, for the scholarly view of education, the economy, the government, and the interactions among them, including the demand of the economy for skilled labor and the adequacy of the education produced by the education system. A full list of interviews is in Appendix B.

Together, the correlational evidence and process-tracing are intended both to compensate for the disadvantages inherent in small-N work by maximizing observations over time and across the education toolkit, as well as leverage the advantages of close case research to establish the causal processes underlying changes in education. Each of the following case chapters begins with the "pioneer" government, whose education policies, unburdened by inheritance, should conform as closely as any government's to the predictions of the framework. I then trace education policy to the year 2000, noting how changes in the vital constituencies changed education policy with evidence on a range of indicators, and supplemented with historical analysis based on secondary sources and detailed interviews with many of the key individuals involved.

CHAPTER 4

Taiwan

Taiwan is an economic success story, and in this story education played an integral part. From 1960 to 2000, only two countries exceeded Taiwan's blazing 6.4 percent annual growth rate in real per-capita GDP.[1] Taiwan's development success rested in large part on skilled laborers manufacturing products cheaply for export, and Taiwan's schools produced abundant supplies of these skilled laborers. The economic usefulness of Taiwan's education system has prompted scholars past and present to look to Taiwan, asking: How did the government do it?[2] And in trying to answer this question, scholars have searched for clues to help policymakers in other countries reorient their education and thereby achieve Taiwan's economic success.

Indeed, Taiwan is an archetypal case for the first of the alternate explanations of education that I discussed in Chapter 1: that with a leadership focused on the economy, an education system will tend toward producing the economically optimal workforce. This explanation is inaccurate. Taiwan's education policies did spur its economic development. But they did not arise naturally from the free functioning of markets, nor from enlightened economic leadership.[3] Thus free markets or economically enlightened leadership are not a recipe for economically optimal education in other countries. Rather, Taiwan's blessing was the makeup of its vital constituency. Taiwan's education policies were the policies the vital constituency wanted: Taiwan's government does not differ from Ghana's or Brazil's in its faithful service to its vital constituency. Taiwan's good fortune was simply to have a vital constituency whose demands for education overlapped substantially with the needs of the economy. Yet while substantial, this overlap was never complete, and it lessened with time. In the 1960s, the educational demands of the vital constituency helped drive Taiwan to spectacular growth, but by the 1980s the vital constituency was demanding the same educational policies, while the economy had developed beyond them and needed a different sort of education policy.

Of the alternate explanations for education introduced in Chapter 1, the economic is by far the strongest in Taiwan. The challenge of this chapter is thus to show that, despite appearances in this explanation's favor, the demands of the vital constituency, not the economy, determined education policy at every point. By contrast, regime type overlaps little with changes in Taiwanese education. This chapter shows the Taiwanese government investing heavily in mass education while its government is firmly autocratic. Taiwan's shift to democracy in 1996 simply continued policies that originated a decade earlier under an autocratic regime.

Instead, this chapter presents evidence that Taiwan's education policy changed according to its vital constituency. Briefly, it shows the following: Taiwan's "pioneer" government, the Kuomintang, took over the island in 1949, after retreating from defeat at the hands of Chinese Communists in the Chinese Civil War. Between 1949 and 2000, the Kuomintang's vital constituency changed twice. Initially it engaged in cross-class political entrepreneurship of the poor and created a cross-class alliance with employers who did not demand skilled labor (type N employers). In the mid-1960s, the Kuomintang stopped its political entrepreneurship of the poor, and ruled Taiwan with an elite vital constituency of elites and employers demanding Broad Worker Training (type B employers). Finally in the late 1980s, the Kuomintang, in response to political entrepreneurship by opposition Taiwanese nationalists, again began cross-class political entrepreneurship of the poor, and ruled with a cross-class vital constituency of elites, the poor, and employers who did not demand skilled labor (type N). Table 4.1

Table 4.1 **Vital constituencies in Taiwan**

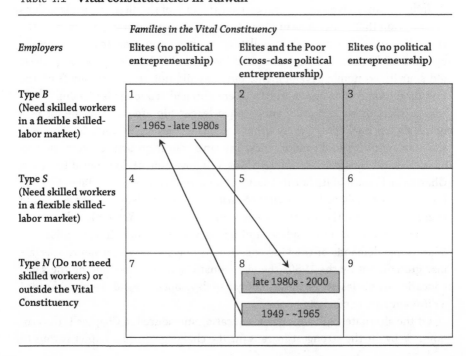

	Families in the Vital Constituency		
Employers	Elites (no political entrepreneurship)	Elites and the Poor (cross-class political entrepreneurship)	Elites (no political entrepreneurship)
Type B (Need skilled workers in a flexible skilled-labor market)	1 ~ 1965 - late 1980s	2	3
Type S (Need skilled workers in a flexible skilled-labor market)	4	5	6
Type N (Do not need skilled workers) or outside the Vital Constituency	7	8 late 1980s - 2000 1949 - ~1965	9

summarizes the vital constituencies. If the framework is accurate, these vital constituencies should have led Taiwan's government to initially produce an All-Levels education system, to shift that system in the mid-1960s to a Top-Down system with Broad Worker Training, and to return to an All-Levels system in the late 1980s.

This is largely what occurred. In this chapter and the two that follow, I offer evidence of three types. The first is enrollment, which describes access to education. The second is spending, which describes resources. In combination, spending and enrollment are the most important pieces of evidence, for they show the resource commitment of the government to a student in a certain type of schooling, relative to students in other types of schooling. The third is the education toolkit. The toolkit describes the *how* of government education policy. It is no substitute for enrollment and spending, which show the reality of the system available to students. But it provides the micro-level evidence that the policies behind enrollment and spending are as predicted. Repeatedly I make reference to exams, teachers, financial aid, tracking, and the other elements of the toolkit to show how the government created its education system, in order to support my contention that the design of the system flowed from the political logic theorized in Chapter 2.

The chapter proceeds as follows. In the first section below, I describe the country and the education system the Kuomintang inherited in 1949. I begin the analysis in Section 2, with an analysis of the vital constituency of Taiwan's "pioneer" government, the vital constituency with whose support the government ruled until the mid-1960s. Section 3 describes the education system in that initial period. In the mid-1960s, the vital constituency changed: Section 4 describes that change, and Section 5 analyzes the corresponding changes to the education system. The late 1980s brought another change to the vital constituency, and Sections 6 and 7 analyze that change and the effects on the education system. Section 8 concludes.

1. The Scene in 1949

When Chiang Kai-shek retreated to Taiwan with the government of the Republic of China, the island's existing inhabitants had been free from their previous occupiers, the Japanese, for only a few years, and were finding their new Chinese government even less likable. For centuries Taiwan had been a backwater of the Qing Dynasty, but following the Japanese takeover of the island in 1895 as a spoil of the first Sino-Japanese War, the Japanese had made the island something of a show colony.[4] They built railways and schools, and bought huge quantities of Taiwanese rice. Later, in the 1930s, they built arms factories and textile mills to equip their imperial armies. They first tried assimilating the Taiwanese as somewhat lesser Japanese citizens, but later nurtured and won over a small Taiwanese middle class and elite. These selected Taiwanese learned Japanese and became expert practitioners of Japanese social mores and customs. They prospered from Japanese business and, in turn, they infiltrated the social structure and allowed Japan to keep control over the island with a minimum of repressive force.[5]

In education, as in the economy, growth was steady under the Japanese. Most of it was primary. Three years after they took the island, the Japanese had already established a network of common schools. By 1930, the primary enrollment rate for children aged 6 to 14 was 37 percent. By the end of World War II, enrollment was 71 percent (Woo 1991).

The program in these primary schools was heavily Japanese, and as the war raged, Chinese education became increasingly scarce. All Chinese education was removed from the public curriculum in 1937, and all private schools for Chinese education were banned in 1940 (Chu and Lin 2001).

Higher education was limited and exclusive. The first junior high school for Taiwanese was not founded until 1915, and by 1939 only nine junior high schools enrolled substantial numbers of Taiwanese students (Woo 1991). The single university, Taihoku National University, the predecessor of the National Taiwan University, was for the Japanese only. In 1950 a survey of Taiwanese schooling found only 66 junior high schools, 62 senior high schools, and 77 vocational schools on the whole island. But there were an astounding 1,231 primary schools (Republic of China 2005b).

Although certainly there was resistance to Japanese rule, the 1945 retrocession of the island to China was not because the Taiwanese had fought for and won their freedom, but because the Japanese had lost World War II. On the whole, the retrocession brought more trauma than rejoicing. The pragmatic developmental KMT state that would one day make Taiwan an Asian Tiger was still years from conception; the Chinese government from 1945 to 1949 was by all accounts brutal and inept. Initially Taiwan was not a Chinese province, but a "special military zone." The patronizing military governor, Chen Yi,[6] filled the government positions left empty by the Japanese with mainlanders and "half-mountains" (*ban shan:* Taiwanese who had fought with the Nationalists in the Chinese Civil War),[7] and plundered the island's economy to help Chiang Kai-shek's armies on the mainland. Substantial wealth also found its way into bureaucrats' pockets. Among Taiwanese there was a popular colloquial saying: "the dog [the Japanese] left, and the pig [the Chinese] took over."[8] When on February 28, 1947 Taiwanese elites revolted, Chen Yi—on instructions from Chiang Kai-shek—unleashed the "White Terror" (*bai se kong bu*), during which Nationalist troops killed tens of thousands, a large proportion of whom were well-educated social elites (Chu and Lin 2001; Chen 2003). In the aftermath, Chiang Kai-shek upgraded Taiwan to a full province and assigned a new civilian governor. But the event wiped out much of the Taiwanese elite and bred resentment against Chinese rule among the elites who remained that would resurface often in later years.

2. POLITICS, 1949–1965: Retreat and Rebirth of the Kuomintang

Thus Taiwan in 1949 was not an ideal retreat for the Kuomintang. Nonetheless they came, having nowhere else to go. The exodus added a million-man army and half a million bureaucrats and civilians to a Taiwanese population of about six million, effectively increasing it by a quarter. These were no ordinary emigrants, though; the army excepted, they were administrators, technicians, doctors—the remains of the Kuomintang's governing elite.

The Kuomintang, though fresh from defeat, viewed Taiwan as a temporary refuge from which they would soon retake mainland China. As a result, the government could afford no instability, and it allowed none. The Kuomintang took from its defeat at the hands of the Chinese Communists a lesson about the destabilizing effects of rural poverty, especially with communists around, and almost immediately it moved to head off any threat of a communist insurgency in the Taiwanese countryside (Li 1981; Chu and Lin 2001).

The KMT did so with political entrepreneurship of the poor. Almost immediately after arriving on Taiwan, the KMT reorganized itself: hierarchical party organs were installed at all levels of the state; military commissars were instituted; and party cells were incorporated into every aspect of civil society, from unions to schools to business associations. By the mid-1950s this organization had given the KMT a quasi-Leninist quality that organized the Taiwanese peasantry into the party apparatus. In 1948, in the aftermath of the White Terror, the KMT had began a program of land reform on Taiwan, and it sped up the reform on arrival. In 1949, farm rents were lowered, and land confiscated from the Japanese was resold to farmers in 1951. In 1953, the government began a "land to the tiller" program in which it bought land from landlords at government-determined prices and sold it to tenants (Li 1981).[9]

In this vast redistribution of land wealth lay the roots of Taiwan's vaunted equity and the source of its coming boom in agricultural productivity (Fei, Ranis, and Kuo 1979). But this costly empowering of the peasantry would prove economically valuable only later. In the early 1950s, its payoff was political. The Kuomintang might have kept control of the peasantry much more cheaply through the upper classes, as the Japanese had done. But its brutal treatment of the Taiwanese elite following retrocession hindered an easy alliance with them after 1949. In order to keep any communist insurgency at bay, the KMT had little choice but to organize and court the peasants and continue to repress elites. At the center, the KMT was increasingly autocratic in the 1950s: through a series of "Temporary Articles" enacted in 1948 in advance of its retreat, the KMT had frozen the membership of the three national bodies provided by the 1947 constitution—the National Assembly, the Legislative Yuan, and the Control Yuan—effectively allowing their occupants to sit for life. Additional measures following the KMT's move to Taiwan did away with the two-term limit on the presidency and gave him sweeping power (Chu and Lin 2001). But the autocratic nature of the central government contrasted sharply with substantial local control that empowered Taiwanese farmers. In 1950 the KMT began to hold elections for the heads of townships and city or county councils and magistrates; in 1954, elections expanded to cover the Provincial Assembly—Taiwan's state legislature. These elections helped the KMT to integrate its local governance with farmers' organizations, so that by the early 1960s a substantial portion of provincial and local officials were former elected heads of farmers' organizations (Jacoby 1967, 114).

Thus we have the KMT's early vital constituency: the mainlanders—soldiers and bureaucrats—of the KMT core, and the farmers they made landowners. The Taiwanese elite were outside, and repressed. The vital constituency is in Table 4.2.

3. EDUCATION, 1949–1965: Primary Education for Farmers; Higher Education for the Elite

The KMT's early vital constituency was a classic cross-class alliance. According to the framework, the KMT should have used its toolkit to create an All-Levels education system. This is what the KMT did.

I begin with the lower levels of the system. The KMT's largesse to farmers was not limited to land; the government also gave the farmers schools. Table 4.3 shows the system's expansion. By the time of retrocession the Japanese had succeeded in enrolling over 70 percent of Taiwanese in primary school. The KMT did far better. By 1965, enrollment reached 97 percent. This would be a feat in itself, but it is still more astonishing considering that the population was expanding at 3.3 percent a year (Republic of China 1965). Between 1950 and 1965, the number of primary students in the overwhelmingly public system[10] more than doubled, from a little over 900,000 to almost 2.3 million, as did the number of primary schools, from more than 1,200 to more than 2,100.

Table 4.2 **The vital constituency of Taiwan's pioneer government, 1949–1965**

Political Entrepreneur(s)	Groups in the Vital Constituency[†]	Groups outside the Vital Constituency
Chiang Kai-Shek and the Kuomintang (KMT): courted farmers	Bureaucracy Military Employers (Type N) Farmers [KMT]	Taiwanese Elites

Notes: [†] If a group was empowered with the help of a political entrepreneur, the entrepreneur is in brackets.

Employer types are in parentheses: Type N employers do not demand training of skilled workers.

Educational expansion often comes at the expense of quality. But not in this case. With the massive growth of students, we might expect the government to realize savings from economies of scale, allowing it to devote fewer resources to each student while maintaining quality. In fact, the KMT devoted steadily *more* resources to each primary student—even while enrollment skyrocketed. Adjusting for inflation, the government devoted more than twice as much to each primary student in 1965 as it had in 1950: nearly NT$3,000, compared to NT$1,322 in 1950 (2001 NT$). Naturally, such lavish spending on private education was a drain on public coffers. Adjusted for inflation, government spending on primary education rose from NT$1.2 billion in 1950 to NT$6.6 billion in 1965 (2001 NT dollars).

This commitment to primary education, impressive as it is, is hardly sufficient evidence that the government was acting in the interests of its vital constituency and its vital constituency alone when planning its education system. It could be simply attributed to the favorite claim of *post-hoc* analyses of achievements in education across East Asia: the prime place of education in Confucian values.[11] Indeed, the 1947 constitution of the Republic of China,[12] adopted two years before Chiang's retreat to Taipei, stipulates that the government provide all citizens with an equal opportunity to acquire elementary education.

For evidence of the early education system's devotion to the demands of the government's vital constituency, we need to consider the system as a whole. When we do, it becomes clear that in the early days of its rule, the KMT built two education systems in Taiwan: one to keep the farmers happy, and one to satisfy

Table 4.3 **Expansion of primary education, 1950–1965**

	1950	*1965†*	*Change*
Number of Primary Schools	1,231	2,143	+74%
Number of Primary Students	906,950	2,257,720	+149%
*Primary Gross Enrollment Ratio**	79.98%	96.83%	+21%
Number of Primary Teachers	20,878	53,522	+156%
Number of Primary Classes	16,856	53,338	+216%
Average Students per Class	53.8	42.3	-21%
Student: Teacher Ratio	43.4	42.2	-3%
*Public Expenditures on Primary Education†† *	NT$50,772	NT$1,134,097	+2,134%
*(in 2001 NT$)†† *	NT$1,198,564	NT$6,589,756	+450%
Public Expenditures on Primary Education per Student	NT$55.98	NT$502.32	+797%
(in 2001 NT$)	NT$1,321.53	NT$2,918.77	+121%

Notes: * Enrollment of children aged 6 to 11; † Fiscal Year 1964–65; †† NT$1,000

the mainlanders. As noted earlier, the mainlanders, soldiers aside,[13] were an exceptionally educated group already, and the Japanese concentration on primary education left the Taiwanese education system ill-equipped to deal with mainlanders' demands. Thus the decade and a half from 1950 to 1965 saw the rapid growth not simply of primary education, but of higher education as well. The number of junior high schools quadrupled, from 66 in 1950 to 272 in 1965, and the number of senior high schools more than doubled, from 62 in 1950 to 142 in 1965. In 1950 Taiwan had a single university; by 1965 it had ten. Colleges went from 3 to 11; junior colleges, from 3 to 20 (Republic of China 2005b). The growth of students in post-elementary education grew just as fast. There were 61,000 junior high school students in 1950, and 427,000 in 1965. Senior high school students went from 19,000 in 1950 to 116,000 in 1965. In 1965 there were 30,000 junior college students, and 55,000 in undergraduate programs, where in 1950 there had been only 1,286 junior college students and 5,374 undergraduates—an increase in tertiary enrollment of almost 1,300 percent (Republic of China 2005b).

For students entering junior high school, the likelihood of continuing into higher education was high, and it got higher as the years progressed. In 1950, 63 percent of junior high school graduates entered senior high school; by 1965, it was 96 percent. A senior high school graduate had a 73 percent chance of entering university, college, or junior college in 1950; in 1965, the likelihood was slightly less, 70 percent, but this is somewhat of a fluke: the next year the likelihood was 74 percent.[14]

Faced with a vital constituency that included both farmers and mainlanders, the KMT was severely circumscribed in how much it could restrict access to higher education just to mainlanders. Nonetheless, in its very early days on Taiwan, it did enact policies the effects of which gave mainlanders certain advantages. These fell into two categories: social and monetary. The Japanese system inherited by the KMT had, as noted, focused heavily on Japanese instruction to the exclusion of Chinese. The KMT unsurprisingly reversed this focus and designated Mandarin Chinese as the exclusive language of instruction. The main losers from the reversal were, once again, the native elites, who were often fluent in Japanese language and customs. But the reversal also affected anyone who had been educated at the Japanese common schools. The advantage for native Mandarin-speakers was short-lived; eventually the other students learned Mandarin, just as students in the 1930s and 1940s had learned Japanese. Nonetheless the advantage was there; ability to understand the instruction in primary school was crucial to passing the standardized Junior High Entrance Exam—the only way into junior high school—and fluency in Mandarin was crucial to understanding the instruction.

The second advantage was monetary. Civil servants, teachers, or those in the military could receive special educational loans from the government at highly subsidized rates.[15] Although at this time primary education was free (aside from some incidental fees), no other level was. Those with access to cheap loans were therefore at a substantial advantage. Mainlanders made up an overwhelming proportion of those in the bureaucracy and the military. This was not simply because of the wholesale relocation of the KMT army, or because many of the mainlander bureaucrats in the pre-1949 Republic of China government had taken up new positions in the bureaucracy when the government moved to Taiwan. It was also because until 1962 the government hired bureaucrats based on a formula that allotted spots to residents of various provinces in all of China according to their populations in 1947. Since Taiwan represented 3.5 percent of China's population in 1947, Taiwanese were allotted only 3.5 percent of civil service openings (Luoh 2003).

These advantages had effects in education. Recent analyses of educational achievement are in almost universal agreement that mainlanders who attended school in these early years did better than can be explained by their socio-economic status, their parents' education, or where they lived (the usual factors that account for educational achievement in later years). Using data from the 1990 census, Luoh (2001) shows that the proportion of mainlander males born in 1935—thus turning 18 in 1953—attending college was more than 20 percent; the proportion of Taiwanese males born in that same year was less than four percent. For mainlander males born between 1943 and 1947—turning 18 between 1961 and 1965—the proportion attending college was nearly 40 percent; for Taiwanese males it rises slightly from six to eight percent.[16] Figure 4.1 shows these trends.

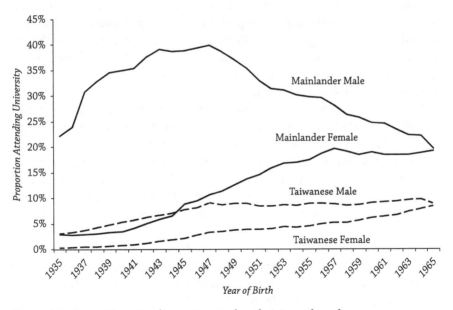

Figure 4.1 Proportion attending university, by ethnicity and gender.

Source: Luoh (2001, 127). Data are from the 1990 Taiwan Census.

A government that is beholden to a group as highly educated as the mainlanders would, if this book's framework is accurate, need to provide exceptional higher education. And in fact, the education the Taiwanese government provided to students who were able to make it into junior high school and above was excellent—and highly subsidized. In 1950 the KMT government spent NT$55.3 million on secondary schools, more than the NT$50.7 million it spent on primary education, even though the primary system was servicing more than 900,000 students while the secondary system had less than 80,000. Spending on higher education was even higher: the government lavished NT$23.7 million on 6,665 students. By 1965, the discrepancies were somewhat less, but still enormous. Nearly 2.3 million primary students were allotted NT$1.2 billion; 661,000 secondary students got NT$1 billion; and 85,300 students in higher education got NT$600 million.

Table 4.4 shows the growth of secondary and higher education. In Figure 4.2, I compare the amount of public education funds devoted to each student in higher education to the amount devoted to a primary student, a secondary student, and a higher-education student. The figure shows that in 1950 the average student in higher education was receiving nearly 87 percent of every education dollar. As the government invested in public primary schools this number fell sharply through 1956. But thereafter the government accelerated spending on higher education to meet increased demands, and the ratio levels off. While there are no rate-of-return studies for this period, there is no reason to suspect that college degrees were not handsomely rewarded by high-paying employment in either the public or the private sector. There is also anecdotal evidence that Taiwanese students who went to the United States and Europe for post-graduate study (Taiwanese universities offered few masters' degrees and no PhDs in this period) competed favorably with the best students there.[17] Higher education seems, if anything, to have been *too* good for the Taiwanese economy to make full use of it: the "brain drain" in this period is substantial and increasing.

Throughout this chapter and those that follow, I follow the analysis of each period with a look back at how well the evidence fits this book's framework. The Evidence Summary for Taiwan 1949–1965 is in Table 4.5.

Table 4.5 shows support for the framework. Taiwan's pioneer government built an All-Levels education system of very high quality. The system grew to service most of the population with primary education, and although enrollment did not quite reach 100 percent at the upper levels its growth was still spectacular.

There are three areas, however, where the framework receives less support: Mandarin instruction, fees for higher education, and accompanying subsidized loans for civil servants to help them afford those fees. An All-Levels system should not provide those inside the vital constituency with any disadvantages, and Mandarin instruction and fees for higher education disadvantaged Taiwanese farmers, who were generally poor and whose children, if they attended primary

Table 4.4 **The expansion of secondary and higher education, 1950–1965**

	Secondary School			Higher Education		
	1950	*1965[†]*	*Change*	*1950*	*1965[†]*	*Change*
Number of Schools[*]	205	544	+165%	7	56	+700%
Number of Students	114,385	660,594	+478%	6,665	85,346	+1,181%
Number of Teachers	6,207	26,153	+321%	964	5,622	+483%
Number of Classes	2,626	12,970	+394%	—	2,270	—
Average Students per Class	43.6	50.9	+17%	—	37.6	—
Student: Teacher Ratio	18.4	25.3	+37%	6.9	15.2	+120%
Public Expenditures[††]	NT$55,303	NT$1,022,270	+1,748%	NT$23,651	NT$576,166	+2,336%
(in 2001 NT$)[††]	NT$1,305,526	NT$5,939,977	+355%	NT$558,324	NT$3,347,856	+500%
Public Expenditures per Student	NT$483.48	NT$1,547.50	+220%	NT$3,548.54	NT$6,750.94	+90%
(in 2001 NT$)	NT$11,413.44	NT$8,991.87	-21%	NT$83,769.57	NT$39,226.86	-53%

Notes: [*] Secondary School: Junior and Senior High School; Higher Education: Junior College, Colleges, and Universities; [†] Fiscal Year 1964-65; [††] NT$1,000.

schools prior to 1950, were studying in Japanese. Yet another prediction of the framework is that a government should also restrict access to those outside the vital constituency, and the primary effect of these two policies was to restrict access by the Taiwanese elite. They were the Taiwanese who had truly learned to operate in Japanese, and thus who would have had the most difficult time adjusting to Mandarin instruction. For the children of Taiwanese farmers, who generally spoke Taiwanese at home, Mandarin instruction was likely no more onerous than Japanese. As for the fees, it took some time before significant numbers of farmers' children were ready to enter the highest levels. In the meantime, it was the better-educated children of the Taiwanese elite, whose land the government had just taken away, who were most affected by high fees with no access to subsidized loans. Thus these two policies provide partial support for the framework: although they did somewhat disadvantage farmers'

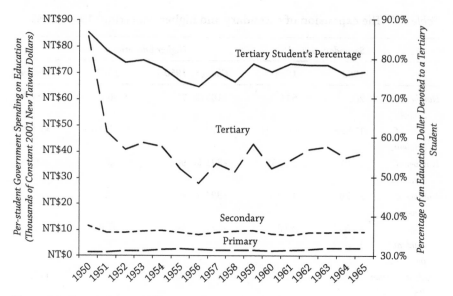

Figure 4.2   Per-student spending at primary, secondary, and tertiary levels, 1950–1965.

Source: Republic of China (2005b); my calculations. Amounts were converted to 2001 NT$ using the Consumer Price Index series from Republic of China (2005a); index values for prior to 1959 are from the Provincial Bureau of Accounting and Statistics, cited in Jacoby (1967, 286, table C.16). Secondary education is junior and senior high schools and vocational schools; tertiary education is junior colleges, colleges, and universities. In 1954 the government changed its accounting from calendar to fiscal years; thus the figure for 1954 is doubled to reflect annual spending.

children, their primary effect was to exclude the children of the Taiwanese elite from higher education.

In its first few years of operation, this two-tiered education system satisfied the important education demands of farmers and mainlanders—the two sides of the KMT's vital constituency. But the system had an inherent flaw, which became increasingly apparent in the late 1950s and early 1960s: farmers were not content with their children receiving only elementary school. In 1950, a mere 32 percent of elementary school graduates entered junior high school; by 1965 it was 57 percent (Republic of China 1988). Seeing the vastly higher social and pecuniary benefits accruing to those with higher education, farmers naturally encouraged their children to apply to higher levels. Because farmers were members of the vital constituency, the KMT government in the 1950s would have been loath to enact measures to overtly exclude their children from junior high school and higher. But as farmers' children studied increasingly hard to pass the entrance exams, it became less and less likely that elite parents could be sure of their children making it into the upper levels of education. In Luoh's (2001) analysis of the 1990 census, the proportion of mainlander males going to college begins a

Table 4.5 **Evidence summary, 1949–1965**

Indicator	Characteristics	Conforms to Framework?
A. Enrollment	Increasing at all levels	■
B. Per-student spending	Increasing at all levels	■
C. The toolkit		
1. Schools	High-quality at all levels	■
Teachers	High-quality at all levels	■
Physical resources	High at all levels	■
Location	Lower levels widely available in urban and rural areas; higher levels concentrated in urban areas	■
2. Fees[†]	Primary: only incidental fees	■
	Other levels: high fees	□
3. Access restrictions and discriminatory pricing		
Quotas	None	
Exams	Exams regulate access between levels, but passage is relatively easy, especially after junior secondary	■
	All exams are in Mandarin	□
Financial aid	Special loans to civil servants permit them to afford higher levels of education	□
4. Tracking	None	■
5. Outsourcing (domestic or foreign; to firms or non-profits)	Minimal—the vast majority of schools are public; there are a few elite preparatory schools, a few private vocational schools, and some elites send their children to universities abroad	■

Notes: ■: fully conforms to the framework; ◨: partly conforms to the framework; □: does not conform to the framework.

[†]Fees are for enrollment, books and other equipment, uniforms, activities, school improvements, etc.

sharp decline for those born after 1947 (so entering college in 1965), a decline that would have begun three years earlier for mainlander males applying to senior high school. Hsu Shui-teh, the county executive for education in Pingtung County in 1965, described these years as "exam hell," with families complaining constantly of the pressure.[18]

At the same time, pressure on the education system itself from students wanting admission to junior high school and higher gradually was reaching a breaking point. (Net enrollment figures for this period are unavailable, so it is impossible to know how many students retook their junior high school exams year after year to gain entrance.) Over the previous decade and a half the government had managed to devote steadily more of the national product to education, until by 1965 education spending took 3.4 percent of GNP—nearly double, relative to GNP, the proportion in 1951. With its coffers strained the government was finding it impossible to provide high quality post-elementary education to all the members of its vital constituency who wanted it. The demands of farmers and mainlanders were colliding. One side would have to give.

4. POLITICS, 1965–1987: The First Vital Constituency Shift: From Farmers to Industry and Local Factions

The eventual resolution to this dilemma was apparent, politically, by the late 1950s. The losers would be the farmers. The KMT government had arrived on Taiwan in 1949 battered and chastened by its defeat at the hands of the Chinese Communists. It is hard to overstate the precariousness of their position. The KMT had to impose Martial Law from May 19, 1949 in an effort to gain control over the population, but this risked alienating the population even further. Most observers—including the American government, the KMT's later patrons—assumed that they were soon to be finished off by the Chinese Communist Party (Chu and Lin 2001).

But then: Korea. Almost immediately the United States took a new view of the struggle of what became known as "Free China" against the rogue communist government on the mainland. U.S. economic and military assistance began pouring into Taiwan. By 1965, when American aid ceased, the United States had given Taiwan $1.5 billion, equivalent to 6.4 percent of Taiwan's entire GNP over that period, or about $10 per capita per year. Even more important was a simultaneous U.S. pledge to defend Taiwan if it was attacked, formalized in the 1954 US-ROC Mutual Defense Treaty. In July 1954, the KMT successfully repulsed an assault by the Chinese Communist forces on Quemoy.

Economically and politically, the KMT was also on much firmer footing by the mid-1950s. In 1951, inflation was 57 percent; two years later it was 4.5 percent. The KMT's political entrepreneurship of the peasantry had succeeded in heading off the threat of a communist uprising. But the KMT was also realizing that its stay on Taiwan was going to be longer than it had hoped.[19] In part, this was the price of American aid and security guarantees: the United States in the late 1950s increasingly pressured the KMT to abandon any plans for military action on the mainland, which President Chiang eventually agreed to in 1962. With its position on Taiwan seeming ever more permanent, the KMT sought firmer control over the local population by substituting its political entrepreneurship for "local factions": generally Taiwanese politicians and other elites and leaders in local communities.[20] With these factions it maintained a patron-client relationship: allied local factions were expected to produce votes for local elections, which they did through various vote-buying schemes; in exchange, they were given various economic spoils, and a blind eye was turned to their efforts to buy votes, which, of course, were technically illegal. To ensure that no faction became too powerful, often two or more factions were nurtured in the same area.[21] Beginning in the late 1950s, the system worked perfectly: with few exceptions it won the KMT at least two-thirds of popular votes and three-quarters of seats in all elections (Chu and Lin 2001, 33). By the 1960s, local elites in local factions were firmly in the vital constituency. The support they provided among the local population was sufficient that the KMT no longer needed the support of farmers. It consequently altered the nature of its relationship with farmers' organizations. I noted above that by the early 1960s provincial and local officials were often former elected heads of farmers' organizations (Jacoby 1967). But thereafter the KMT swiftly halted the overlap, by prohibiting farmers' association officers from simultaneously holding elected local government posts, and by allowing local government supervisory agencies to unilaterally terminate officers' posts in farmers' associations. In time, farmers' associations became quasi-state bodies (Chu and Lin 2001).

The removal of farmers from the KMT's vital constituency coincided with agriculture's decline in economic importance. In 1951 agriculture (including forestry and fisheries) was the dominant economic activity, contributing 38 percent of GNP. Industry (including mining) contributed 24 percent. After the land redistribution programs in the early 1950s, agricultural production soared, to more than double its 1951 level by 1964. But industry grew faster, reaching in 1964 more than five times its 1951 output. The reasons are complex, well-studied, and not worth repeating in detail here,[22] but in brief involved a sharp decline in consumption, which allowed the agricultural surplus to be invested rather than consumed. The agricultural surplus was augmented by U.S. aid inflows, 60 percent of which went to industrial materials and another 25 percent to capital goods (Jacoby 1967; Fei, Ranis, and Kuo 1979). Gross capital formation rose from 14 to 18 percent by 1963, and net capital formation from 10 to 12 percent. By 1963, in just over a decade, agriculture's share of GNP had dropped to 24 percent, while industry's had increased to 33 percent.

As the industrial sector grew, so did its importance, politically, to the KMT. Unlike the years after its arrival on Taiwan, the KMT by the late 1950s was no longer primarily concerned with stabilizing the island as a base for retaking the mainland. By the late 1950s, its political fortunes were increasingly tied to industry. Public industry not only generated resources for the KMT itself, but provided jobs and economic spoils for the local factions that were becoming central to the KMT's strategy for solidifying its rule. By the 1960s, industry too was inside the vital constituency.

That, unsurprisingly, meant that the workers in the new industrial sector were out. Obviously substantial unhappiness among workers would be contrary to industry's interests, so workers were not brutally treated, but their conditions were not ideal. The average worker worked six and a half days a week, nine to ten hours a day,[23] in safety conditions that Harry Weiss, then U.S. deputy assistant secretary of labor for international affairs, described as "quite inadequate" when he visited Taiwan in 1963 (Weiss 1964, 9). With a substantial labor surplus in agriculture, Taiwanese industry could initially count on having plenty of unskilled workers to hire, and did not need to treat them well.

But around 1965 two things happened. The first was that wages started to skyrocket. Until 1965 unemployment had held steady at around six percent; after 1965, it declined sharply. (The economy would reach full employment in 1971, with unemployment of 1.2 percent.) More than two-thirds of the increase in the labor force was absorbed into manufacturing and related industries (Kuo, Ranis, and Fei 1981). Consequently wages, which were falling in the 1950s, began to increase in the 1960s. From 1960 to 1970, manufacturing wages increased on average by seven percent a year. Figure 4.3 shows the change.

The second change was that the fuel powering the growth of Taiwanese industry became exports of finished industrial products, products that required far more skilled workers to manufacture than had the agricultural goods that had until then dominated Taiwan's economy. In 1953 the percentage of exports in GNP was 9 percent, and 92 percent were agricultural products. By 1980, exports were 49 percent of GNP, and more than 90 percent of them were industrial products. The share of rice and sugar in exports dropped from 74 percent in 1952 to 3 percent in 1970, while textiles and electronics together made up 41 percent of exports by 1979 (Kuo, Ranis, and Fei 1981).[24]

Thus industry in the early 1960s was at the wrong end of a two-pronged labor crunch: at the very time Taiwan's labor surplus was evaporating and wages skyrocketing, it needed to employ increasing amounts of more-expensive skilled labor to produce the industrial products it wanted to export.

In Chapter 2, I argued that an increase in the cost of skilled labor is not on its own enough for industry to want government action in education. Education takes time and can be very expensive, and there are two far faster and less expensive solutions to a labor shortage. The first is to import workers. Taiwan's international isolation would have made this difficult, and Taiwanese industrialists have long emphasized a culture and work ethic that they have not often found in foreign workers.[25] The requirement for cultural affinity also prevented most Taiwanese firms from taking their manufacturing abroad, and investment in mainland China

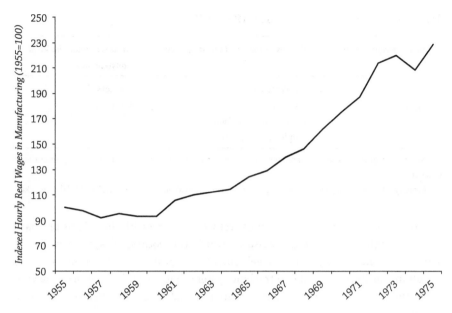

Figure 4.3 Real hourly manufacturing wages, 1955–1975

was not an option. Taiwanese industry was thus left in the 1960s to rely only on increasingly expensive Taiwanese labor.

In short, by the 1960s, the KMT had moved away from its reliance on farmers and toward the vital constituency that would carry it through almost until the 1990s: industry, local elites in the "local factions," and, of course, the army and bureaucracy. Table 4.6 shows the new vital constituency. In the 1960s, neither of the vital constituency's two new groups was happy with the education system— local factions (like mainlanders themselves) because they could not be guaranteed of their and their supporters' children making it into the highly subsidized upper levels of the system; and industry, because it was facing skyrocketing labor costs and increasing demands for skilled workers at a time when it was trying to export its way to prosperity. If the framework is accurate, major changes to the system could not be far off.

5. EDUCATION, 1965–1987: "Manpower Planning" and Two-Track Education

Resolution of the government's education dilemma came in a complete reorientation of the system. The 1960s were a time of drastic reforms—reforms that created a new system of vocational education to serve industry while reserving an increasingly well-resourced academic track for the children of the vital

Table 4.6 **The Vital Constituency, 1965–1987**

Political Entrepreneur(s)	Groups in the Vital Constituency[†]	Groups outside the Vital Constituency
None	Bureaucracy	Farmers
	Military	Workers
	Local Taiwanese Factions	
	Employers (Type B)	

Notes: [†] If a group was empowered with the help of a political entrepreneur, the entrepreneur is in brackets.

Employer types are in parentheses: Type *B* employers need skilled workers in a flexible labor market.

constituency. This section details these reforms. I begin with the origins of "manpower planning,"[26] under the guise of which the vocational system was constructed. I then analyze the development of vocational education, and the simultaneous development of a tracking system that gave the children of the vital constituency access to the academic system, which was both cheaper and more valuable.

MANPOWER PLANNING AND THE ORIGINS OF VOCATIONAL EDUCATION

Beginning about 1960, the year that manufacturing wages began to inch up, industry started to make noises about something then known as "manpower planning." The idea underpinning manpower planning is that it is possible to predict the quantity and quality of skills that an economy will need, and to adjust the education system to provide workers with those skills. By many accounts, Taiwan would become a model for its possibilities (Li 1981; Woo 1991).

The KMT government's manpower-planning approach grew out of a general framework of long-term economic planning that was in vogue at the time and was a common characteristic, in particular, of large-scale U.S. AID programs (Jacoby 1967).[27] In the context of this larger focus on economic planning, the United States in the early 1960s urged the KMT government to add manpower planning to its other planning capacities. Harry Weiss's above-mentioned visit to Taiwan in October 1963 was a crucial part of this effort. Afterward, Weiss wrote that "[t]he most important conclusion which I have reached is that the Government of the Republic of China . . . urgently needs a manpower plan" (Weiss 1964, 10). In the aftermath of this visit, in January 1964, the government set up a Manpower Development Committee under the auspices of the Council for International Economic Cooperation and Development (CIECD), the central economic planning organization—exactly as Harry Weiss recommended. This organization produced in 1966 the first Manpower Development Plan, which the government promptly endorsed and began to implement through the education system. The government followed this plan with a second, far more sophisticated version in 1968 and continued developing plans roughly every two years until the late 1980s.

Taiwan's use of manpower planning appears to signal the government's commitment to shaping education according to the needs of the economy. But a closer look reveals that the timing and character of the sort of manpower planning the KMT eventually adopted placed it squarely in the service of the vital constituency, not the economy. Harry Weiss was by no means the only voice pushing for manpower planning, but his views were influential,[28] and I use them here as an easy way of organizing the process that unfolded over the next few years.[29]

Weiss was very clear about the reason he saw a need for manpower planning: the economy could not absorb all the university graduates that the education system was producing. "As a result [of lacking the capacity for manpower planning] the universities and other educational institutions may be developing skills which are not needed in the present or the future economy of Taiwan. . . . Judged simply from the fact that approximately 85 percent of the students sent to the United States for graduate work do not return, it would appear that there is an overemphasis on some branches of higher university education" (Weiss 1964, 11, 13). At the same time, Weiss recommended expanding compulsory education from six to nine years.

Weiss, in other words, was recommending a refocusing of educational priorities that would have been anathema to two key groups in the vital constituency: local factions and mainlanders. Both were already chafing under the pressure of getting their children into the highly subsidized higher education system; to move resources from higher education to primary and secondary would have only increased the competition by increasing the number of well-prepared students, and lowered the quality of the education that students could expect if they did make it into higher education.

Another of Weiss's recommendations, however, fit well with interests in another corner of the vital constituency. He observed that although many excellent vocational schools existed in Taiwan in 1963, a large proportion were underutilized. Noting the stereotypical characterization of Chinese as thinking far more highly of academic than vocational employment, Weiss concluded that the government needed to do more to encourage students to attend these schools, and to make them aware of the job opportunities that awaited vocational graduates.

If it was acting as predicted by this book's framework, the KMT government should have adopted the second of these recommendations—expanding vocational education—and ignored the first—shifting resources away from higher education. It should furthermore be clear that, while the expansion of vocational education had economic benefits, the government effected it in order to serve its vital constituency, not because the economy needed the workers. I take up these issues in turn. The point is to show that wherever the economy and the vital constituency's needs did not overlap, the government adjusted its policy to serve the vital constituency, not the economy.

THE EXPANSION OF VOCATIONAL EDUCATION

During its first two years of operation, the Manpower Resources Committee of the CIECD was tasked with projecting the immediate future demands of the economy for skilled labor and making recommendations for how to meet those demands. Although the staff was small (seven, with two secretaries), they were aided by both the U.S. Department of Labor and the International Labor Organization and enlisted over a hundred experts from the Directorate-General of Budget, Accounting, and Statistics, and the Ministries of the Interior, Education, and Economic Affairs. The plan they came up with in their two years of work was comprehensive and thorough, and it set the stage for all future plans. It recommended, among other things, an increase in compulsory education from six to nine years, and the expansion of vocational education. Both of these became immediate priorities of the government. But the implementations of both proceeded in very particular ways, ways that ensured that the two goals mentioned above—restoring the elite higher education system, and providing industry with abundant skilled labor through Broad Worker Training—were met.

The most important innovation was the expansion of the senior vocational high school and the five-year junior college. The latter enrolled graduates of junior high schools in five-year, mostly technical courses. Under the new system, modeled after education systems in Germany and Japan, graduates of junior high school would take a Joint Entrance Examination, the results of which determined whether they would go to a senior (academic) high school, a senior vocational high school, or five-year junior college. In the decade after the first MDP was adopted, fifty new vocational schools opened, and enrollment went from a little over 74,000 to more than 282,000. The expansion of junior colleges was even more dramatic: their number shot from 20 in 1965 to 76 in 1975; enrollment went from 29,500 to 150,200 in 1975 (Republic of China 2005b).

Facing, for reasons I discuss shortly, unmitigated demand for entrance to the academic track, the Manpower Development Plans set target ratios for the number of academic students to the number of vocational students. The goal of the first plan was to reduce the ratio of academic students to vocational from 3:2 to approximately 2:3.[30] Successive plans sought to reduce it further: in the third MDP, from 4.5:5.5 in 1970 to 2:3 in 1980; and in the fourth and fifth, to 3:7 by 1980 (Hou 1978).

Although local governments ostensibly have responsibility for lower levels of education in Taiwan, control over the system was highly centralized in this era, allowing the Ministry of Education substantial authority in reaching the MDP goals. At the primary level, the Ministry controlled the finance, personnel, curriculum, tuition, and entrance examinations. It used its power to establish curriculum guidelines to mandate teaching hours, methods, goals, and objectives in each subject, for primary and secondary education. All textbooks were published by the National Institute for Compilation and Translation. Primary school principals and teachers even went through a central government distribution system to get their assignments (Young 1995).

Using this authority, the goals of the MDP were met in large part, if not precisely (Woo 1991). In 1972, the ratio of academic to vocational high school students was 48:52; by 1980 it was 36:64. By the fourth MDP (1972), the Plans began establishing specific student quotas for the Ministry to implement. The fourth plan recommended that the number of students entering senior high school should be frozen, and the rate of increase in students in colleges and universities held to five percent per year. In the fifth (1976) plan, the target rate of increase was reduced to three percent (Hou 1978).

OUTSOURCING VOCATIONAL EDUCATION
TO THE PRIVATE SECTOR

To create the needed expansion in the vocational education system, the KMT did something it had not previously done much of in education: it turned to the private sector. In the decade after the first MDP was adopted, 59 private vocational schools opened, while the number of public vocational schools actually fell by nine. Simultaneously the number of junior colleges went from 15 in 1963 to 76 in 1973—56 of which were private. By 1976, 58 percent of senior vocational high school students and three-quarters of junior college students were in private institutions.

There were at least two simple reasons for the decision to rely on the private sector. The first was speed. Industry was facing rapidly increasing wages and wanted immediate relief. Knowing the pent-up demand for secondary schooling, the private sector was well equipped to expand quickly.[31] The second reason was political: the KMT was already courting the support of local factions, for whom education promised to be a substantial business opportunity.[32]

More broadly, the decision allowed the KMT to solve one piece of the fundamental dilemma I posed at the end of Section 3. By 1965, the post-elementary education system was overwhelmed by applications from graduates from the expanded elementary system, threatening the chances for the children of elites. In opening a new vocational track of education, the KMT was able to channel this demand away from the academic system, greatly relieving the stress on it. The graduates from this new system provided industry with the skilled labor it badly needed to maintain productivity, solving (seemingly) a second piece of the dilemma.

The difference between vocational and academic education was not in control—the Ministry of Education tightly controlled every aspect of the costs and education provided by both private and public schools—but in cost to the government and in quality. In 1974, the first year separate records were kept on government subsidies, private senior vocational high schools got about a quarter less per student in government subsidies than public academic high schools. Vocational students themselves had to pay more: the average academic senior high school student faced fees totaling NT$3,061 (about NT$14,000 in 2001 NT$) in 1971, while the average vocational high school student faced NT$4,175 (about NT$19,000 in 2001 NT$) in fees, an amount roughly equivalent to one-and-a-half times the average monthly salary of a 40-year-old vocational-school graduate (Gannicott 1973). By 1987, the subsidy to a private vocational high school student was 56 percent of that to a public high school student. Public senior vocational schools fared better than private ones—in later years sometimes even exceeding the subsidization of public senior high school students—but these enrolled far fewer students. Among junior colleges, the discrepancy was still higher. In 1976, the first year separate records are available, private junior college students got 36 percent of students in public junior colleges, though private junior colleges enrolled more than three-quarters of students. Compared to a student at one of the elite public universities, government spending on that junior college student was 30 percent in 1976, and 6 percent by 1987. Table 4.7 shows the expansion of vocational education after 1965.

The one exception to this general pattern of public schools exceeding private ones in quality and funding was in senior high school. At that level, a number of established, elite private schools of extremely high quality received large amounts of government funding. These schools played a key role in tracking elite children into higher education, which I consider below. The schools were kept private despite their high level of government funding because this status freed them from curriculum restrictions set up by the Ministry of Education and allowed them instead to teach courses designed almost solely to prepare students for passing the Joint Entrance Exam to the universities (Young 1995).

Table 4.8 shows the increasing subsidies to academic high school and college, and Figures 4.4 and 4.5 show the trends in per-student government spending.

Despite the higher natural cost of fully educating a vocational student (World Bank 1993), government spending was usually much lower in vocational education, both public and private. Spending was low largely because more money just was not available for vocational education. In 1972 the government imposed on businesses a tax of 1.5 percent of total payroll, to be applied to a Vocational Training Fund. This clear assault on the profitability of industry—part of the government's vital constituency—was predictably short-lived; the tax was abandoned less than two years later. With its money tied up providing highly subsidized academic education to other groups in its vital constituency, the government did not have much more money to devote to vocational students.

The lack of funding unsurprisingly resulted in a vocational education that was far from exceptional, but which was very valuable to industry. Evidence abounds of the low quality of most vocational schools. Instructors were generally poorly paid compared to what they could earn in industry, and consequently of low

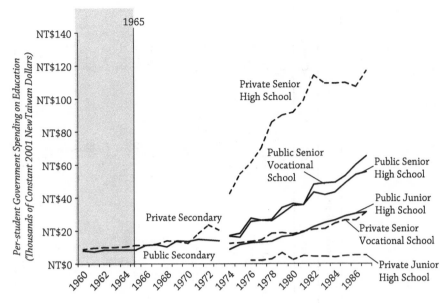

Figure 4.4 Government per-student spending on secondary students, 1960–1987

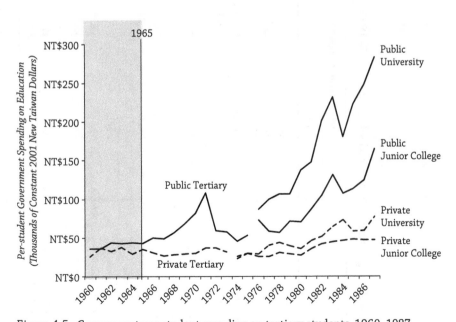

Figure 4.5 Government per-student spending on tertiary students, 1960–1987

Table 4.7 **Expansion of vocational education, 1965–1987**

	Senior Vocational High School			Junior College		
	1965	1987	Change	1965	1987	Change
Number of Schools	130	209	+61%	35	68	94%
Number of Private Schools	41	115	+180%	20	56	180%
Proportion of Private Schools	32%	55%	+74%	57%	82%	44%
Number of Students	74,114	447,328	+504%	29,534	256,610	769%
Number of Students in Private Schools	23,208	270,144	+1,064%	18,022	203,894	1031%
Proportion of Students in Private Schools	31%	60%	+93%	61%	79%	30%
Number of Teachers	6,212	17,366	+180%	1,706	10,038	488%
Number of Teachers in Private Schools	1,256	7,134	+468%	750	7,483	898%
Number of Classes	2,583	9,708	+276%	677	5,049	646%
Number of Classes in Private Schools	642	5,829	+808%	361	3,869	972%
Average Students per Class - Public	26.2	45.7	+74%	36.4	44.7	23%
Average Students per Class - Private	36.1	46.3	+28%	49.9	52.7	6%
Student: Teacher Ratio - Public	10.3	17.3	+69%	12.0	20.6	71%
Student: Teacher Ratio - Private	18.5	37.9	+105%	24.0	27.2	13%

Government Expenditures	Senior Vocational High School			Junior College		
	1976*	1987		1976*	1987	
Public††	NT$1,342,220	NT$8,128,037	+506%	NT$1,077,452	NT$6,110,944	+467%
(in 2001 NT$)	NT$3,458,439	NT$11,545,507	+234%	NT$2,776,223	NT$8,680,318	+213%
Private††	NT$892,007	NT$5,928,117	+565%	NT$1,175,352	NT$6,807,495	+479%
(in 2001 NT$)	NT$2,298,395	NT$8,420,621	+266%	NT$3,028,477	NT$9,669,737	+219%
Public per Student	NT$10,677.88	NT$45,873.43	+330%	NT$28,237.34	NT$115,922.00	+311%
(in 2001 NT$)	NT$27,513.21	NT$65,161.12	+137%	NT$72,757.89	NT$164,661.93	+126%
Private per Student	NT$5,222.77	NT$21,944.29	+320%	NT$10,141.17	NT$33,387.42	+229%
(in 2001 NT$)	NT$13,457.27	NT$31,170.86	+132%	NT$26,130.31	NT$47,425.32	+81%
Private Spending as Proportion of Public per Student	49%	48%	-2%	36%	29%	-20%

Notes: * Fiscal Year 1975–76 was the first in which separate records were kept for spending on public and private vocational high schools and junior colleges; †† NT$1,000.

121

Table 4.8 Increasing subsidization of academic education, 1968–1987

	Senior High School			College and University		
	1968†	1987	Change	1968†	1987	Change
Number of Schools	177	171	-3%	22	39	+77%
Number of Private Schools	98	95	-3%	12	14	+17%
Proportion of Private Schools	55%	56%	+0.3%	55%	36%	-34%
Number of Students	152,877	206,019	+35%	81,881	208,054	+154%
Number of Students in Private Schools	35,643	51,805	+45%	41,914	123,320	+194%
Proportion of Students in Private Schools	23%	25%	+8%	51%	59%	+16%
Number of Teachers	9,862	14,130	+43%	4,993	12,811	+157%
Number of Teachers in Private Schools	3,043	5,767	+90%	1,799	4,702	+161%
Number of Classes	3,209	4,104	+28%	2,138	4,828	+126%
Number of Classes in Private Schools	697	1,047	+50%	883	2,430	+175%
Average Students per Class - Public	46.7	50.4	+8%	31.8	35.3	+11%
Average Students per Class - Private	51.1	49.5	-3%	47.5	50.7	+7%
Student: Teacher Ratio - Public	17.2	18.4	+7%	12.5	10.4	-16%
Student: Teacher Ratio - Private	11.7	9.0	-23%	23.3	26.2	+13%

Government Expenditures	Senior High School			College and University		
	1976*	1987		1976*	1987	
Public††	NT$1,458,031	NT$6,025,680	+313%	NT$2,066,558	NT$16,910,570	+718%
(in 2001 NT$)	NT$3,756,844	NT$8,559,205	+128%	NT$5,324,808	NT$24,020,696	+351%
Private††	NT$868,536	NT$4,261,238	+391%	NT$945,642	NT$6,727,570	+611%
(in 2001 NT$)	NT$2,237,918	NT$6,052,895	+170%	NT$2,436,594	NT$9,556,207	+292%
Public per Student	NT$10,024.35	NT$39,073.50	+290%	NT$33,510.48	NT$199,572.43	+496%
(in 2001 NT$)	NT$25,829.28	NT$55,502.12	+115%	NT$86,344.97	NT$283,483.56	+228%
Private per Student	NT$23,805.94	NT$82,255.34	+246%	NT$11,299.48	NT$54,553.76	+383%
(in 2001 NT$)	NT$61,339.71	NT$116,839.97	+90%	NT$29,114.86	NT$77,491.14	+166%
Private Spending as Proportion of Public per Student	237%	211%	-11%	34%	27%	-19%

Notes: † 1968 was the first year in which separate records for teachers are kept for senior and junior high school;

* Fiscal Year 1975–76 was the first in which separate records were kept for spending on public and private vocational high schools and junior colleges; †† NT$1,000.

caliber and experience. Materials and equipment were in short supply: according to an analysis by Djang (1977), only 14 of the 173 vocational training institutes in 1965 had adequate training facilities and equipment, and all were either public or operated exclusively by large public enterprises. By 1974, only eight additional vocational training institutes had opened which provided high-quality training. In 1972, private industry developed a series of tests through the mostly private National Vocational Training Fund Board and its affiliated Institutes—agencies set up with the money collected during the brief operation of the Vocational Training Fund.[33] In its four years of testing, the NTFSI tested nearly 33,000 skilled workers. Less than half were rated "qualified."[34]

The government did take steps to improve the quality of vocational training, but these seemed only to highlight its general mediocrity. One of the most often-cited government measures was a series of competitions to raise the profile of vocational training. Between 1968 and 1975 the Ministry of the Interior held six national competitions, which were covered heavily in the KMT-controlled media. But when winners were then sent to international vocational competitions, they initially did quite poorly (Djang 1977; Li 1981). (Though by 1973 the eleven workers selected to attend the 21st International Vocational Training Competition in Munich won seven medals.)

The average Taiwanese vocational graduate may not have done well on tests or in international competitions, but he was still a great asset to Taiwanese industry. Vocational education and industry were closely linked, so that the general skills training could be supplemented with firm-specific skills. Indeed many vocational schools—particularly private schools—were integrated with specific companies, even plants, whose facilities were available to the vocational schools for training, and who generally would hire the students upon their graduation. Overall, industry made extensive use of vocational graduates. The average unemployment rate in Taiwan was four percent from 1967 to 1980 (Woo 1991), and early rate-of-return studies indicate that vocational education was good enough to provide an average private return of more than 13 percent, a rate that beat the return on academic senior high school education—though it was still far below the return on academic tertiary education, to which most academic senior high school graduates eventually progressed (Gannicott 1973).

THE EXPANSION OF JUNIOR HIGH SCHOOL AND ELITE TRACKING

The mere establishment of two tracks of education would not, on its own, do much to ensure that the academic track was reserved for the children of the vital constituency. That assurance came with additional changes to the basic education system. These changes came in two categories: a calculated expansion of compulsory education to nine years; and elite tracking within compulsory education.

Prior to 1968, compulsory education was six years. After that, even those who passed the junior high school entrance exam faced considerable costs and fees to attend junior high school. That ended in 1968. Thereafter the government abolished tuition for junior high school and made it compulsory.

The expansion was, however, of quite a different caliber than the expansion of elementary schools in the early 1950s, and reflected the new configuration of the vital constituency, which dictated that only the demands of the mainlander elites and local Taiwanese factions were fully considered. Whereas the total cost to students of attending elementary school was very low—NT$265 in 1971—the only cost eliminated in 1968 for junior high school students was tuition, which was only NT$120. Students still were required to pay a large number of additional fees, for physical education, notebooks, textbooks; for the library; for air raid precautions; for "contributions to military welfare"; and for school uniforms. These fees added up, on average, to NT$1,796 (or around 2001 NT$8,200) a year—half the average monthly salary of a 40-year-old vocational graduate, and slightly more than the average monthly earnings of a 40-year-old with no schooling (Gannicott 1973).

The continuing high fees did not prevent a flood of new students from entering junior high school; education had high returns and it was the shortage of places, not high fees, that had prevented many students from attending before.[35] There are numerous stories in this period of the sacrifices native Taiwanese families with limited resources made to give their children as much education as they could. In the next decade, the number of junior high school students more than doubled, from 500,000 in 1967 to 1,100,000 in 1978 (Republic of China 2005b).

To serve the flood of new students, local regions, and the local factions that controlled them, gladly engaged in the business of building hundreds of new schools, using money made from the sale of free land that the central government gave them for the purpose.[36] But the quality of the education awaiting these new students was not as impressive as the effort to build new classrooms. The government prepared for the launch of nine-year compulsory education in less than two years. College graduates, particularly junior college graduates, were enlisted by the thousands to become teachers, and soldiers could get early discharge from the military if they would agree to take a two-month training course and then teach.[37]

Elite students did not suffer, however, for at this time most junior high schools introduced tracking. Junior high schools were judged on the basis of how successfully their students performed on the Joint Entrance Examination to senior high school, and recognizing this they began separating students judged likely to do well on the exam from students judged likely to do poorly. The latter, destined for vocational schools, were largely neglected, while the former were lavished with the best teachers and resources the school could offer. Though tracking students was technically against Ministry of Education regulations, the Ministry turned a blind eye to the practice.[38]

Tracking in junior high schools gave elite students advantages, but it was at least partly meritocratic: students looking to enter academic senior high schools still had to pass a difficult exam. Those children of the elites who fell through the cracks had another option, however: private academic high schools. Private high schools were extremely expensive—making them accessible only to elites—but offered superb education, and their nominally private status allowed them to offer a curriculum entirely geared toward the entrance exams to universities, entrance to which was the ultimate purpose of going to an academic high school (Woo 1991). Private high schools were, in a sense, a safety net, available to catch the children of elites for whom their other advantages had not been sufficient.

As a result of the new elite tracking, during this period a person's family background—particularly their education—quickly overshadowed all other factors in determining how likely a student was to enter college. This fact is supported by a large and growing body of econometric evidence (Chen and Lin 2004; Chen 2005; Luoh 2001; Gannicott 1973). Ethnicity, by contrast, is of small and predictably lessening importance in this period, as the vital constituency now was firmly settled on mainlander elites and Taiwanese local factions.[39]

THE NEEDS OF INDUSTRY VS. THE NEEDS OF THE ECONOMY

The vocational system may have done an excellent job providing the KMT's supporters in industry with the skilled workers they needed. But this does not mean that the system was what the economy needed. In fact, the needs of the employers inside the KMT's vital constituency were not the same as the economy's. The distinction is important for the accuracy of this book's framework. If the Taiwanese government implemented policy because the economy needed it, then it was not acting in the interest of its vital constituency. Naturally industry's needs did overlap with the economy's. Thus the challenge is to show that the needs of industry and the needs of the economy did not always overlap, and that where they did not, the Taiwanese government always sided with industry, not the economy, in creating education policy. Evidence on these points comes both from the value of various types of education over the period of vocational expansion, and from the manpower planning process itself, which ostensibly had the economy's needs as its exclusive concern.

It was the nature of the manpower planning process that it created the resources and data to do its job as it went. In 1964 there were no accurate surveys of the manpower needs of the current Taiwanese economy, let alone accurate projections of its needs years away. There were the recommendations by Harry Weiss and, earlier, a report by a group of Stanford economists, both of which suggested that the Taiwanese education system was imbalanced and should put more emphasis on secondary education. But there were few specifics, and the basic message was that Taiwan needed manpower planning capacity— not what the manpower plan should be. The Manpower Resources Committee of the CIECD thus spent much of its first two years of operation getting a sense of what the economy needed.

In practice, this meant getting a sense of what industry needed. In half a dozen interviews with senior figures involved with economic planning in this era, I was told that the way the Manpower Resources Committee came to understand the need of the economy for more vocationally-trained workers was by asking large companies what kind of workers they needed.[40] These companies told the committee of their needs, and by some accounts added the complaint that they were being given college graduates to employ, when what they needed were workers and foremen. The committee then analyzed the output of the education system and determined where there were discrepancies.

Given this method of gathering information on the economy's needs, it is not at all surprising that the resulting plan recommended a shift in priorities to vocational education. But the committee also had little choice, since it was starting from scratch, and by all accounts the committee did make every effort to devise a thorough plan for creating the labor force it believed Taiwan would need.[41] It is notable that the initial plan endorsed the expansion of compulsory education from six to nine years and recommended the creation of a more permanent Manpower Planning Unit that could gather data and make accurate predictions for future education targeting.

Thus it is not the plan itself, but rather its implementation, that provides the first hint that the needs of industry and the rest of the vital constituency, not the economy, were foremost for the government. As I noted, there was a shift in the ratio of vocational to academic students and resources. But this shift should not be confused with a shift *away* from academic education. The quality and the funding available to a student in the academic track did not decline in order to free up resources that could be made available to vocational students, as the early manpower planning reports recommended. On the contrary, the amount allocated to each academic student went up—way up. A parallel process occurred in the expansion to basic education, where new junior high schools were set up, but the high private costs and tracking allowed elites more, not less, of a chance of making it into the academic side of post-secondary education.

On the vocational side, the spotty and generally poor quality of the training is more evidence for the central role of industry. Original plans for industry to contribute to a central fund to pay for some of the cost of the huge new vocational system were, as noted above, quickly scrapped. Instead, the resources that were available were put into educating a large volume of workers, even if this meant each one was less than ideally qualified. This is the hallmark of Broad Worker Training described in Chapter 2, and, for Taiwanese employers, it was the right balance. In fact, there is good reason to think that Taiwanese employers preferred somewhat less education in their workers. Some give credit for this view to an ancient Chinese notion that academic education breeds a disconnect from society and real-world concerns.[42] Other employers seem not to have wanted the questioning and lesser respect for authority that they expected from more-educated workers.[43] For example, in the 1970s, when a number of Taiwanese émigrés to the United States returned to Taiwan, those with technical masters' degrees found that they had a difficult time getting work, and most businesses flatly refused to hire those with PhD's.[44]

But because the original manpower plan was devised with so little knowledge and data on what the economy actually needed, it is difficult to separate the needs of the economy from the needs identified in the plan, let alone to make a judgment on whether the plan was intended to benefit the whole economy or just industry. That evidence would come once the Manpower Planning operation was well-established and data-rich enough to start making robust predictions and recommendations.

This does not take long. The first comprehensive study of rates of return to education was conducted in 1972. But rather than showing underprovision of vocational education, which would have vindicated the government's concentration on vocational education, it showed that the returns to the academic track— both the private and the social returns—remained far higher. University education had a social return of nearly 18 percent, on top of a 12.6 percent return to senior high school. Vocational high school, which was usually terminal, had a return of 13.2 percent (Gannicott 1973). Studies conducted by the government in 1974 and 1977 both found the same: that academic high school plus college offered a higher social rate of return than vocational high school or junior college (Republic of China 1974, 1977). Considering that these studies incorporated the vast subsidies given to academic high school and college students, they are strong refutation of the argument that vocational education should have been expanded still further.[45] In fact, students who had reached the pinnacle of the vocational track—junior colleges—found it much more difficult to find a job than university graduates: in a survey from the 1970s, almost half of junior college graduates reported that it was either "very difficult" or "somewhat difficult" to find a job, compared to less than 30 percent of university graduates (Kao, Hsu, and Lee 1976).[46] Yet the government continued to expand vocational education, while pouring resources into and restricting access to the academic track.

Further evidence comes from the manpower plans themselves. As the Manpower Planning operation became more sophisticated, it generated detailed forecasts of needs and outputs. These forecasts were consistently inaccurate, underlining how difficult it is to predict the future growth patterns of an economy. But it is the nature of their inaccuracy that is of interest. Almost without exception, each plan after the first overestimated the number of graduates and students in senior high schools and colleges, and underestimated the number in vocational schools and junior colleges. Yet each plan without exception recommended a further tightening of the ratio between academic and vocational high schools. In many cases the magnitudes are enormous. The second plan (1968) predicted less than 60 percent of the actual number of vocational senior high school graduates in 1971–1972, while it predicted 90 percent of the senior high school graduates and seven percent more college graduates than there actually were. The third plan (1970) was more accurate, though it still predicted 98 percent of the senior high school graduates from 1973–1974, while forecasting only 87 percent of the vocational high school graduates and 17 percent more college graduates than the actual. In its longer-term projections, though, the 1970 plan estimated 8 percent more senior high school graduates and 3 percent more college graduates than there were in 1975–1976, but only 81 percent of the actual number of vocational high school graduates.

Since predicting the labor force growth of an economy is an exercise so fraught with error, it is understandable that the Manpower Planning Unit's estimates were off. But the use of the reports to recommend exactly the opposite of what they seem to recommend is further evidence that the economy's needs were not the reason the Kuomintang kept expanding the vocational system.[47]

WRAPPING UP

In short, the Taiwanese government responded to the 1960s change in its vital constituency by radically altering the education system. The system was divided into two tracks, each serving different members of the KMT's vital constituency. On the one hand there was the academic system, which retained and later improved its quality after the pressure of the early 1960s. Through tracking in junior high school, Joint Entrance Examinations before senior high school and college, and highly subsidized academic high schools and colleges, the KMT government provided a high-quality, low-fee academic education system and restricted access to it to mainlanders and local Taiwanese factions. On the other hand, those outside the vital constituency were channeled to vocational training to provide skilled labor to an industrial sector facing rising labor costs.

These changes generally fit the predictions of the framework. The Evidence Summary for the period 1965–1987 follows in Table 4.9. In keeping with the division of the system into academic and vocational tracks, the table describes the two tracks separately.

The period provides evidence for the framework in most areas. There are only two areas of disagreement. The first is the high fees charged to students at private high schools: the framework predicts that fees should be low for all students inside the vital constituency. But the fees make sense once we know that they were complemented by enormous government subsidies, and that private high schools acted as a safety net for elite children who, despite substantial advantages, had not made it into the public senior high schools. Low fees would have opened up these schools to everyone, while high fees restricted access to them to the elite. At the same time, their nominal private status allowed them to teach a curriculum wholly geared toward helping their students pass their university exams. Because the fees serve these important purposes, they are partial support for the framework. The second area of disagreement is more severe: the government continued to provide subsidized loans to the civil service and the army but did not extend them to the industrial elite, who in this era were newly inside the vital constituency. It is possible to argue that industrial elites were far more able to afford educational fees than either civil servants or soldiers and that industrial elites were also harder to delineate: it would be hard to design a policy that

Table 4.9 **Evidence summary, 1965–1987**

Indicator	Characteristics	Conforms to Framework?
A. Enrollment	Academic: stagnant or slightly increasing at all levels	∎
	Vocational: increasing at all levels	∎
B. Per-student spending	Academic: high	∎
	Vocational: low	∎
C. The toolkit		
1. Schools		
Teachers	Academic: highly paid and qualified, except in the expansion of junior high schools	∎
	Vocational: poorly paid and poorly qualified	∎
Physical resources	Academic: high	∎
	Vocational: minimal—below objective standards of quality	∎
Location	Lower levels widely available; higher levels concentrated in urban areas	∎
2. Fees[†]	Academic: low, aside from private senior high schools; low but still substantial in junior high schools	◻
	Vocational: high (from junior high school on)	∎
3. Access restrictions and discriminatory pricing		
Quotas	None	
Exams	Academic: difficult at entrance to senior high school and university	∎
	Vocational: access to vocational determined by poor performance on academic exams	∎
Financial aid	Subsidized loans to civil servants and the military	☐
4. Tracking	Two tracks, academic and vocational; tracking began within junior high schools and then separated into different schools at the high school level	∎
5. Outsourcing (domestic or foreign; to firms or non-profits)	Academic: private high schools	∎
	Vocational: private high schools and colleges	∎

Notes: ∎: fully conforms to the framework; ◻: partly conforms to the framework; ☐: does not conform to the framework.

[†]Fees are for enrollment, books and other equipment, uniforms, activities, school improvements, etc.

awarded loans only to industrial elites. But the fact is that the loan policy was not extended to them, and this might be considered a strike against the framework.

The education system established in the crucial decade of the 1960s worked well for twenty years. Subsidies to the academic system soared while access restrictions were retained, even tightened. Vocational education provided industry with Goldilocks training for workers: not too little, not too much.

But by the late 1980s, two things were happening that would lead to radical changes in the education system. First, industry was increasingly able to ship its production abroad, and the production that remained had upgraded to the point where its skill demands were outstripping the skills provided in the vocational system. And more important, the vital constituency was changing. The KMT was losing its grip on power.

6. POLITICS, 1987–2000: The Second Vital Constituency Shift: The KMT Slips from Power

In 2000, the Kuomintang lost an election for the presidency of the Republic of China. The seeds of this previously unthinkable loss were sown long before, in the 1970s and 1980s, when domestic and international instability lessened the Kuomintang's ability to repress native Taiwanese elites. As these elites gradually reemerged, they began to act as a political entrepreneur to the poorer Taiwanese middle and lower classes, particularly manufacturing workers, organizing them around a nationalist message that portrayed the Kuomintang as mainlander oppressors. Taiwanese whose votes could formerly be bought through the local factions were gradually reorganized around this message, forcing the Kuomintang to compete directly for their votes. As political competition expanded, so did the Kuomintang's constituency, until by the late 1990s it was essentially the entire country: the Kuomintang could not abandon a single group's interests without losing power. But across this massive vital constituency were competing interests, and although the Kuomintang did its best to satisfy everyone, it simply could not. The 2000 electoral defeat was the result.

This section describes the vital constituency's gradual expansion beginning with the background conditions that led to the Kuomintang's momentous lifting of Martial Law in 1987. Then I consider politics and economics after 1987.

A GROWING OPPOSITION

Recall that the mid-1960s, the start of the previous era, was a time of stability for the KMT. Domestically, it had successfully repressed the native elites and nurtured new local elite factions that allowed it to secure its rule over the population. Internationally, the United States was a firm ally, and the "Republic of China" was in the ascendancy against the Communist state on the mainland. The Kuomintang held the Chinese seat in the United Nations and maintained official relations with most of the world.

But by the late 1960s, it was clear in most capitals that the KMT was not going to retake the mainland, and many countries began to switch their diplomatic recognition to the PRC. In 1971, the PRC was given China's U.N. seat, and Richard Nixon followed a year later with his famous visit to China. Instability was also on the rise at home. Even as the KMT came to rely increasingly on the economy for the resources to buy political stability, economic growth was slowing. The oil crisis fueled inflation—which spiked to nearly 50 percent in 1974—and the resulting international recession robbed Taiwan of crucial foreign capital. GNP per-capita grew 10.7 percent in 1973, and actually fell 0.7 percent in 1974 (Republic of China 1982), though growth recovered to 11.2 percent by 1976.

Since the White Terror in 1947, tensions had simmered among a small and isolated group of former native-Taiwanese elites. These elites had generally supported Japanese rule of Taiwan, but after their repression by the KMT they began to develop an ideology of Taiwanese nationalism (Chen 2003; Chu and Lin 2001). Seeing opportunity in the KMT's difficulties, this opposition began again to raise its head. By 1975, members of this group began publishing the *Taiwan Political Review* to create a shared consciousness among Taiwanese by pointing out their disadvantaged place relative to mainlanders. In 1976, other, more socialist elites began publishing *China Tide* to expose the harsh conditions of workers and peasants in both Taiwan and mainland China and push for social-welfare programs.

In another era the Kuomintang might have moved swiftly to crush such activities. But in the 1970s its preferred strategy was cooption. The party was busily deepening its ties to local factions and elevating friendly native-Taiwanese elites to higher office, a process of "nativization" that somewhat countered the opposition's claims of the KMT's exclusive preference for mainlanders. The process did indeed increase the proportion of native Taiwanese in key positions. For example, in 1972, faced with the death of rising numbers of the permanently-seated main-lander legislators, the government held a special election for three-year seats on the Legislative Yuan. Thirty-six of the new members—nearly 9 percent of the Yuan—were native Taiwanese. In 1975, the government held a second round of special elections, which yielded 9.3 percent of seats to Taiwanese. On the Central Standing Committee, 9.5 percent of places were held by Taiwanese in 1969; 14.3 percent in 1974; and 18.5 percent in 1976 (Chen 2003). This indigenization brought many Taiwanese closer to the mainstream of the party, and created, for the first time, an economic middle class of Taiwanese.

But the KMT's cooption and nativization did not stop native elites from continuing to organize. In 1977, in preparation for the third round of supplementary elections to the Legislative Yuan, several disparate opposition groups formed the *Dangwai* Campaign Corps. Though the groups were only loosely organized, they were nonetheless electorally successful. In Chungli, a riot even stopped vote-rigging (Chu and Lin 2001).[48] A year later, in 1979, the now-unified opposition began publication of another political journal, *Formosa*, which quickly became Taiwan's most popular and influential, and the island-wide offices of which doubled as the nucleus of the opposition's increasingly organized political struggle against the KMT.

As native Taiwanese elites increasingly became a viable political entrepreneur, the Kuomintang watched with growing alarm. In 1979 it cracked down. On December 10, International Human Rights Day, an opposition demonstration in Kaohsiung turned violent, and in the weeks after this "Formosan Incident" the government rounded up leaders of the opposition, charged them with sedition, and locked them up.

The Formosan Incident, with its similarity in targets, if not in scale and violence, to the February 28, 1947 massacre three decades before, brackets the period of the KMT's successful subjugation of the native Taiwanese elite class. Although the party co-opted many elites into its vital constituency, it never bought off the opposition completely, and those who remained outside the vital constituency grew harder to repress with each passing year. In 1980, in the aftermath of the Formosan Incident and despite widespread repression, the opposition won a third of popular votes in elections for the National Assembly and the Legislative Yuan in 1980. Thereafter, political opening proceeded steadily. Demonstrations were virtually unknown in the early KMT state; from 1983 to 1988, there were nearly 3,000, with 1,200 in 1988 alone (Chen 2003). In 1984 and 1985, the opposition opened two ostensibly illegal organizations: the Association of Policy Studies and the Association of Campaign Assistance. When, in 1986, the opposition moved to open chapters of the Association of Policy Studies in many towns in Taiwan, the government responded with dialogue, not repression. Simultaneously, President Chiang Ching-kuo set up a political reform committee in April 1986, which recommended a shortened schedule for democratization and endorsed key opposition demands. Five months after the formation of the reform committee, in September 1986, the opposition gave itself a party: in English, the Democratic Progressive Party, or DPP. Once again legal coverage came after the fact: in October, Chiang Ching-kuo suggested in a public interview that new political parties might be allowed to exist if they were to agree to three principles: acceptance of the 1947 constitution; rejection of Taiwanese independence; and opposition to communism.[49] In the same interview, President Chiang also suggested he might be willing to loosen restrictions on government-controlled newspapers. And he hinted that a lifting of Martial Law might be in the offing.

The KMT's defensive stance was due at least partly to uncertainty about its leadership. In the 1980s, for the first time in its rule on Taiwan, the KMT faced a succession crisis. In the late 1960s, power had passed from Chiang Kai-shek to his eldest son Chiang Ching-kuo—a succession two decades in the making. But by the 1980s, Chiang Ching-kuo too was growing old and had not chosen a successor. By this point, the nativization of the regime had reached a point where the only politically sensible choice for a successor would be a Taiwanese. Thus in March 1984, less than a year before Chiang Ching-kuo's deteriorating health became widely known to the public, Lee Teng-hui, a native Taiwanese, was nominated as vice president. Though Taiwanese, Lee Teng-hui was far from a vocal Taiwanese nationalist; in fact, his views were unknown, his leadership untested, and he was without loyalties or bases of support either inside or outside of the vital constituency. Rather, he was technocrat with a PhD in agricultural economics from Cornell who had entered and risen in Taiwanese politics thanks to Chiang Ching-kuo's nativization policies. He was, in short, seemingly an ideal choice.

As the decade wore on, the difficulties facing the KMT were clear: a weakened leadership; domestic instability and international isolation; and an opposition that was proving an effective political entrepreneur of poorer Taiwanese, whom the KMT's local factions had until then been able to control. These difficulties came together in the summer of 1987. In July, Chiang Ching-kuo declared an end to the Martial Law under which Taiwanese had been governed since 1949. Six months later, Chiang Ching-kuo was dead, and Taiwan had a Taiwanese president. The result was an entirely new political landscape.

THE VITAL CONSTITUENCY EXPANDS

The old guard of the KMT watched the events of the 1980s with some anxiety. But Lee Teng-hui seemed a Taiwanese who would help them restore the old order. He turned out not to be. Instead, he courted Taiwanese moderates, expanding the KMT's vital constituency until the party broke in two. In the face of the increasingly powerful opposition, neither of the fragments could muster majority support in the population. In 1996, the KMT lost the legislature, and in 2000, the presidency.

The difficulty the old guard would have with Lee was apparent almost immediately. Even as they tried to quash the growing opposition by pushing for laws curbing free speech and assembly, President Lee was building alliances that stretched the bounds of the KMT's vital constituency. He courted reform-minded Taiwanese elites, developmental technocrats in the party, capitalists and local factions, and even the opposition Democratic Progressive Party (DPP). He expanded the access of Taiwanese to the top echelons of the party and government, and offered generous pensions to national representatives to induce them to retire, which allowed their replacements to be elected via the local factions. In this way he expanded the reach of patronage politics, which had until then been mostly local, to the national government. His tenure was consequently marked by increasing allegations of corruption and the influences of "black gold," or mafia politics, on policy. Lee's strategies were invariably oriented toward Taiwanese, particularly moderates in the middle classes and local factions. This pursuit of the center had far-reaching effects, both on the KMT and on the opposition DPP.

To the opposition, Lee's outreach was competition. Their response was to become more radical. As Lee courted moderates, the DPP began appealing to Taiwanese to see themselves as ethnically, economically, and politically marginalized, and as citizens of a latent Republic of Taiwan. The DPP did not provoke the KMT by supporting independence outright. Instead it pledged to support independence if and only if one of the following occurred: the KMT engaged in party-to-party negotiations with the Chinese Communist Party; the KMT "betrayed" Taiwan; or the CCP attempted to unify with Taiwan by force. From behind these seemingly sensible conditions, the DPP cultivated a constituency among those disposed to support Taiwanese nationalism and independence.[50]

To the KMT, Lee's cooptation of the middle ground among Taiwanese threatened party unity. It caused the KMT to gradually split into two wings: "mainstream"— Lee and his supporters—and "non-mainstream"—the old guard. Lee's "mainstream" wing gradually gained the upper hand. Starting in 1990, Lee negotiated a series of constitutional reforms, the cumulative effect of which was to remove the old guard's control over the national legislative bodies and create a popularly elected presidency and thus shift Taiwan from a nominally parliamentary to a semi-presidential democracy. The reforms represented a delicate balance. Rather than allow popularly elected representatives to engineer the reforms, the National Assembly, dominated by the old guard, met one final time to establish a framework highly favorable to them under which the constitutional reform would proceed. But once the new assembly was seated, Lee's "mainstream" wing of the KMT aligned with the DPP to push for free elections for mayor of Taipei and Kaohsiung and popular election of the president, both of which were vigorously opposed by the KMT's "non-mainstream" old-guard wing.

For a time, Lee kept the two factions together, despite his moves in favor of the "mainstream" wing. He declared an end to the "Temporary Articles," which had effectively suspended the constitution since 1948. But simultaneously he appointed as prime minister Hau Pei-tsun, a military strongman, who with some success tried to curtail incipient labor and environmental movements in an attempt to lessen their threat to industry.

Yet as Lee tried to maneuver, the population was growing restless with the pace of change, and demonstrations of thousands of marchers were becoming a regular fixture in Taipei. The appointment of Hau Pei-tsun as Prime Minister, for example, drew 10,000 students to the streets. It increasingly became impossible for Lee to court moderate Taiwanese while keeping the "non-mainstream" wing inside the party. After Lee responded to popular pressure to dismiss Hau Pei-tsun, a large group of the "non-mainstream" faction simply left the KMT and formed the "New Party." In 1995 elections, the New Party commanded the loyalties of large numbers of mainlander voters and robbed the KMT of 21 seats in the Legislative Yuan. The KMT, under Lee, had to increase its appeals to Taiwanese voters to maintain its hold on power, and though that decision made electoral sense—there were vastly more of them than mainlanders—the DPP was competing on the same turf, and doing so very effectively: it captured 54 seats. The KMT, left in the middle, won just 85 of the 164 seats, the first time its share fell below 50 percent.

The KMT's difficulty was that in the face of the DPP challenge, it was losing the support of much of its vital constituency. Lee's expansion of the vital constituency had created a coalition with competing interests: as the party moved to the center, the right broke off. Flanked by the resulting New Party on its right, and the DPP on its left, the remains of the KMT could not capture a majority.

But for the moment, the KMT still had the presidency, and it responded to the loss of the legislature by making the presidency more powerful (Chen 2003; Chu and Lin 2001). The third-phase constitutional reforms, completed in alliance with the DPP, put the presidency up for direct election and gave the president the power to appoint and dismiss the premier and the heads of government branches without approval of the legislature. In the next round, completed in July 1997, the president gained the power to dissolve the Legislative Yuan entirely. These reforms were somewhat risky: by tying its fortunes to the presidency, the "mainstream" KMT was banking on Lee's ability to win by popular vote.

The test came in 1996, Taiwan's first direct presidential election. In the campaign, Lee courted a new vital constituency with little regard for the old. He referred publicly to the KMT as an émigré regime, promoted Taiwanese art, and stressed officially the national importance of teaching native Taiwanese history and culture. He described the "misery of being a Taiwanese"[51] and the shared identity of the four Taiwanese ethnic groups—native peoples, Hoklo, Hakka, and mainlanders—built over four hundred years of external rule. And he campaigned with a message of *zhu quan zai min*—sovereignty rests with the people.

It worked. In a four-way contest, Lee won a landslide victory with 54 percent of the vote. But the victory also came at a cost: the KMT won the presidency in 1996 only by reinforcing among Taiwanese the sense of nationalism that the DPP had worked for a decade to foster. In 1989, only 16 percent of the Taiwanese population identified themselves as "Taiwanese"; in 1997, 55 percent did (Chen 2003).

Lee's victory also did nothing to stem the party's difficulties in the legislature and set up the unusual situation that, from 1996 to 2000, the KMT's vital constituency was much of the citizenry: its minority position meant that the KMT could not govern without allying with either the New Party or the DPP. Such a hold on power could scarcely have been less stable. Nonetheless the 1996 strategy had accomplished its goal: the KMT was, at least for the moment, still the ruling party.

In sum, the era from 1987 to 2000 was one of a rapidly and steadily expanding vital constituency. This, for my purposes, is the era's primary political feature. The KMT began the era with a vital constituency very similar to the one it had established in the mid-1960s: a stable coalition of local factions, employers, and the military and bureaucracy. But in the midst of international and domestic instability, the KMT lost its control of the native elite opposition, undermining the KMT's governing strategy—which depended on the local factions' ability to deliver votes—forcing it to compete with the opposition for the support of average Taiwanese. But adding new members to the KMT's vital constituency simply angered the old members, splitting the KMT and costing it the legislature and later the presidency. Table 4.10 shows the KMT's vital constituency after 1987.

THE END OF THE SKILLED LABOR SHORTAGE

There was one other notable change in the vital constituency in this period: the demands of employers. Recall that employers in the previous era were of type *B*: in Taiwan's flexible labor market, they needed to hire large numbers of skilled Taiwanese workers, and thus demanded Broad Worker Training. But the same political opening that expanded the KMT's vital constituency ended the skilled labor crunch by changing the economic environment faced by employers in two important ways. The first was that it prompted the return of tens of thousands of highly educated Taiwanese émigrés. The second was that it led to a thawing of relations with mainland China.

In the latter half of the twentieth century, an estimated 100,000 Taiwanese sought higher education abroad, especially in technical fields (O'Neil 2003). Few returned when they graduated. The political environment kept many away, and Taiwanese employers placed little premium on higher technical training, limiting job prospects for those who would have wanted to return. But with Taiwan's gradual political opening, many émigrés began flocking back: 50,000 returned in the late 1980s. These returnees brought business savvy and entrepreneurial zeal, and they established many of the successful small and medium-sized enterprises that before long pushed Taiwan's manufacturing sector into high technology. We will see in the following section that these returnees also provided valuable high-level labor of a kind that the maturing Taiwanese economy was beginning to demand, and which it did not get from the KMT's vocational training system.

Demand for less-skilled workers also fell in this period, but for a different reason: the opening of China. Thawing relations with China was a part of the lifting of Martial Law in 1987: for the first time, Taiwanese families were allowed to visit their relatives on the mainland. At the same time, the mainland government's coastal development policy opened up the country to foreign investment, and Taiwanese investors saw as clearly as any the vast profits waiting to be made by using cheap Chinese labor. China did all it could to encourage small and medium-sized Taiwanese enterprises to shift their labor-intensive production to China, and Taiwanese businesses—facing higher wage costs and more assertive worker and environmental movements at home—happily obliged. Even before the KMT removed its ban on direct trade in 1991, Taiwan was already the second largest foreign investor in China (Hsiao and So 1996).

Thus labor unrest and environmental activism, though costly, were far more successfully weathered by Taiwanese industry than they would have been a decade earlier. Initially, diversification of labor sources shielded Taiwanese companies from labor shortages at home; low-skilled, labor-intensive production could move offshore, relieving competition for the high-skilled workers necessary for the

Table 4.10 **The Vital Constituency, 1987–2000**

Political Entrepreneur(s)	Groups in the Vital Constituency†	Groups outside the Vital Constituency
1. The KMT	Bureaucracy	None
2. Taiwanese Nationalists: the	Military	
Democratic	Local Taiwanese Factions	
Progressive Party (DPP)	Employers (Type *N*)	
	Taiwanese Middle Class [DPP]*	
	Taiwanese Nationalists [KMT; DPP]*	
	Farmers [KMT]*	
	Workers [KMT; DPP]*	

Notes: † If a group was empowered with the help of a political entrepreneur, the entrepreneur is in brackets. Political entrepreneurs: "KMT": *Kuomintang* (Chinese Nationalists); "DPP": Democratic Progressive Party.

*These groups entered the vital constituency gradually over the period 1987–2000; they are firmly inside by the mid-1990s.

Employer types are in parentheses: Type *N* employers do not demand training of skilled workers.

skill-intensive production that remained. Later, even high-skilled production moved offshore. One example is the manufacture of laptops. Taiwan was once a powerhouse producer of laptops, but the last laptop production line in Taiwan had closed by September of 2005.

Taiwanese industry remained a key part of the KMT's vital constituency from the 1960s, and therefore would have had as much of a say over the government's education policy after 1987 as before. But access to Chinese labor, coupled with the return of tens of thousands of highly-trained Taiwanese from abroad, would, by this book's framework, shift industry from type *B* to type *N*, causing it to cease demanding Broad Worker Training. Not only is abundant labor educated at another government's expense cheaper to industry than labor educated by its own government, but foreign labor is available instantly, not after years or decades of schooling. Thus Taiwanese industry in the 1980s and 1990s should have demanded far less government education of vocational workers than at any time since the 1950s.

Now that we have established the vital constituency for 1987–2000, it remains to see whether Taiwanese education responds as the framework predicts.

7. EDUCATION, 1987–2000: Education Reform for Everybody, but Pleasing Nobody

The years 1987 and 2000 bracket a period of nearly continuous transformation in Taiwanese education. Creeping reform sought to reconcile irreconcilable demands, intensifying dissatisfaction and leading to further reforms that were always inadequate. In the end, an education system that was once a source of substantial pride to Taiwanese became disliked by nearly everyone.

Viewed through the lens of this book's framework, the reforms' substantial length, variation, and difficulties were all largely predictable. The KMT government was fighting for its life throughout this period, forced to rely on a shifting and expanding vital constituency whose demands often conflicted. The government did its best to meet those demands in education, but pleasing one group often meant displeasing another, and since displeasing any group was increasingly dangerous, further reform was always politically essential. The KMT's education system was a gerbil running on a wheel, chasing food forever out of reach.

The framework also sheds light on the nature of the reforms. The KMT's changing vital constituency meant that it no longer needed to produce just a Top-Down education system that ensured the sons and daughters of bureaucrats, soldiers, and members of local factions a high probability of getting a good, low-cost college education. Instead, it needed to produce an All-Levels system, as it had in its early days on Taiwan. As the 1990s wore on, the KMT had to develop a system that also improved the quality of primary and secondary education for those formerly relegated to the vocational track, and that increased access to higher education. The KMT simply did not have the money to do both. Nor, with its vital constituency ever in flux, did it have the time to do any reform well. As a consequence, its reforms were fast and on the cheap. While clearly geared toward meeting the changing vital constituency's demands, each reform was underfunded and inadequate, necessitating a further round of reform once the vital constituency wised up or shifted again.

The one corner of the vital constituency that provided some relief was industry. Industry's newfound access to cheap mainland-Chinese labor, aided to a lesser extent by the tens of thousands of highly educated Taiwanese who returned to Taiwan in the 1980s and 1990s, largely removed the impetus for industry's push for vocational education. As I noted at the end of the previous section, this change meant that Taiwanese industry shifted in the 1980s from type *B*—desiring Broad Worker Training—to type *N*: employers without demands for worker training. With industry's demands lessening, the KMT government was freer to meet the labor-market demands of students, instead of industry. Since the jobs remaining in Taiwan required higher-quality vocational education than industry had demanded in the past, students demanded better vocational education to prepare them.

The KMT's reforms proceeded in two overlapping stages: improvement of vocational education; and improvement in primary and secondary education combined with increased access to higher education. I consider these stages in the following two sections. The reforms resulted in a steady and substantial increase in the resources available to students in schools that had formerly been relatively neglected by the government—those at the lower levels and in the vocational track. These increases were paid for by lowering per-student spending in the formerly privileged higher levels of the system. Figures 4.6 and 4.7 show the trends: Figure 4.6 shows the increasing per-student spending at the primary and secondary levels; and Figure 4.7, the stagnant spending on tertiary students in junior colleges and declining per-student spending on public university students. Figure 4.8 puts the numbers into the broader historical context, and here the break is clear: after allotting a remarkably stable percentage of each education dollar to tertiary students since

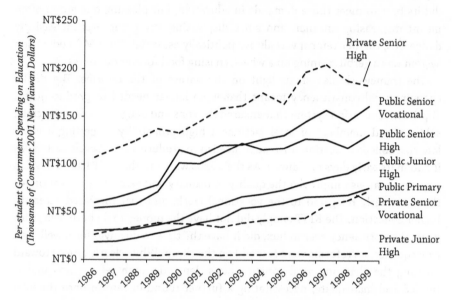

Figure 4.6 Per-student spending in primary and secondary schools, 1986–2000

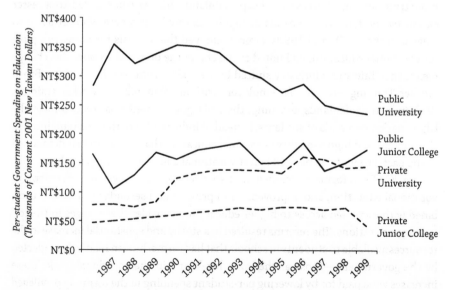

Figure 4.7 Per-student spending in tertiary institutions, 1986–2000

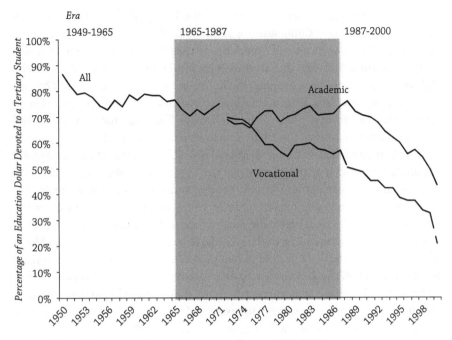

Figure 4.8 Relative spending on tertiary students, 1950–2000

1950—exempting the aforementioned falloff in vocational per-student spending after the mid-1960s—spending begins a precipitous fall after 1987.

IMPROVED VOCATIONAL EDUCATION

Dissatisfaction with education was widespread by 1987, and nowhere more so than among those attending vocational schools. As the vital constituency expanded to cover increasing numbers of Taiwanese, the vocational system was the first target of reform.

For vocational students and their parents, dissatisfaction with vocational education was not primarily about quality. It was about being vocational students. It was the rare vocational student who wouldn't have preferred access to the far more prestigious, inexpensive, and lucrative academic track, rather than improvements in vocational training. But in 1987 the KMT's vital constituency was just beginning to include those receiving vocational education, and industry had only recently attained access to cheap Chinese labor. Thus improving vocational education was as far as the KMT was initially willing to go. Politically, this tactic was unsustainable: demands of the vital constituency cannot be so inadequately addressed and it was only a matter of time before the academic track would indeed be opened up. But in 1987 the KMT had time to maneuver: vocational education had for so long been neglected that any attention to it pleased its patrons.

Reform began almost immediately after the lifting of Martial Law. In July 1987, the ailing Chiang Ching-kuo appointed Mao Kao-wen the new minister of education. Mao brought unique experience to the job. He had a PhD in chemical engineering from Berkeley, and, after working for General Motors, was one of the highly-educated Taiwanese émigrés who had returned to Taiwan in the 1970s. He was also past president of the only higher institute of technical education in Taiwan and was an opponent of the Manpower Planning that had dominated vocational education since the 1960s. One consequence of the dominant place of existing industry in determining vocational education was that the education did not upgrade as quickly as the economy. In the 1970s and 1980s, as new industries came online, new companies formed that demanded new and higher skills. But the vocational system was developed to serve the dominant industries, not the upstarts, and for the most part it did not try to provide those skills. Mao had seen this recalcitrance first hand. In the late 1970s, he had conducted a study to address what he saw as the lack of foresight in Manpower Planning; he projected ten years out the demands of the Taiwanese economy for scientists and engineers based not on linear trends derived from current demands for labor, but by taking account of the changing nature of Taiwanese industry and the possibilities of high-quality education for creating jobs and spurring economic growth. His report went on a shelf.[52]

But by 1987, the politics had changed. In fact, the government had already signaled that it was taking the quality of vocational education much more seriously. The Ministry of Education had undertaken triennial assessments of junior colleges and vocational schools since 1977, [53] but the results were purely informational; yearly entrance to junior colleges was fixed at 3,600 students.[54] In 1985, though, the Ministry began relaxing enrollment requirements for junior colleges that ranked at the top of the Ministry's assessments; in enrolling more students, these colleges could make more money, and profit was thereby tied to quality for the first time.

When he was appointed minister, Mao Kao-wen's views on education and the need for reform, particularly to vocational education, were well-known.[55] Mao's appointment was therefore a signal that the government wanted real reform. On taking office, Mao moved swiftly to increase spending and quality. Students in the academic track benefited, as they always had, with increased resources, but, quite unusually, vocational students often benefited more. From 1986 to 1990, the amount spent on a student at a public senior vocational school nearly doubled, from NT$60,000 to NT$115,000 (constant 2001 NT$). Mao also quadrupled the government's budget for private vocational education. Per-student spending in private vocational schools rose 43 percent, from NT$26,300 to NT$37,700. By 1993, per-student spending on public vocational high school students actually pulled ahead of spending on public academic high school students (see Figure 4.6).

Table 4.11 shows the improvements to the vocational track, and Table 4.12 compares spending increases in the vocational and academic track.

Table 4.11 **Improvement of vocational education, 1987–1990**

	Senior Vocational High School			Junior College		
	1986	1990	Change	1986	1990	Change
Number of Schools	204	216	+6%	77	75	-3%
Number of Private Schools	115	121	+5%	56	62	+11%
Proportion of Private Schools	56%	56%	-1%	73%	83%	+14%
Number of Students	437,924	449,111	+3%	244,482	315,169	+29%
Number of Students in Private Schools	268,179	271,006	+1%	190,946	264,500	+39%
Proportion of Students in Private Schools	61%	60%	-1%	78%	84%	+7%
Number of Teachers	16,721	17,703	+6%	10,444	12,409	+19%
Number of Teachers in Private Schools	7,023	7,022	0%	6,914	9,494	+37%
Number of Classes	9,456	9,897	+5%	4,831	6,387	+32%
Number of Classes in Private Schools	5,691	5,919	+4%	3,612	5,263	+46%
Average Students per Class - Public	45.1	44.8	-1%	43.9	45.1	+3%
Average Students per Class - Private	47.1	45.8	-3%	52.9	50.3	-5%
Student: Teacher Ratio - Public	17.5	16.7	-5%	15.2	17.4	+15%
Student: Teacher Ratio - Private	38.2	38.6	+1%	27.6	27.9	+1%
Expenditures - Public[†]	7,132,949	15,856,481	+122%	4,662,550	6,619,993	+42%
(in 2001 NT$)	10,184,108	20,454,697	+101%	6,656,982	8,539,723	+28%
Expenditures - Private[†]	4,940,412	7,911,099	+60%	6,269,651	11,813,514	+88%
(in 2001 NT$)	7,053,701	10,205,236	+45%	8,951,529	15,239,311	+70%
Expenditures per Student - Public	42,021.56	89,028.84	+112%	87,091.86	130,651.74	+50%

(continued)

Table 4.11 (continued)

	Senior Vocational High School			Junior College		
	1986	1990	Change	1986	1990	Change
(in 2001 NT$)	59,996.51	114,846.28	+91%	124,345.89	168,539.40	+36%
Expenditures per Student - Private	18,422.07	29,191.60	+58%	32,834.68	44,663.57	+36%
(in 2001 NT$)	26,302.21	37,656.86	+43%	46,879.90	57,615.54	+23%
Private Spending as Proportion of Public per Student	44%	33%	-25%	38%	34%	-9%

Notes: [†] In thousands of NT dollars.

Though most of the reforms in this period focused on vocational education, Mao also pushed more generally and less successfully for changes in other areas of education. One was access to the academic track; Mao suggested that the ratio of academic to vocational, which had fallen to 30:70 by the start of his tenure, be increased to 50:50. This was a reform for which the government was not yet ready, and it failed in the face of opposition from industry and Manpower Planning officials.[56] Reform to the academic track was consequently minimal and largely cosmetic. An example is the regulation for studying abroad. Prior to Mao, and with the exception of a brief period in the early 1950s, no one was allowed to study abroad until they had graduated from university. This restriction effectively allowed only members of the vital constituency to send their children abroad to study. Under Mao the Ministry of Education amended the "Regulations for Overseas Study" in 1989 and abolished them entirely in 1990 (Republic of China 2005b). The change was meaningful, but it was hardly the kind of sweeping reform that the KMT's expanding vital constituency wanted and to which the KMT would later acquiesce.

In fact while Mao's concentration on vocational education made political sense in the late 1980s, by the early 1990s the politics were still shifting. Taiwanese—particularly the Taiwanese middle class that would soon enter the KMT's vital constituency—wanted not just better second-class education; they wanted increased access to the prestigious academic track. And in the early 1990s they were getting more vocal about their demands. Improved vocational education was not going to keep them quiet.

REFORM OF THE ACADEMIC SYSTEM

Alongside the general growth in Taiwanese civil society, there grew a grass-roots movement specifically interested in reforming education. By 1994 this movement reached the apex of its annoyance to the KMT. In that year, more than 30,000

Table 4.12 **Comparison of academic and vocational tracks, 1986–1990**

	1986	1990	Increase 1986–1990
VOCATIONAL	[NT$]	[NT$]	
Senior Vocational High School			
Expenditures - Public[†]	10,184,108	20,454,697	101%
Expenditures - Private[†]	4,940,412	10,205,236	107%
Expenditures per Student - Public	59,997	114,846	91%
Expenditures per Student - Private	26,302	37,657	43%
Junior College			
Expenditures - Public[†]	6,656,982	8,539,723	28%
Expenditures - Private[†]	8,951,529	15,239,311	70%
Expenditures per Student - Public	124,346	168,539	36%
Expenditures per Student - Private	46,880	57,616	23%
ACADEMIC			
Senior High School			
Expenditures - Public[†]	8,131,780	15,617,046	92%
Expenditures - Private[†]	5,387,253	7,337,933	36%
Expenditures per Student - Public	54,059	101,506	88%
Expenditures per Student - Private	107,367	133,037	24%
College and University			
Expenditures - Public[†]	19,684,018	39,559,996	101%
Expenditures - Private[†]	7,054,425	12,123,006	72%
Expenditures per Student - Public	248,297	338,777	36%
Expenditures per Student - Private	124,346	168,539	36%
PER-STUDENT SPENDING RATIOS	[Ratio]	[Ratio]	
High School			
Vocational to Academic - Public	1.11	1.13	2%
Vocational to Academic - Private	0.24	0.28	16%
College			
Junior College to College/ University - Public	0.50	0.50	-1%
Junior College to College/ University - Private	0.38	0.34	-9%

people marched in the streets. The demonstration, which began on April 10 and became known as the April 10, or 4/10 Movement, was unprecedented not just in its size, but in its membership: it was led by a university professor and dominated by the middle class. Mothers marched with baby strollers.

The Movement presented the government with four demands: improvement and modernization of primary and secondary education; smaller classes; a central

Education Law to redefine the purpose of education as bringing out the potential in every child (not simply providing workers for industry); and more academic high schools and universities. The four demands were united by a sense that the Top-Down nature of the education system was leading to widespread failures at the lower levels. Pressure to get into the top senior high schools and universities was so fierce that teachers taught only to the exams, and students spent their childhoods going from school to cram school to their bedroom desks in a frenzied effort to pass. Even the fourth demand, which ostensibly dealt with higher education, was actually intended as a way of improving primary and junior high school education by relieving pressure on schools to orient their education toward getting students into high school and college.[57]

Many of the 4/10 marchers were inside the vital constituency. Thus it is reasonable to ask: why did they need to march at all? Why did the government not simply meet their demands, before they had to go to the streets? The answer is that the government tried, but was hemmed in by two limits: its capacity, and the inflexibility of education. We saw in Chapter 3 that these are two of a number of limits on a government's educational choices. In this case, the Taiwanese government simply did not have the resources to change the education system quickly or completely enough. The demands of 4/10 went right to the heart of the system that for decades was designed to provide workers. Teachers, tracking, curricula, funding—all needed reform.

The government had, in fact, already recognized that its reforms to the vocational track would not be sufficient and was beginning to reform the primary and secondary systems. An important step was the replacement of Education Minister Mao Kao-wen in 1993 with Kuo Wei-fan, a soft-spoken former president of the National Taiwan Normal University, the country's top institution for training teachers. Much of the population's impatience with the education system centered around the quality of teaching in primary and secondary schools, which was based around lecturing and rote memorization, with a heavy emphasis on sometimes violently enforced order. Taiwan's teachers were socialized to that method of teaching through training in a system that was as close to a meritocracy as anything in Taiwan. The highly coveted positions in the network of Normal universities were allotted to the highest scorers on tests; those admitted received free education and a living stipend, and a secure job after graduation.[58] At the time, the prevailing wisdom held that greater competition for teaching positions would help raise the quality of teaching. Under the new leadership of Minister Kuo, the Ministry of Education proceeded to do just that. In 1993 the KMT passed a revised Teacher Training Law that allowed any college or university to establish a teacher training course. Most, knowing the huge demand for teaching positions, quickly did, and teaching-course graduates more than tripled.[59]

It was only in the aftermath of this new responsiveness by the government to demands for education reform that the 4/10 Movement was launched. It is possible that the KMT underestimated the urgency of the population's dissatisfaction with the education system. If so the march quickly informed them otherwise. The movement's demands went well beyond isolated changes like a new Teacher Training Law, or the string of other smaller changes that preceded it.[60] But the government was dealing with an increasingly difficult situation. Its expanding vital constituency was requiring it to provide quality education for an increasing share of the population. With limited resources and an education system resistant to quick adjustments, its capacity for actually meeting 4/10's demands was very limited. Chapter 3 theorized that governments faced with such situations enter a period of "churning," the governmental equivalent of panic. When the vital constituency's demands exceed the government's capacity, there is not much it can really do, so it stalls for time and implements reforms that try to soothe the vital constituency's dissatisfaction.

The Taiwanese government's reaction to 4/10 is a clear instance of churning. Two months after the 4/10 march, the Education Ministry held a nationwide conference on education attended by more than 300 social and educational leaders. The ministry then followed the conference with more than 40 regional conferences, in which local community leaders could air their views. And in September, the government made its most momentous educational decision of the 1990s: concluding that systematic change was necessary, but not yet sure how far it would need to go, it appointed the blue-ribbon Commission on Education Reform, headed by Nobel Laureate Lee Yuan-tseh, who had just returned to Taiwan from the United States to become the president of Academia Sinica, Taiwan's premier research institution.

The appointment of the commission bought the government valuable time to figure out its next move, and the commission's prestige—particularly the prestige of its revered chairman, Professor Lee—did take much of the wind out of the sails of the 4/10 Movement.[61] The commission was granted considerable autonomy; it operated directly out of the premier's office, not through the Education Ministry, and had two years to conduct its business. Every six months it would present its recommendations to the government, at which time the Education Ministry could comment on them, but support by the government for the commission's work came right from the top: from President Lee. When Minister Kuo registered minor objections in the first two of the commission's four reviews, he was removed as minister and made the country's representative to France.[62] Kuo's replacement was Wu Jin, a completely unknown and untested figure in Taiwan, but one whose resume suggested that he would be more amenable to the commission's viewpoints: he had spent all of his professional life as a scientist in the United States and had only recently returned to Taiwan to take up the presidency of one of the national universities.[63]

The commission's membership was deliberately light on educational professionals, particularly teachers, and heavy on economists. Professor Lee, the chairman, had little experience in education, not to mention education reform, though he was certainly a successful product of the Taiwanese education system. That, in fact, was the point: the government at this stage was abandoning its traditional emphasis on vocationally oriented education, and wanted—or, rather, its vital constituency wanted—a system that would give every child the chance at the kind of academic success that Professor Lee had enjoyed. The selection of Wu Jin was of a piece with this logic; as another successful academic with no experience with Taiwanese education and no established views on education reform, he was likely to favor the kind of reforms the commission was developing.

In the end the commission recommended major reforms in almost every area of education. The reforms, which were generally couched as decentralizations, tried to shape the Taiwanese system into something closer to the American system, in which Professor Lee had spent his career and which Taiwanese generally hold in high esteem: they emphasized increasing access to higher education, concentration on science and technology, teacher autonomy, deregulation of diplomas and textbooks, and "pluralism," "democracy," and "humanism" in schools—direct responses to the 4/10 Movement's criticisms of the harsh and undemocratic nature of Taiwanese education.

In the previous section I noted that the two years the commission operated were years in which the KMT's vital constituency shifted dramatically in the direction of Taiwanese—particularly elites and nationalists—a shift represented by the KMT's President Lee. With this in mind it is not surprising that the commission's recommendations were embraced by President Lee but met with skepticism by those "non-mainstream" members who had remained with the KMT, and by the education bureaucracy, which had been entirely left out of their development. The split, that is, exactly mirrored the larger one between the two wings of the KMT's vital constituency.

The implementation of the commission's recommendations was selective, and in later years it changed virtually in lock step with the KMT's ever-shifting vital constituency. The KMT's dilemma was that it could not implement any reform that would lower the quality of education available to anyone in the vital constituency. It therefore implemented only those commission recommendations that had a rough Pareto optimality for the vital constituency.

The first was the expansion of access to college. As it dealt with competing interests, expanding access to college was a politically dangerous reform. The academic education system had satisfied elite demands for education only at the price of exclusivity. After 1996, the KMT could afford to alienate no one in society, including these elites, and their demands had not changed. Thus the KMT had to expand access to college in a way that could maintain exclusivity. Its solution, as in the 1960s, was to turn to the private sector. The private sector was well-placed to effect the expansion quickly and cheaply using its existing network of junior colleges. Although technical in nature, a junior college education had some of the aspects of higher education. And just as the private sector in the 1960s was eager to profit from pent-up demand for secondary education, the private sector in the 1990s was chomping at the bit to service students desperate for academic higher education.

As most junior colleges offered three-year courses, the government settled on an easy solution: it simply allowed junior colleges to add a fourth year, transforming them into four-year colleges and awarding their graduates college degrees. From 1995 to 2000, as junior colleges upgraded into colleges and universities, the number of private junior colleges fell from 58 to 19, while the number of private colleges and universities shot from 26 to 78. Junior colleges calculated that, with all the pent-up demand for academic education, the quality of education mattered less than the trappings of college. They were right: while neither the nature nor the quality of the education changed much, the extra year, and the diploma, made all the difference. From 1995 to 2000, private colleges and universities enrolled an additional 200,000 students, more than doubling their previous enrollment. At the same time, relaxed enrollment restrictions allowed the few remaining, mostly private junior colleges to enroll vast numbers of students, so that their numbers actually rose by almost 60,000 students.

The result was naturally a decline in the quality of higher education. Class sizes and student-teacher ratios inched up, and per-student spending fell. In absolute terms, budgets at the top public universities increased, but their enrollments increased much faster. From 1995 to 2000, enrollment at public universities increased 45 percent, while the average amount spent on a public university student in 2000 was NT$235,000, NT$40,000 less than in 1995.

In a relative sense, higher education lost even more. For the first time in its history, the KMT government in the 1990s neglected higher education to improve lower education (see Figure 4.8 above). Declining quality and massive increases in enrollments in higher education—even, though to a much lesser extent, at the elite public universities—were at odds with the increasing resources and quality in the rest of the education system.

The rest of the system was flourishing, in fact. Schools across Taiwan—but especially in the rural areas—got face-lifts and new equipment. Wu Jin, the new minister of education, was a master of the media, and made it a point to visit a different—and most often rural—school district nearly each week to inspect its equipment and offer new government resources.[64] Where most media outlets assigned a single reporter to cover several ministers, Wu Jin by the end of his tenure had two reporters assigned just to him: one to cover the continuous stream of developments at the Ministry, and one to cover his trips around the country.[65] The government's attention even extended to Taiwan's long-neglected outlying islands; Wu Jin made headlines when he arranged for island students to visit Taipei on an exchange and have dinner with President Lee.

Continuing its newfound commitment to vocational schools, the government also devoted commensurate increases to them throughout the 1990s and was increasingly outspoken about the need for their improvement. Wu Jin went to the Legislative Yuan to tell legislators that the government had treated vocational workers as "second-class citizens"—a statement, he told me, that no minister before would have dared to make.[66] Yet even as the resources available to vocational schools inched up, enrollment in them was falling, for the vital constituency was far more interested in academic education. The ratio of vocational to academic students at the high-school level reached its apex in 1986, the year before Mao Kao-wen took over as minister of education; thereafter it began a steady fall, and in 2002, academic high school students outnumbered vocational high school students for the first time since 1970.

To the Lee Commission—and to the expanding vital constituency—this trend away from vocational education was entirely positive. But to Wu Jin, there was still a place for vocational education: not every student was destined to be a Nobel Laureate like Lee, nor did Taiwanese companies want a workforce of only scientists and managers. Eventually the two views clashed. In the past, the KMT's choice would have been obvious: it would have chosen vocational education. It is a sign of how thoroughly the political logic had changed that in the late 1990s, the KMT sided with Lee. Wu Jin was ousted as minister in 1998.[67] In the remaining two years of the KMT's control—in 2000, the DPP won the presidency—the minister's office had two relatively weak occupants, and the shift toward academic education continued uninterrupted.

Indeed, for all the churning, all the protests and reforms, once we step back and look at the period 1987–2000 as a whole, the shifts are remarkably steady. Evidence of the gradual change of the 1990s is in the per-student spending figures above in Figures 4.6–4.8. Tables 4.11–4.13 round out the picture. At the lower levels, class sizes fell and resources increased slowly but surely, while at the higher levels access increased steadily without commensurate new resources. And although new resources were devoted to the vocational track, students increasingly chose the academic track. Considering the momentous changes afoot, the gradual pace of change is remarkable. But it is a consequence of the "churning" process brought on the education system by the KMT's political dilemma: it could not please one side of its large and growing vital constituency without displeasing another. It therefore scrambled continuously for new options and stalled for time. But underneath it all, as its vital constituency grew, the KMT served them.

There are a few things of particular note in these tables. First, over the decade, class sizes grew slightly at the higher levels, and fell sharply at the primary and secondary levels (with the exception of the small number of private junior high schools). Second, the number of vocational institutions fell while the number of academic institutions grew: as colleges and universities tripled, junior (vocational) colleges fell by two-thirds; academic high schools rose 65 percent while vocational high schools fell by an eighth. In enrollments the story is similar. Enrollments in colleges and universities tripled, rising 75 percent in academic high schools while falling marginally in vocational high schools. The exception is junior colleges: the few remaining junior colleges that had not been elevated to university status used relaxed enrollment requirements to enroll huge numbers of new students. Third, and most important, is per-student spending, which rose at every level except colleges and universities, and which rose most at the lowest levels of the system. Over the decade, per-student public primary and junior high spending increased two-and-a-half fold; per-student public high school spending rose 190 percent at

Table 4.13 **Expansion of higher education in the 1990s**

	Junior College			College and University		
	1989	*2000*	*Change*	*1989*	*2000*	*Change*
Number of Schools	75	23	-69%	41	127	+210%
Number of Private Schools	62	19	-69%	15	78	+420%
Proportion of Private Schools	83%	83%	0%	37%	61%	+68%
Number of Students	293,204	444,182	+51%	241,860	647,920	+168%
Number of Students in Private Schools	243,690	388,888	+60%	135,820	408,030	+200%
Proportion of Students in Private Schools	83%	88%	+5%	56%	63%	+12%
Number of Teachers	11,624	3,826	-67%	13,957	39,565	+183%
Number of Teachers in Private Schools	8,884	3,533	-60%	5,096	22,743	+346%
Number of Classes	5,886	8,713	+48%	5,555	14,199	+156%
Number of Classes in Private Schools	4,774	7,603	+59%	2,620	7,763	+196%
Average Students per Class - Public	44.5	49.8	+12%	36.1	37.3	+3%
Average Students per Class - Private	51.0	51.1	0%	51.8	52.6	+1%
Student: Teacher Ratio - Public	18.1	188.7	+944%	12.0	14.3	+19%
Student: Teacher Ratio - Private	27.4	110.1	+301%	26.7	17.9	-33%
Expenditures - Public[†]	4,764,421	9,616,764	+102%	25,396,739	56,531,625	+123%
(in 2001 NT$)	5,110,395	9,615,803	+50%	27,240,951	56,525,973	+66%
Expenditures - Private[†]	9,844,656	16,436,055	+67%	7,480,992	58,845,146	+687%
(in 2001 NT$)	10,559,537	16,434,412	+24%	8,024,233	58,839,262	+486%
Expenditures per Student - Public	96,223.71	173,920.58	+81%	239,501.50	235,656.45	-2%
(in 2001 NT$)	103,211.11	173,903.19	+35%	256,893.17	235,632.88	-27%
Expenditures per Student - Private[†]	40,398.28	42,264.24	+5%	55,080.19	144,217.69	+162%
(in 2001 NT$)	43,331.84	42,260.01	-22%	59,079.90	144,203.27	+95%
Private Spending as Proportion of Public per Student	42%	24%	-42%	23%	61%	+166%

Notes: [†] Thousands of NT dollars.

Table 4.14 **Improvements to the secondary levels in the 1990s**

	Senior Vocational High School			Senior Academic High School		
	1989	2000	Change	1989	2000	Change
Number of Schools	214	188	-12%	168	277	+65%
Number of Private Schools	120	93	-23%	90	125	+39%
Proportion of Private Schools	56%	49%	-12%	54%	45%	-16%
Number of Students	438,140	427,366	-2%	204,457	356,589	+74%
Number of Students in Private Schools	259,445	257,886	-1%	52,993	121,951	+130%
Proportion of Students in Private Schools	59%	60%	+2%	26%	34%	+32%
Number of Teachers	17,687	18,812	+6%	14,475	30,471	+111%
Number of Teachers in Private Schools	7,131	7,380	+3%	5,906	11,903	+102%
Number of Classes	9,777	9,956	+2%	4,210	8,252	+96%
Number of Classes in Private Schools	5,785	5,921	+2%	1,066	2,643	+148%
Average Students per Class - Public	44.8	42.0	-6%	48.2	41.8	-13%
Average Students per Class - Private	44.8	43.6	-3%	49.7	46.1	-7%
Student: Teacher Ratio - Public	16.9	14.8	-12%	17.7	12.6	-29%
Student: Teacher Ratio - Private	36.4	34.9	-4%	9.0	10.2	+14%
Expenditures - Public[†]	10,459,293	38,419,138	+267%	8,028,105	39,977,248	+398%
(in 2001 NT$)	11,218,806	38,415,297	+173%	8,611,075	39,973,251	+271%
Expenditures - Private[†]	7,457,473	21,595,392	+190%	5,421,759	21,549,276	+297%
(in 2001 NT$)	7,999,006	21,593,233	+116%	5,815,466	21,547,121	+196%
Expenditures Per Student - Public	58,531.54	226,688.33	+287%	53,003.39	170,378.40	+221%
(in 2001 NT$)	62,781.87	226,665.66	+188%	56,852.29	170,361.37	+139%
Expenditures per Student - Private	28,743.95	83,740.07	+191%	102,310.85	176,704.38	+73%
(in 2001 NT$)	30,831.22	83,731.70	+117%	109,740.27	176,686.71	+29%
Private Spending as Proportion of Public per Student	49%	37%	-25%	193%	104%	-46%

Notes: [†] Thousands of NT dollars.

vocational high schools and 140 percent at academic high schools; and spending rose 35 percent for the few remaining public junior colleges (spending fell on private junior college students). At the same time, per-student spending on colleges and universities fell by more than a quarter. The government also devoted less money to each private student, relative to each public student, at every level except colleges and universities—where, as we have seen, the government initially tried to soak up demand for higher education by elevating private junior colleges but later needed to try to raise their quality as well.

WRAPPING UP

The period post-1987 was a time of turmoil in Taiwanese education. Public dissatisfaction with the system was widespread; a dozen years of reforms in close succession certainly did not assuage the public's concerns, and probably increased them. This "churning" bought the government time, but behind it, shifts in the system proceeded with remarkable regularity from the late 1980s. After initially trying to improve the vocational system, the government began around 1990 to open the formerly privileged academic track, and to shift resources from the highest levels of the system to the lower levels. As quality increased at primary and secondary schools, hundreds of thousands of new students entered colleges and universities. The expansion far outstripped those institutions' resources, many of which were simply junior technical colleges that had been speedily elevated to university status with little preparation.

In most areas, these changes are what the framework predicts. The evidence summary for the period is in Table 4.16. The framework predicts that a change in the vital constituency like Taiwan experienced in the late 1980s—from elites to a cross-class alliance, and from employers demanding Broad Worker Training to employers without skilled-labor demands (from type *B* to type *N*)—will be followed by a shift from a Top-Down education system providing Broad Worker Training to an All-Levels system. After 1987, facing the threat of the DPP, the KMT's vital constituency expanded rapidly, to the point where, by the end of the 1990s, the KMT found its power in unusual and unstable dependence on virtually the whole country: it could abandon not a single interest group without losing power. (The defection of the KMT's old core—the "non-mainstream" faction—in fact cost the KMT the presidency in 2000.) The incorporation of poorer groups into the vital constituency necessitated precisely the shifts in funding and access that occurred, but this incorporation occurred without the government being able to abandon the wealthier groups that had formerly been at the heart of its vital constituency. In a few short years, the government was asked to provide universal education at all levels, and the task exceeded both its capacity and the speed with which it could alter the education system. Its response to the sudden shift was therefore predictably slow and inadequate. Among other consequences, the inadequacy of the response produced the

Table 4.15 **Improvements to the primary level in the 1990s**

	Primary School			Junior High School		
	1989	2000	Change	1989	2000	Change
Number of Schools	2,484	2,600	+5%	691	709	+3%
Number of Private Schools	22	25	+14%	9	7	-22%
Proportion of Private Schools	1%	1%	+9%	1%	1%	-24%
Number of Students	2,384,801	1,925,981	-19%	1,125,238	929,534	-17%
Number of Students in Private Schools	26,151	22,166	-15%	56,060	86,109	+54%
Proportion of Students in Private Schools	1%	1%	+5%	5%	9%	+86%
Number of Teachers	80,849	101,581	+26%	49,824	49,394	-1%
Number of Teachers in Private Schools	834	912	+9%	298	250	-16%
Number of Classes	56,315	62,443	+11%	25,514	26,553	+4%
Number of Classes in Private Schools	484	546	+13%	1,108	1,879	+70%
Average Students per Class - Public	42.2	30.8	-27%	43.8	34.2	-22%
Average Students per Class - Private	54.0	40.6	-25%	50.6	45.8	-9%
Student: Teacher Ratio - Public	29.5	18.9	-36%	21.6	17.2	-21%
Student: Teacher Ratio - Private	31.4	24.3	-22%	188.1	344.4	+83%
Expenditures - Public[tt]	48,800	189,557	+288%	28,910	106,540	+269%
(in 2001 NT$)	52,344	189,538	+189%	31,010	106,530	+174%
Expenditures - Private[tt]	520	1,536	+195%	191	753	+294%
(in 2001 NT$)	558	1,535	+120%	205	753	+194%
Expenditures per Student - Public	20,689.87	99,567.04	+381%	27,039.61	126,318.78	+367%

(continued)

Table 4.15 (continued)

	Primary School			Junior High School		
	1989	2000	Change	1989	2000	Change
(in 2001 NT$)	22,192.28	99,557.08	+258%	29,003.12	126,306.15	+248%
Expenditures per Student - Private	19,880.69	69,275.56	+248%	3,405.28	8,744.79	+157%
(in 2001 NT$)	21,324.35	69,268.63	+159%	3,652.56	8,743.91	+91%
Private Spending as Proportion of Public per Student	96%	70%	-28%	13%	7%	-45%

Notes: [†] Thousands of NT dollars; [††] Millions of NT dollars.

4/10 march and movement, which frightened the regime into the painful churning process that rocked Taiwanese education throughout the 1990s.

The only area where the framework does not predict what occurred is exams to the top universities. The government did take steps to reduce exam competition: the number of university spaces soared. Nonetheless, entrance to the most prestigious universities, like the National Taiwan University, was still governed by difficult exams for which intense preparation was required. The problem was at least partly a lack of capacity to provide All-Levels education. Yet the problem was also that the government was not willing to fully open its most prestigious universities to the newly empowered poor, and that may be considered a partial strike against the framework.

8. Conclusion

I began this chapter by noting that Taiwan seems a good case for an economic explanation of education. The Taiwanese government was famously a developmental state, one that achieved spectacular growth over many decades and that built the country into an Asian Tiger and a model to many developing countries. In large part, this growth rested on human capital, and Taiwan's education policies have consequently been lauded for their seemingly clear-eyed focus on Taiwan's economic needs.[68] Of the explanations I considered in Chapter 1, the economic explanation seems best-suited to explain Taiwan's changing education landscape under the Kuomintang's half-century rule.

Yet I have presented evidence in this chapter that the economic explanation comes up short. Taiwan's government has always acted in the interests of its vital

Table 4.16 **Evidence summary, 1987–2000**

Indicator	Characteristics	Conforms to Framework?
A. Enrollment	Academic: increasing, especially at higher levels	■
	Vocational: shift to academic	■
B. Per-student spending	Academic: increasing at low levels; decreasing at high levels	■
	Vocational: increasing	■
C. The toolkit		
1. Schools		
Teachers	Increasingly competitive, emphasis on "democracy" and "humanism" in the classrooms	■
Physical resources	High, with particular emphasis on rural areas	■
Location	Particular emphasis on rural schools	■
2. Fees[†]	Low, aside from private high schools and colleges; increasing subsidies to private junior college students	■
3. Access restrictions and discriminatory pricing		
Quotas	None	
Exams	Difficult at entrance to top public universities	▢
Financial aid	Scholarships, and need-based loans	■
4. Tracking	Elimination of tracking: While vocational schools still existed, enrollment caps were relaxed in the academic track	■
5. Outsourcing (domestic or foreign; to firms or non-profits)	Private high schools and colleges	■

Notes: ■: fully conforms to the framework; ▢: partly conforms to the framework; ▢: does not conform to the framework.

[†]Fees are for enrollment, books and other equipment, uniforms, activities, school improvements, etc.

constituency, not in the interests of the economy. The education system's service to the economy—which was undeniably substantial—was the result of an opportune overlap between the vital constituency's interests and the economy's. The overlap meant that in many ways the education system did serve the economy. But it also meant that where the interests of the vital constituency and the economy conflicted, the government always made education policy in the interest of the vital constituency, not the economy.

From 1949 to 2000, the Kuomintang had three distinct vital constituencies. In the early days after its defeat in the Chinese Civil War, the KMT depended on a cross-class vital constituency of soldiers and bureaucrats from the mainland, aligned with Taiwanese farmers and against Taiwanese elites. This initial VC gave way in the 1960s to a coalition of mainlanders, export-oriented manufacturing enterprises, and local factions made up of a new class of native-Taiwanese elites nurtured by the KMT. After a succession crisis and the lifting of Martial Law in the late 1980s, this coalition swelled in the 1990s to include much of the population, as the Kuomintang began losing ground to the Taiwanese-nationalist Democratic Progressive Party, whose political entrepreneurship threatened the Kuomintang electorally and forced it to try to organize and court the poor. In 2000, the Kuomintang lost the presidency.

These vital constituencies—a cross-class alliance with employers without skilled-labor demands (type *N*), followed by elites and employers demanding Broad Worker Training (type *B*), and ending again with a cross-class alliance with employers without skilled-labor demands (type *N*)—should have led the KMT to produce an All-Levels system, followed by a Top-Down system with Broad Worker Training, and finally an All-Levels system again. This is largely what occurred. From the heavily primary system it inherited from the Japanese, Taiwan's "pioneer" government built a two-pronged education system: it expanded primary education to serve its farmers and built excellent high schools and universities to serve its mainlander elite. In the 1960s, as the KMT's position on Taiwan grew more permanent and secure, it abandoned farmers in favor of local factions and export-oriented manufacturing industries, who were facing a skilled labor shortage (type *B*). In response, after 1965, the education system siphoned off the workers' and farmers' children into a new vocational training system, leaving the academic system intact for the children of elites. The siphoning was facilitated by a series of access controls and tracking at the junior high school level that ensured that elite children were groomed for academic secondary education, while children of the lower classes were prepared for vocational schools.

This system operated effectively through the late 1980s, delivering academic education to elites and skilled workers to employers. But by the late 1980s, with the thawing of relations with mainland China, employers were shifting types and no longer needed Broad Worker Training. At the same time, the vital constituency was changing, as Taiwanese nationalists forced the KMT to compete for the native Taiwanese lower classes. With this expanding vital constituency—one that incorporated the poor without disempowering the rich—the KMT entered a period of "churning" in education: with no Pareto-optimal improvements available to it, the government struggled to slow the inevitable flow of resources from the upper to the lower levels and the diluting of the formerly privileged upper levels through increased enrollments. Yet despite the churning, the 1990s were a time of steadily increasing resources for primary and secondary students and declining per-student spending at the universities, as resources failed to keep pace with skyrocketing enrollments. At the same time, the vocational level shifted from serving industry to serving the vital constituency: its quality improved, and its enrollment dropped, as tracking no longer relegated to it a mass of poorer students destined for factories. These reforms, while perhaps inevitable given the changing political environment, have led predictably to widespread discontent with education in Taiwan, as increasing access overwhelms the government's ability to provide each student with the quality of education the system had previously provided.

CHAPTER 5

Ghana

Ghana, the first black African nation to gain its independence, began life bursting with optimism and potential. It possessed vast reserves of gold and timber, a booming export trade in cocoa, and a developed infrastructure; its treasury could draw on tens of millions of pounds in cash reserves; and its charismatic president, Kwame Nkrumah, captivated Ghanaians and the world with his vision of a modern, independent nation in Africa. By 2000, however, Ghana's real GDP per-capita was lower than at independence, much of its wealth was still held by its elite, and it had switched from autocracy to democracy or back no fewer than five times.

This book's three case studies were chosen not just to be different—and thus to test the validity of the book's framework in three diverse settings—but also to provide opportunities for the alternate explanations of education policymaking that are common in political economy scholarship. The previous chapter tested the accuracy of the economic explanation in a country that it seems well-equipped to handle: Taiwan. The role of Ghana (and Brazil in the next chapter) is to test the framework in a far different context, one that is better equipped to test another prominent alternate explanation: that policymaking is a function of regime type. Ghana's five regime-type transitions give each type plenty of chances to make its mark on education policy. The chapter will show that regime type does not predict education policymaking in Ghana. In fact Ghana's education policies seem completely uncorrelated with Ghana's regime changes.

Instead, as in Taiwan, the major changes in Ghana's education system were a function of political entrepreneurship of the poor and the labor market conditions faced by employers. Of the two, political entrepreneurship was more consequential for education policy: it led to two periods in which the government invested heavily in mass education. Since 1951, when Ghanaians, although still formally under British control, gained control over their education policies from their British colonizers, Ghana's governments have been affiliated with political entrepreneurs of the poor in two periods. Ghana's impoverished and disbursed masses have tremendous and well-known collective action disadvantages[1]; but despite these, Ghana's two political entrepreneurs were able to organize them into a political force and each ruled Ghana autocratically with their support. The first political entrepreneur, Kwame Nkrumah and his Convention People's Party, built a cross-class alliance until Nkrumah was overthrown in a coup in 1966; the second, J. J. Rawlings and his Provisional National Defense Council, organized a vital constituency of the poor alone and ruled with their support after 1981. During these two periods, the government invested in mass education. In between, from 1966 to 1981, Ghana's governments depended only on elites, and created Top-Down education.

Ghanaian employers, for their part, have never demanded skilled workers on the scale of Taiwanese employers; thus they have never demanded mass education from the government. In some form, employers have always been inside Ghana's vital constituencies, and they have usually needed some skilled workers. (For much of Ghanaian history, the government itself was by far the largest employer of skilled labor.) Because Ghana's labor market has always been inflexible, Ghana's employers have been of Type S—demanding Selective Worker Training—when they needed skilled workers. During a long economic depression in the 1970s, employers did not need any skilled workers and were therefore Type N—demanding no worker training.

Table 5.1 summarizes Ghana's vital constituencies. If the framework is accurate, Ghana's government should have developed an All-Levels system with Selective Worker Training after 1951, and then reformed it into a Top-Down system with Selective Worker Training after 1966. During the economic depression of the 1970s, the government should have abandoned Selective Worker Training. And finally, after 1981, it should have transformed Ghanaian education into a Bottom-Up system, with Selective Worker Training as the economy recovered.

These predictions are largely born out. This chapter presents a great deal of evidence for each of these transformations. But the basic story is simple and is observable in the distribution of literacy in the Ghanaian population today. Figure 5.1 uses data from Ghana's 2003 Core Welfare Indicators survey[2] to calculate, for five-year age groups, the proportion of the population who achieved literacy based on when they would have graduated from the final year of primary school (which in Ghana is grade 6). Overlaid on the figure are Ghana's vital constituencies.

Of the population who would have graduated from primary school in 1951—the year Nkrumah's Convention People's Party took control of education from the British—a little over 30 percent attained literacy. By 1966, this proportion had risen steadily to 51 percent. But thereafter the increase slowed, and then, incredibly—considering that literate parents tend to produce literate children—the proportion who attained literacy actually began to decline, bottoming out at 50 percent for those who would have graduated from primary school in 1981. Starting in 1981, however—the year Rawlings' Provisional National Defense Council took power—the proportion who attained literacy again began to rise, reaching 73 percent for those who would have graduated from primary school in 1996.

Table 5.1   **Vital Constituencies in Ghana**

Employers	*Families in the Vital Constituency*		
	Elites (no political entrepreneurship)	Elites and the Poor (cross-class political entrepreneurship)	Elites (no political entrepreneurship)
Type B (Need skilled workers in a flexible skilled-labor market)	1	2	3
Type S (Need skilled workers in an inflexible skilled-labor market)	4 1966 - 1972	5 1951 - 1966	6 1979 - 2000
Type N (Do not need skilled workers) or outside the Vital Constituency	7 1972 - 1979	8	9

Behind these numbers is a series of policy changes that, though complex, almost always push Ghanaian education in the direction predicted by this book's framework. As in the previous chapter on Taiwan, this chapter relies on evidence of three types: enrollment, resources, and the education toolkit. The chapter is in eight parts. The first sets the scene by describing Ghana's political economy and education system in and prior to 1951, when Ghanaians inherited control over their education system from the British. The second section begins the analysis by considering the political economy—specifically political entrepreneurship and the make-up of the vital constituency—of the first period, 1951–1966. The third section examines whether the education system evolved in line with the vital constituency identified in Section 2. Like the sections on education in Chapter 6 on Taiwan, Section 3 and the other two sections on education end with an "evidence summary" table that outlines all the evidence presented in the section and assesses how well the book's framework did in predicting the reality of Ghanaian education. Sections 4 and 5 then consider the second period, 1966–1981, and Sections 6 and 7 examine the last period, 1981–2000. Finally, Section 8 concludes with a brief summary of the argument and a more detailed analysis of how well the framework predicts Ghanaian education policies compared to alternative explanations.

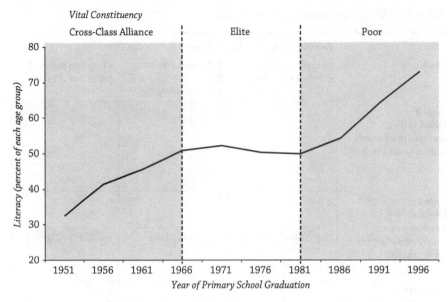

Figure 5.1 The basic story: vital constituencies and progress in literacy, 1951–2000

1. The Scene in 1951[3]

In 1951, when Ghanaians gained a measure of control over their own affairs for the first time since colonization, Ghana's two major political traditions were already firmly established. Ghanaian politics in the decades since has largely been characterized by the struggle between these two traditions. One engaged in political entrepreneurship and governed with vital constituencies that included the poor; the other did not engage in political entrepreneurship and governed with elite vital constituencies. This section outlines the origins of the two political traditions. At the close I add a brief description of the education system Ghana inherited from its colonial period.

In 1951, Ghana was the "Gold Coast," one of the most prosperous colonies in Africa. Its prosperity rested on enormous natural resources of gold and timber and on a booming export trade in cocoa. The roots of Ghana's two political traditions lie in the centuries-long development and trade of these products. Ghana's resources lie mostly in its mid-section, a belt of forests separating the coast and the northern savannah-lands. This forest belt is also the home of the Asantes, Ghana's most powerful tribe. To trade for their resources and slaves, the Portuguese established Elmina Castle, the Gulf of Guinea's first European outpost, in 1482, and over the subsequent five centuries trade grew steadily between the Asante's dominions and a growing European presence on the coast.

The Asantes fiercely resisted colonial influence, even as their trade with the colonial powers increased. Following control by the Portuguese and then the Dutch, the coast of modern-day Ghana became the British Gold Coast Colony in 1874; but it took a series of brutal wars by the British from 1823 to 1896 to defeat the Asantes. Following the last of these wars, Asante lands were forcibly annexed in 1901. The British subsequently plundered the Asante treasury of gold and paired the annexation with a despised Lands Bill that sought to expropriate tribal lands from all over the colony and transfer them to individual ownership. Unsurprisingly, these measures only strengthened Asante resentment of British rule. Historians particularly credit the Lands Bill with spawning the independence movement that would eventually make Ghana the first black African nation to gain independence (Nimako 1991). A year after the Asante annexation, the Gold Coast annexed the Northern Territories, shaping modern Ghana with the addition of a new group of disgruntled tribes.[4]

The years after these annexations brought rapid development of Ghana's natural resources and of cocoa. Cacao trees were introduced to the Gold Coast in 1878; by World War II it was supplying half the world's cocoa and was a wealthy colony. In the last decade of the nineteenth century and the first decade of the twentieth, Ghana's real per-capita GDP grew 1.8 percent annually (Killick, Omaboe, and Szereszewski 1966). But the nature of the development only fueled the discontent. British traders controlled exports and most mining, on which they made enormous profits. By contrast, profits from cocoa production, which was largely in Ghanaian hands, were heavily taxed to pay for development projects and the colonial administration. In 1947, the colonial government set up the Cocoa Marketing Board as a monopsony, ostensibly to stabilize prices; in reality, the board collected vast sums that were deposited in London and helped relieve growing pressure on the British pound (Tignor 2006; Lewis 1953; Nimako 1991).[5] Ghanaian farmers shipped their cocoa to port on British railways, which charged them a far higher rate than British mines. Such exploitation was made possible by co-opted tribal rulers, who acted as middle-men between British entrepreneurs and Ghanaian labor (Nimako 1991). In general the economy developed little autonomous industry,[6] and among Ghanaians there was a widespread perception that Ghana benefited little from its wealth.

The discontent with life under the British fueled Ghana's independence movement and led to the birth of both its political traditions. In 1947, a timber merchant, George (Paa) Grant, and three lawyer friends established the United Gold Coast Convention (UGCC) to push for independence. The UGCC, however, was mostly made up of merchants and lawyers. Realizing that they were unlikely to gain independence unless the Ghanaian masses were with them, they invited Kwame Nkrumah, an eloquent anti-imperialist agitator in the United States and the United Kingdom, to join as general secretary. Under Nkrumah's leadership, and aided by a series of protests and high-profile arrests and terms in jail, the UGCC began organizing as a political entrepreneur of the poor: it set up units in every town and village, and affiliated itself with every major Ghanaian organization— trade unions, women's organizations, social clubs, etc. (Nimako 1991). These efforts transformed the UGCC into a mass movement, but in the process they alienated its elite founders, for whom Nkrumah's goals were too radical. The UGCC's members wished to calmly and gradually replace the British leadership with educated and entrepreneurial persons such as themselves (Nimako 1991; Library of Congress 1994). Nkrumah, by contrast, favored immediate independence, by revolution if necessary. In 1949 Nkrumah's faction split from the UGCC, and formed a new Convention People's Party (CPP). The elite UGCC is Ghana's first political tradition; the CPP and its linkage with the masses are Ghana's second.

The CPP's continual protests helped the British to warm to the idea of at least some local control for the Gold Coast, simply to quiet instability. Britain's main goal was to protect its citizens' interests—not least their financial interests—which meant stopping the protests while maintaining ultimate control. To exploit the independence movement's internal dissention, the British decided to hold rigged elections in February 1951 for a new Legislative Assembly; assuming that no party controlled a majority of seats, they planned to appoint a Brit as the Assembly's "Leader of Government Business" (Nimako 1991). But the British underestimated the CPP's popular support. Even though Nkrumah passed the election in prison, his CPP won 34 of the 38 contested seats; the UGCC won just three.[7] In the election's aftermath, the surprised Gold Coast governor released Nkrumah and he was named the "Leader of Government Business."

It is at this point that the Gold Coast gains some control over its education policies, and it is therefore at this point that this book's framework should begin to explain Ghana's education policies. Nkrumah's CPP government is Ghana's "pioneer" (see Chapter 3).

Before turning to the CPP's educational policies, I briefly examine the kind of education system that the CPP inherited from the British in 1951. That education system was two-pronged: elite and extremely limited higher education paired with somewhat broader primary education. Early Ghanaian primary education was largely parochial; for most of their history Ghanaians themselves saw little need to build schools. In 1876, the Asantehene, the king of the Asantes, remarked, "Ashantee children have better work to do than to sit down all day idly to learn hoy. They have to fan their parents, and do other work which is better" (cited in Kimble 1963, 75). The 1948 census found that only 4 percent of residents of the Gold Coast had ever attended school (Baeta et al. 1967). But with economic development came greater demand for skills and a burgeoning demand by Ghanaians for primary schooling. This demand accelerated most after 1940, apace with the increased economic activity brought by World War II, in which Gold Coast soldiers fought and for which the Gold Coast produced simple war materiel (McWilliam 1959). By 1950 there were a thousand public primary schools and more than 1,300 private primary schools—the majority, simple structures built by local communities that were less than a decade old. These schools enrolled 212,000 primary students and 60,000 middle school students, which probably represented only about 21 percent of the school-aged population (children aged 5 to 14).[8] But the schools were generally low-quality and far from free: fees averaged 15s (about $40 in today's dollars) at the lower grades, and progressed to 30s (McWilliam 1959). Many also lacked adequate materials and trained teachers, though a few older mission schools—catering mostly to the elites—did offer excellent, though more expensive, education.

At the upper levels, education was exclusive and high quality. In 1950 there were just 6,200 students in 56 secondary schools, four-fifths of them private. The few public secondary schools—notably the well-established Achimota College, founded in 1927, and Mfantsipim School, founded in 1876—provided a few elites with a route into the lower levels of the civil service or other white-collar employment (Library of Congress 1994). Despite the growing demand for primary education, the colony had just 19 teachers' colleges enrolling 1,800 students, which was one reason for the lack of trained teachers in the booming primary level. There was also a new university, the University College of the Gold Coast, founded in 1948, a year after the foundation of the United Gold Coast Convention and directly in response to elite pressure (McWilliam 1959). (The British would have preferred to locate the new university in Nigeria, where it would have served all of British West Africa.) The new college enrolled 90 students in its first year and 108 by 1950. It was staffed largely by expatriate professors and held a "special relationship" to the University of London, which gave the exams and granted the degrees. These features ensured an extremely high level of quality.

Table 5.2 outlines the Gold Coast's education system in 1950.

Thus when Kwame Nkrumah took his seat in the new Legislative Assembly in 1951, he took over control of an education system that was clearly elitist. The system also reflected both the growing demand for education and the limited economic opportunities the Gold Coast economy offered Ghanaians. Ghana in 1951 faced no shortage of skilled workers: in fact, graduates of "standard VII"—upper primary—often had difficulty finding jobs, even in the more-developed urban areas of the South (McWilliam 1959). Likewise various schemes to introduce technical schooling had trouble attracting resources or enthusiasm, since the country lacked any manufacturing and had few opportunities for technical graduates.[9]

Kwame Nkrumah transformed this education almost overnight to serve his new vital constituency—a cross-class alliance of the masses and certain elites. The transformation is one of the clearest examples of the operation of this book's framework that we will see in any of the three cases.

2. POLITICS, 1951–1966: Rise and Fall of the Convention People's Party

The CPP took power in 1951 with a cross-class vital constituency. It was Kwame Nkrumah's appeal among and organization of the Ghanaian masses that won his CPP a majority of seats in the critical 1951 elections, and this support sustained

Table 5.2   **Education in the Gold Coast, 1950**

	Primary	*Middle*	*Secondary*	*Teachers' College*	*University*
Schools					
Number of Schools	2,393	511	56	19	1
Number of Private Schools	1,312	0	44	0	0
Proportion of Private Schools	55%	0%	79%	0%	0%
Enrollment					
Number of Students	211,994	59,960	6,186	1,777	108
Number of Students in Private Schools	67,692	0	3,386	0	0
Proportion of Students in Private Schools	32%	0%	55%	0%	0%

the CPP against elite opposition for the subsequent decade and a half. But the CPP's vital constituency was not just the masses; it also had elite elements, many of its own creation. The government sought to "Ghanaianize" the armed forces and the British-dominated Gold Coast economy and created a massive bureaucracy to staff the government, including a large new apparatus for delivering social services to the Ghanaian masses, and, later, myriad new public corporations. In the process the CPP built its own elite, one separate from—though occasionally overlapping with—the traditional elite groups of the colonial era.

In its decade and a half with this vital constituency, the CPP's dominance was never fully secure. The party's pinnacle was undoubtedly March 6, 1957, when Ghana became the first black African state to win its independence and Kwame Nkrumah became an international hero. The nadir was February 24, 1966, when a coup overthrew him and handed power back to rival elites. This section describes the development of the CPP's cross-class alliance after 1951, as well as the nature and strategy of the elites who opposed the CPP government and eventually overthrew it.

Electorally, the CPP began the 1950s in a powerful position and grew still more powerful with time. Its base of support was most of the rural poor, with the exception of most cocoa farmers. Despite the economic importance of cocoa—14 percent of GDP; between half and two-thirds of export earnings[10]—cocoa farmers only accounted for a sixth of the labor force (Lewis 1953) and were heavily Asante. Several of the leaders of the UGCC were also large cocoa farmers. Instead, the CPP courted the more vote-rich rural agricultural workforce (half the workforce) and the large number of migrant workers: mostly young and industrious Ghanaians eager to enter the modern economy. (The latter were dubbed the "veranda boys" because they would gather on the verandas of wealthy homes and businesses looking for work.) These voters had strong tribal loyalties, but the CPP was able, at least for a time, to transcend these and build them into a political force with political entrepreneurship: just as the UGCC had done under Nkrumah's brief leadership, the CPP set up units in every town and village and affiliated with the major Ghanaian civic organizations. And while in power the CPP tried to maintain their support by making policy in their interest—including education policy, as we will see in the next section. By courting these voters the CPP undercut tribal loyalties and won two-thirds of the seats in Assembly elections after 1951—a performance that eventually convinced the British that Nkrumah enjoyed overwhelming support and that they should grant independence under his leadership (Colonial Secretary 1956).

But the CPP's actual support was nowhere near as overwhelming as its electoral performance. It was broad but not deep. In the 1951 elections the CPP won 34 of 38 openly contested seats, but only half of eligible voters had registered, only half of registered voters actually voted, and even of this small group the CPP won only 55 percent of votes cast (Tignor 2006). In the 1954 and 1956 elections the CPP did only marginally better, winning the support of just 15 percent of adults. Tribal loyalties were simply too deep to be expunged by a decade of nation-building. Rather, the CPP succeeded in building a connection with the masses that was only marginally stronger than the sub-nationalist pull of the regional, tribal parties (Nimako 1991; Tignor 2006).

And this fragile success lasted only as long as the CPP could deliver the goods: the jobs and wages of the modern economy it promised Ghanaians. Immediately after taking office, the CPP began spending heavily on social services (including education), and after independence it embarked on a series of Development Plans designed to industrialize the country with an eye to creating good jobs.[11] This industrialization was government-led. From 1955 to 1960, 30 to 40 percent of gross fixed capital formation was government investment (Killick, Omaboe, and Szereszewski 1966), and after 1960, the CPP's industrialization policy turned overtly socialist: it began creating a huge range of industrial enterprises and increased wages with the first minimum wage laws. The most famous of its new industrial enterprises was an effort to create an aluminum industry, an effort that failed but resulted in the massive Akosombo dam.[12] In addition the government created saw mills and timber processing plants, cocoa processing plants, breweries, cement manufacturers, oil refiners, textile manufacturers, vehicle assembly plants, hotels, and a new bank, the Ghana Commercial Bank, which the government subsidized to allow it to compete with the dominant British banks.[13]

In the course of staffing these new services and public enterprises, the CPP also created a new class of Ghanaian elites—civil servants, teachers, nurses, workers and administrators in the new public corporations. The Gold Coast bureaucracy had always been small—in the hundreds—and heavily British. The CPP did not eliminate these senior bureaucrats, but added a new, much larger professional class of Ghanaian bureaucrats. By 1960, close to 40 percent of all recorded employment in the country was in the public sector, including 83 percent of Ghana's 60,000 professional and technical workers (Nimako 1991; Killick, Omaboe, and Szereszewski 1966).

The lifeline of these CPP initiatives was cocoa. Like the British before them, the CPP saw tremendous opportunity in Ghana's cocoa wealth—for everything other than enriching cocoa farmers. Immediately after the 1951 elections, Nkrumah oversaw a redesign of the Cocoa Marketing Board (CMB), under which cocoa profits would be used to fund Ghana's development. Naturally this plan angered cocoa farmers—among them key leaders of the UGCC—who wanted the board to use its funds to stabilize future price fluctuations, its ostensible purpose. But cocoa farmers were anti-CPP anyway. From 1947 to 1960, the board gave back to cocoa farmers only 52 percent of total proceeds from cocoa sales. Even in the 1956–1957 season, as the CPP won its final test election and independence loomed, the CMB cut proceeds to cocoa farmers by 10 percent, although the board's Stabilization Fund alone had reached an astounding £45 million. In real terms, the price paid to cocoa farmers declined 45 percent from 1957 through 1963 (Killick, Omaboe, and Szereszewski 1966).

Through early 1961, high world cocoa prices allowed Ghana to accumulate a total of £87 million in reserves, which the CPP drew on to fund industrialization (Killick 1966). And with the CPP promising jobs from rapid industrialization, it was able to maintain its support with the masses.[14] But despite the government investment, much of the Ghanaian economy remained inefficient[15]—even the cocoa industry, which had far lower productivity than Nigeria's—and eventually the reserves were exhausted.[16] After 1960, government budgets started to show substantial deficits, and in 1961 the government introduced its first austerity budget, prompting protests by CPP backbenchers and a strike by urban workers—key members of the CPP's vital constituency. Things got worse for the CPP as its budgetary situation deteriorated. Government borrowing fueled high inflation after 1961, and deficit pressures prevented the government from raising wages commensurately. Average real wages peaked in 1960 and then began a steep decline (Killick, Omaboe, and Szereszewski 1966). Declining real wages in turn eroded popular support for the CPP.

Waiting in the wings were the traditional elites: those groups that had been powerful under the British. They fell into four categories: the senior (pre-1951) bureaucracy; foreign companies; the small class of Ghanaian entrepreneurs and lawyers who had formed the UGCC; and the tribal elites. Although these groups lacked numbers, they included the tribal elites and hence could influence the masses through centuries-old tribal loyalties. Initially the CPP had courted the masses by overtly decrying the tribal elites, whom it accused of being complicit in British rule. Nkrumah openly called for the chiefs to get out of Ghana and leave their sandals—key symbols of a chief's authority—behind.[17] Such statements appealed to the masses so long as Ghana seemed a land of modern economic opportunity. But as the economy worsened, traditional elites found more resonance for their nostalgic appeal to tribal traditions.

Fully aware of its vulnerability, the CPP turned increasingly authoritarian. As early as 1957—the year of Ghana's independence—the CPP banned all ethnic, religious, and regional parties. This ban, however, had the unintended consequence of uniting the opposition into a new, nationwide "United Party." In 1958 the government implemented the Preventative Detention Act, by which the prime minister could detain persons of his choosing for up to five years without trial. Nkrumah used this and a similar act in 1962 to silence his political opponents, among them, J. B. Danquah, the most prominent UGCC nationalist, who died in prison in 1965. Kofi Busia, the leader of the UGCC and of its successors, the Ghana Congress Party and the United Party, fled to exile in London.

As the economic situation worsened, the CPP's authoritarianism increased. In July of 1960, the CPP declared Ghana a republic and itself the sole political organization in the state. Nkrumah was named president-for-life. There are no accurate figures on the number of political prisoners the CPP detained, but estimates are between 400 and 2,000 by 1961 (Library of Congress 1994). The CPP's already hostile relationship with tribal elites grew worse; the CPP "de-stooled"—de-throned—many chiefs, and detained many more, particularly Asantes, under the Preventative Detention Act.

Yet despite these measures, in the end the CPP lost the support of the masses. The proximate cause of the CPP's downfall was the loss of support among the armed forces, whom Nkrumah had embarrassed by sending around Africa to assist with independence movements.[18] In February of 1966, while preparing to assist in the overthrow of Ian Smith's regime in Rhodesia, the army overthrew Nkrumah instead. But the coup was widely welcomed, based on the common view that traditional elites could restore Ghana's economic health. (Foreign corporations helped in the coup's aftermath by flooding Ghanaian markets with imported staples such as milk, sugar, and bread, which had grown rare in the CPP's waning days.[19]) In the end, even the Trades Union Congress, whose members owed their jobs to Nkrumah's policies, supported the coup.

The 1966 coup brackets the period of CPP dominance, and thus ends the first of our four periods. During the preceding fifteen years, the CPP had governed with a steady vital constituency of public employees and public corporations, the military, workers in the modern sectors of the economy, and farmers and migrant workers in the traditional economy. Opposed were the elements of the traditional elite—the senior bureaucracy, foreign companies, the few Ghanaian entrepreneurs, and the tribal elite—as well as cocoa farmers. Table 5.3 summarizes the vital constituency from 1951 to 1966.

By this book's framework, a cross-class vital constituency such as the CPP's should have built Ghana's education system from its limited and elitist beginnings into an All Levels system widely available to the population.

Table 5.3 **The vital constituency of Ghana's pioneer government, 1951–1966**

Political Entrepreneur(s)	Groups in the Vital Constituency[†]	Groups outside the Vital Constituency
Kwame Nkrumah and the Convention People's Party (CPP)	Junior Bureaucracy Military Public Companies (Type S) Workers [CPP] Farmers/Migrant Workers [CPP]	Tribal Elites Senior Bureaucracy Foreign Companies Ghanaian Entrepreneurs Cocoa Farmers

Notes: [†] If a group was empowered with the help of a political entrepreneur, the entrepreneur is in brackets.

Employer types are in parentheses: Type S employers need skilled workers in an inflexible labor market.

3. EDUCATION, 1951–1966: Developing All Levels

The CPP, Ghana's pioneer government, inherited from the British a limited and highly elitist education system. Almost immediately, it began transforming that system into one that would serve the Ghanaian masses, urban and rural, in its vital constituency. In the 1944–1945 school year, the Gold Coast Government spent £350,000 on education; by the 1954–1955 school year the government was spending £6.4 million (McWilliam 1959). This spending served three goals. First it increased free access to quality primary education to anyone who wanted it. Second, it developed a higher education system that was accessible and world-class. Finally, it provided trained professional and technical workers to staff Ghana's new modern economy. This section takes each of these in turn.

THE LOWER LEVELS

In February 1951, control of education policy passed from the British civil service to the cabinet of the newly elected Legislative Assembly. In an early signal of how seriously the new government would take education, Nkrumah appointed Kojo Botsio, one of his two closest advisors, the first minister of education. Shortly after, the government released a new Accelerated Plan for Development (ADP) in education, in which it envisioned providing a quality six-year primary education to every Ghanaian child. Then it began to do everything it could to implement that plan. In the following fifteen years the government managed to increase enrollment more than five-fold, from 234,000 in 1951 to 1.13 million in 1966.

One of the first steps was to abolish fees on six years of primary education from January 1, 1952 (World Bank 2004a) and absorb into the public sector 1,400 schools that had previously been run privately, most with untrained teachers and few resources. In that single year, enrollment in public schools more than doubled, from 154,000 to 335,000.[20] And this initial absorption was only the beginning: schools were built so fast they were nicknamed "mushroom schools" (Keteku 2005). By 1966 there were more than 8,000 primary schools in Ghana, enrolling 1.13 million students. At the same time, the number of private schools had shrunk to 99 and enrolled barely 1 percent of the total. Table 5.3 shows the increases.

These steps allowed a massive increase in access to primary school. I noted in Section 1 that according to the 1948 census, only 4 percent of Gold Coast residents had ever attended school (Baeta et al. 1967) and that the 1950 enrollment of 212,000 primary students and 60,000 middle school students probably represented about 21 percent of the school-aged population (children aged 5 to 14). By 1966, primary and middle-school enrollment reached more than 1.4 million—an enrollment rate of over 70 percent,[21] or an astounding 350 percent jump in access even as the population was growing at around 2.5 percent a year (Killick, Omaboe, and Szereszewski 1966). Progress should actually have been even more striking: the government thought it was on track to reach full enrollment by 1957—the symbolic year of independence—but the taking of the 1960 census revealed that Ghana's population was 7 million, not 5 million as originally thought (McWilliam 1959). Even so, the 1960 census found that the number of Ghanaians who had received some education had jumped to 21 percent—or 27 percent of the population over age 6—and that 11 percent of the entire population was in school (Baeta et al. 1967).

Such a huge increase in access might easily have come at the expense of quality, as we saw in Taiwan's universities in the 1990s and as we will see in Brazil's primary schools in the 1960s and 1970s. But the CPP took steps to ensure high quality, among them an extraordinary teacher-training program. In 1950, 19 teacher-training colleges were enrolling just 1,800 students in extensive four-year programs. To ensure a permanent supply of trained teachers, the government expanded these colleges rapidly—by 1966, 83 teacher-training colleges were enrolling more than 14,000 students. The government also opened dozens of temporary training centers to provide basic training to the vast numbers of untrained teachers that had entered the system during its rapid private expansion in the 1940s. Most important, the government paid teachers while they were in training, and once they started teaching it paid them *more* than they could earn in occupations demanding similar qualifications.[22] Test scores from the era testify to the high quality of the education they provided. Only in 2002 did average Ghanaian math scores reach the level they achieved in 1960; English scores have yet to reach that level (World Bank 2004a).

Naturally these investments were expensive. I was unable to find government spending figures for 1950, so I cannot judge precisely how much the government increased education spending in 1951. But in 1951 the government was spending £850,000 on just primary and middle schools (or £4 per student)—more than twice what the government had spent on the whole education system in 1944–1945. By the 1963–1964 school year, spending on middle and primary schools had risen to £23 million, or £17 per student.[23] Shortly thereafter, in 1965, Ghana adopted a new currency, the cedi, and accelerating inflation destroyed its value, so that the inflation-adjusted 1966 spending figures seem to show a decline in per-student spending. But that decline belies the government's steadily increasing commitment to the lower levels: as a percentage of total government spending, spending on primary and middle schools more than doubled, from 3.4 percent in 1952 to 7.4 in 1966. Table 5.4 shows the spending figures.

As the CPP's political and economic fortunes were turning, the CPP again looked to educational investments to maintain its popular support. In 1961—the year of the government's first austerity budget—the government passed a new comprehensive Education Act. The Act again raised teacher salaries, gave the government the right to regulate and absorb any private educational institution, and made primary and middle schooling compulsory (though the government made clear that it would not punish parents who did not send their children to school).

THE UPPER LEVELS

Although the CPP heavily courted the masses, its vital constituency was a cross-class alliance that included some elites, specifically the new, Ghanaianized bureaucracy. In addition, the government also was investing heavily to create a modern industrialized economy, and needed skilled workers. But with workers inside the vital constituency—the Ghana Trades Union Congress was practically an arm of the CPP—wages were set centrally, so employers were type S: they demanded Selective Worker Training of just enough skilled laborers to meet their needs. Thus alongside the CPP's expanded primary system, this book's framework predicts that the CPP should have invested in the upper levels and in technical training, and that these levels should have been easily accessible to graduates of the lower levels. That is, the CPP should have created an All-Levels system, with quality at every level and easy passage from one level to the next.

That is what the CPP did. The government matched its commitment to primary education with a vast expansion of quality higher education, heavily subsidized, to which there were few major barriers. Alongside this system the government developed a limited network of technical institutes, engineered to provide employers with the skilled labor they needed. The remainder of this section describes, first, the investments in higher education, and then the new technical training and its relationship to the labor market.

The upper levels of the Gold Coast's education system had been relatively well-developed under the British: in 1951 Nkrumah's government inherited a new University College, enrolling 108 and granting prestigious degrees from the University of London, and a handful of internationally-renowned secondary schools that had trained much of Ghana's elite, including Mfantsipim, then celebrating its 75th birthday, and Achimota. But the elite pedigree of these schools was, from the CPP perspective, a problem, and it moved swiftly to open the upper levels to more of the population.

Table 5.4 **Growth of the lower levels, 1951–1966**

	Primary			Middle		
	1951	*1966*	*Change*	*1951*	*1966*	*Change*
Schools						
Number of Schools	2,533	8012	+216%	539	2,365	+339%
Number of Private Schools	1,450	99	–93%	0	19	
Proportion of Private Schools	57%	1%	–98%	0%	1%	
Enrollment						
Number of Students	234,492	1,130,731	+382%	66,483	280,866	+322%
Number of Students in Private	80,132	13,888	–83%	308	662	+115%
Proportion of Students in Private	34%	1%	–96%	0%	0%	–49%
Spending (public only)						
Primary and Middle Together	G£859,388	NC24,242,025				
(in millions of 2001 ¢)[†]	¢60,622,171	¢364,215	–99%			
Per Student	G£4	NC17				
(in 2001 ¢)[†]	¢274,886,850	¢260,703	–100%			
Primary and Middle Separately		NC17,914,456			NC6,327,569	
(in millions of 2001 ¢)		¢269,149			¢95,066	
Per Student		NC16			NC23	
(in 2001 ¢)		¢240,991			¢339,274	

Notes: [†] No national price indices are available before 1955; thus spending data for 1951 are deflated using the Retail Price Index for Accra City (Ewusi 1986, table 199).

The first step was the expansion of the "middle school." In the foregoing discussion I described middle schools as part of the primary system, but in fact they served a distinct purpose: to make up for the lack of English proficiency in most students.[24] Middle school students had two chances to apply to secondary schools—in Middle Forms II and III, the middle two years of the four-year program—or they could graduate in their fourth year with a terminal middle-school degree. With that degree, a student could enter either a teachers' college or a technical institute, and either of these could lead to university. By 1960, 90 percent of primary school graduates went on to middle school, from which the overwhelming majority either transferred to secondary schools or graduated (Baeta et al. 1967).

The structure of the system expanded access to the upper levels in two ways. First, the government vastly expanded the secondary level. In 1952 the government added 13 secondary schools to the public system and continued to build more throughout the 1950s and 60s. In 1957, the government created the Ghana Education Trust Fund (GET Fund), endowed with £2.5 million from the Cocoa Marketing Board, and by 1960 it had spent £4.75 million building 24 secondary schools.

Secondary schools were not free—in the 1950s fees averaged £12 a year, with an additional £48–60 in boarding fees, or, in total, about equal to Ghana's per-capita income in 1960. But the government implemented an extensive scholarship scheme to pay the fees and provide "bursaries" to cover living costs for the vast majority of secondary students (Ghana 1962). In 1952–1953 the central government gave out £33,500 in scholarships to secondary school; a decade later it was providing £360,000 a year. In 1954–1955 it added a second scholarship scheme, funded by the Cocoa Marketing Board, and by 1963 the CMB was contributing another £200,000 in scholarships.[25] The 1961 Education Act sought to further lower the cost of secondary schooling by abolishing all secondary school fees, while the government continued to provide bursaries to most students.

As a result of these scholarships, secondary enrollment more than doubled in the CPP's first three years in office and by 1966 had grown fifteen-fold to almost 43,000 students. The resources provided by government funding also gave the public students an education of such high quality that public students consistently performed better on exams than private students—much to the surprise of the latter (McWilliam 1959). The expansion had its desired effect: despite overwhelming advantages for elite children, by 1960 the children of farmers and fishermen—the occupations of most of Ghana's masses—accounted for a third of students in the fifth year of secondary school (Foster 1963).[26]

The second method for expanding access to the top was to create new paths into university. Students had the option of bypassing secondary school entirely and entering university through teachers' colleges or technical institutes, or by studying independently for the exams. As noted above, teacher training colleges expanded rapidly in the fifteen years of CPP control. In addition, the government expanded technical institutes from five to eleven in 1966, enrolling 4,000 students (up from 266 in 1950). These alternative paths meant that many students who had not attended secondary school eventually made it to university.

These new paths would not have meant much if the number of university places hadn't also increased. But it did. In 1950 the University of Ghana was enrolling just 108 students; by 1966 it was enrolling 2,200. In addition the government added two other universities: the University of Science and Technology, which attracted graduates of the technical institutes and was enrolling 1,300 by 1966; and the University of Cape Coast, which enrolled 1,000 by 1966. For the most part these students received free education (Nimako 1991). By 1962 the government was spending almost £5 million on the universities, or more than £1,000 per student. By 1966, spending on universities was almost sixty percent of spending on primary and middle schools. Table 5.5 shows the expansion of the upper levels.

The combination of an expanded number of places and new paths into the university meant that higher education moved within reach for poorer Ghanaians. In 1960 fully a third of students at the University of Ghana had not come there from the last year of secondary school (Baeta et al. 1967). Almost 40 percent of students at the University of Ghana were the children of farmers or fishermen. Ghana in the 1950s and 1960s was a place of real economic mobility.[27] Table 5.6 compares the family background of University of Ghana students to students in the fifth and sixth years of secondary school, and to the working population.

SELECTIVE WORKER TRAINING

Technical institutes and teacher training colleges were not, of course, simply alternate paths into universities: they were also the source of much of the new high-level skilled labor the new Ghanaian government and its burgeoning modern economy required. I have already discussed teacher training; now I briefly consider technical workers and the general needs of the economy.

The skilled-labor needs of the Ghanaian economy were never extensive. Even by 1960, after a decade of industrialization, the vast majority of Ghana's workforce was employed in farming and fishing (see the first column of Table 5.6). Yet the economy was also demanding increasing numbers of skilled workers to staff the bureaucracy and the new manufacturing industries. The bureaucracy's needs were largely white-collar and were met by the secondary schools and universities. Indeed, into the 1970s the university would be widely considered a ticket to a well-paid job in the bureaucracy. But the manufacturing companies needed more technically skilled workers, as did government projects like the Akosombo dam, and it was to serve these needs that the government built the aforementioned network of technical institutes and the University of Science and Technology. The institutes were known for their high quality (McWilliam 1959; Baeta et al. 1967): students took local certification exams, but many went on to pass the exams of

Table 5.5 Expansion of the upper levels, 1951–1966

	Senior Secondary			University		
	1951	1966		1951	1966	
Schools						
Schools	62	164	+165%	1	3	+200%
Private Schools	49	61	24%	0	0	
Proportion of Private Schools	79%	37%	-53%	0%	0%	0%
Enrollment						
Students	6,864	42,280	+516%	108	4,506	+4,072%
Students in Private	3,964	6,965	+76%	0	0	
Proportion Private	58%	16%	-71%	0%	0%	0%
Spending (public only)						
Total Spending	G£145,864	NC8,737,782		G£558,024††	NC13,969,815	
(in millions of 2001 ¢)†	¢10,289,406	¢131,277	-99%	¢39,363,625††	¢209,884	-99%
Per Student	G£50	NC247		G£5,167	NC3,100	
(in 2001 ¢)†	¢3,548,071,182	¢3,717,326	-100%	¢364,478,005,207	¢46,578,782	-100%

Notes: † No national price indices are available before 1955; thus spending data for 1951 are deflated using the Retail Price Index for Accra City (Ewusi 1986, table 199).
†† University spending is from 1952.

the City and Guilds of London Institute. Even today their caliber is widely remembered. Table 5.7 shows the key statistics on public teachers' colleges and technical institutes.

The vast majority of technical graduates found well-paid work, usually with the government or one of the public corporations. The same, however, was not true of those with less education. Indeed, the CPP had built an education system that was years ahead of the economy's needs.[28] Middle-school leavers often had difficulty finding work (Baeta et al. 1967), which encouraged dropping out at lower levels.

Table 5.6   **Family background of secondary and University of Ghana Students**[1]

	Working population	Fathers of students in the fifth year of secondary school	Fathers of students in the sixth year of secondary school	Fathers of students at the University of Ghana
Occupational Categories	*(1960)*	*(1960)*	*(1964)*	*(1964)*
Professional, Administrative, Higher Technical, Clerical	6.9	40.3	55	45.6
Private Traders	3.8	10.3	7.8	3.5
Skilled Workers and Artisans	11.8	12.1	6.3	5.8
Semi-skilled and Unskilled Workers	13.4	1.5	0.2	0.3
Farmers and Fishermen	62.8	32.5	23.3	37.7
Others (including Armed services and Police)	1.3	0.7	2.6	2
No Answer; Don't Know; Retired; Dead	—	2.6	4.8	5.1
Source:	1960 census	Foster (1963)	Hurd and Johnson (1966)	Hurd and Johnson (1966)

[1]Source: Baeta et al. (1967), 236, table 6.10.

Table 5.7 **Expansion of public teachers' colleges and technical institutes, 1951–1966**

	Senior Secondary			University		
	1951	1966	Change	1951	1966	Change
Schools						
Number of Schools	20	83	+315%	5	11	+120%
Number of Students	1,916	16,441	+758%	622	4,956	+697%
Spending						
Current	G£234,184	NC7,207,267		G£66,960	NC1,154,000	
(in millions of 2001 ¢)†	¢16,519,596	¢108,283	–99%	¢1,968	¢17,338	+781%
Per Student	G£122	NC438		G£108	NC233	
(in 2001 ¢)†	¢8,621,918,596	¢6,586,141	–100%	¢7,593,941,783	¢3,498,349	–100%

Notes: † No national price indices are available before 1955; thus spending data for 1951 are deflated using the Retail Price Index for Accra City (Ewusi 1986, table 199).

For example, of the 109,000 students who began primary school in 1955, only 57,800 remained in the sixth year. After all, the promise the CPP had made to the masses was modern, well-paid jobs, for which education was a pre-requisite. The CPP had done well providing the education, but less well providing the jobs. From 1953 to 1962 the modern sector of the economy—overwhelmingly public-sector—grew from only 224,000 to 320,000 positions, while at the time middle schools were graduating 40,000 students annually. Baeta et al. point out in their analysis of Ghanaian education and human capital needs that "the only educational solution [to the problem of unemployment] would be to stop the expansion of education, and in Ghana this has never been a practical possibility for political reasons" (1967, 233).[29]

The CPP made every effort to expand the economy sufficiently to employ the products of its education system. As we saw in the previous section, its policies ultimately failed in the face of inefficiency and a drop in world cocoa prices. But that did not stop the CPP from trying to plan for the needed expansion of the economy—using, in fact, the same sort of "manpower planning" that we saw used in Taiwan.

The use of the same basic techniques by governments with very different vital constituencies provides an illuminating comparison. Recall that manpower planning was adopted in Taiwan in order to lower skilled wages by rapidly increasing the number of skilled workers. In Ghana, the same planning techniques were used but for the opposite purpose: to calculate the number of *jobs* that would be needed to employ all the graduates the education system was producing. For example, the CPP's 1963–1970 Seven Year Development Plan (Ghana Manpower Projects 1964), was calibrated so that, by 1970, the growth of employment would absorb the output of the education system[30]: the plan estimated that there would be a net addition of 500,000 workers to the workforce from the education system over seven years and developed a plan that would demand 490,000 workers (Killick, Omaboe, and Szereszewski 1966). Governments in Taiwan and Ghana used the same strategies but to very different ends—ends that reflect the differences in their vital constituencies.

WRAPPING UP

Ghana's pioneer government, the CPP, developed the limited and elitist education system it inherited from the British into a broadly accessible All-Levels system. This system conforms well to the general expectations of this book's framework. Table 5.8 summarizes the framework's performance on each of the specific indicators I laid out in Chapter 3.

I noted at the start of this section that few periods provide such complete support for the framework as this one. The CPP expanded free primary and middle schools to all areas of the country and provided them with materials and quality teachers through an extensive teacher-training effort and a vast expansion of

Table 5.8 **Evidence summary, 1951–1966**

Indicator	Characteristics	Conforms to Framework?
A. Enrollment	Increasing at all levels	■
B. Per-student spending	Increasing at all levels (or decreasing at all levels when accounting for inflation)	■
C. The toolkit		
1. Schools	High-quality at all levels	■
Teachers	High-quality at all levels	■
Physical resources	High at all levels	■
Location	Lower levels widely available in urban and rural areas; higher levels concentrated in urban areas	■
2. Fees[†]	Primary: free (some incidental fees until 1961)	■
	Higher levels: high fees, but extensive scholarships	■
3. Access restrictions and discriminatory pricing		
Quotas	None	
Exams	Exams regulate access between levels, but most students who want to progress do	■
Financial aid	Extensive scholarships for higher levels	■
4. Tracking	None	■
5. Outsourcing (domestic or foreign; to firms or non-profits)	Minimal—the vast majority of schools are public; there are a few elite preparatory schools, a few private vocational schools, and some elites send their children to universities abroad	■

Notes: ■: fully conforms to the framework; ◨: partly conforms to the framework; □: does not conform to the framework.

[†]Fees are for enrollment, books and other equipment, uniforms, activities, school improvements, etc.

teachers' colleges. The middle-school system provided multiple opportunities to enter the higher levels: two years to transfer to secondary schools, which had traditionally been dominated by elites but which were expanded to allow access to children of poorer backgrounds; and, with a middle-school leaver's certificate, the possibility of going to a teachers' college or a technical institute, and from there to a good-paying job or to university. On every indicator, the CPP's education policies are what the framework predicts.

4. POLITICS, 1966–1981: Elite Rule[31]

The 1966 coup ushered in a decade and a half of elite rule. From 1966 to 1981, Ghana was ruled by no fewer than seven governments, each trying to serve its elite vital constituency with spoils from an economy that was steadily and seemingly irrevocably in decline. Economic growth slowed and then reversed, and by 1981 real GDP per-capita was nearly 15 percent lower than it was in 1966 (World Bank 2007). The period saw two democratic and five military governments, punctuated by myriad coups and counter-coups. At first these governments sought to grow, and then simply to maintain, the elites' share of the economic pie, but as the pie itself shrunk, elites began fighting among themselves, largely along ethnic lines, and control began alternating between two major ethnic groups: Akans (the grouping that includes Asantes) and Ewes (the major ethnic group in the eastern Volta region). Meanwhile the neglected masses grew increasingly desperate, and eventually it was they who ended the cycle. J. J. Rawlings, an upstart flight lieutenant, became a political entrepreneur to the masses after taking power in a 1981 coup (his second): with the masses on his side, Rawlings was able to counter the power of the elites and rule Ghana without interruption for nearly two decades.

Though the period is tumultuous politically, for my purpose there is one important constant: the vital constituency was always elite. That is, although the seven governments had vital constituencies of different groups of elites, they were all elites; no government included poorer groups or engaged in political entrepreneurship. From 1966 to 1981, the poor were outside the vital constituency.

The first of the elite governments took power after the February 1966 military coup that overthrew Kwame Nkrumah. The military's motivation was solely to rid Ghana of Nkrumah; they found his administration wasteful and inefficient and they resented him for embarrassing them during his Pan-African independence campaigns. The coup leaders did not wish to rule; they simply wanted to prepare the ground for a new civilian government. Nonetheless their caretaker government was explicitly a return to pre-1951 elite control: it included representatives from all major elite elements. The primary political body, the eight-person National Liberation Council, had a membership of equal parts military and police and also represented all the major ethnic groups.[32] The bureaucracy and the business community were represented by the National Economic Council, which was created alongside the NLC and took control of Ghana's economic policies; it included five senior civil servants and two financial professionals. The NLC and the NEC ruled in a fashion very similar to the British: bureaucrats were at the center and governed the local level through alliances with tribal chiefs and through centrally-appointed administrators (Nimako 1991).

The NEC unsurprisingly declared a "return" to capitalism (from Nkrumah's socialism) and waited expectantly for foreign capital to flood in.[33] It did not. While foreign governments had disliked Nkrumah, foreign companies had not fled Ghana or substantially scaled back their operations, and they saw few new opportunities after the coup. Rather than partaking of the spoils of new investment, the new government instead began its reign saddled with debts incurred under Nkrumah equivalent to a quarter of GDP (Library of Congress 1994).

In an attempt to spur growth and lower spending, the NEC fired between 40,000 and 50,000 state employees and devalued the currency by thirty percent (Nimako 1991). But these were carefully calibrated steps: the fired workers were generally in the public corporations Nkrumah had created,[34] and the devalued currency helped the cocoa farmers, another key group in the vital constituency. The initial trimming of the state enterprises quickly ended after the NLC's hopes for foreign-investment-fueled free-market growth fell flat; the NLC began, in fact, to create *new* state enterprises. After all, the bureaucracy—the heart of the vital constituency—needed employment. Other economic policies were even more explicit in their service to key groups. After years of Nkrumah skimming off as much of cocoa farmers' profits as possible, the government doubled cocoa prices. Soldiers received almost a total tax exemption on their income and got free electricity and water.

Though many average Ghanaians had supported the coup, the masses were not inside the vital constituency, and the NEC's economic policies failed to serve them. Real wages were allowed to decline—they lost thirty percent of their value from 1963 to 1968 (Kraus 1979, 275). Support for the new government among the Ghanaian masses quickly evaporated, but without political entrepreneurship they were politically disorganized and could do little to oppose the new government.

Governing strained the army. Just a year after the 1966 coup, tensions flared into a counter-coup that failed but killed the 1966 coup leader, Colonel Kotoka. Although rule solidified under the new leader, General Afrifa, the army was eager to return the government to civilians. New elections came in 1969. Aware that many average Ghanaians were beginning to look back nostalgically to Nkrumah's rule, the government banned the CPP from competing. The remnants of Nkrumah's allies instead ran under an umbrella National Alliance of Liberals, led by Komla Gbedemah, an Ewe, and a former CPP finance minister who had broken with Nkrumah in 1961. The NLC's elite alliance was represented by the Progress

Party under Dr. Kofi Busia, the former UGCC leader who had fled to London to avoid detention under Nkrumah.

Busia was close with the Asante leadership, and with support in the Asante regions and on the coast the Progress Party won in a landslide, taking 105 of the 140 seats. Busia took over as prime minister in 1971, returning Ghana to civilian rule. The National Alliance of Liberals won 24 seats, mostly in the Volta region, the Ewe heartland. In the aftermath of the election, however, the supreme court prevented Gbedemah from taking his seat after ruling that he had been complicit in financial crimes of the CPP.

The exclusion of Gbedemah immediately stoked ethnic tensions, for without him, Busia's cabinet ended up with no Ewes. This ethnic homogeneity put Busia in a delicate position. Continuing economic troubles made matters worse. Busia had hoped to spur growth and foreign investment by reducing the rigidities and inefficiencies in the Ghanaian bureaucracy and economy. But he faced impossible pressures from his vital constituency. In an early effort to clear out the bloated senior bureaucracy, Busia fired 568 senior bureaucrats in a purge that became known as "Apollo 568." More than 85 percent of the fired bureaucrats were Ewe, and their dismissal further fueled ethnic distrust. Busia also frightened foreign investors—whose capital the economy desperately needed—by brutally putting down workers protesting the lack of jobs: among other actions, he sent the army to occupy the headquarters of the Trades Union Congress. In the end, Busia had little choice but to continue many of the policies of his predecessors: he kept government spending high, which soothed the bureaucracy, and accelerated the NLC's creation of state enterprises, eventually creating more even than Nkrumah.[35]

But cocoa prices were volatile and efforts to diversify the economy were slow to show progress: the same five commodities that accounted for 92 percent of exports in 1967 still made up 80 percent in 1972. In 1971 cocoa prices plummeted, causing imports to outpace exports by 16 percent. Government debt skyrocketed. In desperation, the government implemented austerity measures, which amounted to shooting itself in the foot. It withdrew housing and car subsidies for civil servants and army officers, introduced a tax of between 10 and 25 percent on foreign exchange transfers, raised gas prices, raised the bank rate, introduced hospital fees, and tried to save scarce foreign exchange by banning imports of many consumer goods, including cars. These measures fell hardest on the bureaucracy, which felt further threatened when in 1971, for the first time, a handful of new university graduates—51 of them—could not find jobs. In the final straw, the government devalued the currency by 48 percent in October of 1971.

Two months later army officers overthrew the government. The coup leader announced to the country, on taking power, that the army had to act because Busia had "started taking from us the few amenities and facilities which we in the armed forces and the police enjoyed even under the Nkrumah regime" (quoted in Nimako 1991, 144).

The January 1972 coup ushered in Ghana's "lost decade." In nine years the country had five governments, none of which was better able than the last to serve its elite vital constituency. As the economy fell apart, elite factions squabbled over the shrinking economy, while life for the average Ghanaian grew desperate. By the late 1970s the country had become an "anarchists' paradise" (Nimako 1991).

The first of these governments was the National Redemption Council (NRC), under Colonel Acheompong, who led the 1972 coup. The NRC represented a return to power for Ewes: though Acheompong was an Akan, Ewes held many of the key positions under the new government. The NRC immediately set out to undo many of the austerity measures put in place by Busia: the government revalued the currency by 42 percent, and sought to prevent the outflow of scarce foreign exchange—which were necessary to pay for the imports treasured by the elites—by repudiating $90 million of Nkrumah's debts to British firms and unilaterally rescheduling the remainder of the country's debt on a fifty-year timescale. Later, the government nationalized all foreign companies. The NRC's vital constituency also differed from the two previous governments in excluding many Ghanaian entrepreneurs; but loyal entrepreneurs were awarded with access to scarce foreign exchange to buy imports and grew phenomenally wealthy reselling the goods on Ghanaian markets.

While these practices did enrich a few, they pushed the Ghanaian economy, most aspects of which depended on imports, further into decline. Matters were made worse by rising oil prices and the aging of cocoa trees, which prevented the economy from taking advantage of a sudden spike in world cocoa prices.[36] Scarce foreign exchange allowed fewer imports of consumer goods and fueled inflation, which rose to 17.8 percent in 1972, 22.1 percent in 1974, and 29.7 percent in 1975. Disillusionment with the government soon spread among the educated elite and further stoked tensions between Ewes and Akans.

By 1975 the NRC had largely lost the support of the bureaucracy, and the army struck out on its own. Under Acheompong, it formed the Supreme Military Council, a body that was strictly military. In an effort to gain control over the bureaucracy, the military installed officers in most key government posts. The SMC also replaced many prominent Ewes, thereby shifting the ethnic makeup of the government back to the Akans. The SMC tried to stifle the elites it had just shut out of the government by banning newspapers and jailing journalists and by repeatedly closing the universities, which, as the training centers of the bureaucracy, had become the heartland of the bureaucratic elite. But these measures only hastened economic decline. The market for consumer goods came to be dominated by a massive underground economy run by a few well-connected businesspeople who practiced "kalabule": buying goods at low government-determined prices and selling them on the black market at a huge markup. Even cocoa farmers had trouble feeding themselves, forcing many to grow food instead of cocoa. Cocoa production in 1978 was half its 1964 peak. Inflation rose to 300 percent.

By 1977, opposition to the SMC was widespread in all corners of the society, and the government, seeing the writing on the wall, began planning a return to civilian rule. After some indecision, it appointed a special commission to draft a new constitution, select a new constituent assembly by November 1978, and hold general elections in June 1979. But the chaos was such that even the army brass could not agree on the way forward, and in July 1978, five months before the intended selection of the constituent assembly, Acheompong was deposed by dissident SMC officers. Yet this new SMC—SMC II as it became known—faced precisely the same pressures that Acheompong faced, and so announced that elections would be held and power handed to a civilian government on July 1, 1979. Once again, though, the army did not hold together: less than five weeks before elections, officers from the lower ranks of the army staged a coup.

The 1979 coup was led by Flight Lieutenant J. J. Rawlings, the man who would rule Ghana from 1981 to 2000. But this 1979 coup, Rawlings' first, was not nearly so successful as his second: the resulting government lasted just four months. With the other coup leaders, Rawlings formed the Armed Forces Revolutionary Council, a reactionary group focused mostly on restoring the good image of armed forces, which they claimed had been tarnished by the SMC. AFRC leaders executed the entire SMC II, as well as the heads of previous military governments. To quash the kalabule of the SMC economy, the AFRC broke into warehouses of politically-connected entrepreneurs, stole the goods, and sold them to the public at fire-sale prices. It also destroyed markets in Accra and Kumasi, the capital of the Ashanti region, and publicly flogged the female traders whom it perceived to be agents of the kalabule. The AFRC had no support base, however, and under pressure from the rest of the army and the public it agreed to give up control and finally hold the promised elections.

Those elections occurred in September 1979. They began Ghana's second experiment with democracy, which turned out to be even shorter than Ghana's first. Parties grouped around the traditional divide between the masses, in the mold of the CPP, and the elites and tribal groups (Nimako 1991). In this instance, however, elites and the tribal parties, fresh from a decade and a half of squabbling, did not unite, and the People's National Party, which claimed the mantle of the CPP, had the edge in the elections.

But the PNP was a far different party from the CPP. It was bankrolled by business and did not engage in the political entrepreneurship of the poor that enabled the CPP's success.[37] And the military closely supervised the election, even barring the PNP's founder, Alhaji Imoru Egala—a former cabinet minister of Nkrumah's—from competing; in his place, the PNP choose Hilla Limann, a former diplomat who was virtually unknown in Ghana. Though Limann won, the dissatisfaction of the populace with its choices was reflected in an abysmal turnout of only 40 percent. The disillusioned population gave the PNP only a razor-thin one-seat majority of 71 seats in the new 140-seat National Assembly.

The new government made competence its mantra, and tried to increase its popularity by quadrupling the minimum wage. But it faced the same difficulties as past governments—scarce foreign exchange, rising inflation, a black market estimated at a third of GDP,[38] and massive budget deficits[39]—and what little support the government had quickly eroded. The PNP's coalition was endlessly dissatisfied.[40] Workers were particularly problematic, striking constantly to protest wages they claimed were no longer enough to allow them even to eat, and in the process bringing productivity practically to a halt. Rawlings, meanwhile, was monitoring the new government's service to the Ghanaian masses with a new group, the "July 4 Movement" (named for the day the AFRC had taken power). Since leaving power, the charismatic Rawlings had carefully cultivated an image as the rare Ghanaian ruler who had fought corruption and then left power voluntarily. Faced with the ineffective PNP government, some elite groups, particularly leftists in the universities, began to warm to the idea of giving him another chance. He took power again on New Year's Eve 1981, and this time stayed for nearly two decades.

The 1981 coup marks the end of Ghana's fifteen years of elite rule. The preceding fifteen years saw seven governments but a relatively consistent vital constituency. Although the particular groups changed, the vital constituency was elite throughout: none of the governments engaged in political entrepreneurship.[41] Table 5.9 shows the particular groups. Elites ruled as a mostly cohesive group through 1972. Thereafter, as the economy deteriorated, elites began fighting with each other, both along tribal lines and among bureaucrats, entrepreneurs, and the military. As the economy collapsed in the late 1970s, Ghana experimented briefly

Table 5.9 **The elite Vital Constituencies, 1966–1981**

Political Entrepreneur(s)	Groups in the Vital Constituency[†]	Groups outside the Vital Constituency
None	Military	Workers
	Public Companies	Farmers/Migrant Workers
	Bureaucracy*	Foreign Entrepreneurs
	Foreign Companies*	
	Domestic Entrepreneurs	
	Tribal Elites[†]	
	Cocoa Farmers[†]	

Notes: [†] Akan (Asante) and Ewe tribal elites alternated in the vital constituency after 1972; cocoa farmers were associated with Akan elites, since the cocoa heartland of Ghana is in the Ashanti regions.

* The bureaucracy and foreign companies exited the vital constituency in 1975. All companies were Type S in until the early 1970s, and then Type N (no demand for skilled labor) as the economy declined.

again with democracy, but eventually some elites opted for the perceived integrity of Rawlings. Rawlings' difference—and the reason he would stay in power where the others failed—is that he quickly abandoned the elites who supported his rise, and opted to act as political entrepreneur to the masses, capitalizing on their disillusionment to secure his power. His rise to power in 1981 thus ends the period of elite rule.

This book's framework predicts that, because they shared an elite vital constituency, the seven successive governments that ruled Ghana after 1966 should have implemented a common education policy: transforming Nkrumah's All-Levels system into a Top-Down system to serve elites. The next section considers this transformation.

5. EDUCATION, 1966–1981: Serving Elites

In the fifteen years following the 1966 coup, Ghana's seven governments served their elite vital constituencies by transforming Ghana's education system from All-Levels to Top-Down. The lower levels deteriorated until they became little more than conduits for salaries for teachers, who as bureaucrats were part of the new elite vital constituency. Simultaneously the upper levels of the system saw growth and new resources. To allow elites easy access to these upper levels, a new system of expensive and selective primary schools allowed elites to bypass the deteriorating lower levels. These trends persisted until the mid-1970s, around the time the bureaucracy exited the vital constituency. Thereafter, a succession of resource-strapped governments reduced resources to all levels but kept them focused on the upper levels. Before 1975 the elite vital constituency also included Ghanaian entrepreneurs, and to serve them the government invested in Selective Worker Training. By the early 1970s, however, economic decline had eliminated much of the demand for skilled labor, and most Selective Worker Training was abandoned.

This section considers these developments. I first describe the decline of the lower levels and then the expansion and improvement of the upper levels. The third subsection deals with the decline in all levels of the system after 1975. The fourth examines worker training before and after the January 1972 coup that began Ghana's "lost decade" of political and economic decline. The final subsection presents the evidence summary of how well the book's framework predicts this period's education.

DECLINE AND DIFFERENTIATION OF THE LOWER LEVELS

The expansion of quality primary education had been a central part of the CPP's strategy for courting the Ghanaian masses, and the new military government began reversing it almost immediately after the 1966 coup. The NLC did not

eliminate primary education; Chapter 3 describes several reasons that governments are unlikely to completely abandon sections of the system they no longer
want. But the NLC closed hundreds of schools, particularly in rural areas. By
1971 it had closed more than 900 primary schools, and primary enrollment had
declined more than 15 percent. In closing these schools the government was explicit about its intentions. In its 1968 Budget Statement, the government wrote
that "[t]he check on indiscriminate opening of new primary schools is being
maintained and wherever possible under-enrolled classes and schools are being
merged" (Ghana 1968, 12). Later it bemoaned "[t]he unplanned and uncon-
trolled expansion of primary education under the C.P.P. Government" (Ghana
1970, 24), and established a new "planning unit" to consolidate "uneconomic
primary schools."

The closing of primary schools benefited another side of the NLC's vital constituency: teachers. Though the majority of Ghana's 50,000 primary and middle
school teachers owed their jobs to the CPP's expansion of primary education, once
hired they became part of the bureaucracy that turned against the CPP in 1966
and that was part of the NLC's vital constituency. Under the CPP, teachers had
often balked at being sent to Ghana's rural outreaches (McWilliam 1959). Under
the NLC they could look forward to more comfortable employment in cities and
towns. There they enjoyed relative freedom to teach, or not, as they wished; supervision was extremely limited, and materials were scarce. Between 1966 and
1970 the budget of the Education Ministry's textbook unit fell by more than half
in real terms, and by the mid-1970s, salaries and allowances accounted for more
than 90 percent of the budget (Nimako 1991). At the same time, the Ministry
encouraged teachers to move up into administration, where, of course, there was
no teaching at all (Addae-Mensah, Djangmah, and Agbenyega 1981). Over just a
single year, from 1967 to 1968, the Ministry's inflation-adjusted spending on central administration rose more than five-fold, to fully 70 percent of the amount the
Ministry was spending on all the primary schools in the country.

These steps led naturally to a decline in the general quality of public primary
education. The decline is clear in Table 5.10, which shows the key statistics for
primary and middle schools from the 1966 coup to 1975, when the bureaucracy
split from the vital constituency. In that decade real per-student spending on primary and middle schools declined by nearly 10 percent.

I argued in Chapter 3 that when a government makes a change from an All-
Levels system to a Top-Down system, it will also open a new track at the lower
levels by which elites can enter the upper levels. This the NLC did with a network
of "special schools." These primary schools were generally expensive,[42] mostly private, paid their teachers two-to-three times better than public school teachers,
and taught a curriculum devised specifically to prepare students to take the
Common Entrance Examination (CEE) to secondary school. Recall that under the
CPP the middle school was designed to give students several chances to enter
secondary school. Most public school students were able to pass the exam only in

Table 5.10 **Depleting the lower levels, 1966–1981**

	1966	1975	1981	Changes 1966–75	Changes 1975–81
Primary					
Number of Public Schools	7,913	6,966	7,848	−12.0%	+12.7%
Number of Students	1,130,731	1,157,303	1,377,734	+2.3%	+19.0%
Enrollment in Private Schools	13,888	28,837*	25,522††	+107.6%*	−11.5%
Proportion in Private Schools	1%	2%	2%		
Spending	NC17,914,456	NC39,002,000	¢131,551,000†		
(in millions of 2001 ¢)	¢269,149	¢245,623	¢91,670†	−8.7%	−62.7%
Per Student	NC16	NC35	¢97†		
(in 2001 ¢)	¢240,991	¢217,661	¢67,793†	−9.7%	−68.9%
Middle (Public Only)					
Number of Schools	2,346	3,888	4,449	+65.7%	+14.4%
Number of Students	280,866	451,462	529,695	+60.7%	+17.3%
Spending	NC6,327,569	NC21,978,000	¢79,278,000†		
(in millions of 2001 ¢)	¢95,066	¢138,411	¢55,244†	+45.6%	−60.1%
Per Student	NC23	NC49	¢150†		
(in 2001 ¢)	¢338,475	¢306,584	¢104,295†	−9.4%	−66.0%

Notes: * Private primary enrollment is for 1970–71, the closest year for which data are available.

† Spending data are for 1979 (school year 1978–79), the last year data are available until 1988.

†† Private enrollments are from an unpublished survey of private schools for 1979–80 and represent responses from only five regions (unpublished data, Ghana Ministry of Education).

Currency Note: In 1965 Ghana split from the sterling and established the cedi, which was pegged at a rate of 2.4 cedis to the pound. The new cedi (NC) was introduced in 1967, partly to remove Nkrumah's image from banknotes. In 1972–73 a new series of banknotes was introduced and the currency symbol changed to ¢.

their eighth, ninth, or tenth year of school (Addae-Mensah, Djangmah, and Agbe-nyega 1981). By contrast students at special schools were permitted to take the CEE in grade six, and, if they failed, to get extra tuition and take it again in year seven. These advantages were usually decisive. The best special schools had CEE pass rates of 90 to 100 percent; on average well over half of all special school students entered secondary school, compared to a pass rate of just 15 percent for public-school students. Special school students were also substantially more likely to make it into the best secondary schools. In 1956 the elite Achimota secondary school admitted 106 students, all from public schools; in 1972, it admitted 182 students from special schools, and just 26 from public schools (Addae-Mensah, Djangmah, and Agbenyega 1981).

Elite parents naturally flocked to special schools. A few special schools appeared in the waning days of the CPP—in 1966 the Ministry of Education registered 33, with an enrollment of just over 6,000—but their number doubled after 1966. In total, private primary school enrollment went from 13,000 in 1966 to almost 29,000 in 1971. Increasingly they came to dominate secondary school admissions.[43] By contrast, passing the CEE became a remote goal beyond the imagination of most public school students.[44]

Table 5.10 tells the story of the decline of the lower levels through 1975: on the one hand, declining resources to primary and middle students, and on the other a tiny but rapidly growing population of private school students, whose elite education gave them overwhelming advantages.

THE INCREASINGLY ELITE UPPER LEVELS

The elite students who passed the CEE entered a largely public system that was a far cry from the resource-strapped lower levels. From 1966 to 1975 the secondary and university levels were expanded and enhanced. Even as it was closing schools at the lower levels, the post-coup governments greatly expanded the secondary system: the number of secondary schools went from 103 in 1966 to 171 in 1975, and enrollment nearly doubled, from 42,000 students in 1966 to 81,000 in 1975. Even in the face of these enrollment increases, the government managed to raise real per-student spending by more than 45 percent over the decade, a feat that entailed a real increase in secondary spending of almost 180 percent. Though primary schools often lacked textbooks, the government proudly touted its ability to put new science equipment and typewriters in all secondary schools (Ghana 1968). Table 5.11 presents the key statistics on the growth and improvement of secondary education.

The government also recalibrated secondary-school scholarships to favor elites. In Section 3, I noted that under the CPP, scholarships had permitted poorer students to afford secondary school. After 1967, the government awarded scholarships solely on "merit"—measured by performance on the CEE, for which the aforementioned "special schools" gave elites overwhelming advantages. At first the government also devoted increasing resources to these scholarships: real spending on secondary scholarships rose 65 percent from 1966 to 1967, and by 1970 spending had climbed to 144 percent over its 1966 level. Thereafter, however, spending fell sharply as the Busia government introduced the austerity budgets that would lead to its overthrow (about which more below).

The elitism of the new system was also reflected in teachers' colleges. Under the CPP, teacher-training colleges had offered poorer students a way of bypassing secondary schools, which elites had dominated under the British. But the NLC and later governments had little interest in providing such alternatives; nor, as primary enrollment dropped, did they need more teachers.[45] In 1969 the government began closing down teacher training colleges and converting most of them into secondary schools.[46] By 1975 there were less than half as many teachers' training colleges as in 1966, enrolling only half the students (Table 5.11). The government also decreed that new teachers would be trained in post-secondary courses. For these students, excellent education awaited: real per-student spending on students in teachers' colleges rose more than 40 percent between 1966 and 1975. But, of course, only secondary graduates were eligible; no longer could a poor student hope for a coveted job in the bureaucracy without first finding a way through the elite juggernaut of secondary education.

Many secondary graduates took jobs immediately in the bureaucracy. But secondary graduates could also try for entrance to one of Ghana's three universities, on which the new government lavished nearly as many resources as on the secondary schools. Real per-student spending on universities rose nearly 20 percent from 1966 to 1971, and in addition the government awarded scholarships to every university student that covered not only tuition, but also room and board, books, clothing, travel, examination fees, and activities' fees, and even provided extra money for the student to use as she wished (Ghana 1971).

The beneficiaries of these excellent universities were overwhelmingly elite. The nature of tracking is that initial advantages are compounded (see Chapter 3). Thus the "special" primary preparatory schools gave elites advantages in entering the best secondary schools, which in turn gave them advantages in entering the universities. Addae-Mensah, Djangmah, and Agbenyega (1981) examined admissions to the most remunerative courses[47] at the University of Ghana from 1970 to 1973, from the 12 secondary schools that got more than 20 percent of their students from the special schools. They found that these 12 accounted for 40 percent of admissions, though they represented just 9 percent of total secondary school places. The top three schools alone accounted for 20 percent of admissions.

But as noted in Section 4, the last years of the Busia administration were a time of austerity budgets that fell hardest on Busia's vital constituency and led to his overthrow in 1972. Education spending was not immune. Although secondary spending continued to rise, universities began to see cuts. In 1969 and 1970 the Busia government tried to implement university fees that would not be covered

Table 5.11 **The elite upper levels, 1966–1981**

	1966	1975	1981	Changes 1966–75	Changes 1975–81
Senior Secondary					
Number of Public Schools	103	171	205	+66.0%	+19.9%
Public Enrollment	42,276	81,250	113,157	+92.2%	+39.3%
Private Enrollment	6,965	6,817*	—	-2.1%	—
Proportion in Private Schools	14.1%	7.7%	—		
Spending	NC5,582,675	NC37,249,000	¢87,998,000†		
(in millions of 2001 ¢)	¢83,875	¢234,583†	¢61,321†	+179.7%	-73.9%
Per Student	NC132	NC458	¢778†		
(in 2001 ¢)	¢1,983,979	¢2,887,178	¢541,909†	+45.5%	-81.2%
Teachers' Colleges (Public Only)					
Number of Schools	83	38	36	-54.2%	-5.3%
Enrollment	16,441	8,382	11,662	-49.0%	+39.1%
Spending	NC7,988,468	NC13,691,000	¢26,771,000†		
(in millions of 2001 ¢)	¢120,020	¢86,222	¢18,655†	-28.2%	-78.4%
Per Student	NC486	NC1,633	¢2,296†		
(in 2001 ¢)	¢7,300,018	¢10,286,553	¢1,599,657†	+40.9%	-84.4%

	1966	1975	1981	Changes	
				1966–75	1975–81
Universities (Public Only)					
Number of Schools	3	3	3	0.0%	0.0%
Number of Students	4,506	7,179	7,946	+59.3%	+10.7%
Spending					
(in millions of 2001 ¢)	NC13,969,815	NC42,517,524	¢101,191,580†	+27.6%	−73.7%
Per Student	NC3,100	NC5,922	¢12,735†		
(in 2001 ¢)	¢46,578,782	¢37,298,071	¢8,874,240†	−19.9%	−76.2%

Notes: * Private senior secondary enrollment is for 1970–71, the closest year for which data are available.
† Spending data are for 1979 (school year 1978–79), the last year data are available until 1988.

by scholarships, as well as a student loan program,[48] but its efforts were thwarted by violent student demonstrations. The 1970 budget cut real spending for universities by 25 percent, and the 1971 budget by another 30 percent.

These cuts added to the general assault on the bureaucracy that the austerity budgets represented, and contributed to Col. Acheompong's 1972 coup (Addae-Mensah 2000; Nimako 1991). Acheompong immediately reversed them, as he did most of the other austerity measures: real spending on universities rose 25 percent after the 1972 coup and reached its 1971 level again by 1975. Still, university enrollments were rising and on a per-student basis spending never recovered: in 1975 it was 20 percent below its 1966 level.

Table 5.11 shows the trends in enrollment and spending for the upper levels: secondary schools, teachers' colleges, and universities.

Of course, Acheompong's coup did not solve the economic woes that had prompted Busia's austerity budgets. On the contrary, in the coup's wake the Ghanaian economy began shrinking fast. I now consider how these declining resources affected the education system.

DETERIORATION OF ALL LEVELS

Section 4 described how economic decline led to struggles among the elites that culminated in a split between the army and the bureaucracy in 1975. Government policy thereafter did little more than oversee the economic decline. This book's framework is about what the government does in education with the resources it has. In Ghana, the steadily reducing resources meant deep cuts at all levels of the education system. The cuts affected all levels in part because by 1975, the government had largely achieved the balance in the education system that its vital constituency wanted. The upper levels of the system were well-resourced and restricted so as to be accessible mostly to elites, while the remainder of the lower levels seemed to exist solely to pay teachers.[49]

Thus the decline in resources affected spending relatively equitably. The figures are in Tables 5.10–5.11: real per-student spending declined between 65 and 85 percent at all levels between 1975 and 1981. It is notable that the government continued to fund the universities at much the same relative level despite their becoming vibrant centers of opposition from the newly disempowered bureaucracy. After 1975 successive governments repeatedly closed the universities, and in 1981 university students and professors would become a key group supporting Rawlings' second coup. Yet in 1981 per-student spending on universities was still 131 times per-student spending on primary schools, down only slightly from the 171-to-1 resource advantage universities held in 1975. In 1978, University of Ghana students, who were still receiving free education, including three free meals a day and their own dorm rooms, took to the streets to protest how much (free) chicken they were being served in the cafeteria (Manu 1998).

In all, the fifteen years post-Nkrumah entirely altered Ghana's education system. Initially universities and secondary schools were showered with new resources, while many primary schools closed and the remainder seemed to exist for little purpose other than paying teachers. At the same time the elite gained access to new "special" primary schools that prepared their children specifically for the gateway exams to the upper levels. The system developed in this way until economic decline intervened. But by the mid-1970s, even as inflation gradually ate away at the real resources available for education, the government maintained the Top-Down character of the system.

Before evaluating how well these changes reflect this book's predictions, there is one remaining part of the Ghanaian education system to consider: its small but important system of worker training.

WORKER TRAINING

Recall that Nkrumah's CPP created a system of limited but excellent worker training to meet its particular labor needs. Graduates of the universities, secondary schools, and teacher training colleges staffed the new Ghanaian bureaucracy, and a network of technical schools provided skilled labor for manufacturing and public works projects. By the 1970s economic decline would remove the need for most of the products of these technical schools. But in the immediate aftermath of the coup the new government somewhat expanded technical education, in keeping with its plans for spurring economic growth. In addition the new government, which, unlike the CPP, had entrepreneurs in its vital constituency, experimented with formalizing apprenticeships. This section considers these two developments, and then briefly the decline of worker training during the economic decline.

The National Liberation Council, which took over after the 1966 coup, had a free-market economic orientation. But, as noted in Section 4, its hopes for free-market growth fell flat when the expected flood of new international investment failed to appear. After an initial period of sell-offs of some obviously inefficient state enterprises—a few mines, the state laundry company—the NLC, and later Busia's administration, began actually to create *new* state enterprises.

The government provided skilled workers for these enterprises with a near doubling of technical education. Table 5.12 shows the expansion through the end of Busia's administration. The government added four new institutes, and total enrollment in technical institutes almost doubled. Under the CPP the government technical institutes were renowned for the quality of their education; the NLC and Busia maintained this quality by increasing resources commensurately. Even with the enrollment increases, per-student spending rose more than eight percent.

The similarity of this Selective Worker Training pre- and post-1966 is unsurprising: both were designed to serve the state sector. But the post-1966 vital

Table 5.12 **Technical institutes, 1966–1981**

	1966	1971*	1981	Changes 1966–72	1966–81
Number of Schools	11	15	20	+36.4%	+33.3%
Enrollment	4,010	7,896	—†	+96.9%	
Spending	NC1,440,331	NC1,716,973	¢5,815,000††		
(in millions of 2001 ¢)	¢21,640	¢23,456	¢4,052††	+8.4%	–82.7%
Per Student	NC359	NC217	—		
(in 2001 ¢)	¢5,396,431	¢2,970,602	—	-45.0%	—

Notes: * I use data for 1971 (school year 1970–71) in lieu of 1972, for which data are not available.
† Enrollment data for technical institutes are unavailable after 1976–77, but enrollment for that year is 8,500, suggesting that the growth in enrollments slowed after 1972.
†† Spending data are for 1979 (school year 1978–79), the last year data are available until 1988.

constituency also included one new group of employers: Ghanaian entrepreneurs. These entrepreneurs engaged generally in distribution and maintenance of imported consumer goods, simple construction, and minor value added to nearly finished imported goods; thus their skill demands were less than the state enterprises. Their educational demand was instead for apprenticeships.

Until depression hit in the 1970s, the post-1966 governments tried to address this need in two ways. The first was through the middle schools. Under Nkrumah, middle schools had been designed to provide extra training for students from poorer backgrounds, helping to level the playing field. But after 1966 the government saw them as new sources of low-skilled workers[50]—and it planned to remodel them as Continuation Schools offering vocational training.[51] These plans were never realized: entrepreneurs' needs remained limited, and the money for remodeling the middle schools was tied up in improving the secondary schools and universities.[52]

Instead, the NLC and Busia governments considered another option: formalizing apprenticeships. Informal apprenticeships had been common under the CPP. They provided training of the level that entrepreneurs needed, but their quality was uneven and their informality left entrepreneurs wondering about the quality of the workers they were hiring. In response, the Busia government, with help from the International Labor Organization, created the National Vocational Training Institute, a small network of a training centers offering formal apprenticeships in fields of use to entrepreneurs—like carpentry, dress-making, auto repair, and catering—and administering its own exams to certify the quality of graduates.[53]

But Busia's efforts were cut short by the 1972 coup. Perhaps without the coup they would have led to a more regular stream of skilled workers for entrepreneurs. But by 1972, as the economy began its downward slide, the need for such workers was dwindling anyway. In fact the 1972 coup marks the end of the government's interest in Selective Worker Training. In the decade after 1971, real spending on formal technical institutes fell to just 17 percent of its 1971 level, while enrollment stagnated (Table 5.12). With the economy shrinking, the government had its hands full finding employment for bureaucrats, let alone for newly graduated skilled workers. Likewise the depression curtailed entrepreneurs' demands, and it was not until the late 1980s that talk of formally regulating apprenticeships resurfaced.

WRAPPING UP

This section has described a wholesale reorientation of the Ghanaian education system, from All Levels to Top Down. This is generally what the book's framework predicts when a vital constituency changes from a cross-class alliance to elites. The evidence summary for 1966–1981 is in Table 5.13.

Ghanaian governments from 1966 to 1981 acted as the framework predicts in most areas. After 1966, Ghanaian governments adjusted the All-Levels system they inherited from Nkrumah to shift the balance of resources toward the upper levels and instituted a tracking system to help elite students make it into the upper levels. Most of the population, however, had access only to public primary schools that deteriorated to the point where they seemed to exist as little more than excuses for paying teachers. As budgetary pressures increased in the late 1970s, all level suffered, but it was the lower levels that suffered most; while most primary students lacked books and a teacher who showed up every day, pampered university students protested that their state-provided meals were starting to rely too heavily on chicken.

The only areas in which the governments do not act as predicted are at the lower levels, which remained free and in which enrollment, after an initial contraction, began rising again in the mid-1970s. The framework, by contrast, would have predicted a contraction across the entire period and would not have anticipated that free education would remain after 1966. I argued in this section that in general the primary system provided education of extremely low and steadily declining quality after 1966, but that the system stayed in place in large part because teachers were an important group in the vital constituency. Thus rather than fire them, the government continued to pay them, while reducing their responsibilities and the resources going to primary schools: in real terms spending per primary student in 1981 was less than a fifth of its 1966 level. In addition, the period immediately after the coup did see a substantial decline in primary enrollment, as the government closed schools, mostly in rural areas where many teachers did not want to be posted. Between 1966 and

Table 5.13 **Evidence summary, 1966–1981**

Indicator	Characteristics	Conforms to Framework?
A. Enrollment	Increasing at upper levels	■
	Decreasing then increasing at lower levels	◻
B. Per-student spending	Increasing at upper levels; decreasing at lower levels; decreasing at all levels after 1975	■
C. The toolkit		
1. Schools	High-quality at upper levels; low quality at lower levels	■
Teachers	High-quality at upper levels; low supervision and expectations at lower levels	■
Physical resources	High at upper levels; low at lower levels	■
Location	Higher levels concentrated in urban areas; lower levels consolidated closer to urban areas	■
2. Fees[†]	Primary: free	◻
	Higher levels: high fees but merit-based scholarships	■
3. Access restrictions and discriminatory pricing		
Quotas	None	
Exams	Exams regulate access between levels, for which elite students are given special training	■
Financial aid	Extensive merit-based scholarships for higher levels	■
4. Tracking	Yes—"special schools" offer elites training for the entrance exams to the higher levels	■
5. Outsourcing (domestic or foreign; to firms or non-profits)	Minimal at upper levels; at lower levels, many of the "special schools" are private and expensive; some elites send their children to universities abroad	■

Notes: ■: fully conforms to the framework; ◘: partly conforms to the framework; ◻: does not conform to the framework.

[†]Fees are for enrollment, books and other equipment, uniforms, activities, school improvements, etc.

1972, enrollment fell almost 14 percent. Nonetheless, the increase in enrollments over the entire 1966–1981 period in schools that remained free is not
what the framework predicts.

By 1981, when J. J. Rawlings took the helm, both Ghana's economy and its
education system were in shambles. While Rawlings was not initially a political
entrepreneur of the poor, his coup succeeded where others had failed because
he quickly became one—and not just any political entrepreneur, but the kind
of anti-elite political entrepreneur that we will see only one other time in this
book's three countries (in Brazil, in the early 1960s). Though nearly two
decades at Ghana's helm allowed Rawlings to raise the living standards of some
of the poor to the point where, by 2000, his vital constituency was closer to a
cross-class alliance, Ghana's poor were always the heart of Rawlings coalition,
and Ghana's traditional elites—the senior bureaucracy, the entrepreneurs, and
the tribal elites—were always outside it. Thus the framework predicts that
Rawlings' government should have transformed Ghana's education system
from the Top-Down system he inherited to a Bottom-Up system, and then
gradually to an All-Levels system, as some of the poor in the vital constituency
were raised into the middle class. The next two sections take up the politics
(Section 6) and the education system (Section 7) of the final period for Ghana,
1981–2000.

6. POLITICS, 1981–2000: J. J. Rawlings[54]

After the political turmoil of the 1960s and 1970s, Ghana had one leader for
nearly two decades. J. J. Rawlings, a low-level military officer, took power in 1981
and ruled until 2000, first as a military dictator and then as elected president. On
taking power in 1981, Rawlings' vital constituency was not terribly different from
the elite that had supported Ghanaian governments since 1966. But soon after,
Rawlings abandoned this constituency and organized a new one, made up of the
disgruntled poor, who had not been organized since Nkrumah. After Nkrumah,
Rawlings was Ghana's second political entrepreneur of the poor. And though in
the ensuing two decades Rawlings succeeded in raising the incomes of many of
the poor to the point where they were middle class and his vital constituency was
closer to a cross-class alliance, Rawlings stayed a political entrepreneur of the
poor throughout.

    Section 4 noted that the Ghana of 1981 was an "anarchists' paradise," and ripe
for another coup (Nimako 1991). The democratically elected government of the
People's National Party had been hamstrung by Ghana's moribund economy and
its slim, one-vote majority in the legislature and had been unable to right the
economy or reduce government spending on the bureaucracy. Meanwhile Rawlings
and his "July 4 Movement"—named for the date of Rawlings' first coup—were

watching and waiting. On New Year's Eve, 1981, they struck again, joined by the army ranks, with whom Rawlings was widely popular, and by the New Democracy Movement, a group of Marxist-leaning university lecturers and former state bureaucrats who shared the July 4 Movement's belief that the country's problems stemmed from the bureaucracy's corruption and economic mismanagement. Together the three groups formed the "Provisional National Defense Council" (PNDC), a government with a Marxist orientation intent on fighting corruption and removing the perceived yolk of Western influence over the economy.

The three groups were hardly a viable vital constituency. The July 4 Movement had only about 1,000 members; the New Democracy Movement about 300. With so few supporters, it was not at all apparent that Rawlings' 1981 coup would be any more successful than his 1979 one. Arrayed against the PNDC was nearly the entirety of the traditional elite: the bureaucracy and the entrepreneurs, whose corruption and incompetence the PNDC blamed for Ghana's economic woes[55]; foreign companies, who were quite naturally unnerved by the new government's socialist rhetoric; and the tribal chiefs.[56] Without additional support the new government probably would not have survived. But after taking power Rawlings and his PNDC added to their political support by doing something that previous governments had not: they organized, and served, the poor.

The PNDC organized the poor by means of a series of new, semi-socialist-democratic governing organizations meant to bypass the traditional, elite-dominated governing structures and give the masses local decision-making power. In place of the courts, the PNDC created Public Tribunals to try those accused of anti-government acts, and Citizens' Vetting Committees. New People's Defense Committees, Regional Defense Committees, and National Defense Committees replaced the parliament, and Workers' Defense Committees organized workers democratically,[57] as did Forces' Defense Committees in the armed forces and police. Membership in these committees was restricted to non-elites by excluding chiefs and the "exploiting classes" (Library of Congress 1994). The new structures brought the masses into the political process in the first meaningful way since Nkrumah's Convention People's Party.

The process was hardly smooth. The poor had been isolated politically since the 1960s and had suffered tremendously in the economic decline. They were angry. And as the economy failed to recover in 1983 and 1984, their anger occasionally turned on the PNDC. In addition the new Workers' Defense Committees grew militantly anti-management, interfering with the productivity that the Ghanaian economy desperately needed. In late 1984, as criticism grew, the PNDC eliminated the WDCs, PDCs, and NDCs, and replaced them with a national network of Committees for the Defense of the Revolution (CDRs) in villages, urban areas, and workplaces.[58] Though the PNDC kept a close eye on them, membership in CDRs was unrestricted; elites could join. In 1985 the government sought to further institutionalize the organization by developing a new system of 110 local District Assemblies, which allowed participation of the masses but whose decisions could be overridden by the national government. The PNDC argued that elite candidates had long appealed to impoverished voters with empty rhetoric. Thus the PNDC's design for the assemblies sought to ensure that representatives would be ordinary people and not members of the old elite. While elites could technically run for office in one of the new District Assemblies, the electoral rules banned anyone who had a record of criminal activity, insanity, or imprisonment for fraud or electoral offenses, or anyone accused of such offenses—criteria that easily excluded those from the old elite. The plan further banned all political parties, as well as any election platforms except those approved by a new National Commission for Democracy. In order to both co-opt and weaken tribal elites, the PNDC reserved one-third of the seats in District Assemblies for tribal representatives, who could only be chosen with the expressed approval of the PNDC.

Of course, efforts at organizing the poor into a political force might have backfired if the PNDC had not been able to restore Ghana's economic health. In 1981 the economy was in shambles and the poor were suffering. The cedi, kept overvalued to allow the bureaucracy to buy imported consumer goods, was trading on the black market at 9.6 times its official rate; the parallel economy was estimated at a third of GDP (Library of Congress 1994). To revive the economy, the most desperate need was for foreign exchange and investment. Initially the PNDC's socialist orientation led it to seek these in the Communist bloc. However, Communist countries were facing their own economic difficulties; they could offer little in aid and were not strong enough to replace the West as the buyer of Ghanaian exports. Reluctantly, Rawlings turned back to the West in late 1982, enlisting the help of the World Bank and International Monetary Fund (IMF). The shift entailed expanding the vital constituency to include foreign companies and abandoning some of the more elite leftist elements that had put Rawlings in power. By 1982, that is, the PNDC was a government of the masses, the army, and foreign companies.

Rawlings deftly engineered the shift from leftist elites to foreign companies. The IMF and World Bank saw potential in Ghana—particularly in its gold reserves. But they had been burned by Ghana many times before—loaning its government money only to have those loans repudiated or unilaterally reorganized—and they would not agree to assist Ghana's economic recovery until it demonstrated that it would hold up its end of the bargain. The PNDC did its best to show that it would: in the darkest days of its economic slump, the PNDC handed over hundreds of millions to cover debts dating back as far as Nkrumah—$220 million in 1982 and $660 million in 1983. With this gesture of good faith, the World Bank and IMF agreed to help. From 1984 to 1990, they structured two Economic Recovery Programs—ERPs I and II—aided by $3.5 billion in concessional loans.[59]

The programs entailed austerity on a scale that made the Busia 1971 budget—the cuts in which had led to his overthrow—look like a drunken sailor's. The government devalued the currency, removed most subsidies, price supports, and import licenses from the bureaucracy and entrepreneurs, and it laid off 70,000 bureaucrats and employees of state enterprises. In the past such measures would certainly have led the government to fall, but the PNDC was unique in that it did not need the bureaucracy's support: it had the masses.

Instead, the PNDC engineered the adjustment so that its costs fell disproportionately on the elites, not the poor. Elements of the ERPs that would have helped its opponents were put on the back burner. For example, although the IMF pushed for liberalization of the cocoa industry to the point where farmers would receive 65 percent of the world price of their product, the PNDC repeatedly delayed and this target was not reached until after 2000, when the PNDC was no longer in charge.[60] At the same time, the PNDC embraced World Bank support for spending ERP money directly on the poor through the Program of Actions to Mitigate the Social Cost of Adjustment (PAMSCAD). And even while the government laid off civil servants who were less than supportive of the PNDC (Nimako 1991), the government emulated Nkrumah's policy of offering the poor public employment. Between 1981 and 1985, the PNDC *hired* 222,000 workers, more than doubling the government payroll from its level of 175,000 in 1981. Payrolls shrunk somewhat during ERP II, but thereafter grew again, reaching nearly 600,000 by 1992. Over the decade, public sector employment accounted for four-fifths of total recorded employment (Library of Congress 1994).[61] In the process of adding hundreds of thousands of workers to the bureaucracy, the PNDC created a new middle class in Ghana, and its vital constituency, while still mostly poor, came to include more elite elements. Naturally Ghana's traditional elites mounted vociferous attacks on all these developments, but as the PNDC increasingly secured the support of the newly organized masses, it was able to ignore the traditional elites.

Though the ERPs were not carried out exactly as intended, they finally secured for Ghana the foreign exchange that its economy had been craving since Nkrumah's overthrow. Aid poured in. Annual aid receipts grew from less than 2.7 percent of Gross National Income (GNI) in 1983 to 14 percent of GNI in 1989, and averaged 8.2 percent of GNI from 1984 to 1989. Helped by these inflows of new capital, domestic investment flourished: gross capital formation grew from less than 4 percent of GDP in 1983 to almost 7 percent in 1984 and 14.5 percent in 1990. And inflation, which topped 110 percent in 1981 and 122 percent in 1983, fell to 10 percent by 1985 and averaged less than 30 percent between 1985 and 1990. GDP per capita, which shrunk 10 percent in 1982 and 8 percent in 1983, grew nearly 5 percent in 1984, and averaged 2.5 percent growth from 1984 to 1989. By the end of the ERPs, international investors began returning to Ghana: inflows, which were minimal throughout the 1980s, reached more than 4 percent of GDP by 1994 (World Bank 2007).

With the economy back in shape, the PNDC faced calls to return to democracy, both from opposition elites and from its own mass base, whose appetites for self-government had been whetted by their experience with the District Assemblies. While Rawlings was initially wary of multi-party democracy, he eventually agreed to it, under a new constitution with a number of features that secured both devolution and the power of the president. The constitution retained the 110 District Assemblies, and gave them some fiscal control with funds from a new "Common Fund," made up of five percent of government revenue, controlled by the central government, and distributed to the districts by a formula that favored the poorest (World Bank 2004a). While the constitution provided for formal separation of powers, the legislative and judicial branches received their funding from the executive, and members of a new 200-member Parliament were prohibited from introducing any legislation that would affect the budget. The president was also empowered to appoint an unlimited number of ministers from the Parliament, who would then be members both of the executive and the Parliament. But the 1992 constitution also included a two-term limit on the president—a provision that Rawlings, who won both presidential elections in 1992 and 1996, would honor in 2000.

Ghana's "Fourth Republic" was inaugurated in elections in 1992. Rawlings won a landslide victory against an opposition of elites riven by longstanding internal grievances and no match for Rawlings' organization of Ghana's poor. Among five presidential candidates, Rawlings won nearly 60 percent of the vote and a majority in all Ghana's regions. Polls clearly demonstrated the reasons for the victory: Rawlings and the PNDC were perceived as restoring Ghana's economy and national image and returning honesty to government, and the public, though it had sacrificed some during the Economic Recovery Programs, felt that the country would have been far worse off without the PNDC's policies (Library of Congress 1994). The elections, in other words, demonstrated the success of the PNDC in winning the support of the masses it had organized. The elite opposition, shocked at the magnitude of its loss—it had, after all, pushed for democratization, remembering perhaps how it had been able to dominate politics in previous democratic periods when the masses were not organized—decided to boycott the parliamentary elections that followed the presidential poll. The candidates of the PNDC ran on a message of "continuity" as the National Democratic Congress— whose initials were deliberately PNDC without the "P"—and swept 189 of the 200 seats.

By 1996, the opposition elites had learned their lesson and united against the NDC as the "New Patriotic Party." This NDC-NPP match-up, which still characterizes Ghanaian politics today, is the democratic incarnation of Ghana's two political traditions, with which I began this chapter. The NPP is the party of the elite, the entrepreneurs, and much of the tribal elite; the NDC is the party of the masses. The difference is that the NDC and the NPP are both nationally-organized parties, which both compete in every area of the country: the NPP, like the NDC, organizes its supporters in every village and town. This is the first time in modern Ghanaian history that the country has had two national parties. Nonetheless the traditional ethnic rivalries are still apparent: the NPP does better among Asantes, historically the region most dominated by elites, while the NDC is strongest in the less-well-off regions of the Ewes and the Northern tribes.

In the 1996 elections Rawlings again won a landslide, taking nearly 60 percent of the vote. But the NPP's candidate, John Kufuor, took much of the remainder—nearly 40 percent—and the NPP, now uniting most of the opposition, won 61 seats in the parliament, still less than half the NDC's 131 but a far better showing than in 1996. After 1996 the NPP continued to grow in strength and organizational capacity. By 2000, when Kufuor was able to face off against a lesser-known NDC candidate, rather than the term-limited Rawlings, Kufuor managed a slim victory—48.4 percent to 44.8 percent—and prevailed in the runoff that followed when no candidate reached 50 percent of the vote. Kufuor's NPP also won a slim 100-seat plurality in the parliament, to the NDC's 92 seats.

The NPP victory was somewhat of a surprise. The overwhelming NDC victories in the past two elections had suggested that Ghana was simply returning one-party rule. But by 2000 the NDC was losing some of its popularity, particularly in the resource-rich Asante heartlands. World prices of cocoa and gold were falling and oil prices were rising, leading to accelerating inflation and declining business confidence. And in a competition that was largely free and fair, the NPP, which ran on its appeal to business and reviving the economy, was able to pull together enough voters tired of the NDC, which again ran on its record—its slogan was "Continuity in Change" (Gyimah-Boadi 2001). Perhaps the greater surprise was that Rawlings and the NDC abided by the results, and on January 7, 2001, power changed hands—the first democratic transfer of power since Ghana's independence.[62]

The transfer of power to the NPP marks the end of Rawlings' and the PNDC/NDC's dominance of Ghanaian politics, as well as the end of the third and last period of analysis for this chapter. This section has described Rawlings as an anti-elite political entrepreneur who created a vital constituency that, other than foreign companies, included only the poor: workers, farmers/migrant workers, and the military rank and file. Eventually some of these constituents became middle-class as they got jobs in the PNDC-controlled public sector, but the heart of the vital constituency always remained the poor. Opposed were the elements of the traditional elite: the bureaucracy, Ghanaian entrepreneurs, and the tribal elite. These were the forces that eventually united in the NPP and successfully countered the NDC in the 2000 elections. Table 5.14 summarizes the vital constituency from 1981 to 2000.

The framework predicts that a vital constituency transition from elites to the poor, such as Ghana's in 1981, should lead the new government to transform its Top-Down system into a Bottom-Up system. Likewise it predicts that, as the need for skilled workers rose with the economic recovery, the government should have invested more heavily in Selective Worker Training, in order to provide employers in Ghana's inflexible labor market with the skilled workers to meet their needs. The next section considers whether the PNDC's education policies fit these predictions.

Table 5.14 **The Vital Constituency, 1981–2000**

Political Entrepreneur(s)	Groups in the Vital Constituency†	Groups outside the Vital Constituency
J.J. Rawlings and the Provisional National Defense Council (PNDC) and National Democratic Congress (NDC)	Military New Junior Bureaucracy* Foreign Companies (Type *S*) Public Enterprises (Type *S*) Workers [PNDC/NDC] Farmers/Migrant Workers [PNDC/NDC]	Traditional/Senior Bureaucracy* Domestic Entrepreneurs Foreign Entrepreneurs Tribal Elites

Notes: † If a group was empowered with the help of a political entrepreneur, the entrepreneur is in brackets.

* The PNDC eliminated many of the jobs of the pre-1981 bureaucracy, while hiring hundreds of thousands of new civil servants and employees in the public enterprises.

Employer types are in parentheses. Type *S* employers need skilled workers in an inflexible labor market. With 80 percent of formal employment in the public sector, wages were determined politically in this period.

7. EDUCATION, 1981–2000: Reviving the Lower Levels, Expanding Access to the Upper Levels

In its two decades of control, Rawlings' PNDC (*cum*-NDC) radically altered Ghana's education system. The system it inherited was Top-Down to an extreme: per-student spending on universities was 131 times per-student spending on primary schools, many of which seemed to exist only as excuses for paying teachers. But the PNDC was a government whose vital constituency was overwhelmingly poor—initially its only elite element was foreign companies, and only after years in power did it begin to incorporate a new middle class of its own creation. Thus the PNDC transformed Ghana's education system into a Bottom-Up system. By 2000, Rawlings and his PNDC—by then the democratically-elected National Democratic Congress—had increased primary enrollment by more than 50 percent and almost tripled per-student spending on primary schools. Per-student spending on universities, by contrast, was cut in half, as the universities were forced to take on nearly five times as many students as they had enrolled in 1981.

The PNDC did not tackle education right away; it spent its first few years grappling with the moribund economy. It turned its attention to education only in the mid-1980s, when the economy began slowly returning to life. Thereafter it undertook extremely ambitious, even over-ambitious, reforms. These taxed both Ghana's resources and the economy's ability to make use a flood of newly educated workers. The reforms had two effects: they improved the lower levels, and they increased access to the upper levels. I take each of these in turn.

REVIVING THE LOWER LEVELS

In 1985, the PNDC formed a commission to examine how to improve Ghanaian education. Section 5 gave a sense of the daunting task they faced, and a few other statistics underline the point. In 1988, the World Bank surveyed primary schools. It found that less than half of schools could use their classrooms in the rain and two-thirds reported shortages of chalk. Only 13 percent of English students and 21 percent of math students had a textbook (World Bank 2004a). The Bank estimated that the majority of students who graduated from primary school were illiterate (World Bank 1995).

But the PNDC was already putting massive resources into restoring the primary system. By 1986 its spending on primary schools was more than twice, in real terms, what the government had been spending in 1981; by 2000 spending on primary would be almost four times its 1981 level. By 1986 the government had already added 500 schools to the public system, and by 2000 it would add another 3,500, bringing to the total to 50 percent more than in 1981 and making schools available in remote regions that had not been served since Nkrumah's day. With schooling more accessible, students began flocking to the schools: enrollment rose 50 percent from 1981 to 2000.[63] But government spending more than kept pace: real spending per student rose 160 percent from 1981 to 2000. Table 5.15 shows the key enrollment and spending statistics. In 2003, the World Bank again surveyed Ghanaian schools, and found that two-thirds of classrooms could be used in the rain and less than five percent reported shortages of chalk; 72 percent of English students and 71 percent of math students had at least one textbook. Student performance increased apace: for example, in identical English tests, two-thirds of primary school graduates in 1988 could not outperform guessing; in 2003, less than a fifth scored as poorly as if they had simply guessed (World Bank 2004a).

The reason the World Bank was closely monitoring Ghana's primary education system, and providing excellent statistics with which to judge its progress, was because it was helping to execute, and fund, the improvements. From 1986 to 2000, the World Bank offered Ghana more than $240 million in grants and concessional loans for basic education, catalyzed another $320 million from other donors, and offered invaluable technical assistance in designing the reforms, building schools, distributing resources, and administering the system.[64] It helped the government cut its bloated central education bureaucracy by identifying 13,000 non-teaching staff who could be let go and another 6,000 "ghost workers"—workers who didn't exist but were receiving a paycheck. It helped the Ghana Education Service (GES) develop a new distribution

Table 5.15 **Reviving the lower levels, 1981–2000**

	1981	1986	2000	Changes 1981–2000	1986–2000
Primary					
Number of Public Schools	7,848	8,347	11,916	+51.8%	+42.8%
Public Enrollment	1,377,734	1,295,900	2,114,981	+53.5%	+63.2%
Private Enrollment	25,522**	51,937*	—		
Proportion in Private Schools	2%	4%	10%***		
Spending (millions of current ¢)	¢132†	¢8,616††	¢273,853		
(in millions of 2001 ¢)	¢91,670†	¢192,345††	¢363,966	+297.0%	+89.2%
Per Student (current ¢)	¢95†	¢6,649††	¢129,482		
(in 2001 ¢)	¢66,537†	¢148,426††	¢172,089	+158.6%	+15.9%
Middle/Junior Secondary (Public Only)					
Number of Schools	4,449	4,890	6,054	+36.1%	+23.8%
Number of Students	529,695	539,300	736,251	+39.0%	+36.5%
Spending (millions of current ¢)	¢79†	¢6,907††	¢148,181		
(in millions of 2001 ¢)	¢55,244†	¢154,178††	¢196,941	+256.5%	+27.7%
Per Student (current ¢)	¢150†	¢12,806††	¢201,264		
(in 2001 ¢)	¢104,295†	¢285,886††	¢267,491	+156.5%	−6.4%

Notes: * Private primary enrollment for 1986 is for 1987–88, the closest year for which data are available.

** Private enrollments are from an unpublished survey of private schools for 1979–80, and represent responses from only five regions (unpublished data, Ghana Ministry of Education). *** Private percentage is an estimate from *World Development Indicators*. † Spending data are for 1979 (school year 1978–79), the last year data are available until 1988. †† Spending data are from 1988, the closest year to 1986 for which data are available.

system for textbooks and other materials, which was a part of the reason for their increased availability (at the start of the reforms, the GES system for distributing textbooks was so broken that the PNDC had to mobilize the army to deliver them).

The reforms worked well in providing materials, building new schools, and rehabilitating old ones. Teachers, though, were a thornier problem. As members of the old-guard bureaucracy they were clearly outside the vital constituency, and yet their participation was needed for real improvements to the primary system. The PNDC tried in part to solve the problem by training thousands of new teachers: over its two decades in power, enrollments in teacher training colleges nearly doubled, and per-student spending on them more than doubled as well. Table 5.16 shows the enrollments and spending. With these investments in teacher training the government managed to reduce the number of teachers who were untrained from half to less than 13 percent by the 1990s.[65] But teachers—particularly those who were hired prior to 1981—still resisted their new obligations and supervision. Teachers' absenteeism rose dramatically. In 2003, only 16 percent of schools reported having no problem with absenteeism—down from 85 percent in 1988 (World Bank 2004a). The World Bank judged that teacher resistance was the major reason that the reforms to primary schools did not make even more of a difference in educational quality.

Table 5.16 **Teachers' colleges (public only), 1981–2000**

	1981	1986	2000	Changes	
				1981–2000	1986–2000
Number of Schools	36	38	38	+5.6%	0.0%
Enrollment	11,662	16,692	21,410	+83.6%	+28.3%
Spending (millions of current ¢)	¢27[†]	¢598[††]	¢52,151		
(in millions of 2001 ¢)	¢18,655[†]	¢13,350[††]	¢69,311	+271.5%	+419.2%
Per Student (current ¢)	¢2,296[†]	¢35,826[††]	¢2,435,814		
(in 2001 ¢)	¢1,599,657[†]	¢799,757[††]	¢3,237,333	+102.4%	+304.8%

Notes: [†] Spending data are for 1979 (school year 1978–79), the last year data are available until 1988.

[††] Spending data are from 1988, the closest year to 1986 for which data are available.

Improving primary schools is only one expectation for a government that is converting its education system from Top-Down to Bottom-Up; a second expectation is that the government increase access further up the system, to the limit of the education budget (see Chapters 2 and 3). Recall that the vast majority of Ghanaian students who progressed on from primary school went to middle schools, which had been designed under Nkrumah to offer a few extra years of schooling to prepare poorer students for the upper levels, but which became a dead-end in the late 1960s and 1970s. The PNDC solved that problem by simply eliminating the middle school altogether. In its place, the government created the "junior secondary school" (JSS), a three-year school that combined the first three years of the old secondary schools with vocational and technical training intended to prepare students for the self-employment that, since the economic depression, was the only real employment option available to most of the poor.[66] The JSSs were dubbed "secondary schools of the village," and villagers, who associated vocational and technical training with well-paid work, greeted the new schools enthusiastically.[67]

The vocational aspect of the JSS education never reached its potential—the government never managed to provide the workshops it promised.[68] But it did provide academic and some vocational education to increasing numbers of students. It added more than a thousand schools and increased enrollment by 40 percent, with more than commensurate resources: per-student spending rose more than 150 percent from 1981 to 2000. And the new schools served one other purpose: they helped lower the advantage elite children had in gaining access to secondary school. In Section 5, I noted that, prior to the introduction of the JSS, students in elite "special schools" were taught curricula specifically designed to help them pass the CEE to secondary school, and applied to secondary school from primary grade 6 instead of middle school. But the introduction of JSS applied to all schools, including special schools: students there now were required to complete the same curriculum as everyone else.[69] (For a time, the government even forbade private schools from charging special fees and tried to force private schools to use the same GES teachers who taught in the public schools—though these measures were revoked after vehement protests from well-connected parents.[70])

The government fought a constant battle to keep public primary and new junior secondary schools free. Even with new materials and new or better school buildings, and even with increased per-student spending, the improvements often fell short of what parents wanted, and in the 1990s, in an effort to raise more resources, many schools began surreptitiously charging fees for incidental expenses—uniforms, books, activities fees, etc. The government took steps to combat these fees: in 1996, it introduced fCUBE: "free"—that is, fee-free—"Compulsory Universal Basic Education," and afterward conceived of a "capitation grant," a grant to schools for each student to cover the fees.[71] But schools continued to complain of a lack of resources and fees were continually an issue.

Nonetheless the reforms completely transformed the lower levels, improving their quality and vastly expanding their reach, particularly for the poor. By the World Bank's 2003 survey, 92 percent of those who entered the first year of primary completed junior secondary school (grade 9). In 1988 only 60 percent of the poorest quintile attended school; by 2003 it was 77 percent. (Of the top quintile, 80 percent attended in 1988; 94 percent in 2003.) Differences in test scores between poor and wealthy students declined, and the gender gap was completely eliminated (World Bank 2004a).

EXPANDING THE UPPER LEVELS

At the upper levels the story was far different. The previously elite system of secondary schools and universities was forced to take on thousands of new students without commensurate new resources.

Initially, with the government focused on the primary and the new junior secondary schools, the traditional secondary schools, accustomed to lavish government attention, were neglected. With the introduction of the JSS, the curriculum at the traditional secondary schools, now known as "senior secondary schools" (SSS) was reduced to three years. By 1992 real spending on these SSSs was only three percent higher than in 1988.

Yet as the lower levels improved, increasing numbers of students were graduating from JSSs and seeking admission to SSSs, and the PNDC was eager to give as many of them admission as possible. At the turn of the decade the PNDC began a massive building campaign that would eventually almost double the number of secondary schools in Ghana. In 1988 there were 241 secondary schools in Ghana, enrolling 146,000 students; by 1991 there were 404, enrolling 200,000 students, and by 2000 there were 464. Fees were lowered, and under new government regulations secondary schools both new and old were required to reserve at least 30 percent of their places for residents of their immediate communities.[72] And in keeping with the PNDC's emphasis on providing practical education, SSS curricula, which had always been proudly academic, were revised to include vocational courses—though, as with the JSSs, the government often had difficulty providing the necessary equipment. In fact, as the government continued to pour its resources into the lower levels, per-student spending on SSSs fell by a fifth from its 1981 level. Table 5.17 shows the statistics on schools, enrollments, and spending over the 1981–2000 period.

Harder hit were the universities, the highly subsidized oases where privileged children had trained to be privileged bureaucrats. In 1988, on a recommendation from its "University Rationalization Committee," the PNDC removed all food and living subsidies from university students, instead agreeing to loan students the money at subsidized rates. Later, tuition was introduced. Per-student spending fell by half, as the government forced the universities to take on tens of thousands of new students: enrollment shot from a little over 8,000 in 1986 to more than 36,000 in 2000. (See Table 5.17.)

Table 5.17   **Opening the upper levels, 1981–2000**

	1981	1986	2000	Changes 1981–2000	Changes 1986–2000
Senior Secondary (Public Only)					
Number of Schools	205	233	464	+126.3%	+99.1%
Number of Students	113,157	130,007	204,626	+80.8%	+57.4%
Spending (millions of current ¢)	¢88[†]	¢3,500[††]	¢66,530		
(in millions of 2001 ¢)	¢61,321[†]	¢78,137[††]	¢88,422	+44.2%	+13.2%
Per Student (current ¢)	¢778[†]	¢26,923[††]	¢325,128		
(in 2001 ¢)	¢541,909[†]	¢601,023[††]	¢432,114	-20.3%	-28.1%
Universities (Public Only)					
Number of Schools	3	3	5	+66.7%	+66.7%
Number of Students	7,946	8,193	36,221	+355.8%	+342.1%
Spending (millions of current ¢)	¢101[†]	¢2,320[††]	¢111,385		
(in millions of 2001 ¢)	¢70,515[†]	¢51,798[††]	¢148,037	+109.9%	+185.8%
Per Student (current ¢)	¢12,735[†]	¢283,205[††]	¢3,075,153		
(in 2001 ¢)	¢8,874,240[†]	¢6,322,174[††]	¢4,087,050	-53.9%	-35.4%

Notes: [†] Spending data are for 1979 (school year 1978–79), the last year data are available until 1988.

[††] Spending data are from 1988, the closest year to 1986 for which data are available.

Much of the growth in enrollment was at the well-established universities. From 1988 to 2000, the University of Ghana's enrollment grew more than three-fold, from 3,700 students to almost 12,000; the University of Science and Technology grew almost as fast, from a little less than 3,500 to 9,500; and the University of Cape Coast grew almost six-fold, from 1,500 students in 1988 to 8,200 in 2000. The universities struggled to acclimate to the bulging enrollments:

students slept four or even eight to a dorm room, and class sizes rose into the hundreds. Professors saw their salaries eaten away by inflation and wistfully recalled the 1970s, when they had time to do research.[73] Unsurprisingly both students and professors protested vehemently and regularly went on strike. But the government was insistent. In the 1995–1996 academic year, the government even closed the universities in the face of a strike, even though the following year was an election year. The government knew that its efforts to open the universities to the masses only made it more popular with its poor vital constituency.[74]

But in addition to offering more places in existing universities, the government took further steps to increase access to tertiary-level education. In the Northern Region—a long-neglected area of the country that was a key source of PNDC support—the government founded an entirely new university, the University of Development Studies. It also formed a second new "University College of Education" from a group of existing specialty post-secondary colleges in Winneba, and it upgraded to tertiary status eight public polytechnics (Ayisi 2001; World Bank 2004a). It also encouraged the growth of a few private tertiary institutions in fields where there was excess demand—institutions which helped siphon from the public universities, which had nowhere near the prestige of the public universities, upper-class students who could afford to pay.

The expanded access had an impact. Of the 50 senior secondary schools that provided 58 percent of admissions to the University of Ghana in 1999, only 35 had been top providers of admissions in 1985, before the reforms. In 1985 these 50 schools made up nearly a fifth of all the secondary schools from which any students gained admission to the University of Ghana; in 1999, they were only 7 percent of the secondary schools from which any students gained admission (Addae-Mensah 2000).[75] The best secondary schools still gave students a substantial leg up, but the boost was not nearly as high as it had been.

THE WORLD BANK'S ROLE

The World Bank and other donors were enthusiastic backers of these developments: they fit perfectly with the Bank's prevailing preference for investments in primary education in poorer countries.[76] But their roots in the PNDC/NDC's political logic were not lost on the World Bank. That is, if the reforms just described seem in general to be just what the Ghanaian government would have wanted to do to serve the vital constituency I described in the Section 6—laying off redundant bureaucrats, improving the primary schools, expanding access at the upper levels— the World Bank noticed it too. While the World Bank counts Ghana's education reforms as a crowning achievement, it does not over-estimate its influence in effecting them. In its 2004 evaluation of its educational aid to Ghana, it concluded that "[t]he strong commitment showed by government, and firm actions it took to implement the reforms, demonstrate the high degree of ownership.

In that favorable context, the Bank's financing reinforced the government's position" (World Bank 2004a, xvi), and that "the reforms made sense given the political position of the ruling Provisional National Defense Council (PNDC) at the time" (World Bank 2004a, 26).

And while there was a great deal of convergence between the Bank's recommendations and the PNDC's political logic, the overlap was not complete, and where they did not overlap Ghana simply did not adopt the World Bank's recommendations. In the previous chapter I noted that Taiwan picked selectively from the advice it received on implementing "manpower planning"—making use only of the advice that served the firms in its vital constituency. In the same way, the PNDC did not allow the Bank's counsel or aid to interfere with its service to its vital constituency. For instance, the PNDC gladly removed the subsidies to university students, but it was loath to introduce similar user fees for the primary level, which the World Bank also wanted. The Bank eventually gave up this point, and in 1996 the Ghanaian government explicitly adopted its fCUBE policy. The lesson of Ghana, like Taiwan, is that a government accepts international help when that help serves its vital constituency or when it can manipulate that help to serve its vital constituency.

SELECTIVE WORKER TRAINING

The final element of the PNDC/NDC's education system was its revitalization of Selective Worker Training. Under the PNDC, reforms to Ghanaian education were driven mostly by demand for education by citizens, not employers.[77] Nonetheless, after Ghana's economy began to revive, there was some need for skilled workers. Of the groups in the PNDC/NDC's vital constituency, two were employers who needed skilled workers: foreign companies and the PNDC government itself. As Ghana's labor market remained highly inflexible in this period, these employers' demand were for Selective Worker Training. This the government provided by expanding the number of students who could be accommodated in the existing network of technical institutes, which, as noted in Section 5, became dilapidated by the 1970s. After 1986 enrollment in technical institutes increased by more than 50 percent to 15,000, while real per-student spending rose by more than 40 percent. Table 5.18 shows the statistics. In addition foreign companies with particular needs, such as mining companies, often provided their own, specialized training with government subsidies, as did many of the more skill-intensive public corporations—like the Volta Aluminum Company (Valco), which put all its workers through a two-year training course. Among economists in Ghana there is a general sense that Ghanaian employers have access to the skilled workers they need.[78]

In fact, the government did make some efforts to expand technical and vocational education in the 1980s, even beyond the addition of courses to junior and senior secondary schools. In 1991 the government formed a new National Coordinating Committee for Technical and Vocational Education and Training

Table 5.18 **Technical institutes (public only), 1981–2000**

	1981	1986	2000	Changes 1981–2000	Changes 1986–2000
Number of Schools	20	26	23	+15.0%	−11.5%
Number of Students	—*	9,988	15,078	—	+51.0%
Spending (millions of current ¢)	¢6†	¢216††	¢7,797		
(in millions of 2001 ¢)	¢4,052†	¢4,817††	¢10,363	+155.7%	+115.1%
Per Student (current ¢)	—*	¢21,606††	¢517,136		
(in 2001 ¢)	—*	¢482,323††	¢687,303	—	+42.5%

Notes: * Enrollment data for technical institutes are unavailable after 1976–77 (enrollment for that year is 8,500). † Spending data are for 1979 (school year 1978–79), the last year data are available until 1988.

†† Spending data are from 1988, the closest year to 1986 for which data are available.

(NACVET) to try to regulate all aspects of technical and vocational training—which included everything from the public technical institutes to informal apprenticeships and small private schools teaching specific skills—and to integrate these with industry needs. But workers had a tough time finding work—companies didn't need them—and the committee eventually decided that all it could do was "help the graduates become self-employed,"[79] much like the JSS and SSS training was intended to do.

WRAPPING UP

This section described the transformation of the Ghanaian education system under the PNDC, and its successor the NDC, from Top-Down to Bottom-Up. That type of transformation is what this framework predicts. Table 5.19 is the evidence summary for the period 1981–2000.

The framework is accurate about most of the specifics. The PNDC radically reformed Ghana's education system, making efforts to improve the primary schools physically and academically, provide materials, improve teacher training, expand schooling in previously-neglected areas, remove the tracking that had allowed "special school" students to apply to secondary school early, and increase per-student spending. At the upper levels, the government expanded access while lowering subsidies and per-student spending.

On some of the specifics the framework is not as accurate. Bowing to elite pressure, the government did not completely eliminate subsidies to university

Table 5.19 **Evidence summary, 1981–2000**

Indicator	Characteristics	Conforms to Framework?
A. Enrollment	Increasing at all levels; biggest proportional increases at the upper levels	■
B. Per-student spending	Increasing at lower levels; decreasing at upper levels	■
C. The toolkit		
1. Schools	Increasing quality at lower levels; decreasing quality at upper levels as schools packed increasing enrollments into the same facilities	■
Teachers	Lower levels: increases and improvements in teacher training; increases in supervision; but limited in effect by teacher resistance	◻
	Upper levels: wages eroded by inflation; increasing responsibilities and class sizes	■
Physical resources	Increasing at lower levels; decreasing at upper levels	■
Location	Expansion of all levels into previously underserved areas (particularly rural areas at the primary level)	■
2. Fees[†]	Primary: free	■
	Higher levels: increasing fees, decreasing assistance, but government subsidized loans	◻
3. Access restrictions and discriminatory pricing		
Quotas	None	
Exams	Exams regulate access between levels; elites have decreased but still important advantages in passing exams	◻
Financial aid	Loans for upper-level fees	◻
4. Tracking	The introduction of JSS is an explicit effort to remove tracking	■
5. Outsourcing (domestic or foreign; to firms or non-profits)	Elite schools remain at lower levels;[1] some private colleges in the 1990s; some elites continue to send their children to universities abroad	◻

Notes: ■: fully conforms to the framework; ◻: partly conforms to the framework; ◻: does not conform to the framework.

[†] Fees are for enrollment, books and other equipment, uniforms, activities, school improvements, etc.

[1] By the early millennium, there was an explosion in the growth of private primary schools: by 2003, a fifth of primary students were in private schools. But this explosion began around the end of the NDC's tenure: as late as 1998, private schools had only five percent of primary students (World Bank 2004a).

students; instead it instituted subsidized loans to help students afford the new fees. This decision is widely traced to the widespread protests that surrounded the removal of the subsidies, and was clearly an effort to preserve social stability. And as increasing numbers of students from the poorer ranks of the PNDC's vital constituency made it into the bulging universities, the loans helped them, too. Nonetheless the loans did offer assistance to elite students, which is not what the framework predicts. Likewise, while the government took steps to eliminate the tracking that had allowed elite students from "special schools" substantial advantages in gaining access to secondary schools and universities—the government forced all students, including private students, to go through the same junior secondary school curriculum, and it increased the number of places at the secondary schools and the universities to allow more of the poor access—elite students maintain huge advantages to this day. The top 50 secondary schools, to which elites are much more likely to gain admission, still account for the majority of admissions to Ghana's universities. The framework predicts that the government would have done more to level the playing field.

Lastly, teachers held back the progress of the reforms. In Ghana, as in Taiwan, teachers were one of the least malleable aspects of the education system. Their resistance to reforms was perhaps unavoidable, as teachers went from being largely unsupervised to being asked to do more and harder work, often in the remotest parts of Ghana's rural regions. The government took steps to work around their resistance, training thousands of new teachers and insisting on new standards and supervision even of teachers who resisted. But since these efforts did not create a body of truly effective teachers for the vital constituency, they can only be considered partial evidence of the accuracy of the framework.

In a sense, all these disconnects are related to a single problem, to which I alluded at the start of this section: Ghana's massive reforms outstripped its capacity. It is not that the government did not do its best to level the playing field between elites and the poor, or develop a corps of effective teachers; it simply did not have the time or the resources to fully do the job.[80] In only a few years, the government completely reoriented its education system; and while it rapidly increased the proportion of economic output devoted to education—in 1986, before the reforms began, the government was spending 2.2 percent of GDP on education; by 2000 it was spending 4.6 percent—the speed of the reforms severely taxed the government's capacity for funding and implementation.

The reforms outstripped Ghana's capacity in another way: they exceeded the economy's capacity to make use of the flood of new graduates. Though hundreds of thousands were hired into the bureaucracy, private-sector employment increased little and the self-employment that fueled demand for the vocational side of junior secondary school remained the primary sort of employment awaiting most graduates. World Bank analysis shows today that the economic return to a primary or junior-secondary degree is, incredibly, zero (World Bank 2004a). And an astonishing 1999 survey of young people found "living, working, and sleeping on the streets of Accra," Ghana's capital, found that only seven percent had never attended school, while 40 percent had graduated from junior secondary school and 10 percent from senior secondary school (Amankrah et al. 1999). There is no doubt that Ghanaians wanted education when it was first offered to them: they saw education as a ticket to a good job and flocked to school in record numbers. But once it became clear that the number of skilled jobs had not increased nearly as fast as the number of school places, their demand softened: primary enrollment peaked in 1995, and thereafter declined as parents began to question the value of education. Today many new secondary schools sit virtually empty: 75 have student bodies of less than 100 (Addae-Mensah 2000). The last chapter ended with a discussion of the widespread dissatisfaction of Taiwanese with their education system, which tried to do too much and educated Taiwanese beyond what the Taiwanese economy could productively use. The same, unfortunately, may be said of Ghana.

8. Conclusion

At the start of this chapter I presented a figure, from the 2003 Ghana Core Welfare Indicators Survey, that sums up this chapter's argument. The argument is that the vital constituency—and in particular whether the government was affiliated with a political entrepreneur of the poor—explains education policy in Ghana. From 1951 to 2000, Ghana's educational development has gone through three periods. In the first, the Convention People's Party and Kwame Nkrumah, a cross-class political entrepreneur, built an All-Levels system. It made quality primary schooling widely available and expanded access to the upper levels, which elites had dominated under the British. But the 1966 coup ended Nkrumah's political entrepreneurship of the poor, and in the period thereafter, a string of elite governments transformed Ghanaian education into a Top-Down system, improving the upper levels and creating an elite track into them at the lower levels, while hollowing out the rest of the lower levels until they were little more than conduits for paychecks to teachers. Political entrepreneurship returned to Ghana in 1981, when J. J. Rawlings and his PNDC government began organizing the poor. An anti-elite political entrepreneur, Rawlings reversed the pattern of the preceding governments, transforming Ghanaian education into a Bottom-Up system that opened the elite upper levels while shifting resources into the lower levels to extend their reach and improve their quality. Today's Ghanaians are living testimony to these periods. In the Core Welfare Indicators Survey, those who were in primary school before 1966 and after 1981 achieved literacy at increasing rates. But literacy rates actually decline for those who were in primary school between 1966 and 1981—an incredible statistic, considering that literacy is highly heritable. This living evidence of a half century of Ghana's education policies encapsulates the argument.

Could these changes have been the result of the needs of Ghana's economy or of its regime type? Or, indeed, could they have been the result of collective action but not of political entrepreneurship—that is, could they have been the result of changes in the relative ease with which its poor could act collectively on their own, without the assistance of a political entrepreneur? I consider these alternative explanations in this concluding section.

THE NEEDS OF THE ECONOMY

Chapter 1 detailed the argument that education follows the economy's needs, or, in more-political form, that it will do so when its government is particularly committed to growth. Ghana is not a country that is usually held up as an example of either economically-optimal education or, more generally, of enlightened economic government (among my cases, that country was Taiwan). In the periods I examine, Ghana's education system has never been in synch with the economy's needs. For much of Ghana's modern history—specifically before 1966 and after 1981—government policy seemed to invest too *much* in education, at least from an economic perspective. In its early days, there are no rate of return studies, but economic advisors as eminent as W. Arthur Lewis warned Nkrumah of the impossibility of his plans for rapid industrialization, and it would only have been with the complete success of these plans that the Ghanaian economy would have been able to provide jobs for all the graduates of its expanding education system (Lewis 1953; Tignor 2006; Killick, Omaboe, and Szereszewski 1966). Indeed I noted above in Section 3 that Ghana's efforts in the 1960s at "manpower planning" were the opposite of Taiwan's, in the following respect: their goal was to create employment for all Ghana's educated workers, rather than the more traditional formula of educating enough workers to meet industry's needs. In the interim years, from 1966 to 1981, the government did reduce its emphasis on expanding education, but the concomitant shift in focus to upper-level academic education could hardly have been less suited to the country's weak and deteriorating economic situation. After 1981, the government returned the focus to the lower levels, which did coincide with the prevailing wisdom that poorer countries should invest in primary education.[81] But there is little doubt that even if these investments were of the right type, they went too far for the economy to handle. I noted in the previous section that the return on basic education in Ghana today is zero (World Bank 2004a). In other words, Ghana today faces the same problem it faced in the 1960s: an over-educated workforce.

REGIME TYPE

The regime-type argument is that more democratic governments are more likely to invest in mass education. This argument has several opportunities for confirmation in Ghana: the country has had three democratic periods, from 1969 to

1971, from 1979 to 1981, and after 1992 (Przeworski et al. 2000). But politically the regime-type periodization is not very meaningful. I have described how the coalition behind the democratically-elected Kofi Busia was virtually the same as of the autocratic National Liberation Council, which allowed and supervised his election (while barring the Convention People's Party from competing). The government of president Hilla Limann (1979–1981), which ruled for less than a year and a half, was also democratically elected, but again the military took a heavy hand in the election—Limann was the candidate of the People's National Party only after the Supreme Military Council banned the PNP founder from running for office— and the government's fragile and razor-thin one-vote majority in the legislature meant that it could not alienate elite groups in Ghana and thus continued to govern in their interest. The regime-type argument does best at predicting the constituency of Rawlings' NDC, which did indeed include the masses. But Rawlings built this constituency (as a political entrepreneur) a decade before the transition to democracy and long before his government envisioned democratization: again, the change in regime-type does not cause or even coincide with a change in the government's constituency.

Because regime type does not predict the government's constituency, it also does poorly at predicting education. Busia's government largely continued the educational policies of the NLC: investment in the upper levels and consolidation of the primary schools. Limann's PNP had little time in its short rule to do much with education. And Rawlings' NDC largely continued the educational trajectory initiated by its autocratic PNDC predecessor: investment in and expansion of the lower levels, and increasing access to the upper levels. The difficulty the regime-type argument has with Ghana's educational development is easily seen in Figure 5.1. Figure 5.2 shows the same data as in Figure 5.1, overlaid by Ghana's regime types. In the two early, short periods of democracy, the performance of primary schools is poorer than in the prior period—in the 1979–1981 period, performance is even declining—and in the longer period of democracy after 1992, performance increases but at the same rate begun more than a decade before.

COLLECTIVE ACTION WITHOUT POLITICAL ENTREPRENEURSHIP

Finally, it is worth considering whether the changes in Ghanaian education could have been due to changes in the inherent ability of Ghana's masses to act collectively regardless of whether they were receiving help from a political entrepreneur. Several important works in political science explain policymaking by looking to the inherent ability of groups to organize themselves (e.g., Bates 1981; Rogowski 1989; Rudra 2002, 2008). In particular, Ghana was one of the cases that Bates (1981) used in arguing that inherent collective action ability explains the urban bias in African agricultural policy: those living in urban areas have an easier time organizing themselves.

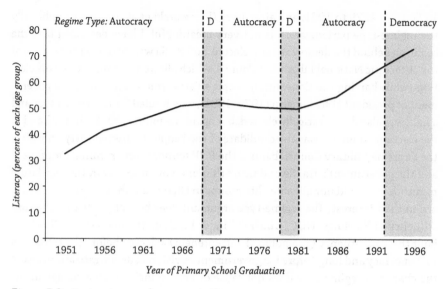

Figure 5.2 Regime type and progress in literacy

The problem with an argument purely about collective action, at least in Ghana, is that it is difficult to use it to explain over-time variation in education. Because it looks simply at collective-action advantage—and not at how an actor like a political entrepreneur can help a disadvantaged group to overcome its collective-action costs—the collective-action argument implies that policy should be elitist unless and until there is an increase in the inherent organizational capacity of the poor. I have presented evidence in this chapter that Ghana implemented mass education policies in the 1950s and 1960s, and again in the 1980s and 1990s. The collective-action argument provides no reason for these pro-poor periods, unless we can also argue that Ghanaian peasants had an easier time organizing themselves in the 1950s and 1980s than in the 1960s and 1970s. That is a difficult argument to make. In reality, peasants in Ghana have faced much the same organizational disadvantages ever since Ghana's independence, and if anything these disadvantages only grew worse in the economic depression of the 1970s—the period immediately before the mass education policies of the 1980s. Thus an argument purely based on collective action ability predicts that Ghana should have implemented elitist education policy since its founding—a prediction that is clearly at odds with the reality of Ghana's education.

Instead of alternate explanations, I argued in this chapter that the key to education policymaking in Ghana—as in Taiwan and Brazil—was political entrepreneurship of the poor and the labor market conditions faced by employers. Ghana's poor did face tremendous disadvantages in organizing; but with the help of two political entrepreneurs, they overcame these disadvantages and helped support governments in two long periods, from 1951 to 1966, and from 1981 to 2000. And because these governments depended on the poor's support, they invested in mass education.

CHAPTER 6

Brazil

Brazil is unequal. Regionally, its impoverished northeast lives in the shadow of the prosperous southeast, which, if it was its own country, would easily qualify for the ranks of the world's richest nations. Within each region, major cities boast wealthy downtowns of glass skyscrapers and $300-a-night hotel rooms but are ringed by slums lacking even basic sanitation. Until very recently, Brazil's Gini coefficient hovered at or over .6, a level surpassed only by a handful of other nations. In 1969, São Paulo, even then one of the most modern cities on earth, had an infant mortality rate of 84 per 1,000 births; in 1971, in Recifé, the northeast's most modern city, the rate was 264 per 1,000 births, 60 percent higher than the highest national rate—Chad's—recorded by the U.N. (United Nations 1968; IBGE 1972).

Brazil has also seen long periods of both democracy and autocracy. Since 1930, the year my analysis will begin, Brazil has been through three regime transitions. But unlike Ghana, which switched between autocracy and democracy over only a few years, each of Brazil's regime transitions—in 1945, 1964, and 1985—has led to a stable government. The continuous coups and instability of Ghana are largely absent from Brazil.

This inequality and institutional stability are Brazil's particular advantages as a case for testing the framework. I chose Taiwan, Ghana, and Brazil both because they allow for testing the framework in three very different settings, and because their differences allow for comparing the framework's accuracy to the common political-economic explanations of policymaking outlined in Chapter 1. For these common explanations, Brazil offers similar opportunities to Ghana, but arguably in an even more advantageous setting. Brazil's changes in regime type are not undone after only a few years or months but have time to settle and should have time to make their mark on policy. And, as in Ghana, Brazil's masses are scattered and impoverished, facing tremendous difficulties organizing themselves into a politically potent force.

Yet while Brazil's vast lower classes have always faced daunting collective-action challenges, Brazil has often invested heavily in mass education. Likewise, changes in Brazil's commitment to mass education change with its regime type in only one instance: 1964. Instead, the predictive factors in Brazil, as in Ghana and Taiwan, are political entrepreneurship of the poor and the labor market conditions faced by employers. Brazil has had two periods of cross-class political entrepreneurship. The first was from 1930 to 1964. After Brazil's Revolution of 1930, Getúlio Vargas and unions organized urban workers; thereafter workers joined elites in a cross-class vital constituency until 1961 and formed the vital constituency on their own for a brief period from 1961 to 1964. From 1964 to 1990, there was no political entrepreneurship and elites ruled unchallenged. But again in the 1990s, unions and their political party, the PT, organized workers, peasants, and the urban poor. Although the PT did not take over the national government until after 2000, when my analysis ends, they were making significant inroads with state governments in the 1990s and using them to change Brazilian education. Thus from 1930 to 1961, federal policy was geared to providing an urban All-Levels system that served industrial elites and workers with education, and left everyone else out. After 1964, an elite government transformed Brazilian education into a Top-Down system. And in the 1990s, the system began, very gradually, to return to an All-Levels system—but this time one that served most of Brazil's population in both urban and rural areas.

These policies were how Brazilian governments served the families in their vital constituencies. What of employers? Chapter 2 argued that their demands depend upon the flexibility of the labor market faced by those employers who need skilled workers. Brazil's heavily state-led and unionized skilled labor market has always been inflexible (Birdsall, Bruns, and Sabot 1996),[1] and thus Brazilian employers have always been Type *S*, demanding "Selective Worker Training"— worker training that trains just the number and type of workers that employers need, and trains them well. We will see in this chapter that Selective Worker Training is indeed what the government provided.[2]

Table 6.1 summarizes Brazil's vital constituencies.

As in previous chapters, I present three types of evidence: enrollments, spending, and the education toolkit. In Brazil, the toolkit is an especially important piece of the story, because Brazil's governments have not always treated its education system as a tool for education. Instead during long periods some parts of Brazilian education have been little more than means of delivering jobs and construction contracts to political supporters, similar to what the lower levels of Ghanaian education became in the 1970s. These parts of the system have not provided "education" in any recognizable sense of the word. The government's intention comes across clearly from its decision-making on exams, teachers, financial aid, tracking, and the other elements of the toolkit.

Brazil differs from Ghana and Taiwan in scale, and its government has a federal structure. During periods when there was little political entrepreneurship in Brazil, I present evidence that federalism did not have much of an effect on Brazilian education: state policy echoed the elitism of federal policy. But during several

Table 6.1 **Vital constituencies in Brazil**

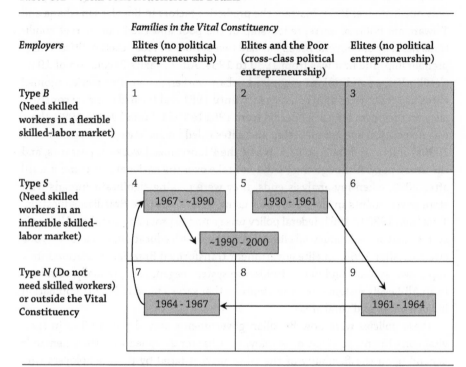

	Families in the Vital Constituency		
Employers	Elites (no political entrepreneurship)	Elites and the Poor (cross-class political entrepreneurship)	Elites (no political entrepreneurship)
Type *B* (Need skilled workers in a flexible skilled-labor market)	1	2	3
Type *S* (Need skilled workers in an inflexible skilled-labor market)	4 1967 - ~1990	5 1930 - 1961 ~1990 - 2000	6
Type *N* (Do not need skilled workers) or outside the Vital Constituency	7 1964 - 1967	8	9 1961 - 1964

Note: The period ~1990–2000 straddles boxes 4 and 5 because the transition between vital constituencies was gradual and ongoing in this period.

periods state governments were affiliated with political entrepreneurs while the federal government was not, and policy in these states diverged from federal policy. For example, as the federal government in Brasília in the 1960s was pursuing a Top-Down education policy, the state government in São Paulo was for a short time still affiliated with a cross-class political entrepreneur, and was consequently making All-Levels education policies—until the Brazilian federal government succeeded in stopping the political entrepreneurship. Once the PT began to gain control of state governments in the 1990s, the education policy in the states that it controlled began to diverge again from federal policy. I illustrate the effects of this state-level political entrepreneurship by focusing on education in two states: São Paulo, and Bahia. These two provide wide variation on important economic and political dimensions. São Paulo is Brazil's richest and largest state: it has more than a fifth of the country's population and alone produces a third of its GDP; at R$15,000 (US$7,000), its per-capita GDP is 50 percent higher than Brazil's average. Bahia, in past centuries the most important state in Brazil, is today archetypal of the poor northeast: with 8 percent of the country's population, it produces only 4 percent of Brazil's GDP; its per-capita GDP is a bit more than half of Brazil's average, and a third of São Paulo's. São Paulo is a sleek, modern state with a large and relatively efficient, if sometimes corrupt, government, which is often at odds with federal administrations in Brasília, while for four decades Bahia's government was a personality cult run, through various official and unofficial capacities, by one man, and was closely aligned with, and an important source of support for, most federal governments in Brasília. In this chapter I incorporate the politics and education policies of these two states into the discussion to illustrate the effects of differences in political entrepreneurship at the state level.

This chapter has nine sections. The first section describes the scene in politics and education in 1930, when Brazil's "pioneer" government—the first government to try to create a modern education system—took power. The second begins my analysis by considering the politics of the vital constituency of that pioneer government, which governed Brazil for three decades, until 1961. The third section considers the education policies of the pioneer government. Section 4 looks briefly at the politics and education policies of the short period of worker ascendancy, from 1961 to 1964, when a coup brought the military to power. Sections 5–8 then examine politics and education in the remaining two periods: 1964–1990 and 1990–2000. The last section concludes and compares the performance of the framework to the alternate explanations of policymaking.

1. The Scene in 1930[3]

Before I begin the analysis, this section sets the stage by outlining what came before 1930: in economics, politics, and in education.

The Revolution of 1930 was a revolution of the modern, urban middle class against the old agricultural order.[4] That order was of a small class of agrarian oligarchs and a tiny bureaucracy that managed their affairs.[5] The power of the oligarchs was centuries old and rooted in an economy that was almost purely agricultural—before World War I, 95 percent of Brazil's exports were of four products: coffee, rubber, sugar, and cocoa. The tiny elite dominated the country's politics, but they were not a coherent group. The elites of the coffee-growing south competed against the sugar-growing north, and elites in the various states of the south competed against each other. Just below the elites were a second group, a tiny bureaucratic middle class who administered the country and the economy. They received their positions through elite patronage; Pereira (1984) calls them the "parasitical middle class" because of their reliance on the elites. Though Brazil from 1891 to 1930 was technically a "republic," in which only those who could read and owned land could vote, and which for decades kept control firmly in the hands of the elites and this parasitical middle class. These two groups—the elites and the parasitical middle class—were Brazil's vital constituency on the eve of the Revolution of 1930.[6]

The revolution was facilitated by limited economic modernization in the early twentieth century that gave birth to a new middle class. The modernization began with a shift in economic importance from sugar to coffee, and therefore from the northeast to the southeast. In the sixteenth and seventeenth centuries, sugar, produced by huge, semi-feudal slave plantations in the northeast, was the dominant product, but in the eighteenth century the sugar industry suffered from fierce competition from new production centers in the Antilles. At the same time coffee production grew in Brazil's southeast. In the centuries of sugar dominance, the colonial capital was in Salvador, in the modern state of Bahia—one of the states whose education policies this chapter will examine. But as Brazil's economic center shifted south, so did its political center: in the mid-eighteenth century the capital moved to Rio de Janeiro, in the southeast, and after 1891, when Brazil became a republic,[7] Brazil was ruled by a series of "coffee presidents" from the southeastern states.

These coffee oligarchs preferred local control and a minimum of meddling from the federal government and each other: the "coffee presidents" alternated among the São Paulo and Minas Gerais by tacit agreement,[8] and the federal government did little other than facilitate the agricultural economy. Its primary activities were national defense; providing investment in needed infrastructure, largely from foreigners[9]; and securing agricultural profits. In the decades before the Revolution of 1930, the government was especially active in securing agricultural profits: after 1906, when over-production of coffee was leading to worldwide price slumps, the federal government began to buy excess coffee and maintain the international price.

The shift from sugar to coffee fueled some limited economic modernization. The coffee regions invested in infrastructure—particularly railroads to bring the coffee to port—and, unlike sugar oligarchs, coffee oligarchs often found it more economical to produce through tenant farming, leading to the emergence of a tiny domestic market and the beginnings of modern commerce. In 1888 slavery was abolished, and sugar plantations in the northeast switched to wage labor. Yet the modernization was limited. Agricultural oligarchs were blessed with high international prices and abundant labor, which allowed them to keep tenant farmers in the southeast and wage laborers in the northeast at near subsistence. By some estimates profits from coffee were as high as 80 percent (Evans 1979), and after 1891 Brazil's per-capita GDP grew faster even than in the United States. In such an environment, the oligarchs felt little pressure to modernize. Brazil produced coffee in 1930 much as it had in 1830, and aside from some peripheral production of non-durable goods—textiles, food, furniture—domestic industry was nonexistent; most durable goods were imported.

Though modernization proceeded at a snail's pace, it did, by the early twentieth century, create a new urban middle class underneath the traditional elites—a class that resented the elites' hold on the government and its largesse. Partly the new middle class was made up of immigrants. The growth of coffee fueled immigration of workers from the declining sugar regions in the northeast and from outside Brazil. After 1880, 4.2 million immigrated, mostly from Japan and Europe. Half went to São Paulo, the state that benefited most from the coffee boom (and the other of the two states whose education policies I examine in this chapter). By 1930, the population of the city of São Paulo was approaching one million (Schwartzman 1989). These immigrants generally brought with them skills and entrepreneurial ambition, and found the *clientelism* of the coffee governments frustrating.[10] The new middle class also included the junior-officer corps of the military, which dates to the Paraguayan War (1864–1870) during which Brazil created a professionalized, national army (Pereira 1984).

The new middle classes gained economic importance during World War I. The war cut off Brazil's access to British imports; to help fill the void, domestic light industrial production doubled during the war. Simultaneously the war reduced world demand for coffee and prices fell, weakening the oligarchs. In 1929, worldwide depression led to another collapse in the price of coffee and a further weakening of the elites. In the past the federal government might have intervened to prop up the domestic price of coffee, but this time it did not—even though the president, Washington Luis, was a Paulista (a native of São Paulo) and himself a coffee planter.[11] Elites instead fought with each other over who would be the next president: Paulistas insisted on keeping the office for themselves, rather than rotating it to Minas Gerais, as would have been customary. Frail and divided, the elites were ill-equipped to resist the ambition of the new middle class. In 1930, the middle class ran their own candidate, and when he again lost an election widely recognized as fraudulent, they revolted and put him in power anyway.[12] That candidate was Getúlio Vargas, the man who would dominate Brazilian national politics for the coming quarter-century.[13]

The Revolution of 1930 marks the end of the rule of the agrarian oligarchs and introduces a federal government that includes, for the first time, the new middle classes, who considered education an investment in future earnings. Thus it is in 1930 that this book's framework should begin to predict Brazil's education policies: Vargas's government is Brazil's "pioneer." The remainder of this section will consider the kind of education system his government inherited.

For much of Brazilian history prior to 1930, education was scarce and oriented toward the training of the "parasitical middle class," as well as providing gentlemen's education for elites who liked the trappings of scholarship. In 1822, when Brazil became independent from Portugal under Emperor Pedro, the country already had several institutions of higher education, including a military academy in Rio de Janeiro, two law schools in São Paulo and Recifé, and medical schools in Rio de Janeiro and Salvador, the capital of Bahia. Elementary education was limited, left to provincial governments, or, more often, to private tutors and Jesuit priests. The first public secondary school, the Colégio Dom Pedro II, was established in Rio de Janeiro in 1838, but secondary schooling remained rare as most gentlemen preferred to get their education back in Europe (Schwartzman 2003). Those outside the elite had little or no access to education: at least

85 percent of the population was completely illiterate, and most of the remainder could not write (Castro 1973).

But as the modern middle and industrial classes grew, urban governments began expanding education. Incipient modernization meant that, in the cities, good jobs were increasingly demanding skills. This educational expansion concentrated on primary and technical education; secondary and higher education still served the elite, and expanded little. On the eve of the 1930 revolution, the system was still very limited, but it had come a long way. I could not find comprehensive statistics on the education system for the late 1920s, but detailed surveys were made of the system in 1912. Table 6.2 summarizes these, and Table 6.3 presents more limited statistics for the eve of the Revolution of 1930. The detailed surveys from 1912 record 50 institutions of higher education (6 federal, 5 state, and 39 private; 1 school of philosophy, 15 law schools, 21 medical schools, and 13 polytechnics), 299 professional schools (31 federal, 52 state, 14 municipal, and 202 private; 50 seminaries, 58 pedagogical schools, 29 liberal arts schools, 89 industrial schools, 33 agricultural schools, 38 commercial schools, and 2 naval academies), and 24 public secondary schools (2 federal, 21 state, and 1 municipal). The surveys include primary schools from only one area, the Federal District of Rio de Janeiro, which had 584 primary schools: 342 municipal and 242 private.

Table 6.2 shows an education system with low enrollment, heavily provided by local and state governments and by the private sector. But it also shows a system of high quality—with low student-teacher ratios and substantial, and relatively equitable, spending—as well as a heavy focus on professional and technical education. Per-student spending was higher on professional students than students in higher education.[14] Spending also reflects a pattern that profoundly affected the later development of Brazilian education: heavy subsidizing of private education. About a fifth of the public spending went to private schools in the form of scholarships and subsidies (Brazil 1927).

Vargas inherited from his predecessors an education system that was still clearly elitist, but whose lower levels were growing fast, fueled by demand from the new urban middle classes and the support of local governments. The Revolution of 1930 brought the federal government under the control of these new middle classes for the first time; thus, by the book's framework, Vargas's government should have developed an All Levels system to serve them. Section 3 will show that the government did indeed build such a system. But first, Section 2 examines the vital constituency of the 1930–1961 period.

2. POLITICS, 1930–1961: Getúlio Vargas

This is the era of Getúlio Vargas. The Revolution of 1930 was the ascendancy of the new middle classes (Pereira 1984), and in its aftermath Vargas built an enduring cross-class alliance. The alliance consisted of workers, the military, and

Table 6.2 **Education in 1912**

	Primary (RJ*)	*Secondary*	*Professional*	*Higher*
Schools	584	24	299	50
Federal		2	31	6
State		21	52	5
Municipal	342	1	14	
Private	242	—	202	39
Students	74,714	4,153	29,472	8,879
Federal		361	4,866	3,818
State		3,738	8,663	658
Municipal	52,843	54	2,397	
Private	21,871	—	13,546	4,403
Teachers	2,156	431	2,859	1,040
Federal		48	430	366
State		364	592	94
Municipal	1,356	19	254	
Private	800		1,583	580
Average Student: Teacher Ratio	35	10	10	9
Federal		8	11	10
State		10	15	7
Municipal	39	3	9	
Private	27	—	9	8
Spending in current Rs	7,984,875,920	4,811,393,771	10,813,933,381	2,814,076,974
Public	6,497,896,829			
Private	1,486,979,091			
Spending in 2004 R$[†]	34,683,512	20,899,014	46,971,950	12,223,368
Public	28,224,594			
Private	6,458,918			
Spending per student (Rs)	—[††]	—[†††]	366,922	316,936
Spending per student (2004 R$)	—	—	1,594	1,377

Notes: * Covers only primary schools in the Federal District of Rio de Janeiro. [†] Figures were converted to 2004 R$ using deflators from IPEA (2006). [††] Per-student primary spending cannot be calculated without total primary enrollment, which is not available for 1912. [†††] Since a substantial portion of the budget subsidized private schools, figures on per-student average spending cannot be calculated without data on the number of students in private secondary schools, which isn't available.

Table 6.3 **Education in 1930**

| | Primary | Secondary | Professional | | | Higher* |
			Industrial	Commercial*	Pedagogic	
Schools	33,049	1,145	151	466*	211	150*
Enrollment	2,084,954	72,541	21,052	46,629*	29,168	15,343*

Notes: * Commercial and Higher use figures from 1929 (1930 is unavailable).

an emerging industrial class of professionals and entrepreneurs. Workers in the lower rungs of the alliance had severe collective action disadvantages, and to them Vargas was a political entrepreneur, assisting their organization through unions and a political party. And between the two groups Vargas was a remarkably successful arbiter, developing a corporatist arrangement that benefited both and spurred Brazil's economic development. This vital constituency remained largely intact for three decades, through, among other things, a transition to democracy in 1945. It ended only when, in 1961, workers and industrialists found they could no longer reconcile their differences, and industrialists linked up with the agrarian elites whom the Revolution of 1930 had deposed.

But Vargas's cross-class alliance was uniquely limited. Unlike the cross-class alliances we saw in Ghana and Taiwan, it did not include the very poor. It did not include the vast ranks of the peasantry—the agricultural workforce of former slaves and tenant farmers—and it did not include Brazil's growing urban poor—peasants who had emigrated to the cities in search of better work. Likewise, quite naturally, it did not include the pre-1930 agricultural oligarchy—the landowners and their "parasitical" middle class—whose power the revolution sought to end. While for the purpose of this book the vital constituency is cross-class, it should also be understood as an urban vital constituency that left out Brazil's rural classes—both the rural elites and the rural poor, including those rural poor who became the urban poor.

The newly ascendant urban middle classes were hardly a homogeneous group, and although they stayed Brazil's vital constituency for three decades, their political power was never fully secure. First, it was threatened from without. The rural masses were disorganized, poor, and not much of a threat, but the agrarian elites were hardly defeated. In 1932 these elites launched a counter-revolt in their stronghold of São Paulo, and fought off federal troops for four months. The vital constituency also faced internal divisions. Early on, a far-left section of the middle class had ambitions for organizing Brazilians around a communist revolution, and fought, often openly, with more nationalist members of the middle class associated with the military and the Catholic Church, which initially was a key supporter of the revolution.[15]

Getúlio Vargas dealt deftly with these divisions and gradually secured political stability through a series of power consolidations. He initially was appointed "provisional president," an office he held for four years, during which time he kept his fractious middle class together by focusing them on writing a new constitution. He also marshaled the military into service to counter the oligarchs. As elected president under the new 1934 constitution, he used the disgruntled leftists in his coalition to further solidify his control. Realizing that Vargas's commitments to a establishing a communist state were less than heartfelt, the leftists launched a series of revolts nationwide in 1935. These revolts were easily put down, but Vargas used the threat of them as a guise for declaring a state of emergency. In 1937, he dissolved the Congress entirely and ruled until 1945 as dictator of the fascist "New State" (*Estado Novo*).

During these years, Vargas built the organizational capacity of workers and developed an economic policy that served both workers and industrialists. The major vehicle for organizing workers was the union.[16] New laws made unionization easy (Pereira 1984), but unions were organized sectorally and hierarchically under government control. Most strikes were illegal, and the government practiced a corporatism by which it regularly raised wages and benefits but simultaneously kept a lid on worker demands.[17]

The emerging professional and industrial classes were also organized, and catered to. In fact, Vargas's government organized a large portion of society in hierarchical organizations: in addition to labor unions, there were business associations and professional bodies, whose members were admitted through stringent certification (Schwartzman 2003). Professionals and industrialists were also well-served. Many professionals found employment in the bureaucracy, which, under Vargas, became regulated by strictly meritocratic examinations. And industry was served with Import-Substitution Industrialization.[18] In 1931 Vargas banned imports in industries with over-production; the government also devalued the currency, raising the price of imports. Industrial entrepreneurs—the majority of whom were recent immigrants[19]—quickly moved in to capitalize: in an environment of suddenly unsatisfied demand, even small workshops, begun with little more capital than one family might raise, grew to meet demands for foodstuffs and other consumer goods, as well as light machinery. Brazilian industrial production grew 27 percent between 1929 and 1935, and 43 percent from 1935 to 1940; in the 1930s, more than 12,000 new industrial establishments were launched, 2.5 times as many as in the previous decade.[20] Thereafter growth slowed somewhat—Brazilian industry was still highly dependent on imported machinery, the supply of which was disrupted by World War II—but production still grew 30 percent between 1940 and 1944 (Pereira 1984).

The corporatist policies spurred economic growth: from 1934 to 1945, annual growth in real per-capita GDP averaged 2.9 percent—a feat, considering that the population was also growing by almost 2 percent a year. Yet mostly the growth touched employed Brazilians in urban areas—a very small proportion of the population. (The 1940 Census found only 12 percent of the population economically active in urban areas (IPEA 2006).) Outside of the major cities, which were concentrated in the South, the rural peasantry was virtually untouched by the government (Skidmore and Smith 1997). The rural elite continued to produce their valuable export products, but each was regulated by an administrative body *(autarquia)* that controlled production and price. For example, the National Coffee Council, established in 1931, sought to maximize export earnings from coffee by alternately buying and destroying excess coffee and expanding production to increase Brazil's share of the world coffee market (Pereira 1984; Ashworth-Gorden 1980).[21]

But despite this economic success, the vital constituency was growing dissatisfied with Vargas's increasingly autocratic *Estado Novo*. The *Estado Novo* was a police state, if a fairly benign one: Vargas banned political parties, instituted censorship, and established a centralized police force that jailed political dissidents. Vargas shrewdly sensed the vital constituency's growing dissatisfaction and eventually attempted to engineer a liberalization that would allow him to remain in power. Using the excuse of the ending of World War II, in which Brazil was nominally one of the Allies, Vargas declared an end to the *Estado Novo* and a return to democracy, with amnesty for political prisoners and legalization of opposition political parties.

In preparation for Brazil's Second Republic, the two ends of Vargas's vital constituency formed two political parties: the Social Democratic Party (*Partido Social Democrático;* PSD), representing the salaried middle class and the new industrial elite; and the Brazilian Workers' Party (*Partido Trabalhista Brasileiro;* PTB), a union-based workers' party. The agrarian elite formed the National Democratic Union (*União Democrática Nacional;* UDN). (The Communists, though diminished from their years of repression under the *Estado Novo,* also formed a party.)

Vargas intended to run for president, but the military, which saw itself partly in a guardian role, felt that Vargas had stayed long enough; they intervened with a bloodless coup in 1945. But the coup was only to ensure democratic elections: the military had no desire to stay in power. And although Vargas was initially barred from running for president, a general whom he supported was elected in 1945, and then in 1950 Vargas himself was elected again by a wide margin. Together the two wings of his coalition, the PSD and the PTB, also regularly won a majority of seats in both houses of the Congress and governed together as the National Parliamentary Front.

Brazil's industrialization after World War II continued largely as it had under the *Estado Novo* (Pereira 1984). Annual growth in real per-capita GDP from 1945 to 1954 averaged 3.8 percent. Again, the beneficiaries were workers and industrialists, at the expense of the rural poor and elite. For example, when coffee prices rebounded after World War II, the government channeled coffee profits into aggressive public investments using exchange rate controls, to the predictable dissatisfaction of the agrarian elites; after 1953 the government adopted a system of multiple exchange rates known as "exchange rate confiscation" (Paiva 1961; Pereira 1984).

Around 1950, sufficient information emerges from censuses and other sources for me to give more concrete dimensions to the vital constituency. These dimensions will be important in the next section in determining whether education policy served only the vital constituency. Using an analysis of the 1950 Brazilian census, Pereira's widely respected (1984) economic history of Brazil divided the country into five classes (Table 6.4).[22]

Pereira's classification is useful less for its exact numbers, which he admits are imprecise, as for the rough proportions it provides. Subtracting the lower classes (70 percent) and agrarian elites, who make up a small but unknowable proportion of the "upper" class, we can conclude that the vital constituency was a little less than 30 percent of the country.

Beginning in the 1950s, this vital constituency began to drift apart. The first problem was economic. Growing national debt and increasing inflation made simultaneous service to workers and the industrial elites increasingly difficult. After doubling the minimum wage in 1954, inflation, which had averaged 11 percent from 1939 to 1953, more than doubled to 26 percent, and Vargas was forced to dismiss his labor minister. Unrest followed, and an isolated Vargas committed suicide that summer.

The second problem was workers, who were emerging as an autonomous political force less dependent on government patronage and less interested in corporatist bargaining. Under the Vargas dictatorship, unions had been prevented from unifying across industries, but democratic Brazil had no such prohibition, and in the 1950s unions formed several alliances.[23] These were led not by government supporters but by a new union leadership bred on the factory floor (Pereira 1984). To their partners the industrialists, these new unions seemed threatening.

Table 6.4 **Social classes, defined by occupation, 1950**

	Population (in thousands)	Percentage
Lower (domestic employees, laborers, lower-ranked military)	11,638	70
Lower Middle (unskilled white collar, skilled workers in industry and commerce)	2,986	18
Middle (mid-level managers and military, supervisors, rural and urban craftspeople)	665	4
Upper Middle (professionals, independent intellectuals, military officers, directors and top management of businesses)	428	2
Upper (owners of businesses, agrarian elites)	779	6

Source: Pereira (1984, 59).

In the 1955 presidential election, workers (represented by the PTB) and the industrial elite (represented by the PSD) united one last time in support of Juscelino Kubitschek, the heir of Vargas's coalition. Kubitschek pushed rapid development that was heavily state-led: the government's share of gross capital formation grew from 28 percent in 1956 to nearly half in 1960. The most famous product of this investment was a new capital city, Brasília, but there are myriad others: a new road network connecting much of the country; hydroelectrics and expanded steel production; and the development of an auto industry, which by 1960 was producing 133,000 cars a year (up from zero in 1950) with more than 90 percent of their content made in Brazil (Evans 1979; Sobrinho 1985; Pereira 1984). Though they nearly bankrupted the government, these policies spurred growth in real GDP per-capita to more than 6 percent between 1956 and 1960 (IPEA 2006), and well-served both the industrial elites and workers.

Yet developments in this era also made further cooperation between workers and industrialists even more difficult. Industry felt hampered by high labor costs, which forced it to become excessively capital-intensive (Birdsall, Bruns, and Sabot 1996). At the same time, workers' ambition grew, fueled in part by industrial elites' rising wealth: in 1960, the ratio of mean income between the upper 20 percent and the bottom 40 percent of earners was 9:1 (World Bank 1979). Strikes became common; in 1960, 500,000 transportation and port workers struck to demand wages on par with the military's (Sobrinho 1985). And unions frightened industrialists by beginning to talk about fundamental reforms: fiscal, banking, and agrarian (Pereira 1984).

As workers and industrialists found less to like in each other, industrialists and the long-disempowered agrarian elites found their interests converging. By 1960, the economic dominance of the industrialists over the agrarian elites was largely unchallenged. In addition, in the late 1950s, overproduction sank world coffee prices. The government's "exchange confiscation" policy, which had formerly used high world coffee prices to transfer agrarian profits into industrialization, suddenly had little to gain from agrarian elites, who in turn had little to gain by opposing the government's policy. This meeting of minds of industrial and agrarian elites, combined with workers' ambitions, portended a defection of the industrial elites from their union with workers into a new union with agrarian elites, and, thereby, the end of the Vargas vital constituency of workers and industrialists.

The end of the Vargas vital constituency occurred in August of 1961. The presidential election of 1960 had brought to power Jânio Quadros, a compromise candidate acceptable to both workers and industrialists. But Quadros resigned in August of 1961, handing power to his vice president, João Goulart, a traditional friend of labor (he was Vargas's labor minister). It is with this transfer of power that the vital constituency split, and Goulart assumed power with an unstable vital constituency of only workers.

Thus it is August of 1961 that ends Brazil's first period. From 1930 to 1961, Brazil's vital constituency was a union of workers and a professional class that

Table 6.5 **The Vital Constituency of Brazil's pioneer government, 1930–1961**

Political Entrepreneur(s)	Groups in the Vital Constituency†	Groups outside the Vital Constituency
Getúlio Vargas, Unions, and the Brazilian Workers' Party (PTB)	Entrepreneurs-cum-Industrial Elites (Type S) Workers [Vargas/PTB] Bureaucracy Military	Agrarian Elites (Type N) Traditional Middle Class Peasants Urban Poor

Notes: † If a group was empowered with the help of a political entrepreneur, the entrepreneur is in brackets.

Employer types are in parentheses: Type S employers need skilled workers in an inflexible labor market; type N employers do not need skilled workers.

eventually came to include a new industrial elite. Vargas built this coalition, delivering political entrepreneurship to the workers through unions and a political party, the PTB, and engineering a corporatist bargain between workers and industrialists that served both and fueled Brazil's development. Table 6.5 shows the groups in the vital constituency.

The framework predicts that a cross-class alliance like Vargas's should have developed an All-Levels system of education to serve the primarily urban working and professional classes in its vital constituency.

3. EDUCATION, 1930–1961: The Development of Modern Education in Brazil

Vargas and his democratic heirs did indeed create an All-Levels system in Brazil. The system provided modern high-quality education to the new modern classes in Vargas's vital constituency, and it provided Selective Worker Training to the emerging industrialists. Because the vital constituency was limited, the education was as well: at the end of Vargas era in 1960, the primary enrollment rate was just 42 percent—just about what was required to serve the vital constituency but not those outside it.[24] This section details the system's development. I begin with primary education, and then consider the upper levels and Selective Worker Training.

PRIMARY EDUCATION

Education was intimately wrapped up in the modernizing creed of the Revolution of 1930. Its politicians and policymakers viewed modernizing education as part of modernizing Brazil (de Oliveira Romanelli 1978), and the Revolution made education a national priority for the first time (Schwartzman 2003). But Vargas's modernization of Brazilian education did not start entirely from scratch. By 1930, many state governments had vital constituencies that included the new middle classes, and they had begun to provide modern education: primary enrollment in 1930 was more than 2 million (Table 6.3). Because this education was mostly provided locally, it lacked uniformity or organization (Sobrinho 1985). The ascendance of Vargas simply elevated these demands to the federal level, bringing to power a government that wanted to provide modern education systematically. Rather than nationalizing the disparate local education systems, the new federal government instead tried to expand and rationalize those systems.[25] In 1930, only shortly after taking power, the new government established a new Ministry of Education and Health to administer Brazilian education,[26] and the constitution of 1934 provided for administrative and financial decentralization in education and appointed the federal government supervisor of the system. To guide the federal government in its supervision of the new system, the constitution required the government to develop a National Education Plan, and to make sure states and municipalities actually provided education the constitution obligated them to earmark 20 percent of their revenues for the education system; the federal government was required to spend 10 percent.[27]

Under the new framework, primary education expanded rapidly through 1938: from a decline of 3 percent in 1931, primary enrollment expanded by 2.5 percent in 1932 and by 7.3 percent in 1933; from 1933 to 1938, enrollment growth averaged 7 percent a year. Over the same period, the number of primary schools increased by 10,000, or by more than a third. Thereafter growth slowed and then stalled during the years of World War II. But in 1944 enrollments began to rise again, and growth averaged 5.2 percent annually through 1960. Most of the growth was in state and municipal primary schools; there were only a few federal schools enrolling less than half a percent of the total. Table 6.6 shows the system's development.

Yet this growth did not lead to universal enrollment; rather, it led to primary education for the middle classes—the vital constituency. The rapid expansion in the 1930s brought primary enrollment to 25.5 percent in 1940; a decade later, in 1950, it was even slightly lower, 24.1 percent.[28] Recall that in Section 2, I presented evidence from Pereira's (1984) analysis of the 1950 Census that the vital constituency was slightly less than 30 percent the population. Assuming that the vital constituency had children at the same or a slightly lower rate than the rest of the population,[29] the education system under Vargas would have done a good job of providing primary education to the vital constituency and only the vital constituency.

The quality of this primary education was high: primary schools in general had resources and good teachers. Spending data are not available for the early Vargas years, but they are available for 1944 and 1960, and I present the figures in Table 6.6. They show that spending was substantial and more than kept pace with enrollment growth. Tellingly, the R$125 (2004 Reais) spent on primary students in 1944 is nearly a third of what Brazilian governments in the late 1990s defined as the minimum level for adequate basic education. And while enrollment more than doubled from 1945 to 1960, per-student spending still increased by 84 percent.

A second source of quality was teachers. Scholars of later years often note the lack of qualified teachers as one of the primary causes of underperformance in Brazilian public schools.[30] But in this era, being a teacher was a high-status job; teachers came from the middle class.[31] Alongside the expansion of schools was a commensurate increase in institutions for training qualified teachers. Primary school teachers were mostly trained in pedagogic, or normal, schools.[32] Graduations from secondary-level pedagogic schools increased, on average, by 4.1 percent annually from 1934 to 1945, and by 7.4 percent between 1934 and 1958. This meant that the supply of trained teachers kept up with the growth in enrollments: average class sizes rose slightly prior to 1945, but actually fell sharply thereafter (Table 6.6).

While there are certainly minor variations in these patterns, the remarkable feature of the 1930–1961 period is the steadiness of its development. Over the years the centralization and uniformity of the system increased somewhat, but its general character did not change (Sobrinho 1985).[33] Instead new developments only reinforced existing trends. Toward the end of Vargas's *Estado Novo*, his powerful minister of education, Gustavo Capanema, passed the "organic laws" to centralize and homogenize the system.[34] And the 1946 Constitution continued the process, giving the federal government the authority to establish educational directives and norms but granting the states the responsibility to organize individually their systems of formal education (World Bank 1979).[35]

Yet in one area, private education, there were, by the 1950s, signs of a subtle change, one that became very important in the 1961–1967 and 1967–1990 periods. Table 6.6 shows a primary system that was overwhelmingly public. In 1945, only 14 percent of primary students were in private schools. But in the 1950s, private schools began to grown in number: private enrollments rose 73 percent between 1945 and 1960. And even though public enrollments grew still faster—in 1960, only 11.5 percent of primary students were in private schools—these private schools began to play a special role in the primary system: they were expensive and catered to the growing elite classes eager to give their student an edge on university entrance exams. (Their growth coincides with the growing inequity between industrial elites and workers, the two sides of Vargas's vital constituency, which we saw in Section 2.) And the federal government's role in funding these schools also increased: in 1951, federal "subventions and auxiliary" spending on primary schools, which includes aid and scholarships for private schools, was just under 2004 R$500,000; by 1960, it was 2004 R$35.5 million.[36]

For the most part, however, it was the public education system that the vital constituency used, and it provided them with excellent primary education. Table 6.6 presents key statistics on it.

Table 6.6 **Development of primary education, 1932–1960**

| | 1932 | 1945 | 1960 | Changes | | |
				1933–45	1945–60	1933–60
Schools	26,945	41,141	95,938	52.7%	133.2%	256.1%
Federal	17	5	454	-70.6%	8,980.0%	2,570.6%
State	15,222	19,459	41,595	27.8%	113.8%	173.3%
Municipal	5,201	13,959	44,624	168.4%	219.7%	758.0%
Private	6,505	5,908	9,265	-9.2%	56.8%	42.4%
Enrollment	2,071,437	3,496,664	7,458,002	68.8%	113.3%	260.0%
Federal	2,250	192[†]	33,871	-91.5%	17,541.1%	1,405.4%
State	1,332,898	1,957,785[†]	4,699,644	46.9%	140.0%	252.6%
Municipal	355,527	782,878[†]	1,863,609	120.2%	138.0%	424.2%
Private	380,762	498,085[†]	860,878	30.8%	72.8%	126.1%
Teachers	56,320	83,825	225,569	48.8%	169.1%	300.5%
Federal	86	7	1,045	-91.9%	14,828.6%	1,115.1%
State	33,171	50,557	141,907	52.4%	180.7%	327.8%
Municipal	8,606	19,645	55,191	128.3%	180.9%	541.3%
Private	14,457	13,616	27,426	-5.8%	101.4%	89.7%
Student: Teacher Ratio	37	42	33	13.4%	-20.7%	-10.1%
Federal	26	27	32	4.8%	18.2%	23.9%
State	40	39	33	-3.6%	-14.5%	-17.6%
Municipal	41	40	34	-3.5%	-15.3%	-18.3%
Private	26	37	31	38.9%	-14.2%	19.2%
Spending (Public Only) [††]		(1944)*			(1944–60)	
Cr$ (thousands)		436,308	17,552,367		3,922.9%	
2004 R$ (thousands)		374,954	1,517,389		304.7%	
Per Student		Cr$ 146	Cr$ 2,661		1,728.5%	
Per Student (2004 R$)		R$ 125	R$ 230		83.9%	

Notes: [†] Breakdown does not add up to 41,141 because 1,810 primary schools are supplementary schools.

* Spending data are from 1944 (per-student spending is calculated with enrollment from 1944).

[††] Calculated with public students only.

THE UPPER LEVELS AND WORKER TRAINING

According to the framework, a cross-class alliance like Vargas's should have provided its vital constituency with an All-Levels system. And indeed, the modernization of education after 1930 was as impressive in the upper levels as at the primary level: Brazil's education system after 1930 developed to provide the vital constituency with higher education as they came to demand it. The integrated system provided both academic higher education and Selective Worker Training that prepared workers from inside the vital constituency to work in the burgeoning industrial sector.[37] Because of the integration, this subsection will examine the academic and professional[38] upper levels together.

I mentioned in Section 1 that higher education in agrarian Brazil was largely a gentlemen's pastime, and in 1930 Vargas inherited a system with a number of elite secondary *colégios* and isolated institutions of higher education. In general these institutions were not the focus of developments in the 1930s; the government's focus was primary schools. For example, these institutions were not included in Capanema's "organic laws" (Schwartzman 1989).

Yet as the economy developed, secondary education took on new value, and demand for it increased. Secondary education developed into two distinct types, academic and professional, a division that was formalized in comprehensive secondary-school reforms in 1942 (Schwartzman 1991). Academic secondary had both scientific and "classical" tracks and led to higher-level employment or the universities. Professional schools were a system of Selective Worker Training: they were vocational and prepared students for mid-level white- or blue-collar employment. Both drew students from the middle classes of the vital constituency, but with time the two stratified socioeconomically, with professional schools taking students from the working class and academic secondary schools from the professional and industrial classes. Both types offered good education and their availability accelerated with economic development. I begin with the professional schools, which provided Selective Worker Training.

Chapter 2 defined Selective Worker Training as providing just the number and type of workers that employers need. The framework predicts that it will develop in inflexible labor markets like Brazil's union-dominated market, in which wages are inelastic to labor supply. And in Brazil, professional schools were indeed closely integrated with the demands of business and industry: they were privately-run but largely publicly-funded, and they provided workers trained to industry's needs (World Bank 1979).[39] Initially, the Vargas administration made some attempts at organizing a formal system of technical education, even hiring instructors from Switzerland (Schwartzman 1989, 2003). But industry was resistant, and the government eventually settled on private provision of worker training; the 1937 Constitution even assigned specific responsibility to employers for training their workers (Verhine 1993). In 1942, industrial technical schools were organized under the National Industrial Training Service (SENAI). Although SENAI was supervised by the Ministry of Labor, and funded by a payroll tax on industrial firms of more than 500 employees, it was run privately by the Federation of Industry in each state, with minor redistribution to the poorest states by a small central office, which also helped design courses. In 1946, the government followed SENAI with SENAC, a similar training apparatus for commercial firms. Both had their own training facilities and supervised training within their firms' plants or businesses. The number of students was determined by the needs of firms, and the education was (and is) widely considered to be excellent (Castro 1975; World Bank 1979; Plank 1996; Verhine 1993; Schwartzman 2003).

Table 6.7 shows the development of professional education of four types: commercial and industrial schools, as well as the normal (teacher training) schools discussed in the previous section and one type I have not discussed: agricultural schools. The middle classes of Vargas's vital constituency were mostly urban and thus not much interested in agricultural schools (Schwartzman 2003), but Table 6.7 shows the tremendous growth of industrial and especially commercial schools.

On the academic side, secondary education also developed quickly, followed by higher education as the market demand for it increased with economic development. In the 1930s growth was concentrated at the secondary level: secondary enrollments took off after 1933, averaging 14 percent annual growth from 1934 to

Table 6.7 **Professional education, 1933–1960**

				Changes		
	1933*	*1945*	*1960*	*1933–45*	*1945–60*	*1933–60*
Schools	657	1,580	3,194	140.5%	102.2%	386.1%
Commercial	388	935	1,392	141.0%	48.9%	258.8%
Normal (Teacher Training)	223	370	1,277	65.9%	245.1%	472.6%
Industrial	40	255	427	537.5%	67.5%	967.5%
Agricultural	6	20	98	233.3%	390.0%	1,533.3%
Enrollment	41,885	121,509	309,249	190.1%	154.5%	638.3%
Commercial	19,493	84,553	194,124	333.8%	129.6%	895.9%
Normal (Teacher Training)	18,069	19,533	93,600	8.1%	379.2%	418.0%
Industrial	3,936	16,764	26,081	325.9%	55.6%	562.6%
Agricultural	387	659	6,850	70.3%	939.5%	1,670.0%

Notes: * This table starts from 1933, as data on professional education are not available for 1932.

1940; higher education, by contrast, rose slightly in the early 30s and then fell, ending the decade with just 20,000 students, 1,500 fewer than in 1932. Higher education had been a luxury of the elite before 1930, and in the 1930s there was little need for graduates of higher education in an economy that while modernizing was still relatively underdeveloped. In fact, aside from two actual universities—the University of São Paulo, founded in 1934, and the University of Brazil, founded in 1937[40]—much of higher education consisted of isolated "faculties of philosophy," and these became effectively teacher training colleges for secondary school teachers (Schwartzman 1998).

The supply of such highly-trained teachers was one reason for the generally high quality of secondary education; another reason was resources. In 1944, per-student spending on secondary schools was R$728 (2004 R$), and it grew by almost 250 percent, to more than R$2,500 per student, by 1960. Table 6.8 shows the details. The table shows spending only on schools, but federal and state governments were also spending an additional R$107.2 million (2004 R$) on secondary education for projects and scholarships and aid to private schools—13 percent of what they were spending on public secondary schools. Seventy-five percent of that spending was by the federal government. And there is no telling how much additional public money actually went to private secondary schools: Brazilian governments at all levels have a long history of channeling public money off-budget to private schools (Plank, Sobrinho, and Xavier 1996).

Secondary education, both professional and academic, was also widely available. Total enrollment increased 250 percent between 1945 and 1960, and more than 1,500 percent between 1932 and 1960 (Table 6.8). And while I could not find figures for this era on enrollment by grade, I did find data on graduations, which allow a very rough estimate of the availability of secondary education. In 1940, for example, 240,000 students graduated from primary schools; in that year, enrollment in schools offering grades 5–8 was 295,000, meaning that even if we assume a drop-out rate of zero, 30 percent of primary graduates went on to a secondary institution—a very high percentage considering how recently the economy had begun to need that level of education. (In fact the percentage of admissions to secondary institutions was likely much higher, since the drop-out rate was much higher than zero: slightly less than 47,000 students graduated from secondary, commercial, industrial, and pedagogic schools in 1944, compared to 74,000 who would have graduated if the drop-out rate had been zero.) Yet the admissions rate did not improve much with time: in 1955, 577,000 students graduated from primary school, and enrollment in schools offering grades 5–8 was 724,000, implying an admission rate of 31 percent if the drop-out rate was zero.

Higher education did not begin to develop rapidly until after World War II, as rapid modernization raised the job-market demand for it (Schwartzman 2003; Sobrinho 1985). The federal government responded thereafter by creating a network of federal universities, at least one in each state, which generally combined the isolated "faculties of philosophy" that had previously dominated Brazilian higher education. The government made large investments in the new universities: even though enrollment shot up 130 percent from 1945 to 1960, to more than 100,000 students, the government increased per-student spending by nearly 60 percent (Table 6.8). Total spending on higher education institutions was R\$375 million (2004 R\$), a 260 percent increase from 1944. And the money spent on institutions was less than half of total spending on higher education: another R\$578 million went to special projects and scholarships and aid to private institutions. More than 96 percent of this funding came from the federal government.[41]

Still, integration of the isolated faculties did not instantly create universities of the quality of those we saw in Ghana and Taiwan. The isolated institutions had structures and cultures that made transforming them into modern universities difficult: academics generally taught part-time and did little research, and much of the control rested with the holders of isolated chairs, which were awarded for life (World Bank 1979; Schwartzman 1998). It would take a major university reform in the 1960s—under a new, elite vital constituency—to transform Brazilian universities into the high-quality institutions of today.

WRAPPING UP

This section described how Brazil's pioneer government, led by Getúlio Vargas and his democratic successors, built an All Levels system to cater to their largely urban cross-class vital constituency of workers and entrepreneurs—an alliance that made up less than 30 percent of the population. In general this is what the framework predicts. This last section will consider whether the framework predicts Brazilian education policy specifically on the range of indicators I laid out in Chapter 3. The evidence summary for 1930–1961 is in Table 6.9.

The Vargas government and successors created a mostly-free system with increasing enrollments and per-student resources at All Levels. And the reach of the system was remarkably in synch with the proportion of the population in the vital constituency, at least judged on Pereira's (1984) analysis of the census. But there are four indicators on which the framework is less predictive. The first two have to do with universities, which, once the demand rose for higher education, the government provided for the most part by simply absorbing isolated faculties of philosophy into a network of federal universities. This method hampered the quality of the education offered. The third area of only partial support is access to secondary education, which was high considering the underdevelopment of the economy but did not appear to rise even as the economy developed. And lastly, the emergence of private and partly subsidized lower-level schools in the 1950s represents the beginnings of a tracking system at the lower levels. While this tracking system was still limited in comparison to the role it will play in the coming sections, its graduates had advantages in gaining access to the upper levels.

Table 6.8 **Development of the upper levels, 1932–1960**

	1933	1945	1960	Changes 1933–45	1945–60	1933–60
Secondary						
(Academic)						
Schools	394	1,282	3,860	225.4%	201.1%	879.7%
Enrollment	56,208	256,467	904,252	356.3%	252.6%	1,508.8%
Proportion in Private		68.1%**	62.4%			
Spending (Public Only)		(1944)*			(1944–60)	
Cr$ (thousands)		63,099	9,457,332		14,888.1%	
2004 R$ (thousands)		54,226	817,579		1,407.7%	
Per-student		847**	28,995		3,322.9%	
Per-student (2004 R$)		728**	2,507		244.3%	
Higher						
Schools	328	587†	1,571	78.9%	167.7%	379.0%
Enrollment	30,496	45,073†	102,971	47.8%	128.5%	237.7%
Proportion in Private		41.6%**	46.8%			
Spending (Public Only)		(1944)*			(1944–60)	
Cr$ (thousands)		120,840	4,332,410		3,485.2%	
2004 R$ (thousands)		103,847	374,534		260.7%	
Per Student		5,022**	79,056		1,474.1%	
Per Student (2004 R$)		4,316**	6,834		58.3%	

Notes: † Higher institutions and enrollment in 1945 are imputed. Data on total higher enrollment and schools are not available between 1941 or 1942 and 1953 (only academic higher is available, which is 26,757 in 325 schools in 1945). Total higher enrollment for 1945 is imputed assuming constant growth from 1941 (29,632) to 1953 (75,956); total higher schools for 1945 are imputed assuming constant growth from 1942 (492) to 1953 (939). * Spending data are from 1944. ** Per-student spending is calculated only for public students, using data on total students from 1944 and assuming that the same proportion of total enrollment are in private institutions in 1944 as in 1954, the closest year for which data are disaggregated into public and private institutions. These estimates are intended only for use in calculating per-student spending.

Table 6.9 **Evidence summary, 1930–1961**

Indicator	Characteristics	Conforms to Framework?
A. Enrollment	Increasing at all levels to cover the vital constituency (less than 30 percent of the population)	■
B. Per-student spending	Increasing at all levels	■
C. The toolkit		
1. Schools	High-quality at all levels, except universities	□
Teachers	High-quality at all levels, except universities	□
Physical resources	High at all levels	■
Location	Mostly towns or urban areas	■
2. Fees[†]	Public is free; private primary and academic secondary charge fees	■
3. Access restrictions and discriminatory pricing		
Quotas	None	
Exams	Exams regulate access between levels; admissions from primary to secondary are high for an underdeveloped economy, but fail to increase with modernization	□
Financial aid	Some scholarships to private schools, especially higher education	■
4. Tracking	None for most of the period; beginnings of tracking in the 1950s from private primary and secondary schools	□
5. Outsourcing (domestic or foreign; to firms or non-profits)	Minimal at lower levels, extensive at secondary and upper, before isolated institutions are absorbed into new federal universities	■

Notes: ■: fully conforms to the framework; ◪: partly conforms to the framework; □: does not conform to the framework.

[†] Fees are for enrollment, books and other equipment, uniforms, activities, school improvements, etc.

The year 1961 marks the end of three decades of rule by governments with the Vargas cross-class vital constituency. With the defection of elites from the coalition, workers held on for three years, but a coup in 1964 put in power a government with an elite vital constituency—that is, a government that, according to this book's framework, should have transformed Vargas's All-Levels system into a Top-Down system to serve elites. Sections 5 and 6 will consider this change in the vital constituency, and the changes to education that it ushered in. But first, Section 4 briefly considers the vital constituency and education of the short period when workers held on to power.

4. POLITICS AND EDUCATION, 1961–1964: Briefly, a Workers' State

By 1964, just three years after the resignation of Jânio Quadros that marked the end of the Vargas cross-class alliance, the military took over in Brasília. But for those three years, workers held on to power. These workers had great ambitions but ruled during a time of economic difficulty, and in the end did not have much of a chance to do anything before the military intervened and Brazil began two and a half decades of elite rule. This section briefly considers the politics and education policies of that period.

POLITICS

Workers' fleeting period in power was largely accidental, the result of the unexpected resignation by a president supported by elites and his automatic replacement by a vice president supported by workers. In Section 2 above, I noted that workers, prompted by rising inequality, had become more demanding in the decade leading up to the 1960 presidential election. While both workers and industrialists benefited from Brazil's economic development, industrialists benefited more, and workers were resentful; they began talking of fundamental reforms to land ownership, bank policy, and public investment. Elites responded aggressively, calling the demands communist and stoking fears of revolution, which workers did nothing to quell by arguing that it might, in fact, be only through revolution that real change would come to the country.

Yet even as the two sides grew further apart, they managed to elect Jânio Quadros, who, though a candidate of the elites, was acceptable to workers. But Quadros resigned in August of 1961 for unknown personal reasons. His resignation elevated the vice president, João Goulart, a worker-friendly leader who was anathema to elites (Pereira 1984).

In a sign of things to come, Goulart was sworn in only after a failed coup by more conservative members of the military. But he was sworn in nonetheless, fueling intense optimism by workers, who thought their time had come. Talk turned to the fundamental changes that workers had agitated for, and in 1963 Goulart proposed major reforms.

Workers, however, were in a weak political position, opposed by elites alongside an increasingly agitated military[42] and facing economic decline. Inflation was on the rise and agricultural and industrial production fell, slowing per-capita economic growth from 5.5 percent in 1961 to 3.6 percent in 1962 and -2.2 percent in 1963. Firms began laying off workers in droves and large-scale unemployment appeared for the first time since modernization (by June 1965, unemployment São Paulo would reach 13 percent[43]). Workers struck to protest, and the official tally of strikes rose from 700 a year in 1962 and 1963, to more than 1,000 in 1964 (Telles 1962; Sobrinho 1985). Interestingly, as we saw with the CPP and the Rawlings governments in Ghana, leftist leaders tried to shore up their political power by organizing a union between workers and peasants: the National Students' Union worked aggressively to organize peasants after 1962 (Sobrinho 1985). But they were not able to do so quickly enough. The military, feeling, as Stepan (1978) puts it, that "no single group within the polity was competent to rule the country," stepped in.[44]

EDUCATION

The framework predicts that a change from a cross-class alliance to a vital constituency of the poor will lead to a change in the education system from the All-Levels of the Vargas years to a Bottom-Up system that was similarly engineered to cover the vital constituency (about 30 percent of the population). The 1961–1964 period was unstable and not long enough to have a fundamental impact on the education system. Nonetheless, there were signs that the Goulart administration may, if it had more time, have concentrated its efforts on improving primary education. The only major policy change in education was the passage, nine months after Goulart was sworn in, of a new basic education law.[45] The law only reinforced the objectives and improved the structures in the Capanema "organic laws" (Sobrinho 1985).[46] But it was notable for doing that: such a law had been on the table for two decades but was constantly thwarted by controversy.[47] The 1961 law affirmed the autonomy of states in operating their schools but set a common school year at 180 days, required that all primary school teachers have at least a secondary degree and all secondary teachers a higher-education degree, and increased the proportion of federal spending earmarked for education from 10 to 12 percent.[48]

Otherwise, education developed largely as before. Table 6.10 shows basic enrollment and spending statistics for the period. The four years saw a large increase in enrollment at all levels but a relatively larger increase at the secondary and upper levels: primary enrollment grew by 25 percent, secondary by more than 50 percent, and higher by almost 40 percent. In nominal terms, per-student

Table 6.10 **Education, 1960–1963**

	1960	1963	Change
Primary			
Schools	95,938	115,710	20.6%
Enrollment	7,458,002	9,299,441	24.7%
Spending			
Cr$	3,274,395*	11,145,249*	240.4%
2004 R$	R$ 283,069*	R$ 266,959*	-5.7%
Per Student	Cr$ 439	Cr$ 1,198	173.0%
Per Student 2004 R$	R$ 38	R$ 29	-24.4%
Secondary (Academic Only)			
Schools	3860	4,607	23.7%
Total Enrollment	904,252	1,246,125	51.3%
Spending			
Cr$	4,612,198*	16,514,518*	258.1%
2004 R$	398,721*	395,567*	-0.8%
Per Student	5,101	13,253	159.8%
Per Student 2004 R$	441	317	-28.0%
Higher			
Schools	1,571	1,285	-16.7%
Enrollment	102,971	126,405	38.6%
Spending			
Cr$	8,837,564*	32,804,953*	271.2%
2004 R$	764,001*	785,766*	2.8%
Per Student	85,826	259,523	202.4%
Per Student 2004 R$	7,420	6,216	-16.2%

Note: * in thousands.

spending more than kept pace, but because of the high inflation of these years real per-student spending fell at all levels by similar amounts.

The 1964 coup ushered in a period of far more stable control under an elite vital constituency. The new government inherited an All-Levels system from the Vargas cross-class alliance and the brief period of worker's rule. The new government should, according to the framework, have changed this system into a Top-Down system. The following two sections examine, first, the politics of the new vital constituency, and then how the government reformed the education system to serve it.

5. POLITICS, 1964–1990: Elite Rule

The 1964 coup began two and a half decades of elite rule in Brazil. The coup cut short the burgeoning political entrepreneurship of Brazil's long-neglected peasantry, and decimated the much-better-established political entrepreneurship of workers that had brought workers into the vital constituency in the Vargas coalition. In place of the Vargas cross-class alliance, agrarian and industrial elites linked arms to support a succession of military governments (Pereira 1984). Through clever institutional maneuvering, elites held power even while continuing to hold elections and used the state to accelerate economic growth, from which they benefited enormously: in the 1960s, the income of the Brazil's wealthiest five percent doubled (Evans 1979). Yet growth slowed into the 1970s, and slower growth weakened industrial elites' satisfaction with their government (Mainwaring 1986), while discontent simultaneously rose among the disenfranchised workers and peasants; as the military's rule weakened they began organizing again, and protesting (Mainwaring 1986; Sobrinho 1985; Brown 1995). The 1980s saw a gradual opening of elections, culminating, in late 1989, with the first direct elections for the presidency.

Ending this period at 1990 is somewhat arbitrary. Political entrepreneurship did not immediately return to Brazil in 1990; in fact a political entrepreneur did not take power in Brazil until 2003. But as I describe in Section 7 below, the 1990s are a time of growing political entrepreneurship that change at the state level and some limited responsiveness by the federal government to the newly organized groups. Because this process is gradual there is no clear start date, and for lack of a better one I have chosen 1990, when the first directly elected president since 1961 took office.

This section considers the politics of the period. These politics were not simple, but the features of the vital constituency underlying them are relatively straightforward. The vital constituency developed through two sub-periods. In the first, which ended around 1974, the military consolidated its rule and undermined the organizations that had enabled political entrepreneurship of the poor in the prior period; for the remainder of the period, the vital constituency grew dissatisfied with the weakening economy and political entrepreneurship returned, first to workers, and then gradually to the peasantry. The next two sub-sections consider the years before and after 1974. The period 1964–1990 is also the first for which I include supplementary analyses of the politics and education of São Paulo and Bahia. Two brief sub-sections at the end consider the politics in each.

STRENGTHENING ELITE RULE TO 1974

In the decade after the 1964 coup, the military solidified its rule, relying on a vital constituency of agrarian and industrial elites. It centralized control in the hands of the federal government, and drove the economy to spectacular growth. The military did not seize power with this path in mind. For its first three years in power, it ruled under a moderate general, Humberto Castello Branco, with the intention only of purging Brazil's politics of their populist—or "communist," in their view—elements, after which they would return the country to civilian rule (Pereira 1984; Brown 1995). The military elevated technocrats above politicians and cracked down hard on political entrepreneurship, especially by union leaders, while building ties to the National Democratic Union (*União Democrática Nacional*; UDN), a right-leaning political party particularly associated with the agrarian elites. The military leadership thought that it could reeducate the public not to listen to the siren song of the populists, after which it could turn the reins over to the civilians. But the reeducation seemed to fail: in litmus-test mayoral and gubernatorial elections in 1965, a year after the coup, the opposition won the mayor's office in the city of São Paulo, the industrial capital, and governorships in three of the four most industrialized states.

Ever since the 1964 coup, hard-liners in the military had wanted to take control for the foreseeable future—unusually for a military that had previously seen itself simply as a guardian or watchdog of civilian governments (Stepan 1971). The 1965 election losses strengthened the hardliners' hand and weakened the moderates'. In the election's aftermath, the two sides struggled over whether to return to civilian rule, and eventually the moderates lost out. Moderate General Castelo Branco caved to hardliner pressure and pushed through the Second Institutional Act (the First had set up the military government after the coup), which created indirect elections by bodies in which the military's support was strongest—the president and vice president by the Congress, and the state governors by the state legislatures. The act also gave the president the power to remove any elected official, and abolished all political parties. In their place, the government fashioned a new two-party system, with a government party, the "National Renewal Alliance" (*Aliança Renovadora Nacional*; ARENA), and a single opposition party, the "Brazilian Democratic Movement," (*Movimento Democrático Brasileiro*; MDB). Castelo Branco, who still wished to return the country to civilian rule, gave the Act an expiration date, 1967, but by then the hardliners in the military had won the internal struggle. Instead of expiring, the Act's major features were formalized in a new constitution, and Castelo Branco was replaced as president by Marshall Artur da Costa e Silva, a hardliner.

With the triumph of the hardliners, the military government began much more actively to court both industrial and agrarian elites. Industrial elites had tolerated Castelo Branco's government, but they had not been represented in it (Pereira 1984). And Castelo Branco's economic technocrats had not served industrial elites particularly well: they were largely monetarists who focused all the government's energy on fighting inflation, by slashing the government investments and subsidies that had fueled growth before 1964 (Pereira 1984). Real per-capita economic growth slowed to just 1.3 percent between 1964 and 1967 (IPEA 2006). After 1967, this economic policy was reversed by the new hardliner administration of

Costa e Silva and his successor, General Emílio Garrastazú Médici (who was selected after Costa e Silva suffered a stroke just a year into his presidency). Under
the hardliners the state quickly became Brazil's largest investor: state development
banks provided more than 70 percent of all investment loans (Baer 1979, 49), and
the military created more state-owned enterprises than any previous government.[49] These corporations greatly enriched the industrial elites by giving them
the lion's share of a growing economic pie. The corporations themselves were generally profitable and productive (Evans 1979): real per-capita GDP growth rose
from 1.3 percent in 1967 to 6.7 percent in 1968, and to an average of 8 percent a
year from 1968 to 1974 (IPEA 2006). And those economic gains went largely to the
wealthy: in just a decade, between 1960 and 1970, the ratio of the mean incomes
of the upper 20 percent to the bottom 40 percent of earners went from 9:1 to 12:1
(World Bank 1979, based on the 1960 and 1970 demographic censuses).

While serving elites, the military further secured its rule by continuing to
repress political entrepreneurship and relying electorally on rural areas. In 1967
Costa e Silva enacted through the Fifth Institutional Act, which briefly closed the
congress and gave the government repressive powers that were used over the subsequent decade to remove 113 federal deputies and senators from office (Brown
1995). The government also brutally repressed protest strikes in Osasco and Con-
tagem, and no further strikes occurred for a decade (Mainwaring 1986). Weakened, censored, and forced to function through the government-controlled
opposition party, the MDB, the opposition was trounced in 1970 elections by the
government party, ARENA.[50]

But by 1974, the military's grip had weakened. The military itself was strained
by governing,[51] and with the worker and peasant movements in ruins even some
industrial elites in the vital constituency were becoming uncomfortable with the
military's continued repression and were calling for democracy (Pereira 1984;
Mainwaring 1986). Fearful that it would lose direct gubernatorial elections in
1974, the military postponed them until 1978. But it went ahead with Congressional elections, where it sustained heavy losses: the MDB increased its seats in
the Chamber of Deputies from 87 to 165 (out of 364 total), and in the Senate from
7 to 20 (Brown 1995).

These elections mark the beginning of a loosening of the military's firm grip
on Brazilian politics. In the election's aftermath, its popular support declined
steadily. Thereafter it stayed in power by continually changing Brazil's formal
institutions,while presiding over a gradual political "opening" (abertura) that would
eventually force it from power.

WEAKENING ELITE RULE AFTER 1974

After 1974, the opposition gained steadily in election after election. In municipal
elections in 1976, the MDB won majorities in the councils of most of Brazil's
major industrial areas, including Rio de Janeiro, São Paulo, Belo Horizonte, Pôrte

Alegre, Salvador, Campinas, and Santos. The military responded by again closing the Congress and introducing a package of constitutional provisions—called the "April Package" after their date of introduction, April 1, 1977—intended to shift representation to the rural areas and the northeast and otherwise secure the government's position.[52] In 1979, the military, which had ironically united the opposition by creating the MDB, tried to fragment it by dissolving the two-party system and introducing a new government party, the Social Democratic Party (*Partido Democrático Social*; PDS), while simultaneously diffusing tensions by granting amnesty to exiles and abolishing the Fifth Institutional Act (Mainwaring 1986; Brown 1995). When the opposition subsequently split into four parties, the military then allowed direct elections of governors and federal senators in 1982. Again this allowed the military to stay in power: in the 1982 elections the PDS stayed the largest party in Congress and maintained a majority in the electoral college, which elected the president.[53] Yet the election also showed the military's weakened position: its party lost the majority in congress, and opposition parties won nine governorships in the most populous states. For the first time, the military thus had to negotiate bills through a congress in which it did not have a majority (Fleischer and Wesson 1983).

The military was also facing rising discontent both from within its vital constituency and from workers. Per-capita economic growth slowed to just over 2.2 percent in 1977 and 1978 (IPEA 2006), causing dissatisfaction with the regime among industrial elites (Pereira 1984). Simultaneously workers, sensing that the military's hold on power was weakening, began re-organizing: between 1977 and 1980, workers and peasant unions cropped up all over the country. With repression and some placating, the military kept these groups relatively weak (Mainwaring 1986). But in 1980 the government faced a debt crisis and recession hit: between 1980 and 1983, real per-capita GDP fell almost 13 percent (IPEA 2006) and inflation reached more than 200 percent a year. In desperation, the government turned to the IMF, but the resulting stabilization package further alienated the industrial elite (Mainwaring 1986). All the while protests grew to an unprecedented scale. In April 1984, a million people in Rio de Janeiro and more than a million in São Paulo all took to the streets demanding direct elections; hundreds of similar marches occurred around the country.[54]

Such strains eventually split the government. In 1985, in presidential elections that were still indirect, a moderate faction from within the regime broke off and joined with the opposition to support the candidacy of Tancredo Neves. With this support, Neves defeated the military hardliners' candidate. In the past, this might have prompted the military to change or ignore the rules so as to maintain control. But the military was weak and Neves maneuvered cleverly to placate them— his new cabinet included representatives of centrist and right-wing political parties of the industrial elites and the agrarian elites, and excluded workers, who were represented by a new "Workers' Party" (*Partido dos Trabalhadores*; PT). Seeing Neves as acceptable, the hardliners' acquiesced, and military rule was over.

Neves's victory was an important development. Yet even as the military ceded control to civilians in 1985, the vital constituency did not change appreciably. In the first place, Neves did not end up being president: he was old and died the day before his inauguration. Instead, the vice-presidential candidate, José Sarney, ascended to the presidency. Sarney, however, was not a moderate like Neves: he was the leader of the government's party, the PDS, after 1979, and was a leader in the military tradition. As president, he governed largely like the military leaders who preceded him. As before, the Sarney government tried to serve the industrial elites in the vital constituency despite the turmoil in the economy, and as before it sought to placate workers, who were outside the vital constituency. Industrial elites remained dissatisfied as average real per-capita growth slowed to zero from 1986 to 1990 (IPEA 2006) and inflation, fueled by public spending, continued to rise—even though the government implemented price controls and changed the currency three times. And although the new government formally considered major socio-economic reforms, it did not pass them: a new labor law died in congress, as did a major agrarian reform, which was killed by rural elites and military ministers (Mainwaring 1986). Indeed the only real reform was institutional: a new constitution, in 1988, that restored freedoms and direct elections, and reversed the centralization of the military years. (Among the areas decentralized was education, which I discuss in the next section.)

In 1990, the first president was directly elected under the new constitution. For the two and a half decades after the 1964 coup, the vital constituency was a largely stable alliance of agrarian and industrial elites along with the bureaucracy and military. Outside were the workers, the peasants, and the urban poor, whose political entrepreneurs the military succeeded in repressing until the very end of the period. Table 6.11 shows the vital constituency.

With the federal vital constituency defined, it remains only to briefly examine the vital constituencies in Bahia and São Paulo.

Table 6.11 **The Vital Constituency, 1964–1990**

Political Entrepreneur(s)	Groups in the Vital Constituency[†]	Groups outside the Vital Constituency
None	Military	Workers
	Bureaucracy	Peasants
	Agrarian Elites (Type N)	Urban Poor
	Industrial Elites* (Type S)	

Notes: [†] If a group was empowered with the help of a political entrepreneur, the entrepreneur is in brackets. * Industrial elites were not represented in the technocratic military government that ruled from 1964 to 1967.

Employer types are in parentheses: Type S employers need skilled workers in an inflexible labor market; type N employers do not need skilled workers.

VITAL CONSTITUENCIES IN BAHIA AND SÃO PAULO

Bahia and São Paulo provide important variation in Brazil's vital constituencies. Bahia is in the poor northeast, a region that the military counted on to deliver it crucial electoral support, especially as its support in the more industrial states waned. São Paulo, by contrast, is an industrial state, and was a center both of worker agitation and of the industrial elites who grew increasingly dissatisfied with the military's repression and economic policies.

Bahia[55]

In most parts of the poor northeast, the military courted powerful agrarian elites.[56] But in some states, agrarian elites, who had been battered in the decades prior to 1964, were vulnerable to clever political operatives. This was the situation in Bahia, where Antônio Carlos Magalhães ("ACM") outsmarted the agrarian elites to begin forty years of political dominance.

Initially, the military courted agrarian elites in Bahia as elsewhere. In the aftermath of the 1964 coup, the new military government determined that, for reasons of national security, they needed to appoint the mayor of Salvador, the capital of Bahia and a city whose middle class was opposed to the military take-over. ACM was the mayor they appointed—at the urging, ironically, of a pow-erful agrarian oligarch of whom ACM was a protégé. But once in power, ACM maneuvered around the agrarian elites, building a loyal technocracy in Salva-dor and controlling the appointments of mayors and legislators. These mayors and legislators were ACM's vital constituency. He delivered patronage to them and in turn they delivered votes to the federal military governments. In 1985, ACM helped José Sarney establish the Liberal Front Party, (*Partido da Frente Liberal*; PFL), which represented northeastern elites and became a key member of Sarney's governing coalition. The military governments compensated ACM for this support by twice appointing him governor of Bahia, once as the head of the government's electricity agency—an office with tremendous patronage possibilities—and by finally appointing him Minister of Communications in the Sarney government, a post that allowed ACM to distribute valuable televi-sion and radio licenses.

São Paulo[57]

São Paulo is Brazil's most important industrial area, and its vital constituency under the military was the industrial elites. Engineering the state's support was far more difficult for the military governments than in Bahia. I noted above that the state, and particularly its capital, was the center of worker unrest and a host to myriad strikes and demonstrations. It was the birthplace of the PT, the workers' party. And because São Paulo was the industrial capital of Brazil, it was also the home of much of the industrial elite wing of the vital constituency, who, as I noted above, grew increasingly unhappy with the poor performance of the economy under the military government in the 1970s and 1980s.

The military tried to negotiate this dilemma by minimizing the power of the São Paulo state government through a centralization of power at the federal level, and by directly appointing key officials, such as the mayor of the city of São Paulo (as in Salvador, this was justified on grounds of national security). Before 1979, the governor was elected indirectly, by the state legislature, in which more conservative and rural factions were stronger; after 1979, the military also began appointing the governor. When the military again allowed political parties and held direct elections in 1982, these brought to power the Brazilian Democratic Movement Party (*Partido do Movimento Democrático Brasileiro*; PMDB), the party of the industrial elites and middle class.

6. EDUCATION, 1964–1990: Top-Down Education

The coup of 1964 ended the three-decade rule of the Vargas cross-class alliance and brought to power an elitist government in Brasília. According to the framework, the change should have led to a shift in Brazilian education, from the All-Levels system that Vargas and successor governments built to a Top-Down system to serve the elites of the new vital constituency.

This it did—to an extreme. Indeed, with the possible exception of Nkrumah in Ghana, no government in this book so drastically reoriented its education system as the Brazilian military after 1964. In twenty years, the primary and secondary levels of Brazil's public education system went from serving their target populations adequately and relatively equitably to being bloated, woefully under-funded, and extremely poor. Resources and teacher quality in particular fell to abysmal levels. The story is the reverse at the upper levels, where increased public funding and university-governance reforms created world-class education, offered free to those who passed its entrance exams. Developments in the private system ensured that it was generally elites who passed. On the one hand, the private sector created an exceptional elite track of expensive primary and secondary schools, assisted by increasing amounts of public money and the high demand of wealthier parents who wanted their children to enter the public universities. On the other hand, poor-quality, but also costly, private institutions of higher education (*faculdades*[58]) emerged to soak up demand for higher education by ambitious middle-class children whose education in the crumbling public primary and secondary school systems offered them little chance of passing the public-university entrance exams.

All these developments are what the framework predicts. But in another way the period seems to offer a fierce rebuttal of the framework, for 1964–1990 is also a period of rapidly expanding investments in and access to primary education, particularly for Brazil's rural poor. In this section I present evidence that there is no contradiction: this expansion of "education" mostly benefited elites, not students. First, the expansion provided elites with two important things: construction contracts and jobs as teachers in a bloated education bureaucracy that could be given to supporters. And second, it offered no threat to the education of the new elite vital constituency: as countless studies have previously noted, and as test scores still attest, the new schools largely failed to educate.[59] In this way the expansion served elites.

This section details these developments. The first sub-section considers the lower levels of primary and secondary education. The second sub-section examines Selective Worker Training, and the third sub-section examines universities. The fourth sub-section describes educational developments in the states of Bahia and São Paulo. Lastly, the fifth sub-section presents the evidence summary for this period.

DETERIORATION AND INEQUALITY IN PRIMARY AND SECONDARY EDUCATION

The 1964 coup stopped the implementation of the new Basic Education Law passed in the brief period of worker rule (see Section 4). In its place the new military government began a process of centralizing control and transforming the lower levels of the public education system from a schooling system into a conduit for jobs and construction contracts. The centralization began almost immediately and accelerated with the 1967 constitution, which gave the president almost complete control over education spending. The previous pattern of earmarking a certain proportion of federal spending for education was largely abandoned—the government argued that such mandates unnecessarily limited the executive's powers—and new sources of funding for education that were presented to the National Congress were regularly rejected (Cunha 1991; Brown 1995). For this reason, Brazil's federal structure was less influential under the military, and the transformation of Brazilian education under the military was mostly at the behest of the federal government.

The transformation that the military engineered was a massive expansion and deterioration of the lower levels of public education. In the quarter century after 1964, the number of primary schools rose almost 60 percent. Federal per-student spending on primary education rose by 54 percent from 1964 to 1972, and by 465 percent from 1972 to 1985; spending on secondary education rose 57 percent between 1964 and 1985. The number of students in grades 1–8—which, after reforms in 1972, became the grades designated as "basic education"—rose nearly 140 percent. The remaining three grades of secondary education, grades 9–11, grew by even more, nearly 200 percent, though enrollment started from a much smaller base. Particularly in the lowest grades, this expansion was almost entirely in previously under-served rural areas, primarily in the poor Northeast. Table 6.12 shows the massive expansion of primary, or basic education; Table 6.13 shows secondary education.

Table 6.12 **Primary ("basic") education, 1964–1989**

	1964	1972	1989	Changes		
				1964–72	1972–89	1964–89
Schools	(grades 1-4)	(grades 1-8)	(grades 1-8)			
Total	124,946	165,051	196,638	32.1%	19.1%	57.4%
Federal	448	849	725	89.5%	-14.6%	61.8%
State	52,125	56,454	50,367	8.3%	-10.8%	-3.4%
Municipal	61,600	98,160	134,345	59.4%	36.9%	118.1%
Private	10,773	9,588	11,201	-11.0%	16.8%	4.0%
Enrollment						
Grades 1-4*	10,217,324	13,605,365*		33.2%		
Grades 1-8*	11,670,995**	18,370,744*	27,557,542	57.4%	50.0%	136.1%
	(grades 1-4)	(grades 1-8)	(grades 1-8)			
Federal	37,927	134,664	140,983	4.7%		
State	6,435,539	10,894,288	15,755,120	44.6%		
Municipal	2,520,001	4,923,979	8,218,455	66.9%		
Private	1,223,857	2,417,813	3,442,984	42.4%		
Teachers	(grades 1-4)	(grades 1-8)	(grades 1-8)			
Total	336,903	525,628	1,201,034	56.0%	128.5%	256.5%
Federal	1,305	2,638	5,802	102.1%	119.9%	344.6%
State	215,777	327,832	668,450	51.9%	103.9%	209.8%
Municipal	79,102	151,858	366,132	92.0%	141.1%	362.9%
Private	40,719	43,300	160,650	6.3%	271.0%	294.5%
Student: Teacher Ratio	(grades 1-4)	(grades 1-8)	(grades 1-8)			
Average	30	35	23	15.2%	-34.3%	-24.3%
Federal	29	51	24	75.6%	-52.4%	-16.4%
State	30	33	24	11.4%	-29.1%	-21.0%
Municipal	32	32	22	1.8%	-30.8%	-29.5%
Private	30	56	21	85.8%	-61.6%	-28.7%
Spending[†]	(grades 1-4)	(grades 1-8)	(1985) [†††] (grades 1-8)		(1972–85)	(1964–85)
Current (thousands)[††]	25,748,106	500,947	7,360,399[††††]			
2004 R$ (thousands)	325,397	901,879	6,866,684	177.2%	661.4%	2,010.3%

(continued)

Table 6.12 (continued)

	1964	1972	1989	Changes		
				1964–72	1972–89	1964–89
Spending[†]	(grades 1-4)	(grades 1-8)	(1985) [†††] (grades 1-8)		(1972–85)	(1964–85)
Per Student[††]	2,520	27	297,211			
Per Student (2004 R$)	32	49	277	54.2%	464.8%	770.6%

Notes: * Beginning in 1972, the first four years of secondary education were combined with the four years of primary, creating a new level of "basic" education with 8 grades. ** This figure is calculated to allow constant comparison of the growth of "basic education" over the period; it is the sum of grades 1-4 from this table and grades 5-8 from Table 6.8. † Spending is only from the Ministry of Education: it does not include spending on education by other ministries. Spending figures include all reported "subventions" to private schools; thus per-student figures are calculated for *all* students, not just students in public schools. †† Nominal spending, unadjusted for currency changes in 1967 and 1986, each of which removed three zeros from the currency. ††† I present 1985 spending in lieu of 1989, which is unavailable. Per-student spending is calculated with 1985 enrollment of 24,764,918. †††† in millions.

Yet this expansion was not an expansion in "education" by any reasonable definition. Most of the new schools operated in shifts of less than four hours each, with few materials and teachers who had not finished primary school. By 1972, 70 percent of Brazil's school buildings were one-room schoolhouses; these served 90 percent of rural students (World Bank 1979). In 1979 the World Bank published this stylized description of a typical Brazilian rural school:

> The school is a one-room house where groups of students (officially in different grades) sit and stare. The instructor is unlikely to have advanced beyond basic level education and is paid less than the minimum wage. She is supposed to teach the entire program of studies in all grades, but her knowledge of the subjects is, at best, a product of sheer repetition. The room is overcrowded. There are no textbooks: some volumes were produced but have not been distributed; they are too expensive. Unquestioning repetition of the teacher's words is equated with learning. When this is achieved, the reward is moving to the intermediate or back rows of the classroom (a sign of grade promotion). The price of failure is to stay in the same row or drop out. (World Bank 1979, 31)

The expansion built such schools because they were of the most benefit to rural elites—members of the government's vital constituency. We can see this by looking

Table 6.13 **Secondary education, 1964–1990**

	1964	1972	1989	Changes 1964–72	1972–89	1964–89
Enrollment						
Grades 5-8**	1,453,671	4,288,646		195.0%		
Grades 9-11**	439,040	1,299,937	3,478,059	196.1%	167.6%	692.2%
	(grades 5-11)	(grades 9-11)	(grades 9-11)			
Federal	51,881	53,722	97,777		82.0%	
State	716,938	633,021	2,170,832		242.9%	
Municipal	62,006	58,023	152,981		163.7%	
Private	1,061,886	555,171	1,056,469		90.3%	
			(1985)†††		(1972-85)	(1964-85)
Spending†	(grades 5-11)	(grades 9-11)	(grades 9-11)			
Current (thousands)††	34,179,629	253,122	1,154,586††††			
2004 R$ (thousands)	431,951	455,708	1,077,140	5.5%	136.4%	149.4%
Per Student††	18,059	195	382,803			
Per Student (2004 R$)	228	351	357	53.6%	1.9%	56.5%

Notes: * Unlike in previous tables, "secondary" in this table refers to all secondary institutions, not only academic. ** Beginning in 1972, the first four years of secondary (*médio*) education were combined with the four years of primary, creating a new level of "basic" education with 8 grades; thereafter secondary (*colegio*) is only grades 9-11. † Spending is only from the Ministry of Education: it does not include spending on education by other ministries. Spending figures include all reported "subventions" to private schools; thus per-student figures are calculated for *all* students, not just students in public schools. †† Nominal spending, unadjusted for currency changes in 1967 and 1986, each of which removed three zeros from the currency. ††† I present 1985 spending in lieu of 1989, which is unavailable. Per-student spending is calculated with 1985 enrollment of 3,016,138. †††† in millions.

a bit deeper into the nature of the expansion. First, it was heavily biased in favor of local governments in the Northeast. Table 6.12 shows that the vast majority of the new schools were municipal—i.e., run by local towns. And later sub-sections on the education in Bahia and São Paulo show the Northeastern bias of the expansion: Table 6.15 shows that Bahia's municipal basic-education schools expanded by more than 130 percent over the period, to more than 20,000; by contrast, São Paulo's *declined* by more than two-thirds, to just over 600. Recall, from Section 6, that industrial and agrarian elites were the key groups in the military's vital constituency. These new municipal schools provided contracts for politically powerful construction companies, run by the industrial elites, with projects in the areas controlled by rural elites, particularly mayors (Plank 1990; de Mello e Souza 1989).[60]

The federal government also created projects to provide textbooks and other resources to the new schools. But these, too, generally just aided the elite vital constituency. For example, the federal government spent exorbitantly to buy textbooks from politically powerful textbook companies: the federal Student Assistance Foundation (*Fundação de Assisténcia ao Estudante*; FAE) spent more on textbooks and instructional materials for schools and students than the Ministry of Education transferred to state governments for basic education, and two-thirds of what it transferred to municipalities (Plank 1990). Yet the books were low-quality, could not be used for more than a year, and tended to arrive toward the end of the school year, if at all. Other federal money budgeted for providing schooling materials was simply diverted to other uses entirely: Plank (1990) reports, for instance, that in 1987 up to 40 percent of transfers from the Ministry of Education to municipalities for basic education were distributed off-budget for "special projects." The majority of the Ministry's discretionary resources went to projects in the Northeast (Plank, Sobrinho, and Xavier 1996)—where, to be sure, the needs were greatest—but only a tiny fraction actually reached classrooms (CEC/IPEA 1987). Xavier and Marques (1987) report that in 1987 only half of resources allocated to the Northeast for education actually reached classrooms. In other words, federal funds for basic education were largely a boon to elites, not to the students they were ostensibly meant to serve.

The new schools were a boon to mayors and other rural elites in another way: they provided jobs that could be distributed to political supporters (Hanushek, Gomes-Neto, and Harbison 1996; Birdsall, Bruns, and Sabot 1996; Plank 1996; Harbison and Hanushek 1992).[61] Some of these jobs were in an incredibly bloated bureaucracy. In many Brazilian states the education system employed half of all government employees; by the late 1980s, Brazil's education system was the country's largest employer, and in some states the ratio of non-teachers to teachers was as high as 2:1 (Birdsall, Bruns, and Sabot 1996). These officials were chosen politically, not for their educational skills,[62] and their quality was generally poor (Plank, Sobrinho, and Xavier 1996).

Thousands of additional jobs were for teachers. In a poor village, a teaching job was coveted employment: it was one of the only jobs that provided steady wages, even if these were low.[63] By doling out teaching jobs to political supporters in villages, mayors were able to shore up their political support (Harbison and Hanushek 1992). But the clientalistic method of hiring teachers only further weakened the basic education system. Prior to 1964, teaching had been a prestigious occupation, well-paid and aspired to by the middle class (see Section 3). After 1964, teaching became a low-paid[64] occupation for less-qualified students from lower socio-economic backgrounds (Schwartzman 1991). Average teacher quality fell sharply. By the early 1980s, 60 percent of rural primary teachers in northeast Brazil had not themselves finished primary school (Harbison and Hanushek 1992).

The cumulative effect of these developments on Brazilian basic schooling was catastrophic. Student performance sank, while enrollment rates registered only minor increases. In 1970, enrollment of 5- to 14-year-olds was 56 percent, up substantially from 42 percent in 1960; but by 1980, enrollment had risen by just 1.5 percentage points, to 57.5 percent.[65] The reason was that hardly any students actually completed school. Birdsall, Bruns, and Sabot (1996) report that in 1950, 60 percent of Brazilian primary students completed primary school; in 1976, it was just 15.8 percent. By 1972, 12 percent of students in rural one-room schools were dropping out during their first year, and another 25 percent failed out at the end of their first year.[66] Others simply failed to show up the next year: only half of rural first graders made it to second grade in 1972 (World Bank 1979); by 1982, it was only a third (Harbison and Hanushek 1992). Many rural schools did not even offer more than two grades (Gomes-Neto and Hanushek 1996). By the 1980s, more than half of Brazilian students had to repeat the first grade; in the rural Northeast it was 73 percent (Fletcher and Ribeiro 1989). In the rural Northeast, by the mid-1980s, the average student starting fourth grade had already been in school for 7.6 years (Hanushek, Gomes-Neto, and Harbison 1996).[67]

The transition to civilian rule in 1985 did little to change these trends. After 1985 the Ministry of Education was consistently headed by a member of the Liberal Front Party (PFL), the party established by President José Sarney and Bahia's ACM to represent the Northeastern rural elites (Schwartzman and Klein 1993; and also see Section 5). In 1986, after opposition parties won 25 of the 26 governorships, the federal government responded by simply shifting much of federal education spending onto municipalities: total federal transfers to municipalities skyrocketed 600 percent, and municipal control over basic education was enshrined in the 1988 Constitution (CEC/IPEA 1987; Plank 1990). Even a large infusion of new resources ostensibly intended to improve basic education in the *Educação para Todos* ("Education for All") program, which was developed by the Sarney government, were lost to the same clientalism and corruption that had absorbed basic education spending for the previous quarter century (Plank 1990).

Had there been no other option, the precipitous decline in the quality of the lower levels of public education would have harmed not only the Brazilian middle and lower classes, but also the children of the military's elite vital constituency. But even as the public basic education system was deteriorating, a private elite track opened up that allowed elite children primary education that was world-class (Birdsall, Bruns, and Sabot 1996) and provided superb preparation for taking the entrance exams to universities. In 1964 there were 1.2 million students in private schools in grades 1–4, and another million in grades 5–11; in 1989 there were 3.4 million in grades 1–8—the grades of "basic education" after the 1972 reform—and another million in grades 9–11 (see Tables 6.12 and 6.13). Tuition to private schools was regulated to limit profits but be high enough to ensure outstanding quality, which also had the side effect of making it generally unaffordable to anyone below the upper middle class.[68] In 1982, for example, the average family income of a private school student was three to five times that of a public school student (de Mello e Souza and do Valle Silva 1996).

Yet although private school was expensive, its quality was far better than its tuition would have allowed, because the government heavily subsidized it. In Section 4, I noted that the 1961 Basic Education Law allowed public education money to go to private schools; although post-1964 governments stopped the implementation of most of the law, this provision remained. Private educational expenses were tax-deductible (World Bank 1979)—a benefit that went overwhelmingly to the top earners.[69] In addition, private schools themselves were exempt from paying income and wage taxes intended to support public education, and various governments developed countless ways to assist private schools or purchase "places" in private schools.[70] Myriad sources of scholarships cropped up, some controlled individually by federal officials or members of the federal Congress. In 1989, federal transfers to private schools were estimated at a third of all federal spending on basic education (Plank, Sobrinho, and Xavier 1996). This private track did its job well. I show in the next section that public university students were overwhelmingly upper class graduates of private basic and secondary schools.

Both the increased resources to private education and the new public schools, teachers, and projects were expensive: Table 6.12 shows steadily increasing resources devoted to basic education, and Table 6.13 the increasing resources to secondary education, both in total and per student. Much of the money came from general revenues, but two additional sources are worth mentioning: a new education tax on workers' salaries for basic education, and foreign aid. The tax, called the *salário educação*, was first conceived in 1964 and first collected in 1969. Until the mid-1970s it was 1.5 percent of payrolls, and 2.5 percent thereafter. Two-thirds of the money was transferred to the states on a need-based formula that meant that most went to the Northeast; the remaining third went into a National Fund for Educational Development, which helped fund the aforementioned projects.[71] Businesses were not required to pay the *salário educação* if they spent the same amount in scholarships to private schools for their employees or their employees' children, or in otherwise educating their employees; after 1975 they could deduct twice as much as they spent (World Bank 1979; FNDE 1990; Velloso 1988).[72]

The second source of additional financing was foreign aid. Until the 1970s, USAID contributed millions for basic education, particularly in the Northeast, and thereafter the World Bank began pouring in money. Although I am not aware of a comprehensive estimate, the region received hundreds of millions in basic education as part of high-profile projects, such as the Bank's *Projeto Nordeste*.[73] In general this funding furthered the developments already discussed: it helped build schools and provide materials for schools that generally failed to educate. Consequently, the aid is usually judged to have been wasted.[74] For example, in the most exhaustive study of the impact of an educational aid project in the northeast, Harbison and Hanushek (1992) found that the $100 million EDURURAL project, part of which the World Bank helped finance, made almost no measurable impact on student achievement.[75] Coupled with the astounding success of basic education aid to Ghana over some of the same period, which we saw in the previous chapter, the wastage of aid in Brazil strongly suggests that aid for education will not help unless it fits the government's political logic.[76] Indeed, other educational aid to Brazil was extremely successful: for example, in the 1960s and 1970s, the Inter-American Development Bank helped Brazil build unified federal universities throughout the country (Schwartzman 1998)—a development I consider in the next section.

This period's twin developments in the lower levels of education—the deterioration of the public system while the private system provided excellent and highly-subsidized education—vastly increased the inequality of Brazilian education. Birdsall, Bruns, and Sabot report that "almost all of the decline in average quality over the past two decades is attributable to a worsening at the bottom of the quality distribution" (1996, 26). Earnings inequality increased substantially even as education inequality ostensibly declined (Lam and Levinson 1991)—a surprising result from an economic perspective. Finaly, intergenerational mobility declined precipitously in the 1970s and 1980s (Pastore and Zylberstajn 1996; Adelman et al. 1996).[77]

WORKER TRAINING

In one respect, the vital constituency of the 1964–1990 period was the same as the prior period: it included employers who demanded skilled workers in an inflexible labor market. Thus the framework predicts that the government should have continued the Selective Worker Training policies of its predecessors.

The military government did in fact continue Selective Worker Training. The SENAI and SENAC systems continued to provide excellent workers to industry, and the government took additional steps to aid companies that wanted to train their workers themselves. I alluded to one of these above: firms could deduct whatever they spent—and, after 1975, twice what they spent—on training their workers from their taxable income (World Bank 1979).[78] And whenever a shortage of skilled labor appeared, the government provided the missing labor—for example, creating an aerospace engineering school to staff its new aerospace industry.[79] There was little sense at the time that Brazilian industry faced a shortage of skilled workers or pressured the government to provide additional workers.[80]

In this period, entrepreneurial government economists and other technocrats (called *técnicos*) tried to implement a sort of Broad Worker Training—a policy for which, according to this book's framework, Brazil's economy had little need. I argued in Chapter 3 that policymakers generally cannot successfully make policies that do not serve the vital constituency. The efforts of these *técnicos* to implement Broad Worker Training is a good example: it was largely a failure. The government began trying to tie education and the economy together by starting "manpower planning" in 1965 (e.g., Brazil 1965)—around the same time that the governments in Taiwan and Brazil were experimenting with such planning. Seven plans followed, each predicting educational needs based on forecasted economic development (Sobrinho 1985), and in 1972 the *técnicos* tried to reorient the secondary education system in line with the plans. Alongside the reforms that added grades 5–8 to "basic" education, the government tried to remake the remaining secondary grades 9–11 into technical training: all secondary schools were required to offer vocational and secondary courses. The *técnicos* envisioned that the secondary level would become a technical level, preparing graduates for specialized occupations in 130 different subjects, whose enrollments would be determined by the manpower plans. But most secondary schools did not receive new teachers or equipment funding to implement the new courses, and the few federal technical schools that received disproportionate federal money saw their graduates, mostly from elite families, continue to take university entrance exams instead of becoming skilled workers. The program was largely abandoned in 1974 and was formally reversed in a "devocalization" law passed in 1982 (Brown 1995; Sobrinho 1985; World Bank 1979; Schwartzman 2003).

WORLD-CLASS UNIVERSITIES

While education got progressively worse for the average public primary and secondary student, it got progressively better for public university students. Recall, from Section 4, that at the time the vital constituency changed in 1964, public universities had only recently become a government priority: higher education had long been a gentleman's pastime for elites, and only in the 1950s did the Brazilian economy develop to the point where wages for college graduates began to make higher education seem to be a good investment. At that time, as I noted in Section 4, the federal government began organizing disparate private and state institutions of higher education into a series of federal universities, but the quality of these universities was hampered by the structure of the institutions they incorporated: teachers taught part-time and did little research, and administrative power was in the hands of unaccountable holders of life-time chairs (World Bank 1979; Schwartzman 1998).

This book's framework predicts that after a change to an elite vital constituency such as Brazil's in 1964, the new government should have done all it could to address the problems in higher education. That is what happened. Just after the

1967 triumph of the hard-line faction of the military—when the military government decided to stay in power, not simply prepare the country for a transition back to civilian rule—the government tackled higher education. In 1968, it passed a new higher education law, intended to transform Brazilian education along the American model. The law abolished the chair system in favor of academic departments, introduced a credit system, and created common facilities, campuses, and a uniform administrative structure under the control of a rector appointed with the blessing of the federal government. Academics were given full-time appointments, with combined research and teaching responsibilities, and a post-graduate tier was created for masters and PhD courses (Schwartzman 1998, 2003; World Bank 1979).

At the same time, the government pumped money into the system, some from general revenues, and some from funds that would, under pre-1964 earmarking procedures, have gone to primary education (Brown 1995). Spending by the federal Ministry of Education on higher education rose nearly 160 percent between 1964 and 1972, and another 130 percent from 1972 to 1985. And this spending was only a part of total spending on higher education. Additional money came from other ministries: for example, the Ministry of Planning's National Fund for Scientific and Technological Development (FNDCT) took care of all equipment costs and student scholarships, and paid a supplement for researchers' salaries. FNDCT was managed by the Financing Agency for Studies and Projects, FINEP, a competent and agile bureaucracy that, unlike the administration of the basic and secondary levels, operated largely free of political influence. FINEP also funded research, which it chose strictly on merit, though it had plenty of money: until 1977 the supply of research funding actually *exceeded* the demand, on average, by nearly 15 percent annually (Schwartzman and Klein 1993). A handful of other government agencies also handed out generous scholarships and stipends to graduate students and researchers.

The contrast in funding between the upper and lower levels was drastic. In its 1979 report, the World Bank noted ironically that "while most rural primary schools must do without piped water and basic sanitation facilities, almost all public universities in Brazil have swimming pools, sports facilities, pleasant cafeterias, and other social amenities" (World Bank 1979, 36). Table 6.14 shows data on the expansion and improvement of public universities. Even while the number of places in public universities rose 200 percent between 1964 and 1972, and 750 percent between 1964 and 1989, spending kept pace: spending per student on universities from just the Ministry of Education—i.e., not including all the other sources of funding for higher education—dropped only 15 percent between 1964 and 1972, and rose 2.5 percent from 1972 to 1985.

Above I characterized private basic and secondary education after 1964 as an "elite track" that prepared students for entrance exams to these excellent and luxurious public universities. The sign of the success of such a track is the proportion of its students who make it through the entrance exams. Judged on this criterion,

Table 6.14 **Improvement of the upper levels, 1964–1989**

| | 1964 | 1972 | 1989 | Changes | | |
				1964–72	1972–89	1964–89
Enrollment	144,281	700,560	1,573,237[1]	385.6%	124.6%	990.4%
Graduate	142,386	690,402	1,521,710[2]	384.9%	120.4%	968.7%
Post-Graduate	1,895	10,158	48,480	436.0%	377.3%	2,458.3%
Public	86,315	262,788	738,212	204.5%	180.9%	755.3%
Private	57,966[3]	437,772[4]	835,024[5]	655.2%	90.7%	1,340.5%
Percentage in Private	40.2%	62.5%	53.1%			
Spending (Public only)[†]			(1985)[†††]		(1972–85)	(1964–85)
Current (thousands)[††]	80,500,616	1,451,695	6,495,370[††††]			
2004 R$	1,017,342	2,613,558	6,059,679	156.9%	131.9%	495.6%
Per Student[††]	932,637	5,524	10,927,497			
Per Student 2004 R$	11,786	9,946	10,195	-15.6%	2.5%	-13.5%

Notes: [†] Spending is only from the Ministry of Education: it does not include spending on education by other ministries. Per-student figures are calculated only for students in public universities, which receive the vast majority of public funding for higher education. [††] Nominal spending, unadjusted for currency changes in 1967 and 1986, each of which removed three zeros from the currency. [†††] I present 1985 spending in lieu of 1989, which is unavailable. Per-student spending is calculated with 1985 enrollment of 3,016,138. [††††] in millions.

Imputation: some of the enrollment figures for higher education are imputed, as follows: 1989: [1] Enrollment data are not available; the figure assumes trend growth between 1988 (1,550,443 students) and 1990 (1,596,366 students); [2] Assumes trend growth between 1988 (1,503,560 students) and 1990 (1,540,080 students); [3] Assumes the proportion of students in private institutions is the same in 1964 as in 1962, the closest year for which data are available; [4] Assumes the proportion of students in private institutions is the same in 1972 as in 1974, the closest year for which data are available; [5] Assumes trend growth between 1988 (918,209 students in private institutions) and 1990 (759,376 students in private institutions).

Brazil's elite track was exceptional. Only 10 percent of university admissions went to students whose fathers were "working class"—unskilled or skilled workers or supervisors of manual workers. By contrast, the proportion of the student population beginning primary school whose fathers were working class was about the same as in the overall population: 60 to 70 percent (World Bank 1979).[81] Plank, Sobrinho, and Xavier (1996) report that in the late 1980s in the Federal University of Ceará, a Northeastern state, 88 percent of students in the most prestigious faculties—Engineering, Medicine, and Data Processing—had graduated from a private secondary school.[82]

But it is not that those outside the vital constituency had no access to higher education. In fact, the expansion and improvement of public universities is only half the story of higher education under the military. This period also saw a large expansion in private higher education. In 1964 there were just 58,000 students in private higher education, or two-thirds as many students as in the public universities; by 1972, students in private higher education outnumbered public by nearly 60 percent, and by 1989, there were 835,000 students in private higher education, a 1,340 percent increase in 25 years. (See Table 6.14.) Unlike the public universities, these new private institutions provided those *outside* the vital constituency with higher education, albeit of far lesser quality.

Why, given its vital constituency, would the post-1964 government have allowed this expansion? Although the new Brazilian private institutions (like those in Ghana and Taiwan) were far inferior to public higher education, they did provide some education—they were not like the public lower levels, which seemed not to be educating at all. This book's framework predicts that a government will sometimes increase the availability of education to a group outside its vital constituency in order to preserve social stability (see Chapter 3). This was the Brazilian government's motivation. As I noted in Section 5, the 1960s were a time of great social unrest by newly disenfranchised groups, particularly the middle and lower-middle classes. One of their main grievances was, in fact, a lack of educational opportunity. The vast expansion of primary and secondary education prior to 1964, in combination with greater job-market demand for university degrees, created a glut of qualified students for whom there were not enough places in universities. In the mid-1960s, these students, called *exedentes*, protested angrily. Facing growing unrest, used its outsourcing tool: "[T]he military government acted quickly. To answer middle-class demands, the government turned towards the already established private sector" (Vahl 1980; Brown 1995, 163).

To ensure rapid growth in private higher education, the federal government dropped accreditation standards to nearly nothing (Brown 1995). From 1968 to 1976, the peak of its leniency, the Federal Council of Education approved 73 percent of around 1,500 requests for new private courses in higher education (Schwartzman 1998). At the same time, it regulated fees so that they would be accessible to middle-class families. Private institutions consequently expanded to the point that they were taking basically anyone who could pay: the World Bank (1979, 133) cites a study by economist Cláudio de Mauro Castro showing that admission was extended even to those whose scores on entrance exams were barely above guessing. With fees capped, private institutions specialized in low-cost education, taught by part-time teachers and requiring only a room and a chalkboard—mostly law, social sciences, and humanities (Brown 1995). Graduates of these institutions were regarded not much more highly than secondary-school graduates (World Bank 1979).[83]

Turning to the private sector in this way had two advantages. First, it calmed social tensions by providing education that cost the government little and was inferior enough not to be a threat to the elites graduating from the better public universities. Second, it made a great deal of money for the business elites in the government's vital constituency.

In sum, in this period, developments of the public and private systems at the lower and upper levels were mirror opposites. On the one hand, excellent private basic education led to free public universities. On the other, students who managed to make it through the poor-quality public basic and secondary schools—students whose inferior education ill-equipped them for public university entrance exams—usually had to settle for paying to attend a mediocre private institution.

BAHIA AND SÃO PAULO

In most respects, Bahia and São Paulo reflected the regional pattern of education that I outlined above. Bahia, with its elite vital constituency, followed the North-eastern pattern: at the lower levels, its rural schooling expanded dramatically, but the overall quality of its public lower levels fell and a great deal of public money was given to private schools or wasted; at the upper levels, the system was almost entirely public and dominated by the children of elites. In São Paulo, where the vital constituency was cross-class through the late 1960s, the govern-ment continued to improve primary education; after the military began appoint-ing São Paulo's governments, their attention shifted to technical and higher education.

Bahia

The most notable developments in the lower levels of Bahian education (as else-where in the Northeast) were the expansion and deterioration of public education and the siphoning off of public money to private schools that served the govern-ment's elite vital constituency. In the 1950s and early 1960s, public primary and secondary schools were few but highly regarded, with teachers who were well-qualified and well-paid.[84] But beginning in the 1960s, the system grew and its quality plummeted. Table 6.15 shows that the growth was nearly all in municipal schools, which grew 130 percent from 1964 to 1989, by which time they accounted for 83 percent of all schools in Bahia. 19,230 of the 20,759 municipal schools were in rural areas. Many of the new rural schools were like those in the World Bank description I cited above: one-room, perhaps offering only one grade,[85] and taught by an unqualified, politically appointed teacher.[86] Those that were not often oper-ated in as many as four shifts per day and admitted students in three yearly cohorts beginning in January, March, and June.[87] Thus despite the growth of schools, the enrollment rate in Bahia among 5- to 14-year-olds, which had risen

Table 6.15 Education in Bahia and São Paulo, 1964–1989

	Bahia				São Paulo			
	1964	*1972*	*1989*	*Change 1964–89*	*1964*	*1972*	*1989*	*Change 1964–89*
Primary								
Schools	12,483	17,678	24,969	100.0%	17,008	25,089	14,020	-17.6%
Federal		23	43			10		
State	2,532	2,529	3,024	19.4%	14,092	21,218	12,028	-14.6%
Municipal	8,981	14,104	20,759	131.1%	1,830	1,989	602	-67.1%
Private	970	1,022	1,143	17.8%	1,086	1,872	1,390	28.0%
Enrollment								
*Grades 1-4**	664,307	1,009,706*			2,071,097	2,432,760*		
*Grades 1-8**		1,149,200*	2,023,601			3,877,412*	5,788,565	
Federal	(gr. 1-4)	(gr. 1-8) 3,261	(gr. 1-8) 8,642		(gr. 1-4)	(gr. 1-8) 3,457	(gr. 1-8)	
State	250,927	444,023	868,921	246.3%	1,752,470	3,248,705	4,575,807	161.1%
Municipal	340,545	587,297	913,948	168.4%	137,181	280,174	536,942	291.4%
Private	72,835	114,619	232,090	218.7%	181,446	345,076	675,816	272.5%

	Bahia				São Paulo			
	1964	1972	1989	Change 1964–89	1964	1972	1989	Change 1964–89
Secondary								
Enrollment								
Grades 5-8*	62,710	179,494*			413,154	1,444,652*		
Grades 9-11*	19,953	65,894*	191,976	862.1%	127,358	376,854*	957,419	651.8%
In Private	43,845	22,827	46,092	5.1%	252,588	124,984	285,067	12.9%
% Private	53.0%	34.6%	24.0%		46.7%	33.2%	29.8%	
Higher	(1963)				(1963)			
Enrollment								
Graduate	4,763	20,303	45,497[3]	855.2%	34,085	273,843	485,757[7]	1,325.1%
Post-Grad.	83	135[1]	—		543	5,346[5]	—	
In Private	—	11,782[2]	19,242[4]		—	211,780[6]	349,108[8]	
% Private	—	57.6%	42.3%		—	75.9%	71.9%	

Notes: * Beginning in 1972, the first four years of secondary education (*ginasial*) were combined with the four years of primary, creating a new level of "basic" education with 8 grades; thereafter secondary (*colegio*) is only grades 9-11. -- No data available.

Imputation: some of the enrollment figures for higher education are imputed, as follows: *Bahia:* [1] The figure assumes trend growth between 1971 (104 students) and 1974 (228 students); [2] Assumes the proportion of students in private institutions is the same in 1972 as in 1974, the closest year for which data are available; [3] Assumes trend growth between 1988 (45,990 students) and 1990 (45,009 students); [4] Assumes trend growth between 1988 (20,640 students) and 1990 (17,938 students); *São Paulo:* [5] The figure assumes trend growth between 1971 (4,153 students) and 1974 (8,861 students); [6] Assumes the proportion of students in private institutions is the same in 1972 as in 1974, the closest year for which data are available; [7] Assumes trend growth between 1988 (474,487 students) and 1990 (497,294 students); [8] Assumes trend growth between 1988 (383,320 students) and 1990 (317,950 students).

from 31.1 percent to 42.1 percent from 1960 to 1970, actually fell from 1970 to 1980, from 42.1 percent to 39.2 percent.[88]

What the schools did do was fuel patronage networks. Recall from Section 4 that Bahia was a state run almost entirely by one man, ACM, through a patronage network of civil servants and mayors. These mayors knew the powerful effect that a new school had on a village.[89] One secretary of education for the state in the 1990s told me that villagers would usually see the school as a gift, because the taxes that paid for it were hidden in the price of goods; the quality of the education the school would provide was naturally not apparent when it opened.[90] These schools were largely impervious to efforts to improve them, as Harbison and Hanushek's (1992) study of the EDURURAL project shows.

On the other hand, the private system flourished: enrollment grew nearly 220 percent between 1964 and 1989. And the system received tremendous amounts of public money: in 1986, Bahia's secretariat of education estimated that 40 percent of all educational expenditures went to support private schools (Plank, Sobrinho, and Xavier 1996), a percentage that had risen steadily over the previous five years (Plank 1990).

The remaining areas of education—worker training and higher education— developed in a way similar to the national pattern. Training of skilled workers, the demand for which was not very high in Bahia, was almost entirely through SENAI schools, which produced workers tailored to employers' demands: often the schools had agreements with firms to provide training inside company facilities and factories.[91] In higher education, Bahian enrollments grew only slightly more slowly than the rest of Brazil, with a somewhat lower percentage in private institutions (Table 6.15). For much of the period Bahia had one federal university, but the university leaned left and had a contentious relationship with ACM. In the 1980s the government added a new state university, created by absorbing ten teaching colleges in smaller towns where support for ACM was strong.[92]

São Paulo

Unlike Bahia, which was firmly under the control of ACM, São Paulo was one of the most difficult states for the military to control. Its governments engaged in political entrepreneurship through the late 1960s, and education policy by governments in São Paulo contrasted sharply with federal policy. Paulistas tried to improve the quality of equity of primary and secondary education, experimenting with a "cycle" of first and second grade to reduce repetition of first grade, and eliminating the entrance exam between fourth and fifth grade years—a step the federal government would take in 1972, but for which at the time it denounced São Paulo's government as communist.[93] From 1960 to 1970, São Paulo's enrollment rate among 5- to 14-year-olds increased from 52.2 to 66.3 percent, a rate higher than all but two of Brazil's other states.[94]

But as the military repressed political entrepreneurship in São Paulo and solidified its control over the state in the 1970s, the state's education policies shifted into line with the federal government's. The public universities saw new resources and improving quality. São Paulo was already home to several excellent state universities, including the University of São Paulo, Brazil's best, and was therefore well-positioned to benefit from the reforms and meritocratic funding structures implemented by the military in higher education.[95] Table 6.15 shows that by 1972, 40 percent of all the students in higher education in Brazil were in São Paulo. São Paulo also accounted disproportionately for the increase in private higher education, as it was the home of many of the middle and working class students whose protests had prompted the military to open up the private sector after 1968: three-quarters of the state's higher-education enrollment was in private institutions in 1972.

At the same time, at the lower levels, the government began shifting attention away from broad public education—after rising more than 14 percentage points in the previous decade, the enrollment rate among 5- to 14-year olds rose only 3.7 percentage points from 1970 to 1980[96]—and toward technical education of workers for industrial elites. In 1969 the state government opened the first of what would become a large network of "Centro Paulo Souza" schools that offered specialized secondary and higher-education courses in technical and service skills. (Today there are 138 secondary and 39 higher-education institutes scattered in 118 cities around the state.) But the rest of public basic education deteriorated. In 1974, after education was expanded to eight years, the government redistributed students into new schools that offered grades 1–8 under one roof, a step that necessitated building many new schools (providing large numbers of construction contracts) and closing old schools—hence the seeming decline, in Table 6.15, in the number of basic schools in São Paulo from 1972 to 1989, even as enrollment rose by almost two million. The change led to overcrowding, and, as in Bahia, schools worked in shifts. Average quality was dismal.[97] (Unlike in Bahia, most lower-level schools were run by the state government; the number of municipal schools actually fell by two-thirds between 1964 and 1989, and almost 80 percent of the remainder were in urban areas.) As elsewhere in Brazil, money ostensibly intended for education ended up paying for everything but: for example, for paving a road that passed a school, or paying the electricity bills of buildings in the school's vicinity.[98] Elites generally sent their children to private schools, enrollments in which rose 270 percent between 1964 and 1989.

After years of federally appointed governors, a directly-elected governor took power again in São Paulo in 1983, and thereafter the state's governments appointed more powerful secretaries of education who again tried to improve the quality of basic education. The system introduced cycling in grades one and two to reduce repetition, built new schools and rehabilitated old ones, instituted new curricula and teacher training courses, fired underperforming teachers, and created new salary structures that rewarded teachers who stayed in the classroom instead of moving into administration. These measures made a difference, though they did not undo the damage to the system.

WRAPPING UP

The 1964 coup brought to power an elitist government. Thus the framework predicts that the new government should have transformed Brazil's education system
from narrow All-Levels to Top-Down. This section has presented evidence that
this is generally what the new government did. Table 6.16 summarizes the
evidence.

In most ways Brazil's governments acted as predicted from 1964 to 1990. But
the period also presents some challenges for the framework. At the lower levels,
the major indicators—enrollment and per-student spending—do not behave as
predicted. Likewise, the massive expansion of the lower levels was concentrated
in rural areas in the Northeast: exactly where the opposite of what the framework
predicts. I have argued that there is a simple reason for these discrepancies: in this
period, the public lower levels largely ceased to educate students, and instead, as
in Ghana, they mostly became conduits for patronage jobs and construction contracts that helped the rural elites in the vital constituency. Consequently the new
schools were the most basic of structures, staffed by unqualified teachers and possessing few materials, and their students learned little. Of the vast sums spent on
these schools, only a trickle actually made it into students' education. Only the
private elite track retained high-quality primary and secondary education, and
there high fees prevented all but the elite from attending. All these features of the
system are evidence of the government acting as predicted. Yet the raw data on
spending and enrollment still are the opposite of what the framework predicts,
and must therefore be considered a strike against it.

In addition, the data raise a question: if, in this period, Brazil's lower levels
were little more than patronage machines, why did Brazil's government decide to
deliver patronage by building schools and hiring teachers? We have seen this kind
of schools-as-patronage before, in Ghana in the 1970s, when schools were
reduced to little more than excuses for paying teacher salaries. But there is a key
difference: in Ghana the schools already existed; in Brazil the government chose
to build schools for students whom it was not already educating. There are four
reasons why schools were an excellent patronage tool in Brazil. The first and most
important reason is foreign aid. Because the World Bank and other donors were
willing to pour hundreds of millions of dollars into school construction, there
was plenty of money available for building schools, and the industrial elites who
ran and staffed Brazil's construction companies were only too happy to build
them. Second, teaching positions were ideal patronage jobs for mayors to distribute: they had few responsibilities, required little education or skills, and, along
with police, were one of only two jobs in a village with a guaranteed paycheck.[99]
Third, as I noted above when discussing Bahian education, the schools were perceived by villagers as gifts from the mayor and enhanced his or her popularity.
And lastly, the quality of the schools was low enough that they were unthreatening to the education provided to the vital constituency. Schools were only one

Table 6.16 **Evidence summary, 1964–1990**

Indicator	Characteristics	Conforms to Framework?
A. Enrollment	Lower levels: increasing	☐
	Upper levels: increasing	■
B. Per-student spending	Lower levels: sharp decline, then increasing	◻
	Upper levels: increasing	■
C. The toolkit		
1. Schools	Lower levels: private: excellent; public: abysmal	■
	Upper levels: private: poor; public: excellent	■
Teachers	Lower levels: private: excellent; public: abysmal	■
	Upper levels: private: poor; public: excellent	■
Physical resources	Lower levels: private: excellent; public: abysmal	■
	Upper levels: private: poor; public: excellent	■
Location	Lower levels: widespread; particular growth in rural areas	☐
	Upper levels: mostly towns or urban areas	■
2. Fees[†]	Lower levels: public is free; private charge high fees	■
	Upper levels: public is free; private charge affordable fees	■
3. Access restrictions and discriminatory pricing		
Quotas	None	
Exams	Exams for public universities favor students from private primary and secondary schools	■
Financial aid	Extensive tax breaks for spending on private education; extensive aid and stipends to students at public universities	■
4. Tracking	Exceptional tracking from private lower levels into public universities	■
5. Outsourcing (domestic or foreign; to firms or non-profits)	Lower levels: extensive, for the elite track	■
	Upper levels: extensive, to preserve social stability	☐

Notes: ■: fully conforms to the framework; ◻: partly conforms to the framework; ☐: does not conform to the framework.[†] Fees are for enrollment, books and other equipment, uniforms, activities, school improvements, etc.

of many patronage tools employed by Brazilian governments in this period (see, e.g., Mainwaring 1986), but for these reasons they were an extremely valuable patronage tool.

There is one other, lesser discrepancy between the framework's predictions and the reality of Brazilian education in this period: the expansion of private higher education. I have argued that this expansion was motivated by social instability, and was engineered to provide education to those outside the vital constituency at little cost to the government, to the great profit of business elites, and of a quality low enough to pose little competition to the children of the elite in the public universities. Still, as the framework predicts that governments do not extend education to those outside their vital constituencies, the expansion of private higher education may be considered a partial strike against it.

On the remaining indicators the framework is largely accurate. Brazil's military government radically transformed Brazilian education to a system that provided excellent and highly-subsidized education to elites right up through universities and graduate school; on the other hand, those outside the vital constituency who could not afford the fees for private primary and secondary schools were relegated to a deteriorating public system that threw up every conceivable barrier to achievement, and which offered at its end only the chance to pay for private higher education that was far inferior.

Brazil's transition to democracy in 1985 did little to change these trends. But behind the scenes, political entrepreneurship was slowly returning to Brazil, led by the new Workers' Party, the PT, and its charismatic leader, Luiz Inácio Lula da Silva. The PT's gradual creation of a new political force in Brazilian politics—an alliance of workers and the rural poor—would soon make an impact on Brazilian education.

7. POLITICS, 1990–2000: Gradual Return to a Cross-Class Alliance

The 1990 election began a gradual expansion of the vital constituency, from the military-era alliance of industrial and agrarian elites to a cross-class alliance that included the middle class and, increasingly, workers and the poor. This expansion proceeded slowly through the 1990s, and, although it took a big step forward with the 2002 presidential election of "Lula," Luiz Inácio Lula da Silva, of the PT, it is still ongoing as I write this. The expansion was prompted by the political entrepreneurship by the PT of Brazil's workers and urban and rural poor. This section details the PT's role as a political entrepreneur, and then gives a brief overview of the makeup of the vital constituency through the political economy of the 1990s.

A NEW POLITICAL ENTREPRENEUR: THE PT

The origins of the PT's political entrepreneurship of the poor date to a series of electoral defeats in the 1980s, which convinced the PT that it needed to organize these supporters intensely and continuously. The party consequently gradually developed a hierarchical structure of local, state, and national organs that linked together its disparate organizational groups and that persisted between elections (Samuels 2004). The military also added, unwittingly, to the PT's incentives for political entrepreneurship. In 1979, during its "opening," or *abertura* (see Section 5), a new election law legalized political parties but established difficult thresholds for legalization—thresholds that did not favor parties with geographically concentrated support, such as the PT. The PT's support was strong in the industrial regions of the Southeast, particularly São Paulo, but weak in the rest of the country. The legalization threshold required that a party have founding conventions in at least a fifth of the municipalities of at least nine states, as well as a national convention and either ten percent of the representatives of the National Congress, or five percent of the total votes in the most recent election to the Chamber of Deputies and a minimum of three percent in nine states. In part to reach the threshold, the PT expanded broadly, moving far beyond its labor roots to link up with leftist groups and social and peasant organizations across Brazil (Keck 1992). The party's growing organization of disadvantaged groups brought it increasing electoral success, particularly in towns and cities. In 1990 it won 35 seats in the 503-seat Chamber of Deputies; in 1994, 49 seats and two governorships; in 1998, 58 seats and three governorships.[100]

The PT's success was naturally threatening to Brazil's larger, centrist parties. In Brazil, local support is crucial to national electoral success: generally local mayors offer their support for national candidates—through endorsements and the help of their political machines—in exchange for promises of federal programs and resources (see Ames 1994, on the 1989 presidential election). The PT's organization was threatening because it competed at the local level with these machine politics.

POLITICS AT THE TOP: THE "DEMOCRATIC ALLIANCE" PARTIES

Parties in control of the national government had long been free to ignore to the demands of Brazil's rural and urban masses. But the PT's threat forced them increasingly to try to placate mass demands.

Though the PT influenced national politics in the 1990s, it did not itself win the presidency or hold sway in the Congress until after 2000 when my analysis stops. In the 1990s, power in Brasília was held by the three parties of the "Democratic Alliance," the coalition that had elected Tancredo Neves in 1985. The first two parties, the PMDB and PSDB, were center-left parties (the PSDB was slightly to the left of the PMDB) that were powerful in the Southeast and represented the industrial elite and middle classes. The third party was the right-leaning PFL, the party in which ACM, in Bahia, played such a prominent role. The PFL represented the agrarian elites and was nearly dominant in the Northeast. After the 1990 election, the PMDB and PFL were the largest parties in the Chamber of Deputies, and after the 1994 elections the PSDB joined them in the top three; together they held 46 percent of the Chamber after 1990, 50 percent after 1994, and 56 percent after 1998. In the mid-1990s, two other right-wing parties joined the coalition, giving it an overwhelming majority of seats but making policy agreement difficult.

The federal government faced an unenviable political and economic situation. The government's vital constituency of elites and the middle class was barely powerful enough to maintain the government in power, and ongoing economic turmoil was threatening the support of that vital constituency. The experience of the first directly-elected president since the 1960s, Fernando Collor de Mello, illustrates the government's political and economic difficulties. In 1989 elections, Mello prevailed in a run-off against Lula by only a slim margin, winning 53 percent to 47. Mello was formerly a PMDB governor, but for the presidential election he formed his own political party, and he therefore lacked a base of support in Congress: his party won only two seats in the Chamber of Deputies and one in the Senate, and while the PMDB and the PFL supported him in the run-off, the PSDB backed Lula.

Mello also inherited an economic mess from his predecessor, José Sarney. During Sarney's administration, inflation had skyrocketed and growth had slowed. Aware that his government was losing the support of the industrial elites in the vital constituency, Sarney had tried to stem the economic decline, instituting price controls, changing the currency three times, closing international markets, and defaulting on foreign debt. But inflation continued to rise—by 1989 it was more than 1,600 percent. Real per-capita growth was negative in 1988 and only 1.2 percent in 1989 (IPEA 2006). In 1990, Collor's first year in office, per-capita growth turned sharply negative, to -6 percent.

Collor's government tried to tackle inflation even more aggressively than Sarney's. Collor froze wages and prices, cut government spending, and privatized several state-owned companies. At the same time, his government tried to spur growth by removing import restrictions and opened the economy, exposing previously sheltered Brazilian companies to foreign competition, against which, for a time, they fared very badly. Per-capita growth stayed negative: -.7 percent in 1991 and -2.15 percent in 1992 (IPEA 2006). Unemployment rose, affecting workers but also the middle class and thus fueling dissatisfaction among a key group in the vital constituency. Collor lost still more support among the elites in his vital constituency by trying to fight inflation by converting large bank accounts into illiquid government bonds. Yet inflation would not subside: after dropping to 460 percent in 1991, it was back up to 1,130 percent in 1992. The vital constituency largely blamed Collor and his policies, and in 1992, he was impeached.

Collor was succeeded by his vice president, Itamar Franco. Franco was a prag-
matist who moved immediately to shore up his support in the Congress by organizing key leaders of the PMDB, PSDB, and PFL into a coalition government. A
year later, he and his new finance minister, Fernando Henrique Cardoso, finally
slayed hyperinflation with their "*Plano Real.*" Inflation had risen to 2,460 percent
in 1993, but fell to 941 percent in 1994, 23 percent in 1995, 10 percent in 1996,
and 4.8 percent in 1997. In 1993, per-capita growth turned positive again: it was
3.3 percent in 1993, and 4.2 percent in 1994 (IPEA 2006). With the economic
recovery, Franco's approval ratings rose sharply. Franco did not run for re-election
in 1994 but instead supported Cardoso, whom the *Plano Real* had made a national
hero. In addition to Franco's backing, Cardoso ran with broad support from the
Democratic Alliance: he was a candidate of the PSDB, but was also supported by
the PFL and much of the PMDB, which joined his coalition after the election. Cardoso won the presidency outright, in the first round. (Lula again came in second,
with 27 percent of the vote.)

Cardoso shared much of Franco's coalition—the PSDB, PMDB, and PFL, as well
as two smaller right-wing parties[101]—and he continued the privatization policies
of his predecessor. But his coalition often had difficulty agreeing, and its disagreement watered-down major reforms to the tax code and the social security system.
Brazil was also hit hard by spillover effects of the Mexican and East Asian financial
crises. The economy managed only 2.4 percent average annual growth in per-
capita GDP from 1994 to 1998, and thereafter growth turned slightly negative.
Cardoso was re-elected in 1998, but thereafter his popularity waned. In 2002,
Lula finally won the presidency.

Table 6.17 shows the vital constituency of Brazilian federal governments in the
1990s.

Table 6.17 **The Vital Constituency, 1990–2000**

Political Entrepreneur(s)	Groups in the Vital Constituency[†]	Groups outside the Vital Constituency
Unions and the Workers' Party (PT); PMDB/PSDB	Military	Workers [PT]
	Bureaucracy	Peasants [PT]*
	Middle Class [PMDB/PSDB]	Urban Poor [PT]*
	Agrarian Elites (Type *N*)	
	Industrial Elites (Type *S*)	

Notes: [†] If a group was empowered with the help of a political entrepreneur, the entrepreneur is in
brackets. * As the PT grows in strength as a political entrepreneur, it brings peasants and the urban
poor into the political arena as forces in their own right. In 2002, the PT wins the presidency in part
with their support.

Employer types are in parentheses: Type *S* employers need skilled workers in an inflexible labor
market; type *N* employers do not need skilled workers.

VITAL CONSTITUENCIES IN BAHIA AND SÃO PAULO

Bahia and São Paulo again help to highlight the important variation in the state vital constituencies in the 1990s. Bahia was the heartland of the PFL, the right-wing party that was a key coalition member of federal governments in the 1990s. In São Paulo, political competition was between the PMDB/PSDB—the parties of the industrial elites and the middle class—and the PT—the party of workers.

Bahia[102]

Section 5 introduced ACM, the overlord of Bahian politics. In the 1990s, ACM was still Bahia's dominant political force, and was increasingly powerful nationally: he was the undisputed leader of the PFL and was president of the federal Senate from 1997 to 2001. (Thereafter corruption scandals forced him to resign, and he began to face competition from previously-allied leaders, both in Bahia and nationally, as well as from the PT.)

In democratized Brazil, as under the military, ACM relied for most of his power on the support of the mayors in the interior, many of whom owed their offices to him. These rural elites, particularly mayors, were the key groups in his vital constituency. They were joined in the vital constituency by the senior Bahian bureaucracy, but urban areas, particularly Salvador, remained ACM's weakest area. Workers and the small urban middle class/junior bureaucracy generally opposed ACM. Their dissatisfaction with him grew stronger in the aftermath of the decentralization of government power that followed from the 1988 constitution. As part of the decentralization, Salvador took on tremendous new responsibilities, but federal transfers intended to provide the resources to meet those responsibilities were slow in coming, causing several years of chaotic and ineffective administration.

São Paulo[103]

In São Paulo, political competition in the 1990s was between the PMDB/PSDB and the PT: as in the rest of the country, the former represented the industrial elites and middle class, and the latter workers. Both competed to some extent for the impoverished urban masses. In later years the PFL, the right-leaning party of agrarian elites that was centered in the Northeast, also made inroads. Given the distribution of the workers and the poor in the state, the PT tended to do better in the city of São Paulo—it held the mayor's office from 1989 to 1992 and won it again in 2001—while the PDMB/PSDB was close to dominant in the state government.

8. EDUCATION, 1990–2000: Minor Equalizing

The previous section described the federal government's vital constituency as expanding gradually and incompletely through the 1990s to incorporate the middle class and, largely as a response to the PT's political entrepreneurship, attempting to placate the Brazilian masses. That is, the vital constituency was still one that preferred a Top-Down system, but from outside the vital constituency the government was facing challenges from increasingly organized groups that wanted a Bottom-Up system. In this section we will see educational developments that reflect these politics: there are some important, placating reforms, but no drastic reorientation of the system and no formidable efforts to equalize it. At the upper levels, quality and access did not change appreciably; at the lower levels, access to the public system increased, but quality only inched up and the private elite track remained. This section, like previous sections, begins with the lower levels, the area in which we will see the most important changes in the 1990s. The second sub-section briefly considers worker training and the third sub-section the higher levels—areas in which there have been fewer developments. The fourth sub-section looks at educational developments in Bahia and São Paulo. Finally, the fifth sub-section weighs the evidence from the 1990s against the framework's predictions.

THE LOWER LEVELS

The 1990s saw increases in both access and quality at the lower levels. As expected of a government that was trying to placate the masses but not serve them, the increase in quality was meager, while the increase in access was more striking.

Recall, from Section 6, Brazil's education system in 1990. In the preceding quarter-century, the system had become two-tracked: for the wealthy, expensive private primary and secondary schools paved the way for good scores on entrance exams to the public universities; for everyone else, poor-quality public schools made it very difficult for most students to achieve, and even the most capable and dedicated students were usually relegated to a spot in a private institution of higher education, paying for an inferior education. Section 6 also noted that not much changed after the transition to civilian rule in 1985.

This inertia continued under the early democratic administrations of Collor and Franco. Enrollment rose 28 percent from 1985 to 1994, a slightly slower pace than under the military (Table 6.18). To the extent that the federal government focused on improving the public lower levels, its focus was largely rhetorical and legal. Brazil's new 1988 Constitution formalized the municipalization of basic education and included several other educational provisions, including an "actionable" right to education and a return to constitutionally-mandated spending on education.[104] And much of the 1988–1995 period was spent debating a new Basic Education Law, which was finally adopted in 1996.

It was not until the Cardoso government took power in 1995 that the federal government began actively to make real changes to the lower levels. After a long line of strictly political appointments to head the Ministry of Education—many of whom, after 1985, came from the rightist PFL, aligned with Bahia's ACM— Cardoso's choice for minister of education was Paulo Renato de Souza, a respected

Table 6.18 Primary ("basic") education, 1989–1999

	1989	1994	1999	Changes		
				1989–94	1994–99	1989–94
Schools	196,638	195,545	183,448	-0.6%	-6.2%	-6.7%
Federal	725	129	50	-82.2%	-61.2%	-93.1%
State	50,367	46,584	34,686	-7.5%	-25.5%	-31.1%
Municipal	134,345	134,873	130,759	0.4%	-3.1%	-2.7%
Private	11,201	13,959	17,953	24.6%	28.6%	60.3%
Enrollment	27,557,542	31,680,595[1]	36,059,742	15.0%	13.8%	30.9%
Federal	140,983	41,530[2]	28,571	-70.5%	-31.2%	-79.7%
State	15,755,120	17,904,237[3]	16,589,455	13.6%	-7.3%	5.3%
Municipal	8,218,455	9,988,422[4]	16,164,369	21.5%	61.8%	96.7%
Private	3,442,984	3,746,406[5]	3,277,347	8.8%	-12.5%	-4.8%
Teachers	1,201,034	1,335,270	1,487,292			
Federal	5,802	1,948	2,091	-66.4%	7.3%	-64.0%
State	668,450	721,467	626,744	7.9%	-13.1%	-6.2%
Municipal	366,132	430,995	638,516	17.7%	48.1%	74.4%
Private	160,650	180,860	219,941	12.6%	21.6%	36.9%

	1989	1994	1999	Changes		
				1989–94	1994–99	1989–94
Student: Teacher Ratio	23	24	24	3.4%	2.2%	5.7%
Federal	24	21	14	-12.3%	-35.9%	-43.8%
State	24	25	26	5.3%	6.7%	12.3%
Municipal	22	23	25	3.2%	9.2%	12.8%
Private	21	21	15	-3.3%	-28.1%	-30.5%
Spending						
Current *(thousands)*[††]		8,240,217	22,652,635		174.9%	
2004 R$ *(thousands)*		19,858,409	38,756,065		95.2%	
Per Student[†]		295	691		134.2%	
Per Student *(2004 R$)*		711	1,182		66.3%	

Notes: [†] Per-student spending is by all levels of government on public students, in current Reais, as calculated by INEP/MEC. [††] Calculated by author as per-student spending multiplied by the number of public students.

Imputation: Enrollment figures for 1994 are imputed, as follows: [1] Assumes trend growth between 1991 (25,354,119 students) and 1995 (28,870,159 students); [2] Assumes trend growth between 1991 (96,728 students) and 1995 (31,330 students); [3] Assumes trend growth between 1991 (16,637,040 students) and 1995 (18,347,733 students); [4] Assumes trend growth between 1991 (8,620,351 students) and 1995 (10,491,096 students); [5] Assumes trend growth between 1991 (3,594,147 students) and 1995 (3,798,579 students).

economist.[105] Under Paulo Renato, Cardoso's administration tried to improve the efficiency and funding of basic education, improved educational statistics, and developed new tests to gauge student performance: the National Basic Education Evaluation System (SAEB)[106] and the National Secondary School Exam (ENEM). But by far the most important development was a constitutional amendment creating a new National Fund for Basic Education (FUNDEF).

FUNDEF, which began operation in 1998, collects three-fifths of the state revenues earmarked for education (25 percent of total state revenues) and distributes them to systems—municipal or state—based on their enrollment in grades 1–8.[107] Linking funding and enrollment naturally encouraged an increase in access to basic education, and by the millennium, Brazil was approaching universal primary enrollment (Schwartzman 2003). FUNDEF also continued to shift education resources from states to municipalities, since constitutionally, municipalities had primary responsibility for grades 1–8.[108] Table 6.18 shows the enrollment increases and the shift from state to municipal schools. In 1994, there were 80 percent more basic-education students in state schools than municipal schools; in 1999, enrollment was almost evenly divided between the two.

Yet while FUNDEF's major effects were to continue existing trends—pushing enrollment increases and municipalization—the amendment also contained something new: additional provisions that sought to increase the quality of basic education. First, FUNDEF included a requirement that 60 percent of the money be spent on teachers, and, to combat the use of education resources to be spent on things only loosely connected to education, defined what could count as spending on education. Second, it defined a minimum level of per-student spending, initially R$315. If a municipality or state fell below that minimum, the federal government would top up the funding. This provision led to real increases in per-student spending on 11 million students (World Bank and IDB 2000).

But the R$315 floor (about $285 at the time) was not enough for quality education.[109] It did, however, make a great deal of political sense. R$315 was higher than existing per-student spending levels only in eight Northern and Northeastern states. The threshold therefore meant federal transfers to municipalities in states where municipal support was crucial to Cardoso's coalition partner, the PFL.[110] (The FUNDEF amendment actually required the government to carry out a detailed analysis to determine the minimum cost of quality education, but in the end it did not, claiming technical difficulties, and it never released the results of the attempted analysis.[111])

In other ways too, FUNDEF led only to very minor improvements in basic education's quality. Generally municipal schools in Brazil are inferior to state schools (see Section 6; and World Bank and IDB 2000), so municipalization itself worked against quality improvement.[112] Second, although FUNDEF led to improvements in teacher salaries of around 50 percent in the Northeast (World Bank and IDB 2000),[113] and FUNDEF money provided for remedial pedagogy courses for under-trained teachers, teacher quality itself responded only minimally: recall that teachers had generally gotten their jobs for political reasons, and raising their salaries or teaching them pedagogy did not suddenly make them good teachers with knowledge of their subjects (World Bank and IDB 2000; Schwartzman 2003; World Bank 2004b).[114]

Thus the general quality of basic education remained very low. Repetition continued to be an enormous problem: by the end of the 1990s, around 7 million students in grades 1–8 were older than they should have been (Schwartzman 2003). And test results continued to show abysmal student performance in basic education. Testing under the new National Basic Education Evaluation System showed no improvement in math scores between 1995 and 2001: more than half of students could not solve simple problems with units of money and time or use data displayed in graphs. In Portuguese, test scores actually declined. In 1997, only 52 percent of eighth and 26 percent of eleventh grade students achieved at the minimum expected level for their grade in Portuguese; in math, 48 percent of eighth graders performed below the expected level for *fourth* graders.

Secondary education fared no better. Enrollments nearly tripled between 1989 and 1999 (Table 6.19)—mostly in state schools, which were given primary responsibility for grades 9–11 in the 1988 Constitution. But the enrollment increase was nowhere near enough to make secondary education universal: by 2001, 43 percent of 18-year-olds were still out of school. And the quality of the education provided to those who were in school was extremely poor[115]—FUNDEF did not cover grades 9–11, so the schooling at that level did not even benefit from the minor quality improvements grades 1–8 enjoyed. In 1997, only five percent of 11th graders achieved at the expected level for their grade (World Bank and IDB 2000).

The poor quality of higher grades in public schools, particularly secondary schools, had the effect of limiting the progress of low-income students relative to those in the elite track of private primary and secondary schools, which continued to provide excellent education at a price out of reach for most Brazilians (Schwartzman 2003; World Bank and IDB 2000).[116] Hence in the 1990s, research into educational attainment continued to uncover virtually unbreakable linkages with wealth.[117] In the late 1990s, a student from the lowest three deciles of the population—roughly the population below the poverty line—had only a 15 percent chance of completing primary education and a 4 percent chance of completing secondary (World Bank and IDB 2000). And those who did make it through were at a substantial disadvantage because of the poor quality of their instruction: even as late as 2005, testing of secondary-school graduates by the National Secondary School Exam (ENEM) revealed that more than three-quarters of those who attended private secondary schools scored in the acceptable range (average, good, or excellent), compared with just a quarter of public-school graduates. Just 18 percent of children whose family income was less than one minimum

Table 6.19 **Secondary education, 1989–1999**

| | 1989 | 1994 | 1999 | Changes | | |
				1989–94	1994–99	1989–94
Enrollment	3,478,059	4,892,295[1]	7,769,199	40.7%	58.8%	123.4%
Federal	97,777	110,695[2]	121,673	13.2%	9.9%	24.4%
State	2,170,832	3,401,016[3]	6,141,907	56.7%	80.6%	182.9%
Municipal	152,981	254,545[4]	281,255	66.4%	10.5%	83.8%
Private	1,056,469	1,126,039[5]	1,224,364	6.6%	8.7%	15.9%
Spending						
Current (thousands) [††]		1,182,604	4,208,329		255.9%	
2004 R$ (thousands)		2,850,003	7,199,969		152.6%	
Per Student[†]		314	643		104.8%	
Per Student (2004 R$)		757	1,100		45.4%	

Notes: [†] Per-student spending is by all levels of government on public students, in current Reais, as calculated by INEP/MEC. [††] Calculated by author as per-student spending multiplied by the number of public students.

Imputation: Enrollment figures for 1994 are imputed, as follows: [1] Assumes trend growth between 1991 (3,725,133 students) and 1995 (5,371,837 students); [2] Assumes trend growth between 1991 (103,243 students) and 1995 (113,296 students); [3] Assumes trend growth between 1991 (2,425,681 students) and 1995 (3,806,569 students); [4] Assumes trend growth between 1991 (173,597 students) and 1995 (289,183 students); [5] Assumes trend growth between 1991 (1,022,612 students) and 1995 (1,162,789 students).

wage—R$300 per month in 2006 (US$140[118])—scored in the acceptable range, compared to 85 percent of those whose families took in more than R$15,000 (US$7,000) per month, the highest income category.[119] By world standards, the lower levels of Brazil's education system were extremely poor and unequal at the turn of the millennium. In 1999 tests by the OECD Programme for International Student Assessment, Brazilian students scored lowest in the world in every area—reading, math, and science (World Bank 2004b). Bourguignon, Ferreira, and Menéndez (2003) calculate that if Brazil replaced its education distribution with the United States', Brazil's Gini coefficient would decline by 6.4 points, more than half of the difference in inequality between the two countries. A 2001 analysis by economist Jorge Abrahão estimates that, at enrollment growth in 2001, by 2011 Brazil would need to spend eight percent of its GDP on education to provide quality schooling at all levels, but estimated that in fact it would spend less than 4.3 percent (2001, 126, table 6).

WORKER TRAINING

Brazil's economic recovery brought greater demand for skilled workers but greater union activity as well (see Section 7), and skilled wages remained highly inflexible. Hence the government continued to provide Selective Worker Training. There was some reduction in the aid to companies to train their own workers: in 1996, amid a debate about the amount of public money seeping into private schools, the Cardoso administration ended the *salário educação* exemption for companies that spent the money training workers or their children (Verhine and Rosa 2002).[120] But companies continued to prefer workers trained in private training facilities, such as SENAI and SENAC or the Centro Paulo Souza schools in São Paulo. Though this training was expensive—costing up to ten times as much per student as regular secondary schooling—the quality of the training was, and remains, excellent, and economists told me that employers generally want it to remain expensive and selective.[121]

UPPER LEVELS

The federal government's interest and involvement in the lower levels was not repeated in the upper levels.[122] The PMDB-PSDB-PFL coalition had a complicated relationship with the universities, which were often centers of support for the PT. But it also faced rising demand from the middle class in its vital constituency to gain access to higher education. The government's solution was to leave the public universities largely as they were and to expand and improve private education.

Maintaining the status quo for the public universities meant, in fact, a slight decline in their quality, for the public universities faced skyrocketing costs in the 1990s from a new source: retirements. In the 1960s, the creation and expansion of the public universities had absorbed 70,000 teachers and professors into the federal university system—all with very generous pension plans. In 1985, these professors began to retire and draw their pensions; by 2001, a third had retired. Keeping up with these pension costs, as well as keeping the salaries of current professors in line with inflation, left the government little room for any additional spending (Schwartzman 2003). In the latter half of the 1990s, per-student spending on universities fell just over a third (Table 6.20).

Still, the decline in quality was minor—Brazil's universities today remain some of the finest in Latin America. Admission stayed restrictive: over the decade enrollment in federal universities rose just 40 percent, enrollment in state universities rose just 57 percent, and altogether public universities enrolled just 832,000 students in 1999 (Table 6.20)[123]—a tiny figure considering that there were 33 million students in public schools in grades 1–8 in 1999. By keeping enrollment restrictive, the government was able to keep quality high.[124]

Table 6.20 **Upper levels, 1989–1999**

	1989	1995	1999	Changes		
				1989–95	1995–99	1989–94
Enrollment	1,570,190[1]	1,822,316	2,453,706[8]	19.8%	34.6%	61.2%
Graduate	1,521,710[2]	1,759,703*	2,369,945	15.6%	34.7%	55.7%
Post-Graduate	48,480	62,613	83,761[7]	29.2%	33.8%	72.8%
Federal	313,317[3]	353,235	442,562	12.7%	25.3%	41.3%
State	192,568[4]	201,974	302,380	4.9%	49.7%	57.0%
Municipal	76,059[5]	43,370	87,080	-43.0%	100.8%	14.5%
Private	835,024[6]	529,353	1,537,923	-36.6%	190.5%	84.2%
Percentage in Private	53.2%	29.0%	62.7%			
Spending						
Current (thousands)		5,490,023	6,997,686		27.5%	
2004 R$ (thousands)[†]		13,182,634	11,790,429		-10.6%	
Per Student		9,172[††]	8,410		-8.3%	
Per Student (2004 R$)		22,103[††]	14,389		-34.9%	

Notes: [†] Spending data from Amaral (2003), converted to 2004 R$ by the author. * Total enrollment figures for higher education in *Anuário Estatístico Do Brasil* for 1994 are larger than the sum of federal, state, municipal, and private enrollments. No explanation is given. [††] Per-student spending for 1995 is calculated using the sum of federal, state, and municipal enrollments.

Imputation: Some enrollment figures are imputed, as follows: 1989: [1] Assumes trend growth between 1988 (1,550,443 students) and 1990 (1,596,366 students); [2] Assumes trend growth between 1988 (1,503,560 students) and 1990 (1,540,080 students); [3] Assumes trend growth between 1988 (317,831 students) and 1990 (308,867 students); [4] Assumes trend growth between 1988 (190,736 students) and 1990 (194,417 students); [5] Assumes trend growth between 1988 (76,784 students) and 1990 (75,341 students); [6] Assumes trend growth between 1988 (918,209 students) and 1990 (918,209 students); 1999: [7] Assumes that growth 1998 and 1999 is the same as between 1997 (71,521 students) and 1998 (77,641 students); [8] This is the sum of graduate enrollment, which is not imputed, and post-graduate enrollment, which is imputed as described in note 7.

Instead of throwing open the doors of public universities, the federal government's solution to increasing middle-class demands was to expand the private higher education sector. Over the decade enrollments in private institutions rose 85 percent (Table 6.20). But this expansion was qualitatively different from the expansion of private higher education in the 1960s and 1970s; this time the government made some attempts to improve the quality of private institutions. The 1996 Basic Education Law was written, at the urging of the Cardoso administration, to include provisions that provided for periodic evaluation of private courses and required all private institutions to provide a teaching staff in which at least a third had masters' degrees and a third worked full-time (Schwartzman 1998). These provisions were not well-enforced, however, and by 2000 around 85 percent of their teachers still worked part-time.[125]

In 1996, the government introduced the *Provão*, an exam for graduates of private institutions intended to reveal to the public the quality of those institutions. The results were comparable across institutions, and were then widely publicized (Schwartzman 2003). Parents and the press strongly supported the plan; private institutions naturally opposed it, and they were joined by associations of public university teachers and students, which feared that the government was trying to shift the focus away from public universities (Schwartzman 2004).[126] (In 2004, the new PT administration greatly altered the *Provão*.) Supporters, however, argue today that private universities responded to the *Provão*, making efforts to increase their quality and thereby their scores.[127] Still, despite the government's efforts, the gap between the quality of public and private institutions remains substantial.[128]

BAHIA AND SÃO PAULO

Bahia and São Paulo illustrate how differences in state vital constituencies in the 1990s translated into variation in the education system. Recall from the previous section that Bahia's vital constituency changed far less over the 1990s than São Paulo's, in which the PT was powerful and even held the mayor's office for a brief period. In keeping with these differences, São Paulo's education system took significant steps toward becoming an All-Levels system, while Bahia's hardly evolved at all.

Bahia
Throughout the 1990s, ACM and his PFL were firmly in control in Bahia, and were prominent coalition partners of the federal government. ACM's vital constituency were rural elites and the senior Bahian bureaucracy, and developments in Bahian education in the 1990s kept the system Top-Down and kept the lower levels as spoils machines through which mayors could dole out jobs and construction contracts. Industry in Bahia remained small and dominated by the state; in general it got its skilled workers from SENAI schools or imported them from the Southeast.[129]

As in most Northeastern states, FUNDEF was a boon to Bahia, and particularly to Bahia's municipalities—and their mayors. Over time the proportion of municipalities receiving benefits rose enormously—in 1998, half of Bahian municipalities got transfers; in 2000, 62 percent did—as did the total value of the transfers: in 2000, Bahia got more than R$17 billion (Verhine and Rosa 2002). Yet in a comprehensive analysis of FUNDEF's effect in Bahia, Verhine and Rosa (2002) conclude that the extra money did little to improve the quality of teaching or the progress of students. (They find that, although 60 percent of FUNDEF money should have been spent on teachers and teacher improvement, teacher salaries rose just 7 percent on average in municipal schools, and actually fell 21 percent in the state system.) In 1997, the average Bahian student reaching fourth grade took more than six years to get there; the average eighth grader took almost 12 years to get there (World Bank and IDB 2000). Of those who made it to eighth grade, only 2 percent met minimum standards in math. Only .2 percent were rated "good."

Instead of raising quality, the main effect of FUNDEF was to shift resources to mayors, who used them as they had long used education money: to build schools and award patronage jobs. Throughout the era school construction was rampant. Table 6.15, which presents key statistics on Bahia and São Paulo side-by-side, shows that nearly 2,500 schools were built between 1994 to 1999, bringing the total number of municipal schools to 23,000, or almost twice the total number of federal, state, municipal, and private basic-education schools in the much-larger state of São Paulo. And mayors continued to exercise a tight grip on the hiring of teachers and principals.[130] Well-meaning efforts to loosen this grip met with partial or total failure. (In 2003, one state secretary of education who tried to sever the grip entirely lasted only three months in the job and left with a nervous breakdown.[131])

On the other hand, the elite track stayed intact and continued to receive large amounts of public money. In one three-year period in the early 1990s, the state government gave out $10 million in scholarships to private schools based solely on political criteria.[132]

São Paulo

In São Paulo, education developed in a way almost opposite to Bahia: while Bahia lagged behind national efforts to improve basic education, São Paulo went further than the national pattern, making progress in improving basic education and opening higher education to the middle class.

In the 1990s, Paulista governments implemented a number of reforms to basic education intended to reduce repetition and improve school and teacher quality. Reforms from the mid-1990s separated schools into those offering grades 1–4 and grades 5–8, implemented new "cycles" of several grades each (within which students were automatically passed from one grade to the next), and increased the hours of schooling from four to five. Teachers were offered extensive training, were paid for meeting time, and were subject to external evaluations every two years, after which teachers who scored poorly would have to attend additional training and teachers and schools that performed well would receive a bonus. Unlike Bahia, the São Paulo government municipalized the lower grades slowly and cautiously, making sure that municipalities had the resources to provide quality education before it transferred responsibility to them. Table 6.15 shows

Table 6.21 Education in Bahia and São Paulo, 1989–1999

	Bahia				São Paulo			
	1989	1994	1999	Change 1989–99	1989	1994	1999	Change 1989–99
Basic (1-8)								
Schools	24,969	25,416	27,172	8.8%	14,020	9,587	12,290	-12.3%
Federal	43	9	3	-93.0%			1	
State	3,024	3,490	2,222	-26.5%	12,028	7,517	6,250	-48.0%
Municipal	20,759	20,653	23,077	11.2%	602	520	3,386	462.5%
Private	1,143	1,264	1,870	63.6%	1,390	1,550	2,653	90.9%
Enrollment	2,023,601	2,701,892[7]	3,702,727	83.0%	5,788,565	6,534,303[13]	6,325,294	9.3%
Federal	8,642	1,856[3]	742	-91.4%			207	
State	868,921	1,220,308[4]	1,291,451	48.6%	4,575,807	5,157,064[10]	4,052,972	-11.4%
Municipal	913,948	1,230,176[5]	2,209,254	141.7%	536,942	630,618[11]	1,511,184	181.4%
Private	232,090	249,551[6]	201,280	-13.3%	675,816	746,621[12]	760,931	12.6%
% Private	11.5%	9.2%	5.4%		11.7%	11.4%	12.0%	
Spending				(1994-99)				(1994-99)
Current[††]		480,988	1,844,400	283.5%		2,607,164	5,328,961	104.4%
2004 R$		1,159,151	3,155,558	172.2%		6,283,102	9,117,242	45.1%
Per Student[†]		178	498	179.8%		399	842	111.2%
PS 2004 R$		429	852	98.6%		962	1,441	49.9%
Secondary (9-11)								
Enrollment	191,976	274,010[8]	504,554	162.8%	957,419	1,453,445[14]	2,047,402	113.8%
In Private	46,092	53,295[9]	54,568	18.4%	285,067	305,731[15]	295,810	3.8%
% Private	24.0%	19.5%	10.8%		29.8%	21.0%	14.4%	

(continued)

Table 6.21 (continued)

	Bahia				São Paulo			
	1989	1994	1999	Change 1989–99	1989	1994	1999	Change 1989–99
Spending		(1994–99)				(1994–99)		
Current††		63,549	241,761	280.4%		460,336	1,400,821	204.3%
2004 R$		153,149	413,625	170.1%		1,109,380	2,396,645	116.0%
Per Student†		232	479	106.6%		317	684	116.0%
PS 2004 R$		559	820	46.7%		763	1,171	53.4%
Higher								
Enrollment	45,497[1]	44,684	73,785	62.2%	485,757[2]	540,716	740,113	52.4%
Spending		(1994–99)				(1994–99)		
Current††		94,010	333,604	254.9%		729,246	1,576,052	116.1%
2004 R$		226,557	570,757	151.9%		1,757,436	2,696,444	53.4%
Per Student†		2,841	7,609	167.9%		2,250	12,981	477.0%
PS 2004 R$		6,845	13,017	90.2%		5,422	22,208	309.6%

Notes: † Per-student spending is by all levels of government on public students, in current Reais, as calculated by INEP/MEC. †† Calculated by author as per-student spending multiplied by the number of public students.

Imputation: Some enrollment figures are imputed, as follows: 1989: *Bahia:* [1] Assumes trend growth between 1988 (45,990 students) and 1990 (45,009 students); *São Paulo:* [2] Assumes trend growth between 1988 (474,487 students) and 1990 (497,294 students); 1994: *Bahia:* Primary: [3] Assumes trend growth between 1991 (1,027,303 students) and 1995 (1,292,389 students); *São Paulo:* Primary: [3] Assumes trend growth between 1991 (1,432 students) and 1995 (2,024 students); [4] Assumes trend growth between 1991 (1,317,612 students); [6] Assumes trend growth between 1991 (208,290 students) and 1995 (265,047 students); [7] This is the sum of the imputed enrollments at in federal, state, municipal, and private schools; Secondary: [8] Assumes trend growth between 1991 (212,746 students) and 1995 (298,770 students); [9] Assumes trend growth between 1991 (43,007 students) and 1995 (57,245 students); *São Paulo:* Primary: [10] Assumes trend growth between 1991 (4,851,574 students) and 1995 (5,263,111 students); [11] Assumes trend growth between 1991 (585,276 students) and 1995 (646,500 students); [12] Assumes trend growth between 1991 (728,307 students) and 1995 (752,827 students); [13] This is the sum of the imputed enrollments at in state, municipal, and private schools (there are no students in federal schools); Secondary: [14] Assumes trend growth between 1991 (269,552 students) and 1995 (318,839 students).

the far slower pace of municipalization. The São Paulo government also undertook a number of smaller initiatives to selectively target certain schools for improvement (generally schools in middle class areas).[133] São Paulo, a wealthy state, was a net loser from FUNDEF. But despite this added budgetary pressure it still increased average real per-student spending on basic education by almost 50 percent (Table 6.15).

These reforms had an impact. The same analysis that found that an average Bahian fourth grader took more than six years to get there found that, in 1997, almost every child who entered first grade in São Paulo would complete fourth grade in four years and had a 71 percent chance of completing eighth grade in, on average, nine years (World Bank and IDB 2000).

The Paulista government devoted less attention to secondary schools, in which enrollment increased but quality lagged; still, enrollment in grades 9–11 in São Paulo was more than two million, 28 percent of all secondary students in Brazil. And in higher education spending and enrollment both soared: real per-student spending rose 300 percent between 1994 and 1999, and enrollment rose to 740,000, or 30 percent of total enrollment in Brazil (84 percent were in private institutions).

WRAPPING UP

The 1990s saw a gradual expansion of the vital constituency from one that was simply elite to one that included the middle class. In addition, the government was facing an increasing threat from the PT's political entrepreneurship of the Brazilian masses.

According to the framework, this vital constituency should have led the Brazilian government to largely maintain the Top-Down system it inherited, while taking minor steps at the lower levels to placate the Brazilian masses in a way that would not be threatening to the vital constituency's education. Table 6.22 is the evidence summary.

In general, the education system's evolution in the 1990s did not change it tremendously, which is generally what the framework predicts. Access to the lower levels increased over the 1990s, but schools improved little in the lower grades and not at all in the upper grades, and there was hardly any improvement in the quality of teachers. Access to the upper levels also increased, but mostly in private institutions that, while better than the private institutions created under the military, still fell short of the standards of the public universities. Most important, the elite track stayed largely intact: elites were far more likely to go to private schools that prepared them to take the entrance exams to public universities. All of this is consistent with maintenance of a Top-Down education system with placating improvements to the lower levels—except in states, like São Paulo, that became affiliated with a political entrepreneur of the poor.

Table 6.22 **Evidence summary, 1990–2000**

Indicator	Characteristics	Conforms to Framework?
A. Enrollment	Lower levels: increasing	■
	Upper levels: private: large increases; public: small increases	❑
B. Per-student spending	Lower levels: increasing, through two channels: federal policy: increasing spending to areas where education was primarily for jobs and construction contracts; state policy: increasing in states like São Paulo where there was political entrepreneurship	■
	Upper levels: declining	■
C. The toolkit		
1. Schools	Lower levels: private: excellent; public: only minor improvement	■
	Upper levels: private: some improvement; public: excellent	❑
Teachers	Lower levels: private: excellent; public: abysmal	■
	Upper levels: private: poor; public: excellent	❑
Physical resources	Lower levels: private: excellent; public: only minor improvement	■
	Upper levels: private: small improvement; public: excellent	■
Location	Lower levels: widespread; particular growth in rural areas	■
	Upper levels: mostly towns or urban areas	■
2. Fees†	Lower levels: public is free; private charge high fees	❑
	Upper levels: public is free; private charge affordable fees	■
3. Access restrictions and discriminatory pricing		
Quotas	None	
Exams	Exams for public universities favor students from private primary and secondary schools	■
Financial aid	Extensive tax breaks for spending on private education; extensive aid and stipends to students at public universities	■
4. Tracking	Exceptional tracking from private lower levels into public universities	■
5. Outsourcing (domestic or foreign; to firms or non-profits)	Lower levels: extensive, for the elite track	■
	Upper levels: extensive, to increase availability while preserving the public system's quality	■

Notes: ■: fully conforms to the framework; ❑: partly conforms to the framework; ❑: does not conform to the framework.† Fees are for enrollment, books and other equipment, uniforms, activities, school improvements, etc.

The areas where framework is less predictive generally have to do with the upper levels. The government was facing pressure from the middle class inside its vital constituency to increase access to the restricted, elite public universities. The government did try to expand the public universities while generally maintaining their quality. But most of the expansion was through the private sector, through outsourcing. While the government tried to regulate the expansion to make the private universities both affordable and high quality, they remained (with a few exceptions) far inferior to the public universities. This development thus provides only partial support for the framework. In fact, we have seen in all three of this book's cases that a vital constituency expansion like the one the PMDB-PSDB-PFL government faced is the most difficult for a government to deal with: it finds itself needing to provide quality education to new members of the vital constituency while continuing to provide existing members with the education they have come to expect.

9. CONCLUSION

This chapter has argued that for 70 years—from 1930 to 2000, when this book's analysis stops—the vital constituency, and particularly political entrepreneurship of the poor, has determined education policy in Brazil. In those 70 years, Brazil has had two political entrepreneurs, both cross-class. The first was Getúlio Vargas, who built a cross-class alliance of workers and industrial elites that lasted until 1961. Vargas built Brazil's modern education system as a narrow All-Levels system: his government expanded quality, public primary, secondary, and, in the 1950s, university education to the vital constituency, which was a little less than 30 percent of the population. In 1961, this coalition split and businesses linked up with agrarian elites. Workers held on to power until the military stepped in and ended unions' organization in 1964, not allowing them to stay in power long enough to make much of an impact on education. Thereafter Brazil was ruled by elite governments: first military, then civilian. These elite governments radically transformed the narrow All-Levels education system they inherited into a Top-Down system, reducing the quality of the lower levels to the point where they largely failed to educate and pouring resources into improving the universities. An elite track of exceptional private primary and secondary schools ensured that students in these federal universities were overwhelmingly children of elites, while the few middle-class students who made it through the abysmal public primary and secondary schools, and who wanted to go further, had to settle for an expensive and deficient education in a private institution of higher education. The second political entrepreneur of the poor was Lula's Workers' Party, which organized not only workers but also the previously-ignored rural and urban poor. As this organization brought the PT electoral success at the state levels, education in these states began to shift toward All-Levels education; at the federal level, this success led to some placating of mass demands for access and quality at the lower levels, but in ways that did little to threaten the Top-Down education that the federal government's vital constituency wanted.

This chapter opened with the claim that this book's framework does better at explaining Brazilian education policies than alternative explanations of policymaking. To further support that claim, in the remainder of this concluding section I will briefly argue that the educational developments described in this chapter cannot be understood as the result of Brazil's economic development or its regime type, and that the political entrepreneurship of the poor, not changes in the inherent ability of the poor to organize themselves, was the key to their political power.

THE NEEDS OF THE ECONOMY

The needs of the economy do not correspond to developments in Brazilian education. Brazil's education system has never provided Brazil with the economically optimal workforce, even when its policymakers were committed to improving the economic benefits of the system.

First, economists have long argued that Brazil's education system harms the economy by forcing it to become excessively capital intensive (see, e.g., Birdsall, Bruns, and Sabot 1996). Brazil's system of Selective Worker Training provided a steady supply of well-trained workers tailored to specific industries or corporations, but this system was expensive. By contrast, the rest of the education system, aside from the elite track, provided graduates with few skills of value to employers—particularly after 1964, when the quality of public primary and secondary schools deteriorated. Indeed the parts of the education system that have the highest enrollments—the public primary and secondary schools, and until recently the private institutions of higher education—both offer inferior education.

Brazilian policymakers have often recognized these problems but have seemed not to be able to do much about them. We saw in this chapter that economically-motivated efforts to increase the supply of skilled workers—the Vargas government's attempts to create formal technical education; the 1970s reforms by economic policymakers to implement "Manpower Planning" and to make all secondary education technical; the more limited effort in the 1990s by Paulo Renato de Souza, the minister of education, that tried to focus federal technical secondary schools on technical education—have all been failures. Rather than educating workers with a coherent vision for economic development, the most the Brazilian government has been able to do is selectively reduce "bottlenecks to economic growth."[134]

REGIME TYPE

Brazil seems to provide more evidence in support of the regime-type argument—that more democratic governments will make more pro-poor education policy—than Ghana or Taiwan. The transition to military rule in 1964 certainly shifted the government's attention away from primary education, and the federal government's renewed attention to primary education in the 1990s did follow Brazil's return of democracy, which, by various measures, occurred in 1979 (Przeworski et al. 2000) or 1985 (Marshall and Jaggers 2000). In fact, Brazil has inspired some work in political science linking primary education investments and regime type (Brown 1995; 2002).[135]

Yet this coincidence of education policies and regime type in Brazil is likely spurious, for two reasons. First, there is no evidence that regime type explains education policymaking before 1964. Brazil was an autocracy from 1930 to 1945 and a democracy from 1945 to 1964 (Marshall and Jaggers 2000). But its education policy was largely constant throughout this period; it shows no break after 1945.[136] And to the extent that policy did evolve after 1945, it evolved in the wrong direction: beginning in the late 1950s, the government began to focus a great deal of attention and resources on higher education, an area it had neglected to that point.

Second, while resources for primary education did rise after the transition to democracy in 1979 or 1985, I presented evidence that the kind of primary education in which the government was investing was extremely poor quality—so poor that few students who went to the schools learned much at all. In this sense, the primary education the government was investing in after the transition to democracy was not qualitatively different than the primary education it had provided prior to the transition.

The central difficulty with regime type, as I have argued elsewhere in the book, is that it is a poor predictor of the government's constituency. For this reason, it is a poor predictor of the government's education policymaking.

I also argued in Chapter 1 that the regime-type argument fails to predict the government's constituency because the government's institutional structure cannot supersede the overwhelming collective-action advantages of elites over the poor. These advantages go a long way toward explaining why Brazil's education policies have left out the vast majority of the population for much of its history, under both democratic and autocratic institutions. Brazil's working classes and its urban and rural poor have faced collective-action disadvantages that were generally too severe for them to surmount without help.

But elites' collective action advantages have not always been decisive in Brazil, because in several periods political entrepreneurs were able to help poor citizens to organize. In Brazil, as in Ghana and Taiwan, political entrepreneurship has allowed poorer groups to overcome their collective-action disadvantages, and during those periods Brazilian education policy was not elitist. Prior to 1964, a political entrepreneur organized workers, and Brazilian education policy provided workers with excellent education. In the 1990s, a political entrepreneur again organized workers and was beginning to organize the urban and rural poor—and, where that political entrepreneur gained control of state governments, it began provide quality education to those groups.

Thus the evidence from Brazil shows that rather than the needs of the economy or the type of the regime, the labor market conditions of employers of skilled labor and, especially, political entrepreneurship of the poor are the key factors behind Brazilian education.

CHAPTER 7

Conclusion

This book has proposed a new answer to an old question of political economy: When will a government invest in its citizens? The book examines the question by developing a framework for understanding how governments decide to make education policies, a framework that is rooted in political organization and labor market conditions. The framework successfully explains most educational decisions taken across a half-century or more by governments in three very different developing countries: Taiwan, Ghana, and Brazil.

In the framework, two factors jointly determine education policy. The first is the success of political entrepreneurs at organizing the poor into a political force. This determines whether the government will depend for its power on poorer groups, more elite groups, or a cross-class alliance, and thereby determines most of the key features of the education system the government will try to create—for example, whether the system will concentrate on primary education, higher education, or try to provide all levels. The second factor is the flexibility of the labor market faced by employers who need skilled workers, which determines the nature and extent of any worker training the government will try to provide.

The evidence from Taiwan, Ghana, and Brazil both supports this framework in very different contexts and casts doubt on explanations of policymaking that are common in analyses of the political economy of development—emphasizing regime type and the needs of the economy. Taiwan, Ghana, and Brazil collectively provide settings in which these alternate explanations should do well: all have been through one or more regime transitions; and they include one country whose education system is widely thought to be the product of wise economic management and two whose education systems are not. In addition, the three countries vary on other important dimensions: they cover nearly the full range of inequality in the world; they are on three continents; and they have different cultures and colonial histories.

Despite these differences, the book demonstrates that in each of the three countries, over a half-century or more, governments facing similar conditions of political entrepreneurship and employer demands adjusted their education policies similarly, regardless of other factors. This similarity extends not only to the common indicators of an education system—enrollments and per-student spending—but also to what I labeled the government's "education toolkit": the sorts of schools, teachers, exams, fees, and access restrictions in the system, as well as the role of the private sector. Indeed, it seems not to matter much which country we examine: once we have determined entrepreneurship and employer demands, the government's education policies seem to develop as a matter of course.

In addition to explaining education policy, the results also suggest some more general insights into several issues central to political economy: into the circumstances in which international institutions and ideas can affect domestic policy-making; into the inability of democratic institutions to produce pro-poor policies; into the roots of a government's constituency; and into how a government makes policy to serve that constituency, not just in education, but generally. In this final chapter, I briefly explore these points, in an effort to lay the ground for more rigorous research into them.

1. International Influence

Do international ideas influence a government's education policies? Can international actors prod a government to make better education policies, or lure it with foreign aid? Chapter 3 theorized that governments make policies that serve its vital constituency, regardless of international ideas and pressure. The implication is that governments will use international ideas that serve their vital constituency and will accept international assistance only if the donor's goals coincide with the government's, or if it believes it can manipulate the aid's use or siphon it off to other uses.

Taiwan, Ghana, and Brazil provide some evidence on these points. For example, all three countries implemented "manpower planning"—using the education system to produce a workforce in anticipation of the economy's needs. But all cherry-picked or reshaped the technique so that it served the vital constituency; none implemented it purely to serve the economy. The Taiwanese government used manpower planning to justify the expansion of vocational education—an expansion that helped stem the rise in skilled wage premia—but the government simultaneously increased, rather than reduced, the restrictiveness and resources in the academic track, which was exactly the opposite of what the manpower planning recommended. In Brazil, manpower planning led the government to try to make all secondary schooling technical in the early 1970s, but properly funding the effort would have required equipping and improving secondary schools for those outside the vital constituency and requiring those inside the vital constituency to learn technical subjects instead of preparing for university entrance exams. Consequently the effort was abandoned after only a few years. And in

Ghana, the Convention People's Party's manpower planning in the 1960s inverted manpower planning's basic formula: instead of trying to educate a workforce that would meet the economy's needs, it calculated the growth in employment that would be necessary to employ the workforce it was educating.

Another example of the centrality of the vital constituency is the efficacy of foreign aid. Two of the book's three cases, Brazil and Ghana, received large amounts of foreign aid to improve primary education. In Brazil, the general consensus is that the aid was mostly wasted, while in Ghana, it helped tremendously. Brazil received hundreds of millions of dollars of aid for basic education in the 1960s, 70s, and 80s, at a time when, as we saw in Chapter 6, the Brazilian government's vital constituency had substituted workers for agrarian elites. These elites secured their control in the northeast through extensive patronage networks, and it was those patronage networks, not any student's education, that foreign assistance primarily served. The very most that can be said for the aid is that it facilitated the construction of schools and that some students attended schools who would not have otherwise. What cannot be said is that these students received primary education by any minimal standard (Harbison and Hanushek 1992; Hanushek, Gomes-Neto, and Harbison 1996).

Contrast Brazil's aid with Ghana's. In the 1980s, Ghana's primary education was arguably in worse shape than northeast Brazil's. Ghana, though, had a vital constituency of the poor. In 1986 the World Bank offered to assist Ghana with improving its basic education, and in the subsequent decade and a half provided invaluable technical expertise and lent Ghana $260 million for primary education. With the Bank as catalyst, other donors joined up, more than doubling the bank's contribution. And this aid was a tremendous success—largely because of Ghana's politics, as the World Bank itself acknowledged (World Bank 2004a).

These examples strongly suggest a general conclusion: if a donor's goals coincide with the government's, the donor will see its aid used effectively. Thus the success in Ghana. But if a donor's goals are at odds with the government's, the government will only accept the aid if it believes it can manipulate its use or siphon it off to other uses. The government serves its vital constituency, not the donor or the international community, and it will not allow any aid it receives to do otherwise. Thus, as in Brazil, where the government's goals differ from the donor's, the donor will likely watch unhappily as its aid is either misused or wasted.[1]

2. The Limits of Democracy

In theory, democracies should serve the poor. In any country with the standard right-skewed distribution of income, the income of the median voter will be less than the mean, and the median voter will therefore favor some measure of redistribution; to win over that voter, the government should allocate more of its resources to social policies that serve the poor. By contrast, an autocratic ruler is not institutionally accountable to the poor and might safely ignore them. This belief is a large part of the reason that development theorists are generally so optimistic about democracy and supportive of democratization.

The evidence in this book strongly suggests that the conventional optimism about democratic institutions needs re-evaluation. In all three countries, democratization fails to predict pro-poor education policies: more often than not, autocratic governments implement pro-poor education policies, and democratic governments do not. And each period of pro-poor education policymaking by a democratic government was simply a continuation of the policy of a previous, autocratic government. Democratic institutions plausibly caused pro-poor education policy only for a short period in Brazil, where they can largely explain elitist education policy following the 1964 coup. But democratic institutions cannot explain pro-poor policy prior to the coup or the failure of democratic governments in the 1980s and 1990s to provide anything more than placating improvements to the lower levels. In Ghana, two democratic periods—from 1969 to 1971 and from 1979 to 1981—fail entirely to correspond to periods of pro-poor education policy, which occurred much earlier while Ghana was an autocracy; another democratic period began in 1992, six years after the introduction of pro-poor education, when few were predicting that Ghana would democratize. And in Taiwan, democratic institutions fail to predict pro-poor education before the 1960s, when Taiwan was an autocracy, and are ten years late in predicting pro-poor education that began in the 1980s.

Democracy clearly has much else to recommend it: its attendant freedoms of association, voice, and choice are valuable and may ultimately help the poor to organize. But on its own, democracy seems to be neither necessary nor sufficient to serve the poor.

3. Political Entrepreneurship and the Origin of The Vital Constituency

This book argues that the government's constituency is shaped by the interaction of collective action and political entrepreneurs, who subsidize the collective-action costs of disadvantaged groups. Specifically, I have argued that it is the success of political entrepreneurs affiliated with the government at organizing poor citizens that determines whether the vital constituency will be elites, the poor, or a cross-class alliance. The success of political entrepreneurship in determining the vital constituency and predicting education policymaking, at least in Taiwan, Ghana, and Brazil, raises interesting questions about political entrepreneurship itself. What conditions make affiliated political entrepreneurship more or less likely? When are entrepreneurs prone to being cross-class or anti-elite?

Can interested outside parties—international agencies, for example, or concerned citizens—encourage political entrepreneurship?

In this book, I use political entrepreneurship only to identify the vital constituency; I did not select cases in a way that would allow me to say anything concrete about the origins of political entrepreneurship or the conditions behind its success. Still, my three cases suggest some promising possibilities. Taiwan's Kuomintang, for example, played political entrepreneur because of competition among elites, and elite splits also led to political entrepreneurship in Brazil and Ghana. These instances of political entrepreneurship fit well with existing scholarship on the relationship between elite splits and mass mobilization.[2]

A second possibility is democracy. I argued that the incentives created by democratic institutions for rulers to court the poor are never strong enough to overcome the incentives of rational rulers to serve elites—unless and until political entrepreneurs are able to organize the poor into a locus of countervailing political power. But democracy is more than elections and the electoral incentive to serve the poor; it also leads to freedom of speech and association.[3] These freedoms do not cause the organization of the poor, so democracy is no substitute for organization; but they may make that organization easier, and perhaps more sustainable. In the past two decades, democracy has spread to all three of the countries I examine. In two of the three, Ghana and Taiwan, political entrepreneurship long preceded democratization, so democratization was not plausibly a cause of political entrepreneurship. But it is surely not a coincidence that, once the poor were organized, in both countries they pushed for democracy. Similarly, Brazil's Vargas, a political entrepreneur to workers, ruled with authoritarian institutions in the 1930s and early 40s, but democratized under pressure from his base after World War II. And Brazil's democratization in the 1980s, while not caused by political entrepreneurship of the poor, may have helped the PT as it organized the rural poor in the 1990s. On the other hand, without democratic freedoms, political entrepreneurship of the poor seems to be harder. In three of the five instances of political entrepreneurship under autocracy the country eventually democratized—Ghana in 1992, Taiwan in 1996, and Brazil in 1945.[4] The evidence from these three countries suggests that, while democratic institutions are not necessary to a vital constituency that includes the poor, they may help the poor to organize and stay organized.

If this is the case, it would suggest a way to reconcile the findings in this book with the body of cross-country analyses showing a tendency for democracies to make pro-poor policies. Political entrepreneurship of the poor both causes pro-poor policy and may be associated with democracy. The challenge for future research is to examine the role of democracy alongside other plausible factors behind political entrepreneurship of the poor: outside influence, for example, or the idiosyncratic rise of a leader capable of building an organization of poor citizens.

A second issue involves the incentives behind political entrepreneurship. The incentives will likely be different for the two types of political entrepreneurship—

cross-class and anti-elite. For cross-class entrepreneurship, the key question is: when will elites want to link up with disadvantaged groups? Certainly the political entrepreneurship required for a cross-class alliance will not be elites' ideal option, since political entrepreneurship takes effort and expense. There is not simply the organizing itself: by bringing a group into the vital constituency, elites are also entitling the group to government largesse and policy, leaving themselves with a smaller share. Since elites will therefore have competing interests with disadvantaged groups, we are not likely to see elites helping disadvantaged groups to organize unless they have to. It thus seems reasonable that cross-class political entrepreneurship may be the consequence only of a situation in which elites are unable to work out their differences, and some elites find themselves outside the vital constituency: an elite split, like those in all three of my cases. In an elite split, one faction may try to organize the poor in an effort to tip the balance of political power in its favor, in a manner similar to Przeworski's (1991) reasoning on democratization.

Anti-elite political entrepreneurship will likely stem from different causes. Anti-elite political entrepreneurs are less common than pro-elite: in my cases there were only two (Rawlings in Ghana; workers in Brazil from 1961 to 1964), and a cursory look around the world suggests that there are not many true anti-elite governments. What are the circumstances that give rise to it? The common explanations—great deprivation, oppression, civil war—are possibilities. But the organizing by entrepreneurs in these circumstances can often be ephemeral, lasting just until elites regroup and restore themselves to the presidential palace—as in Brazil in 1964. The challenge is to examine the causes of more lasting anti-elite entrepreneurship, such as with Rawlings in Ghana.

These are only a few of the issues and challenges that would concern an investigation of political entrepreneurship. But this book itself may provide a starting point. It shows the importance of political entrepreneurship in identifying the vital constituency across long periods in three very different countries. Thus it suggests that further study of political entrepreneurship may yield valuable insights into government constituencies across the developing world.

4. Explaining Pro-Poor Policymaking

The success of this book's framework in explaining education policymaking also suggests that the framework may provide a basis for a more general theory of distributive policymaking—not just in education, but in many areas relevant to sustainable development. I argued throughout this book that a central difficulty with current theories of policymaking is that they have difficulty identifying the government's constituency. From decades of work across the social sciences, we today have a reasonable idea of the kinds of policies different citizens will demand—in education policy and many other policy areas. This book relies on such research to determine the demands of different citizens for education policies. But there is nothing unique about education: social scientists today have just as good a sense of who will favor land reform and the right to own property in general, who will want open borders, and who will support investments in roads and hospitals. We also know that a government will generally make the policies that its constituents demand: a government's supporters—its vital constituency—are its lifeline, and to maintain their support it will do its best to serve them. The hard part is identifying that constituency. Thus, development policymaking today often has an air of mystery: governments that should make developmental policies often do not, and governments that should not often do.

If it is possible to create a general, empirically verified theory of political entrepreneurship, that theory may provide the basis for a more general theory of policymaking—a theory that would enhance our ability to understand and to predict the actions of governments in developing countries over a wide range of policies vital for successful development. Indeed, in these three cases there are myriad examples of policymaking in other areas that follow the same logic as policymaking in education. One such example is land reform in Taiwan. In 1953, the Kuomintang forced elite Taiwanese landlords to sell vast tracts of farmland and gave the land to Taiwanese serfs. As with the Kuomintang's education policies, today's most accepted political-economic theories predict that this government should not have implemented land reform—the serfs themselves were far too poor to organize themselves into a political force, and the Kuomintang itself was a brutal, anti-democratic regime, bent not on developing Taiwan's economy but on retaking mainland China from the Chinese Communists. But Chapter 5 argued that the Kuomintang needed the support of Taiwanese peasants to secure Taiwan against the insurrectionist Taiwanese landowning elite, from whom it had wrested power when it retreated to Taiwan. It therefore organized the peasants, and they became citizens on whom the Kuomintang's power depended—a part of its vital constituency. And as a result, it made policy on land rights, like education policy, in their interest.

In this way, a more general theory of political entrepreneurship may help to predict not only whether a government will invest in primary schools, but also whether it will flout property rights, lower tariffs, close borders, build roads, invest in hospitals, or do any of the other things that make life better or worse for its citizens. If the purpose of researching development is to uncover how the world's poor and disadvantaged may advance their potential, freedom, and happiness, no subject in development research is more central than how governments make development policies. Individuals power the economy and society, but the government creates their environment: their safety, their access to health care and skills, their freedom to think and own property—in short, their ability to live their lives to the fullest and push their nation forward. The government's decisions are at the heart of development, and to understand development we need to understand its policymaking incentives. And any accurate understanding of these incentives begins with knowing whose support the government needs to survive.

The conclusion and lessons suggested in this chapter are only speculative. I hope this book serves as a starting point for tackling them. The book provides a framework for predicting government behavior in education, one of the driving forces of economic development and human fulfillment. It demonstrates that the keys to understanding education policymaking lie in political entrepreneurship of the poor and the labor market conditions faced by employers who need skilled labor. These factors determine the educational demands of the particular groups on which the government's power depends—demands that the government, to secure its power, will try its best to meet. Across five decades or more, in countries on three continents with widely varying economies, institutions, cultures, and histories, governments consistently made similar education policies when faced with similar political entrepreneurship and labor market conditions. In the modern world, much of a country's development success depends on its education. This book shows both why governments make the education policies they do, and the political conditions that would be necessary for them to chose different education policies.

Appendix A

SELECTION OF TAIWAN, GHANA, AND BRAZIL

By design, Ghana, Brazil, and Taiwan have little in common. The logic of selecting cases as different as possible so as to test the common effect of one independent variable is related to two well-known methods of inquiry in political science: J. S. Mill's "Method of Agreement" and the case-selection advice in King, Keohane, and Verba (1994). Following Mill's Method of Agreement, if a phenomenon occurs in settings that have only one circumstance in common, we may conclude that the circumstance causes the phenomenon.[1] With the advice of King, Keohane, and Verba (1994), we may refine this method by seeking "unit homogeneity"—that the same value of the explanatory variable will cause the same effect on the dependent variable in all cases[2]—and by making an effort to limit selection bias. Together the two works point to selecting cases with some randomness but with an eye to providing maximum variation on the key explanatory variables.

My key explanatory variable is the "vital constituency." As there is no measurement of the vital constituency across countries, there was little possibility of selection bias on the independent variable. This benefit—inherent in my reliance on a new concept—does not, of course, negate the need to maximize the variation of the sample, but it did leave me free to maximize the variation among my cases in a way that served a second goal: testing plausible existing hypotheses in political economy about policymaking. In choosing cases with maximum variation, I tried to provide each of the explanations discussed in Chapter 1 with conditions favorable to its confirmation.

I began with regime type. If regime type explains education policymaking, regime changes should predict changes in education policymaking. I narrowed my search to those countries that had been through at least one democratic or autocratic transition in the last half-century. Using the industry-standard ALCP regime-type variable (Przeworski et al. 2000), I determined that 128 countries have had at least one regime transition between 1950 and 2000.

I further divided these 128 countries by inequality. I first removed from the 128 countries any country without inequality data for the 1980s. (I took the 1980s as a reasonable middle period for case selection, since it is late enough that surveys of income inequality had become common but early enough not to be skewed toward the present day.) Of the 128, I could find Gini coefficients for 45.[3] I divided the sample of 45 into three groups: low inequality (Gini of less than .35), medium inequality (Gini of between .35 and .55), and high inequality (Gini of greater than .55). Using these Gini cut-offs, the low-inequality group contained 16 countries, from Belarus (Gini .23) to Pakistan (Gini .34); the medium group contained 21 countries, from Nigeria (Gini .39) to Bostwana (Gini .54); and the high group contained eight countries, from Honduras (Gini .55) to Sierra Leone (Gini .63).

Finally, to account for explanations that rely on economic development or the dedication of policymakers to economic performance, I selected three countries— one from each inequality group—that were at low, medium, and high levels of economic development by the 1990s, and one of which is an economic success story. In its most politics-free form, the economic explanation is that all education systems should tend toward economic optimality. Because returns are higher to primary education in less-developed countries, the less-developed a country is, the greater should be its relative investments on primary education over tertiary. A more political form of the explanation is that education should tend toward economic optimality when governments are economically enlightened or committed to development. The obvious choice for the success story was Taiwan, an Asian Tiger often touted for its sound economic governance of an economy that *averaged* 6.4 percent annual growth in real per-capita GDP between 1960 and 2000—a blazing rate exceeded only by two countries: Botswana (7.2 percent) and Oman (6.5 percent) (Republic of China 2007; World Bank 2007). This growth rate made Taiwan, by 1990s, a high income country according to the World Bank's income classifications for 2000. (High income countries had GDP per capita of greater than 2000 US$9,265.) Taiwan is also a country in the low inequality group (Gini of .3 in the 1980s). Thus the remaining two cases needed to be countries of medium and high inequality and medium and low economic development.

I began by looking for a country with high inequality, and choose Brazil. Few countries are more unequal than Brazil: in fact, among the 45 in my sample, only two had Gini coefficients higher than Brazil's .58 for the 1980s: Guatemala (.59) and Sierra Leone (.63). Sierra Leone's unrest made it a dangerous place to do research, and Brazil had the advantage over Guatemala of having a very well-researched education system.[4]

Brazil is a middle-income country—its GDP per capita for the 1990s of 2000 US$3,246 puts it at the low end of the World Bank's "upper-middle-income" category, which has a lower bound of $2,996. Thus my remaining country needed to be lower income (per-capita GDP of lower than 2000 US$755) with medium inequality. Of the 21 countries in my sample that had medium inequality in the 1980s, five had per-capita GDP in the 1990s of less than $755: Ghana, Nigeria, Mauritania, Madagascar, and Côte d'Ivoire. Of these, I choose Ghana. It is stable and English-speaking, and it has the lowest per-capita GDP of the five (just $227 over the 1990s).

Table A1.1 shows key statistics on the three countries. Figure A1.1 shows where the three countries rank by inequality, among the 45 countries from which they were chosen.

One final note on the selection of Brazil. Both Taiwan and Ghana are relatively small countries in which most education policy is determined centrally. But Brazil is an enormous country with a federal government, in which power over education is shared by the local, state, and federal governments and varies over time. To understand education policy in Brazil, it is not sufficient to study simply federal policy. Thus the selection of Brazil entailed a further layer of analysis and an additional selection of cases. In Chapter 6, in addition to examining Brazilian education at the federal level, I also examine two Brazilian states: São Paulo, and Bahia. The logic of selecting these states from among Brazil's 26 was similar to the logic just described in selecting Taiwan, Ghana, and Brazil: the two states provide wide variation on the important economic and political dimensions. São Paulo is Brazil's

Table A1.1   **Regime transitions, inequality, and income classifications in Taiwan, Ghana, and Brazil**

	Taiwan		*Ghana*		*Brazil*	
Regime-type transitions since 1950	1		5		2	
Inequality (1980s)	.3		.48		.58	
Income classification (*World Bank*)	High Income		Low Income		Upper Middle Income	
	1960s	*1990s*	*1960s*	*1990s*	*1960s*	*1990s*
Economic Indicators						
GDP per-capita (*2000 US$*)	1,255.8	12,938.7	264.7	227.4	1,606.4	3,511.2
GDP per-capita growth (*% annual*)	6.2	5.1	-0.1	1.6	3.0	0.3
GDP (*2000 US$, millions*)	16,238.1	273,692.1	2,123.9	3,998.4	134,205.9	563,637.9

Sources: Regime-type: Przeworski et al. (2000); Inequality: for Taiwan: Luxembourg Income Study (accessed from *World Income Inequality Database*); for Ghana: Ghana Living Standards Surveys (Deininger, Squire, and World Bank 2004); for Brazil: *World Development Indicators*; Basic economic statistics: for Brazil and Ghana: *World Development Indicators*; for Taiwan: Republic of China (2007), deflated with Consumer Price Index data from Republic of China (2005a).

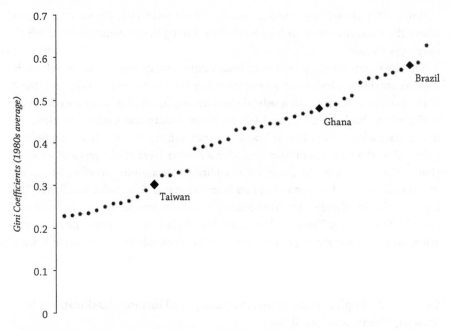

A1.1 Countries that have been through regime changes since 1950, ordered by Gini coefficients
Source: World Development Indicators and World Income Inequality Database.

richest and largest state, with a large and relatively efficient, if sometimes corrupt, government, which is often at odds with federal administrations in Brasília. Bahia, in past centuries the most important state in Brazil, is today archetypical of the poor northeast. For decades its government has been a personality cult, run by one man in various official and unofficial capacities, and is closely aligned with, and an important source of support for, many recent federal governments in Brasília.

Appendix B

LIST OF INTERVIEWS

	Government	Academia	Civil Society
Taiwan	*Education*	*Education*	*Education*
	Wu Jin (吳京), former Minister of Education	Chen Peiying (陳佩英), Assistant Professor, Center for Teacher Education, National Tsing Hua University	Shih Ying (史英), Founder, Humanistic Education Foundation
	Chang Pei-chi (張不繼), former Director, Manpower Planning Department, Council for Economic Planning and Development, Executive Yuan		Huang Yushi (黃武雄), founder, 4/10 Movement
	Kuo Wei-fan (郭為藩), former Minister of Education	*Other*	*Other*
	Mao Kao-wen (毛高文), former Minister of Education	Ching-hsi Chang (張清溪), Economics Professor, National Taiwan University	Yu-bin Chiu (邱毓斌), former labor activist
	Liou Ching-Tien (劉清田), former secretary to Mao Kao-wen	Lin Jih-Wen (林繼文), Political Scientist, Institute of Politics, Academia Sinica	
	Fan Sun-lu (范巽綠), former Deputy Minister of Education	Chi Huang (黃紀), Chair, Political Science, National Cheng Chi University	
	Lee Chung-Chi (李重志), Senior Executive Officer, Minister Li-yeh Fu, Executive Yuan		

(continued)

List of Interviews (*continued*)

	Government	Academia	Civil Society
Taiwan	*Other* Fredrick Chien (Chien Fu) (錢復), former Foreign Minister and President of the Control Yuan Hsu Shui-teh (許水德), former Minister of the Interior, President of the Examination Yuan Hsu Li-teh (徐立德), former Chairman of the Council for Economic Planning and Development		
Ghana	*Education* J. S. Djangmah, former Director-General, Ghana Education Service and former Vice Chancellor, University of Cape Coast Paul Effah, Executive Secretary, National Council on Tertiary Education Ivan Addae-Mensah, former Vice-Chancellor of the University of Ghana F. K. Buah, former Minister of Education Henrietta Mensah-Bonsu, Law Professor at the University of Ghana and member of President Kufuor's Committee for the Review of the Education Reforms	*Other* Kwesi Jonah, Head, Governance Centre, Institute for Economic Affairs, and Professor of Political Science, University of Ghana Ernest Aryeetey, Director, Institute of Statistical, Social, and Economic Research, University of Ghana A. Baah-Nuarkoh, Professor of Economics, University of Ghana William Baah-Boateng, Economist, University of Ghana Evans Aggrey-Darkoh, Political Scientist, University of Ghana	*Education* Nancy Keteku, Regional Educational Advising Coordinator for Africa, US Embassy, Accra Eunice Dapaah, Lead Education Specialist, World Bank, Accra Judith Sawyer, former principal of Ghana International School, Accra *Other* E. Acquaah-Harrison, former president, Association of Ghana Industries

	Government	Academia	Civil Society
Ghana	*Education (continued)*		
	William Kofi Ahadzie, Research Fellow, Centre for Social Policy Studies and member of President Rawling's Education Reform Committee		
	Nikoi Kotei, former Executive Secretary of National Accreditation Board		
	John Budu-Smith, former principal of Accra Technical Training Center, Director of Technical Education for the Ghana Education Service (GES), and Deputy Director General of GES for Academics (field operations)		
	James K. Glover, Director, and Edwin Billy Akorli, Assistant Director, NACVET (National Coordinating Committee for Technical and Vocational Education and Training)		
	Fosuaba A. Mensah Banahene, Administrator, Ghana Education Trust Fund		
	Other		
	Anthony Yaw Baah, Head of Policy and Research, Ghana Trades Union Congress		

(continued)

List of Interviews (*continued*)

	Government	Academia	Civil Society
Brazil	*Education*	*Education*	*Education*
	Paulo Renato de Souza, former Minister of Education	Yvonne Maggie, Professor of Education, Federal University of Rio de Janeiro (UFRJ)	Violeta Monteiro, Observatorio Universitario
	Eunice Ribeiro Durham, former federal Secretary of Higher Education	Ruben Klein, Cesgranrio	Alberto Rodriguez, Lead Education Specialist, World Bank
	José Amaral Sobrinho, Coordinator of Formulation and Implementation of Programs, Fundescola, Ministry of Education (MEC)	Paulo Corbucci, economist, Institute of Applied Economic Research (IPEA)	
	Reynaldo Fernandez, President, National Institute of Educational Research and Study (INEP), MEC	Sergei Soares, economist, IPEA	
	Linda Goulart, Director of Public Affairs, INEP, MEC	Jorge Abrahão, economist, IPEA	
	Anamélia Lima Rocha Fernandes and Zuleide Araújo Teixeira, Education and Culture Committee, Federal Chamber of Deputies	Antônio Carlos da Ressurreição Xavier, economist, IPEA	
		Romualdo Portela de Oliveira, Professor of Education, University of São Paulo (USP)	
		José Marcelino Pinto, Professor of Education, USP	
		Other	
		Denisard Alves, Professor of Economics, USP	
		Creso Franco, Professor of Economics, Pontifícia Universidade Católica (PUC), Rio de Janeiro	

Government	Academia	Civil Society
Brazil		
	Other (continued)	
	Alberto de Mello e Souza, Director of the School of Economics, State University of Rio de Janeiro (UERJ)	
	Ricardo Barros, economist, IPEA	
	Argelina Figueiredo, Professor of Political Science, University Research Institute of Rio de Janeiro (IUPERJ)	
	Ladislau Dowbor, professor of economics, PUC-São Paulo	
Brazil – São Paulo *Education*	*Education*	
Rose Neubauer, former São Paulo State Secretary of Education	Bernadette Gatti, Coordinator of the Department for Education Research, Fundação Carlos Chagas, São Paulo	
Moacir Gadotti, former chief of staff to Municipal Secretary of Education Paulo Freire		
Guimar Namo de Mello, former São Paulo Municipal Secretary of Education		
Brazil – Bahia *Education*	*Education*	
Eraldo Tinoco, Vice Governor of Bahia and former Bahia State Secretary of Education and federal Minister of Education	Bob Verhine, Professor of Economics and Education, Federal University of Bahia (UFBA)	
Renata Procerpio, former Bahia State Secretary of Education	Katia Siqueira de Freitas, Professor of Education, UFBA	

(continued)

List of Interviews (*continued*)

	Government	Academia	Civil Society
Brazil – Bahia	*Education (continued)*	*Other*	
	Edilson Freire, Ombudsman of Bahia and former Bahia State Secretary of Education	Celina Souza, Professor of Political Science, UFBA	
	Jansen Teixeira, Project Leader, Education for All project, State of Bahia		
	Edivaldo Boaventura, Director General, *A Tarde* newspaper, and former Bahia State Secretary of Education		
	Other		
	Maurício Campos, Superintendent of Development, Science and Technology, Secretary of Science, Technology, and Innovation, State of Bahia		
	Alexandre Paupério, President, Research Support Foundation of the State of Bahia (FAPESB)		

NOTES

Preface

1. Examples are David Stasavage's (2005) study of Uganda and David Brown's (2002) study of Brazil.
2. For example, Brown (1995; 1999, 2002), Sylwester (2000), Lake and Baum (2001), Baum and Lake (2003), Stasavage (2005), Ansell (2010).
3. World Bank (2004a).
4. Cited in Kimble (1963).
5. For example, Ross (2006) and Mulligan, Gil, and Sala-i-Martin (2004).
6. Lant Pritchett calls this the "Normative as Positive" model of education policymaking (Pritchett 2001).

Chapter 1

1. An entire literature on "new growth theories" in economics deals with the role of education in spurring economic growth through technological change (Romer 1986; Lucas 1988), and standard exogenous growth models (Solow 1957) now regularly include a term for human capital (e.g., Mankiw, Romer, and Weil 1992). Empirically, education and economic growth are highly correlated (Barro 1991; Barro and Lee 1993, 1994). In individuals, education raises earnings, improves agricultural productivity and the management of industry, and increases the capacity of industry to make use of new technologies (e.g., Schultz 1988; Psacharopoulos 1994; Jamison and Moock 1984; Birdsall 1993; Deraniyagala 1995).
2. On this virtuous cycle, see Sen (1999), UNDP (1990), and Ranis, Stewart, and Ramirez (2000). Education's benefits go far beyond its role in economic development. Isaiah Berlin wrote: "The only real remedy for the evil consequences, whether of ignorance or of knowledge, is more knowledge.... Unless men are given the chance to find out what kind of world they live in, what they have made, are making, and could make of it . . . they will continue to walk in darkness and be faced by the unpredicted and sometimes appalling consequences of one another's activities" (1975).
3. For example, Bils and Klenow (2000) find that less than 30 percent of the cross-country relationship between education and growth is the result of individual investments in education based on private returns.
4. Early development scholars argued for increasing technical and higher education even in very poor countries to meet estimated demand for highly trained technical labor (Harbison and Myers 1964; Denison 1962). Recently, economists have argued for investments in higher education to develop indigenous technology or adapt technology developed elsewhere and reduce "intellectual dependency"—the gap in knowledge between developed and

developing countries (World Bank 2002b; Birdsall 1996; also see Altbach et al. 2004). Still, after a half century of economic research on human capital, the most influential view is that the poorer a country is, the more its government should focus its educational investments on primary schools—i.e., expand mass education—because in poorer countries primary education has typically had higher economic returns (Ahmed and Blaug 1973; Psacharopoulos 1973, 1981, 1994). Even those who would like developing countries to provide higher education as well do not advocate that developing countries should focus on higher education.

5.
$$\frac{per - student\ spending\ on\ tertiary}{per - student\ spending\ on\ primary\ +\ per - student\ spending\ on\ secondary\ +\ per - student\ spending\ tertiary}$$

6. The hypothesized connections between educational demands and culture can be very specific. In dynastic China, imperial exams regulated entry to the prestigious and well-remunerated positions in the Emperor's service—exams that required extensive academic preparation mostly irrelevant to the positions for which exam-takers were applying. Taiwanese officials in the 1960s and 1970s blamed the culture surrounding these exams for the apparent desire of Taiwanese parents to send their children to universities instead of vocational schools (Wan 1972; Gannicott 1973).

7. Psychologist David McClelland's famous book *The Achieving Society* (1961) examined Weber's Protestant Work Ethic as a "special case of a more general relationship" between the value a society accords to individual achievement and the development success of that society. In testing that value, which McClelland dubbed "*n* Achievement," he found it predicted development in thirty countries, and not the other way around: an achieving culture causes development; development does not cause an achieving culture. But McClelland's basic empirical analysis showing that an achieving culture precedes development has failed to stand up to scrutiny with better data and statistical techniques (Mazur and Rosa 1977; Frey 1984; Gilleard 1989).

8. Downs (1957); Meltzer and Richard (1981).

9. Bueno de Mesquita and his coauthors in fact go to some effort to distinguish their theory of policymaking incentives from standard regime-type theorists, by building it on distinct concepts: the "selectorate" and the "winning coalition." But while they allow for the theoretical possibility that an autocracy could have a large selectorate and winning coalition, their presentation in fact serves to underline the entrenchment of the conventional view. For instance, they write that "most systems with large winning coalitions are democratic, and those with small coalitions and large selectorates are autocratic (monarchies and juntas usually have small coalitions and small selectorates)" (Bueno de Mesquita et al. 2002, 560) and that "[i]n modern mass democracies, the selectorate is the electorate, and the winning coalition is determined by specific electoral rules. In autocratic systems, the winning coalition is often a small group of powerful individuals, and the selectorate is those who have the positions (for example, military rank or party membership in a single-party system) to aspire to make and break leaders" (561).

10. Brown and Hunter (1999) find that, in Latin America, democracies spend more than autocracies on social programs, especially in economic crises; Zweifel and Navia (2000) find that democracies have lower infant mortality rates than autocracies at similar levels of development; Rodrik (1999) finds that, primarily because of political competition and participation, labor's share of manufacturing value-added is higher in democracies. See also Acemoglu, Robinson, and Johnson (2002) and Boix (2003).

11. National being an important distinction in Brazil.

12. See Olson (1984); Skocpol (1995); Grossman and Helpman (1994, 2001); Stigler (1971); Peltzman (1976); Becker (1983); and Moe (1988).

13. North (1990); Przeworski (2004); Huntington (1968, 461).

14. Mulligan, Gil, and Sala-i-Martin (2004) find no difference in economic or social policymaking between democracies and nondemocracies. Ross (2006) comes to a similar conclusion and argues that past studies that claim to find a relationship between democracy and pro-poor policymaking suffer from a particular selection bias: nondemocratic states with good social and

economic policies are far less likely than nondemocratic states with poor social and economic policies to report the statistics that scholars typically use to measure the pro-poor bias of policy.

15. An alternative conception is that meaningful democracy only emerges once inequality is low enough that the poor are not likely to demand much redistribution (Boix 2003; Boix and Stokes 2003).

16. I go into more detail in Chapter 2. Important works around political entrepreneurship include Frohlich and Oppenheimer (1971); Jones (1978); Riker (1986); Noll (1989); Moe (1988); Schneider and Teske (1992); and North (1990).

17. On these judgments, see World Bank (2004a); Harbison and Hanushek (1992); and Hanushek, Gomes-Neto, and Harbison (1996).

18. On Taiwan's development, see Fei, Ranis, and Kuo (1979); Doner, Ritchie, and Slater (2005); Li (1981); and Woo (1991). On Ghana, see Bates (1981b); Nimako (1991); Kimble (1963); Killick, Omaboe, and Szereszewski (1966); the U.S. Army's Country Study of Ghana (Library of Congress 1994); and Kanbur (1994). On Brazil, see Pereira (1984); Evans (1979); Skidmore and Smith (1997); Schwartzman (2003); Castro (1973); Birdsall, Bruns, and Sabot (1996); Plank, Sobrinho, and Xavier (1996); and Plank (1996)

Chapter 2

1. This definition of education is somewhat narrower than the "human capital" with which people contribute to their economy. The pioneer of human capital theory, Theodore W. Schultz, identified five categories of human capital, of which formal education is only one; the others are health, on-the-job training, "study programs for adults not organized by firms," and migration of laborers to adjust to changing job opportunities (Schultz 1961, 9). Although these other categories play some role in the discussions that follow, I am concerned in this study only with education.

2. It is even possible to exclude individuals from education, though this is harder than excluding groups. I return to this issue in the next chapter.

3. Because of the clarity of its immediate beneficiaries, education policy is somewhat different from government policies about which there is more distributive uncertainty. It is not always immediately clear who will benefit from a tight monetary policy, for example, which makes demand for it harder to impute and government response harder to predict— exercises that are key to the following analysis.

4. Education's consumption value is not trivial and for some people it can be the primary reason they acquire education. (No one becomes a political scientist for the money.) But for the vast majority of people in developing countries, the investment value of education dominates.

5. A large number of studies demonstrate that in the less-developed world, primary education has the highest rates of return, and that these returns fall relative to higher levels in more-developed countries (Psacharopoulos 1973, 1981, 1994).

6. For a discussion, see Wiseman (1987) or Ljungqvist (1993). Behrman, Pollak, and Taubman (1989) show this point empirically with financing for college education in the United States.

7. Friedman (1962).

8. World Bank economist George Psacharapoulos used to conduct semi-decadal surveys of rates-of-return studies; the most recent of these, from 1994, showed that, on average, across the world, a primary graduate earned about 18 percent more than a person with no education, a secondary graduate earned 13 percent more than a primary graduate, and a graduate of higher education earned 11 percent more than a secondary graduate (Psacharopoulos 1994).

9. A balance in the demand and supply of skill would mean that the cost of becoming educated to a certain level of skill would equal the discounted present value of the additional earnings a person with that education could expect to earn in the job market (Findlay and Kierzkowski 1983). More on this below.

10. See, for example, Downs (1957), Mayhew (1974), Bueno de Mesquita et al. (2003).

11. This condition is from Findlay and Kierzkowski (1983). Findlay and Kierzkowski derive it using a modified Heckscher-Ohlin/Stolper-Samuelson two-factor, two-good general equilibrium model of international trade (Stolper and Samuelson 1941; Samuelson 1948, 1949; Lerner 1952), in which the traditional two factors "land" and "labor" are replaced by skilled and unskilled labor. In equilibrium, the lifetime earnings of unskilled and skilled laborers are equal, indicating a shortage of neither. The equilibrium condition is valuable for insight into an individual's decision to acquire education as an investment, but it depends on the education system being private (educational capital privately held), on a perfect market for student loans, and on all workers being identical and having no assets at the start of their lives—all nontrivial assumptions that are violated by reality.

12. See, for example, Glick and Sahn (2006).

13. The poor family's demands may differ depending on the country's level of development. In a wealthier country, a poor family might afford a few years of meager-quality secondary education.

14. Workers naturally oppose this policy, which erodes skilled wages. In surveys, workers oppose immigration in countries where immigrants have higher skills than they do (Mayda 2006).

15. The labor market's flexibility is likely to be partly a result of the vital constituency, a point I return to later.

16. See Pritchett (2006).

17. The patterns of skill development in Broad vs. Skilled Worker Training systems echo influential work on the political economy of developed countries in Liberal vs. Cooperative Market Economies (Hall and Soskice 2001). In Liberal Market Economies (LMEs), public policy supports the development of general skills; in Cooperative Market Economies (CMEs), it supports the development of more-specific skills (Estevez-Abe, Iverson, and Soskice 2001). Like my approach, the *Varieties of Capitalism* approach emphasizes the endogeneity of particular governing institutions to the underlying economic relationships and patterns of skills development: for example, CMEs may favor proportional-representation systems, because they facilitate greater redistribution to provide social insurance that, in turn, incentivizes worker investment in specific skills (Iverson and Soskice 2006).

18. The government and its leaders are not the same thing, of course, but to the extent that the "government" has motives set for it by leaders, there is no analytical reason to separate the two, so I refer to them interchangeably.

19. In addition to Bueno de Mesquita et al. (2003), see, especially, Downs (1957); Riker (1962); and Mayhew (1974).

20. To be exact, all governments of *effective states* have a vital constituency. Failed states are another issue, one I leave aside in this book. The government of a truly failed state does not have a vital constituency in the sense that there is no coalition capable of sustaining the government in power. But the government of a failed state is not likely to be providing much education anyway.

21. Przeworski (1991) has an excellent discussion of this point, related to the emergence of democratic institutions in Eastern Europe.

22. See, among others, Grossman and Helpman (1994, 2001); Skocpol (1995); Shaprio (Shapiro 2002); Graetz and Shapiro (2006); Bartels (2010); Hacker and Pierson (2010); Culpepper (2010).

23. See Moore (1966); Huntington (1968); Acemoglu and Robinson (2005).

24. See, for example, Geddes (1999); Przeworski et al. (2000); Lust-Okar (2005); Davenport (2007); Gandhi and Przeworski (2007); Gandhi (2008); Landry (2008); Vreeland (2008); Rudra (2008); Pepinsky (2009); Nooruddin (2011).

25. Notably the work of Steven Levitsky and Lucan A. Way (2002, 2010).

26. In arguing that elites will generally be the vital constituency, I am following work in political science that conceives of economic institutions—of which education might be considered to be one—as arising from elite politics (Knight 1992; Geddes 1994; Bates 1995). I share with

this work the idea that economic institutions stem from *political* dynamics, not from the interaction of private actors seeking to maximize their mutual welfare. I differ, however, in arguing that economic institutions need not arise solely from elite politics, if the poor are also a locus of political power.

27. Bates (1981), for example, predicts that poorer citizens are only able to organize and cause a government trouble when they live in urban areas, where their closer proximity facilitates collective action. But he does not theorize a mechanism by which they translate proximity into collective action. Rogowski (1989) predicts that, where trade conditions advantage a societal group, a political entrepreneur will arise to organize that group, enabling them to translate their new advantage into political power and hence favorable trade policy.

28. Moe (1988) is among the most useful and comprehensive theoretical treatments. Other prominent works include Frohlich and Oppenheimer (1971); Jones (1978); Riker (1986); Noll (1989); Moe (1988); Schneider and Teske (1992); and North (1990).

29. In most theories of political entrepreneurship, political entrepreneurs are assumed to be motivated solely by monetary gain. Hence they help organize latent groups in order to and to the extent to which they can maximize the group's "surplus"—in Moe's (1988) analysis, participant contributions minus the costs of organization and selective incentives. But in the cases I examine, the political entrepreneur's gain comes not from the group's contributions, but from political power, which the group's participation in politics allows him or her to obtain and retain. This is an important distinction but it is not fundamental, as long as we think of political power as providing rewards—either monetary rewards or other goods, privileges, or distinctions that have value to the political entrepreneur. (Moe in fact acknowledges, albeit in passing, the possibility that a political entrepreneur will seek political office (64).) In other words, there is no reason to think of the sort of political entrepreneurs I examine as motivated any differently than other seekers of high political office—as described, for example, in classic analyses like Downs (1957) or Mayhew (1974).

30. Olson would call a group like the "poor," which is mobilized by a political entrepreneur, a "mobilized latent" group—meaning a large group that has "latent power or capacity for action," but has only "been led to act in its group interest . . . either because of coercion of the individuals in the group or because of positive rewards to those individuals" (Olson 1965, 51).

31. Moe (1988) provides an excellent discussion of the incentives for political entrepreneurs to be undemocratic.

32. On subgroups of the poor, see Krishna (2009).

33. See Przeworski (1991) or Waldner (1999).

34. Political entrepreneurship does not determine whether employers are inside the vital constituency. Any of the three vital constituencies in Table 2.2 may include employers.

35. Thus the vital constituency is not necessarily a "minimum winning coalition," as in Bueno de Mesquita et al. (2003) or Riker (1962), or a more-secure "supermajority" (Groseclose and Snyder 1996).

36. See, for example, Przeworski and Wallerstein (1988) and Lindblom (1977).

37. See Rudra (2002, 2008) and Harris and Todaro (1970). Calvo (1978) extends the Harris-Todaro model to include unions, who endogenously determine the urban wage.

38. Those outside the vital constituency have another option: they are free to leave the country. But once those outside the vital constituency leave the country they lose their ability to influence the government.

39. See Levy (2004, 2007).

40. The argument that governments are threatened by the resources, and particularly the education, of those outside the vital constituency goes back at least to John Dewey (1916), and includes Seymour Martin Lipset's (1959) famous argument on the social origins of democracy and more-recent influential empirical work by Robert Barro (1999) and Przeworski et al. (2000). Some more-recent empirical studies have found evidence against this causal link (e.g., Acemoglu et al. 2004).

41. All else being equal—i.e., holding constant inequality, economic advancement, and GDP per capita.

Chapter 3

1. The inspiration for this exercise is David Mayhew's (1974) classic study of the organization of Congress. Mayhew describes his method this way: "I shall conjure up a vision of United States congressmen as single-minded seekers of reelection, see what kinds of activity that goal implies, and then speculate about how congressmen so motivated are likely to go about building and sustaining legislative institutions and making policy" (xxviii–xxx).
2. See, e.g., Prichett (2009); Darden (forthcoming).
3. See Chapters 1 and 2 for a discussion of existing studies of the political economy of education. Prominent examples are Brown (1995, 1999, 2002); Sylwester (2000); Lake and Baum (2001); Baum and Lake (2003); Stasavage (2005); Ansell (2010).
4. Empirical work on the United States finds that the tax-price elasticity of public spending is small and statistically insignificant, with varying signs. Among others, see Bergstrom, Rubinfeld, and Shapiro (1982); Rubinfeld, Shapiro, and Roberts (1987); and Rubinfeld and Shapiro (1989).
5. Thus at the margin, aid is little different from any other source of government revenue (Mosley, Hudson, and Horrel 1987; Boone 1996).
6. For example, see Brown (1995; 1999, 2002); Brown and Hunter (1999); Sylwester (2000); Lake and Baum (2001); Baum and Lake (2003); Stasavage (2005); Ansell (2010). Political-economic models of education spending such as Gradstein (2004) and Levy (2005) follow the logic in the classic Meltzer-Richard (1981) model of redistributive tax policy, in which a rational median voter with income of less than the mean will redistribute income to himself through tax policy, but will not equalize incomes, for doing so would reduce the incentive to work and thereby lower his income. But these models imply that greater income inequality— specifically the poorer the median voter relative to mean income—should mean greater redistribution and hence more spending on public education. The evidence, however, is that inequality is positively correlated with inequality in schooling and negatively correlated with average level of attainment (Becker and Chiswick 1966; Adelman and Morris 1973)— the opposite of what one would expect if education is redistribution from rich to poor in order to minimize future demands for redistribution or keep the poor participating in the labor market. Further evidence shows a negative correlation between inequality and secondary school enrollments (Perotti 1996; Flug, Spilimbergo, and Wachtenheim 1998; De Gregorio and Lee 2002).
7. On the importance of considering this sort of path dependence in political science scholarship, see Pierson (2000, 2004).
8. Because the first government's decisions in building an education system are the freest from the chains of its inheritance, and therefore most fully illustrate the operation of this theory, I try to begin each of the case studies that follow with the government that is most responsible for constructing the country's modern education system.
9. This "stacking of the deck" is a common tactic of governments, especially those with short time-horizons—for example, the majority party in the U.S. Congress (Cox and McCubbins 1993).
10. See, for example, Tullock (1971).
11. For example, scholars have long theorized a causal path from education to democracy (e.g., Dewey 1916; Lipset 1959; Barro 1999; Przeworski et al. 2000; Huntington 1968). But see Acemoglu et al. (2004) for evidence against this causal path.
12. See the discussion in Section 2 of Chapter 2.
13. Kuznets (1955).
14. Others have theorized many conditions, including the presence of an activist or political entrepreneur to guide the disparate disgruntled into a protesting movement, and sufficient information on the viability of protest as a method of effecting change (Lohmann 1994).
15. Often, rational choice theories do not require that actors act rationally, only that they behave *as if* they act rationally (among many others, see Friedman (1953); Cox (2004); Green (2004)). By taking explicit account of actors' motivations, I am trying to set a somewhat

higher bar. My theory contends that policymakers act systematically in the interest of certain groups. While this contention does not require that policymakers have specific thoughts, the theory would be implausible if policymakers did not hold views in accordance with the policies my theory expects them to implement.

16. Downs (1957); Riker (1962); Mayhew (1974).
17. One of the more interesting examples is Musharraf's Pakistan, a country which, despite deplorably inadequate primary schooling, enthusiastically embraced the World Bank's recommendations on improving and investing in higher education, ostensibly because of its likelihood of improving national well-being (Altbach et al. 2004; Rosovsky, Bloom, and Steven 2002, 2000).

Part II

1. See the discussion in Chapter 1. On economic development and education, important works include Lewis (1954); Harbison and Myers (1964); Mincer (1974); Morris and Sweeting (1995); and Pritchett (2001). On culture and education, see McClelland (1961); Dai (1989); Rozman (1991); or Davies (1995). On inequality and education, some works have viewed education as a tool for reinforcing inequality in advanced democracies (e.g., Hyman 1953; Banks 1976) and others implicitly include collective-action while describing the role of other important variables on education policy (e.g., Stasavage 2005, on the role of democratic institutions in education policymaking).
2. Przeworski et al. (2000).
3. On Taiwan's development, see Fei, Ranis, and Kuo (1979); Doner, Ritchie, and Slater (2005); Li (1981); and Woo (1991). On Ghana, see Bates (1981b); Nimako (1991); Kimble (1963); Killick, Omaboe, and Szereszewski (1966); the U.S. Army's Country Study of Ghana (Library of Congress 1994); and Kanbur (1994). On Brazil, see Pereira (1984); Evans (1979); Skidmore and Smith (1997); Schwartzman (2003); Castro (1973); Birdsall, Bruns, and Sabot (1996); Plank, Sobrinho, and Xavier (1996); and Plank (1996).
4. For Taiwan: Luxembourg Income Study (accessed from *World Income Inequality Database*); for Ghana: Ghana Living Standards Surveys (Deininger, Squire, and World Bank 2004); and for Brazil: *World Development Indicators*.
5. Ghana did not gain formal independence from the United Kingdom until 1957, but throughout the 1950s independence was a foregone conclusion and an elected Ghanaian government had control of much of government policy—including education policy—starting in 1951.
6. Recall that boxes 2 and 3 are unlikely to occur (Chapter 2).
7. I rely on regime type as reported by Przeworski et al. (2000). Przeworski et al. do not measure regime type prior to 1945; thus for Brazil prior to 1945, I use the Polity IV measure of democracy (Marshall and Jaggers 2000).
8. Data are occasionally from international sources (World Bank, UNESCO), but, as these often contain errors, I rely more often on official statistics gathered in archives in the three countries. Official statistics, of course, have their own reliability problems, but any bias is likely to overstate consistently the access to or quality of the education system, and is unlikely to systematically favor or oppose my periodizations, which have not existed before now.

These are the major sources for official statistics: Taiwan: Educational statistics come from *Education Statistics of the Republic of China*, various editions (e.g., Republic of China 2005b). I converted spending figures to 2001 NT $ using the Consumer Price Index series from Republic of China (2005a); index values for prior to 1959 are from the Provincial Bureau of Accounting and Statistics, cited in Jacoby (1967, table C.16). Ghana: Educational statistics are from various editions of the *Statistical Yearbook* (e.g., Ghana 1973) until 1969, and from various editions of *Education Statistics, Digest of Education Statistics of the Republic of Ghana* and the *Quarterly Digest of Statistics* (e.g., Ghana 1997) thereafter. Spending figures for most years are from the *Annual Estimates*, which are issued by the Ministry of Finance (e.g., Ghana 1999). I convert them to 2001 cedis using price indices from various editions of the *Quarterly Digest of Statistics* and from Ewusi (1986). Brazil: Educational statistics and spending figures are compiled from various editions of *Anuário Estatísticos do Brasil*, except where otherwise noted. I converted figures to 2004 reais using deflators from IPEA (2006).

Chapter 4

1. The two countries with growth rates exceeding Taiwan's are Oman and Botswana. World GDP data from *World Development Indicators*. Taiwan data from report 93SNA (2007) of the Bureau of Statistics (Directorate General of Budget, Accounting and Statistics, Executive Yuan, R.O.C.). Nominal GDP converted to 2001 NT$ using the Consumer Price Index series from Republic of China (2005a); index values for prior to 1959 are from the Provincial Bureau of Accounting and Statistics, cited in Jacoby (1967, 286, table C.16).
2. The classic account is Fei, Ranis, and Kuo (1979). Others include Doner, Ritchie, and Slater (2005); Li (1981); and Woo (1991).
3. Taiwan was certainly blessed with an education system led by many knowledgeable and hard-working officials. But so are many countries with education systems that serve their economies far less well.
4. To this day, many native Taiwanese maintain far more affection for Japan than for mainland China.
5. For more on Taiwan's experience under Japanese and early Chinese rule, see Chu and Lin (2001); Rigger (1999); and Tsurumi (1977).
6. Initially Chen Yi claimed that the Taiwanese ("Formosans") were politically undeveloped after their years under the Japanese. They thus could not be permitted full political rights (Chen 2003, 73).
7. The "native Taiwanese" ethnic group is actually made up of three distinct groups: a small group of native peoples, and two groups of Han Chinese: Hoklo and Hakka. Even so, political struggles by Taiwanese nationalists starting in the 1970s have forged a Taiwanese identity that pits "native Taiwanese" against mainlanders who emigrated to Taiwan after 1945.
8. Quoted in Chen (2003, 76).
9. In 1949, 60 percent of the Taiwanese population was in farming; of these, 39 percent were tenants, a quarter were part-owners, and 36 percent were full-owners. The average owner, however, owned just 1.4 hectares. Average leases required two years' rent to secure, and average rents were half of total crops. In reality, rents were even higher, because they did not make allowances for crop failures, which were common. Accounting for crop failures, rents were an average of 57 percent of total crops, and could reach as high as 70 percent. Only a tenth of leases were written, so the remainder could be terminated at will by landlords (Li 1981).
10. Only 53 of the primary schools in 1965 were private; in 1950, none were (Republic of China 2005b).
11. See, for example, the discussion in Young (1995).
12. The document written to define the republican government for all of China is, with some amendment, the same document by which Taiwan is still governed today, as it is the remaining embodiment of the "one-China" principle, upholding the Taiwanese government's right to govern all of China. It was ratified in 1947 and recognized at the time by all the major powers (Chu and Lin 2001).
13. The lack of education among soldiers might have affected their education-policy demands, but for the most part soldiers came to Taiwan without their families, and so had no children they wished educated, until years later when many remarried to Taiwanese wives. By contrast the governing elite often were wealthy and influential enough to bring their families with them to Taiwan.
14. Graduates were not always able to enter the next level of education on their first try. In 1950 the net enrollment ratio (current-year graduates entering the next level) was 51 percent for junior high school graduates and 40 percent for senior high graduates. In 1965, the ratios had improved to 79 percent for junior high school graduates, and for senior high graduates had stayed roughly the same at 39 percent.

15. The earliest rate of interest I could find—10.08 percent—was for 1971, though by that year it had already been the established rate for at least several years. This was an extremely low rate for the period (Gannicott 1973).

16. Chen (2005) gets similar results for cohorts born before 1960. Analyzing years of schooling, rather than likelihood of attending college, a working paper by Chen and Lin (2004) finds declining ethnic differences in education attainment for cohorts born after 1944, differences that are insignificant after controlling for parental educational attainment.

17. In an interview, Chien Fu, former foreign minister and president of the Control Yuan, remarked that the education provided by the system was a source of great pride to those who went abroad to study. Mr. Chien himself came to Yale in 1958 to begin a PhD (Chien Fu, personal communication, New Haven, October 12, 2005).

18. Hsu Shui-teh, personal communication, Taipei, January 19, 2006.

19. Accounts variously date the KMT's realization that it faced a prolonged stay on Taiwan to between 1954 and 1956. Jacoby (1967) dates it from around 1956. Before that, he notes, "[t]he dominant aim of President Chiang Kai-shek and his government was to build a socially and politically stable, and an economically capable, base for the recovery of all of China. Indeed, this motive was of such overwhelming weight in the minds of the Republic of China's leaders, at least during the early years . . . that the purpose of developing Taiwan into a viable independent economy did not exist" (Jacoby 1967, 36).

20. See Wu (2003) for more on local factions and their relations with the Kuomintang.

21. Scholars differ on whether the KMT maintained at least two factions everywhere, or just in strategically vital areas. Works such as Chu and Lin (2001) seem to suggest that the former, while other scholars argue that outside important areas factions were bought off as they sprung up (Chi Huang, personal communication, Taipei, February 9, 2006). Certainly some areas were too important to risk faction-based electioneering. Thus in Taipei, after disloyal factions appeared to be gaining ground in the mid-1970s, the KMT simply eliminated elections until the mid-1990s.

22. See the classic accounts in Fei, Ranis, and Kuo (1979) and Wade (1990).

23. Tenth Issue of the *Report of Taiwan Labor Statistics* (cited in Weiss 1964).

24. Ranis (1979) labels these middle years, 1963–1972, the period of Taiwan's "take-off" into sustained economic growth (along the lines of Rostow 1961).

25. When I asked Hsu Li-teh why Taiwanese industry didn't simply import workers instead of going to such trouble to train Taiwanese, he responded that he didn't think it would work to import them, for workers need to be able to relate culturally (Hsu Li-teh, personal communication, Taipei, February 21, 2006).

26. The gendered term is ubiquitous.

27. Jacoby remarks that "[a]fter the passage of the Foreign Assistance Act of 1961, long-term economic planning became an accepted concomitant of U.S. economic aid programs" (1967, 142).

28. See Li (1981, 85–86).

29. Weiss himself remarked that "[t]he conclusions which I have drawn here, for the most part, emanated from discussions with these various officials ["officials of various ministries in both the national and provincial governments"] and are not original to me. If my visit has served any useful purpose, it has primarily been to serve as a catalyst to bring together ideas which have been developed in a number of agencies of the government" (Weiss 1964, 18).

30. The precise ratio in 1966 was 57:43 academic to vocational.

31. Hsu Li-teh, then Deputy Administrative Secretary of the Manpower Resources Group, Council for International Economic Cooperation and Development, described the decision as taken of necessity: the needs of industry for skilled labor were so great that the system had to expand very quickly. Thus the government had to accept that the private sector could make money at it, or it would not make the necessary investments.

32. Another reason for the expansion of private, rather than public, vocational education may be an internal debate that the adoption of manpower planning sparked in the government. The idea of treating education as just another input to economic production was a necessity to officials of economy-centered ministries like the Ministry of Economic Affairs, but unsettling

to officials of the Ministry of Education, who generally saw education as an end in itself. Manpower planning officials were sympathetic to the latter's concerns, but saw Taiwan as a society with very limited resources, the optimal allocation of which was crucial if the country was ever to reach a mature state of development. In the end, with manpower planning's ascendancy, the Manpower Planning Department (the successor of the Manpower Resources Committee) became, over the next twenty years, a bridge unifying and coordinating the policies of the Ministry of Education and the Ministry of Economic Affairs (Personal communications, Hsu Li-the and Chiang Pei-chi).

33. The 36-member board was composed of 12 members representing public enterprises, 12 representing private enterprises, and 12 representing (KMT-controlled) trade unions. Its chair was Chang Kuo-an, owner of the San Fu Motor Car Company.

34. In some fields the pass rate was far lower: among those tested in refrigeration and air conditioning, 13.4 percent passed; among electricians, who made up more than 27,000 of the 33,000 tested, 44.1 percent passed. The highest pass rates were for army apprentices, provincial youth reformatories, and the Tatung Engineering Company and the Taiwan Fluorescent Lamp Company (Djang 1977, 161, table 35).

35. Though it is worth noting that the increase was less than officially forecast, for which the continuing high fees deserve most of the blame (Gannicott 1973).

36. Personal communication, Hsu Shui-teh.

37. Personal communications, Hsu Shui-teh and Ching-hsi Chang. This was during the period when the United States was urging President Chiang to demobilize (Chu and Lin 2001), and teaching was deemed a good alternate occupation for soldiers.

38. Personal communications, Shih Ying, Wu Jin, Chen Peiying, Fan Sun-lu, and Huang Yu-shi.

39. The transformation from ethnicity to family educational history in determining a student's education attainment does not, of course, negate the role of ethnicity: since mainlanders held a significant advantage in education when they emigrated to Taiwan and increased their advantage in the 1950s, children of very educated parents are to this day substantially more likely to have mainlander parents.

40. This was the answer to questions in interviews with Chien Fu, Chang Pei-chi, Kuo Wei-fan, Mao Kao-wen, Liou Ching-tien, and Hsu Li-teh.

41. The commission was also not an insulated government project, but a wide-ranging effort with, as noted earlier, considerable involvement by all levels of government and business, as well as outside assistance from the U.S. Department of Labor and the International Labor Organization.

42. Huang Yu-shi described an article written by a prominent Taiwanese entrepreneur during the education reform movement in the 1990s, which argued against the expansion of university education on these grounds.

43. Shih Ying told me of a friend of his who runs a business, who remarked that he prefers vocational graduates to college graduates because they don't ask questions.

44. Liou Ching-tien, personal communication.

45. Gannicott's study concluded: "Within the educational system, primary and university levels are the most profitable investments under current conditions. There is no evidence for the often heard view that there is a shortage of senior vocational school graduates" (Gannicott 1973).

46. Almost twice as many junior college graduates reported that it was "very difficult" for them to find a job: 14.7 percent, compared to 8.5 percent of university graduates (Kao, Hsu, and Lee 1976).

47. A further example from later underscores the point. Professor Chang Ching-hsi, a labor economist, told me of a study commissioned by the CEPD in the early 1980s comparing the proportion of vocational students to academic students in Taiwan with the proportion in other countries. Taiwan's proportion of vocational students was of course substantially higher. The government somehow used this as indication that Taiwan needed more vocational graduates (which baffled Chang).

48. Chu and Lin (2001) mark this as the beginning of the KMT's "protracted demise."

49. Formal legalization of opposition parties did not come until 1989.
50. More radical DPP members went further in the 1989 elections, even publishing a Constitution of the Republic of Taiwan.
51. From a widely-quoted interview between Lee and a Japanese writer in May 1994 (quoted in Chen 2003, 211).
52. Mao Kao-wen, personal communication.
53. Assessments of junior colleges began in 1975; vocational-school assessments began in 1977.
54. Liou Ching-Tien, personal communication.
55. Mao confirmed this in an interview. When he told President Chiang Ching-kuo, before he was appointed minister, that he believed that the education system had many problems, Chiang replied, "OK, change it" (Mao Kao-wen, personal communication).
56. Industry's resistance is illustrative of a point made earlier about the educational demands of much of Taiwanese industry: they told him "if you upgrade [them], [the workers] won't be practical" (Mao Kao-wen, personal communication).
57. Shih Ying, personal communication.
58. Realistically, there was only one offense for which teachers could be fired: criticism of the KMT. And although the vast majority of teachers were Taiwanese natives—the fully subsidized education made Normal colleges the one area of higher education for which income and occupation were not criteria—the teacher who didn't support the KMT was rare.
59. Discussion from personal communications with Kuo Wei-fan and Lee Chung-chi. Minister Kuo today is skeptical of the change, arguing that it led to an oversupply of teachers and abandonment of a system that had strictly controlled teacher quality. The change in the law did not affect existing teachers, who were a key group in the KMT's vital constituency.
60. One example of such small, case-by-case changes was a story common in textbooks of Wu Fang, a fictional Taiwanese native who was portrayed as primitive; after students protested, Minister Mao removed the story from the textbooks.
61. Huang Yu-shi, the NTU Mathematics Professor who led the 4/10 Movement, remarked to me that it was difficult to keep the movement going after the march. It lacked an institutional apparatus, resources, and a committed core of activists. He did try to continue the struggle through the newspapers, but those were heavily controlled by the KMT and did not, for the most part, oblige (Huang Yu-shi, personal communication).
62. A de-facto ambassador; the KMT did not maintain official relations with France.
63. Wu Jin told me that even he did not know his views on education policy before he became minister (Wu Jin, personal communication).
64. Wu Jin told me that his attention to rural, neglected schools came simply from a concern for the underprivileged, and an acknowledgement that they had long been cut off from the government's largesse, both of which President Lee shared (Wu Jin, personal communication).
65. Wu Jin partly blames this attention for his relatively short (two-year) tenure as minister, as it irked other ministers (Wu Jin, personal communication). Huang Wu-shi noted to me that Wu Jin was so savvy with the media that whenever his 4/10 Movement, trying to regain its momentum, would plan a rally or event, Wu Jin would develop some alternate event to upstage them (Huang Wu-shi, personal communication).
66. Wu Jin, personal communication.
67. Wu Jin gave several reasons for his departure, including the resentment of his fellow ministers and some political missteps in recognizing degrees from universities in mainland China. But the primary reason was that President Lee began to disagree with his policies, especially his continuing efforts to improve vocational education instead of concentrating exclusively on academic education. Wu Jin told me that President Lee offered to allow him to stay on as a Minister without Portfolio, but Wu Jin told him that "if you don't like my policies, I'll just go" (Wu Jin, personal communication).
68. See, among others, the works referred to at the start: Doner, Ritchie, and Slater (2005); Li (1981); and Woo (1991).

Chapter 5

1. These formed part of the basis for Bates' seminal (1981) study of agricultural policymaking in Sub Saharan Africa, where he argued that agricultural policy in African tilted toward the urban areas, because urbanites were better able to organize themselves collectively and threaten the government's rule.

2. The Core Welfare Indicators surveyed a nationally representative sample of 49,005 families on a variety of subjects: health, education, employment, poverty, etc. The survey defined "literate" as being able to read and write in any language. It is not dependent on school attendance (see Ghana 2005a; 2005b).

3. This section draws from Nimako (1991); Kimble (1963); Killick, Omaboe, and Szereszewski (1966); and the U.S. Army's Country Study of Ghana (Library of Congress 1994).

4. Unlike the Asante annexation, the annexation of the Northern Territories was relatively peaceful. For the lack of resistance, scholars credit the lack of organization among the Northern peoples (Kimble 1963) or a cultural tendency among the Northern peoples to be subservient to their conquerors (Nimako 1991).

5. See also Robert Bates' well-known account in his study of agricultural policies in Sub-Saharan Africa (Bates 1981).

6. In the first half of the twentieth century, for example, half Ghana's imports were consumer goods, establishing a pattern of consumption that would come to haunt the economy in later years. Nimako (1991) calls the pattern "trade without accumulation."

7. In the Assembly, 38 seats were directly-elected; 37 were elected by representatives of various territorial or state councils; and nine were appointed by the British Governor. The CPP won 34 of the 38 directly-elected seats; the UGCC won just three (McPheeters 1957).

8. This is my rough calculation. The 1960 census reports that there were 1.7 million children aged 5 to 14 in Ghana (Baeta et al. 1967). Population growth in the 1950s was around 2.5 percent a year (Killick, Omaboe, and Szereszewski 1966). Imputing backwards leaves 1.32 million children in 1950, of which 272,000 students is 21 percent.

9. James K. Glover, director of the National Coordinating Committee for Technical and Vocational Education and Training (NACVET), told me that graduates of the few technical schools in the 1920s and 30s had an impossible time finding work, and that began the Ghanaians' cultural skepticism of technical education (Interview in Accra, September 4, 2006).

10. Killick, Omaboe, and Szereszewski (1966).

11. The plans were designed to increase manufacturing's share of GDP from 10 percent in 1960 to 14 percent by 1970.

12. The dam created Lake Volta, still by surface area the largest man-made lake in the world.

13. In general this was in keeping with Nkrumah's industrialization strategy. Rather than nationalizing foreign industries, the government created Ghanaian industries and tried to skew the playing field in their favor.

14. Indeed, through the late 1950s, Ghana's plans for modern job-creation received widespread endorsement, despite reservations by the British and economic advisors like W. Arthur Lewis. For example, the influential journal *West Africa* endorsed the industrialization plans under the headline "Jobs for All for £G 240 million"—the price tag of the government's five-year industrialization plan—and predicted confidently that the plan "will definitely mean the transformation of Ghana into the near paradise which is the goal of all our efforts" (February 16 and 17, 1959, quoted in Tignor 2006, 163).

15. In 1960 the capital-output ratio was 2.9, far higher than other developing countries and about the same as that of the United States (Killick, Omaboe, and Szereszewski 1966).

16. It was for this reason that W. Arthur Lewis warned, in his prescient report on industrialization in the Gold Coast and later as economic advisor to the Ghanaian government, that the CPP should not invest too heavily in industrialization, but instead concentrate first on improving productivity in agriculture (Lewis 1953). Nkrumah responded that Lewis did not understand the political realities (Tignor 2006).

17. Interview, Evans Aggrey-Darkoh, University of Ghana, Legon, August 30, 2006.

18. In particular, Nkrumah sent troops to the Congo in 1960, where they failed to stop the murder of Patrice Lumumba and from which they returned shell-shocked.

19. Interview with Kwesi Jonah, Institute of Economic Affairs, September 6, 2006; and Library of Congress (1994).

20. 80,000 of these 180,000 new students were transfers from previously private schools; the remainder were new enrollees. Demand for primary education in Ghana had grown fast since World War II, as I noted in Section 1 (see Table 5.2), but the proliferating private primary schools were generally of low quality and yet charged fees that made them inaccessible to many poorer students.

21. Enrollment rate uses the same algorithm as in note 8. Assuming 2.5 percent population growth, the 1960 census figure of 1.7 million 5- to 14-year-olds would be 1.97 million by 1966. Using 1963–1964 enrollment statistics, Baeta et al. (1967) report enrollment of 67.6 percent.

22. A commission set up to deal with the teacher shortage prior to the adoption of the ADP noted: "teachers should command salary scales higher than other persons with similar qualifications, experience and ability in other walks of life. . . . We are aware that such high recognition as we propose is not accorded to teachers in most other countries, but we believe that it is necessary if this country is to develop rapidly and achieve its place among the nations" (quoted in McWilliam 1959, 95).

23. These central government spending figures actually understate the total spending on the lower levels, some of which was local. Local governments—local, urban, and city/municipal councils—spent £1,960.20 in 1960 on basic education, augmenting the central government's spending by almost 60 percent. (Central government spending on primary and middle schools in 1960 was £3,327.50.) In general, local spending went to the school buildings, while central-government spending paid teachers, provided supplies, and helped equalize education in poorer regions, notably the Northern Territories (McWilliam 1959).

24. Regarding the middle schools, McWilliam (1959, 72) notes: "It is the intention that as soon as the standard of English in primary schools can be sufficiently raised, pupils should go direct from them to secondary schools."

25. CMB scholarships were ostensibly reserved for cocoa farmers, but in actuality this was no barrier: anyone who could demonstrate a loose connection to a cocoa farmer was deemed eligible (Addae-Mensah, Djangmah, and Agbenyega 1981).

26. In their extensive analysis, Baeta et al. conclude: "the presence in secondary schools of children of the under-privileged groups is due largely to the fact there are more secondary school places than there are children of the elite to fill them" (1967, 238). See also Addae-Mensah (2000).

27. Shiman's (1971) examined the background of second-generation educated Ghanaians, and finds that a high percentage were children of low SES parents who were educated in the 50s and 60s.

28. As W. Arthur Lewis had warned (Lewis 1953).

29. The authors made the following observation regarding the relationship between the education system and the economy: "The frequently heard argument that the growth of the education system has also been brought about by the needs of an industrializing country for technically skilled manpower is easy to overstate. Certainly an industrializing country has occupational needs which may act as a stimulus to certain sections of the educational system. For example, the rapid expansion of the university institutions and of the secondary schools can be related to the perceived need for high level personnel to staff both the growing administration and the growing industrial sector. But the spectacular growth of the primary school system after 1951, culminating in the establishment of free and compulsory primary and middle school education in 1961, cannot be understood in these terms. There is not at present a high demand for the services of those leaving middle school, although less than 40,000 reach this level annually. Indeed, it is difficult for these young people to find any employment at all. When the annual output of the middle schools rises to a quarter of a million, as is planned by 1970, it is difficult to imagine the economy expanding fast enough to be able to absorb the young people entering the labor market" (221).

30. In the plan, see the tables on the growth of employment (Ghana Manpower Projects 1964, 145) and the output of the education system (146).

31. This section draws heavily from Nimako (1991); Library of Congress (1994); and interviews with Kwesi Jonah (Head of the Governance Centre, Institute of Economic Affairs, and Professor of Political Science, University of Ghana, Accra, September 6, 2006) and Evans Aggrey-Darkoh (Lecturer in Political Science, University of Ghana, Legon, August 30, 2006).

32. Three Ewes; one Asante; three Gold Coast nationalists (2 Gas and a Fante); and one Northerner (Nimako 1991).

33. The coup leaders had guarantees of foreign economic and political assistance from the CIA (Nimako 1991).

34. When workers struck to protest the cuts, the NLC repressed them on the grounds they were making a political protest organized by the CPP.

35. Aryeetey, Harrigan, and Nissanke (2000); and interview with Ernest Aryeetey, Director, Institute of Statistical, Social, and Economic Research, University of Ghana, Legon, October 4, 2006.

36. Many of Ghana's cocoa trees had been planted during the 1940s and 1950s, and by the 1970s were reaching the end of their productive lives (Killick, Omaboe, and Szereszewski 1966). Political turmoil and volatile world cocoa prices had discouraged replenishing of the cocoa stock in the 1960s.

37. Interview with Kwesi Jonah, Accra, September 6, 2006.

38. Library of Congress (1994).

39. For example, the PNP's first budget (for Fiscal Year 1981) projected a budget deficit equal to 30 percent of GDP.

40. Kwesi Jonah told me that the PNP went out of its way to keep the army and the bureaucracy happy, even importing new cars for the bureaucracy (Interview, Kwesi Jonah, Head, Governance Centre, Institute of Economic Affairs, and Professor of Political Science, University of Ghana, Accra, September 6, 2006).

41. An arguable exception is the PNP, which after the 1979 elections made a half-hearted attempt to court workers by raising the minimum wage. But the impact of the policy was negligible (it was quickly offset by inflation) and the party did not engage in any actual organizing of disadvantaged groups—the key criterion of entrepreneurship.

42. Fees ranged from 20 cedis to 100 cedis a term, far outside the reach of ordinary Ghanaians. By comparison, the Ghanaian minimum wage was 1 cedi per day (Addae-Mensah, Djangmah, and Agbenyega 1981).

43. There are signs that many Ghanaians were aware of—and concerned about—the increasing correlation between a student's socio-economic background and his or her likelihood of admission to secondary school. For example, a 1973 commentary in the *Ghanaian Times* noted: "The problem as I see it is whether, by unintentionally setting up two different classes of schools, our society is not widening the gap between the haves and the havenots, the privileged and the less privileged, the 'equals' and the less 'equals.' The child in a public school must be exceptionally bright to enter a first-class secondary school. As a result of this competition, many parents are depriving themselves of some very essential needs to send their children to 'international schools' [one type of 'special schools'] where they are sure their children will be specially prepared to meet the requirements of the Common Entrance" (Kwakwa 1973).

44. One headmaster of public schools in a neighborhood of the capital Accra put it this way: "My pupils are always put through the prescribed Ministry of Education syllabus. The Common Entrance Examination is incidental to the teaching in my school. Only the bright boys and those whose parents wish it, take it, and therefore if we gear our teaching to the examination only, this will affect the progress of the majority of pupils who are not taking the examination. However, we try to arrange special tuition for pupils during the year they are to take their examination, but they have to pay extra money for this private tuition—that is if there is a teacher willing enough to undertake this task. Naturally, we have a high failure rate at the Common Entrance Examination" (Addae-Mensah, Djangmah, and Agbenyega 1981, 37).

45. In 1969 the government worried that "if the disproportionately large training colleges are not streamlined, there is the danger that very soon more trained teachers will be produced than will be required by the system" (Ghana 1969). (This, of course, was only a worry because the government was closing so many primary schools.)

46. The government began closing teacher training colleges even though less than half of primary teachers had not been trained in a teachers' college (these were known as "pupil teachers").

47. Medicine, science, agriculture, law, and administration (accountancy, management, and public administration).

48. Busia, impoliticly, remarked that the student loan program was "part of fundamental reform of the 'everything is free and is a privilege' expectations of the people" (quoted in Wereko-Brobby 1998). Busia himself may have had some personal moral difficulty with the growing inequity in the education system. He remarked that it was "morally wrong for the Government to continue to spend only 20 cedis per child per annum on a primary or middle school child, while it spent 2,962 cedis on a university student" (Busia 1971).

49. As noted above, more than 90 percent of the budget went to teachers' salaries and allowances (Nimako 1991).

50. In this view the government was very similar to Taiwan's (see Chapter 5). Had Ghanaian entrepreneurs had skilled-labor needs as great as Taiwanese entrepreneurs, Ghana's middle schools might have developed much as Taiwan's vocational high schools.

51. From Ghana (1968, 13): "It was . . . envisaged that the present middle school course would be remodeled and renamed Continuation Schools as soon as practicable to place special emphasis on pre-vocational training. The Continuation Schools would be of two years' duration, and would cater for a majority of pupils who fail to gain admission in Secondary Schools or Technical Institutes."

52. From Ghana (1969, 12): "In view of difficulties of obtaining trained staff, materials and buildings only two schools in each region have been selected to attempt the Continuation School Course as an experiment. In view of the prevailing financial circumstances the content of the Course has been modified so as to pay special attention to English, Mathematics, and Science, while additional subjects such as Agriculture, Fishing, Woodwork, Metalwork, Typing, Elementary Book-keeping, Technical Drawing and Home Science are taught where the local conditions require and the facilities can be provided."

53. Djangmah (2005), and interviews: E. Acquaah-Harrison, former president, Association of Ghana Industries in the late 1960s, advisor on industrial and vocational training, Accra, September 18, 2006; William Kofi Ahadzie, research fellow, Centre for Social Policy Studies, November 29, 2005; and James K. Glover, director, and Edwin Billy Akorli, assistant director, NACVET (National Coordinating Committee for Technical and Vocational Education and Training), Accra, September 4, 2006.

54. This section draws, like the previous two political sections, on Nimako (1991); Library of Congress (1994); as well as on Kanbur (1994) and Gyimah-Boadi (2001). Various other sources for specific points are noted in the text.

55. And whose goods Rawlings' short-lived first government, the Armed Forces Revolutionary Council, had stolen and sold to the masses (see Section 4).

56. Initially the PNDC did not try to appeal to the chiefs. Later, in the 1990s, it made some half-hearted attempts as part of its election campaigns, but these were generally unsuccessful, and the chiefs remained outside the vital constituency throughout (Interview, Kwesi Jonah, head, Governance Centre, Institute of Economic Affairs, and professor of political science, University of Ghana, Accra, October 20, 2006).

57. Workers Defense Committees were intended to bypass the Trades Union Congress (TUC), which, despite its Nkrumhist history, had become more associated with the bureaucracy Rawlings blamed for Ghana's economic troubles—of necessity, since the public sector was one of the few sources of formal employment in Ghana in the 1970s. On taking power PNDC supporters beat union organizers and leaders, and the PNDC even tried to dissolve the TUC (Interview, Dr. Anthony Yaw Baah, head of policy and research, Ghana Trades Union Congress, September 22, 2006).

58. Library of Congress (1994); and Interview, Kwesi Jonah, head, Governance Centre, Institute of Economic Affairs, and professor of political science, University of Ghana, Accra, October 20, 2006.

59. Ghana was the third biggest recipient of such loans, after India and China (Nimako 1991).

60. This cherry-picking of the IMF programs to serve the government's supporters and hurt its opponents is consistent with James Vreeland's findings that countries turn to the IMF because of their domestic political considerations (Vreeland 2003).

61. In part these new employees staffed the new organizational organs of the PNDC: the Committees for the Defense of the Revolution and, later, the District Assemblies (Interview, Evans Aggrey-Darkoh, Lecturer, Political Science, University of Ghana, Legon, August 30, 2006).

62. This turnover, in which Rawlings honored his term limit, was an unexpected and fascinating success for Ghanaian democracy. For an excellent account, see Gyimah-Boadi (2001).

63. The World Bank examined the increased enrollment that accompanied lower travel times in several regions in Ghana. It found drastic effects: "in one area surveyed, average travel to the nearest school was cut by 45 minutes with enrollments increasing from 10 to 80 percent. . . . In two other areas average travel time was reduced by nearly 30 minutes and enrollments increased by over 20 percent" (World Bank 2004a, xi).

64. The 2006 value of the yearly disbursements was $288.5 million from the World Bank, and $387.3 million from bilateral donors (disbursements deflated with the unit value of imports from *International Financial Statistics*).

65. Thereafter the proportion of untrained teachers rose slightly and then sharply after 1998, but only because of the growth of new private primary schools, which hired teachers generally not trained in official teachers' colleges (World Bank 2004a).

66. The idea of the junior secondary school was not new: it had first been proposed in 1972 by the Dzobo Commission, but not implemented by governments that were concentrating their resources on the upper levels.

67. Interview, J. S. Djangmah, Accra, September 20, 2006.

68. Teachers were also a barrier. Addae-Mensah (2000) writes: "[S]uddenly, the old middle school teachers who used to teach English and Arithmetic with some smatterings of geography and nature study, found themselves confronted with teaching algebra, geometry, technical drawing, technical skills, general science, agriculture, life skills, a local language which may not be their own, etc., etc. Many of them simply could not cope, and can still not cope" (35).

69. It is telling that the PNDC chose J. S. Djangmah to head the Ghana Education Service from 1986 to 1988, during the introduction of the JSS schools. Djangmah had been an author of the widely-circulated report on the advantages that "special schools" imparted to elite students—a report I cited heavily in Section 5 (Addae-Mensah, Djangmah, and Agbenyega 1981). In an interview, he told me that he was chosen precisely because he held those views (Interview, J. S. Djangmah, Accra, September 20, 2006).

70. Nancy Keteku, the U.S. State Department's Regional Educational Advising Coordinator for Africa, told me a story about the elite Ridge Church School, which her children attended. After the junior secondary school was introduced, the school continued to charge its normal fees, but the ministry came to tell them that they were not allowed to charge fees and that the government would provide their resources and a teacher. They responded that they couldn't offer the quality of education they had on the government subsidy: they were paying teachers more than the government and providing better materials. But the government ordered them to refund the fees that parents had paid. It was only after parents complained that the following year they were again able to charge fees (Interview, Nancy Keteku, Accra, November 29, 2005).

71. This grant was not realized until after 2000.

72. Addae-Mensah (2000). The government decided to lower fees rather than changing the emphasis of scholarships from merit to need (Interview, J. S. Djangmah, Accra, September 20, 2006).

73. An industrial economist, A. Baah-Nuarkoh, told me that professors, who in the 1970s could do research of their own choosing, conduct research now to make money—for example, by writing reports for international donors. He believes that this is one reason that cutting-edge research no longer comes out of the University of Ghana (Interview, Legon, September 6, 2006).

74. The World Bank watched the success of the government in eliminating the entrenched privilege of the universities—which had until then seemed impossible politically—with some amazement. In its 2004 evaluation, it asked, "Why did the PNDC embrace reforms that had proved politically difficult for well over a decade, and how was it able to successfully implement them?" and concluded that "[t]he opposition to the reforms came from the middle class elite, which were not the PNDC's political base" (World Bank 2004a, 26).

75. In fairness, Addae-Mensah (2000)'s conclusion is that the best senior secondary schools still dominate admissions to the University of Ghana. I am re-interpreting the statistics he presents to point out that there was a substantial increase in opportunity for students from poorer secondary schools, even if the increase did not eliminate the advantages of students from the best secondary schools.

76. The preference was based on rate-of-return studies showing that primary education had the highest private and social returns in less-developed countries (e.g., Psacharopoulos 1973, 1981, 1994).

77. Interviews with economists Ernest Aryeetey (Legon, October 4, 2006), A. Baah-Nuarkoh Ahadzie (Legon, September 6, 2006), sociologist William Kofi Ahadzie (Legon, September 18, 2006), and E. Acquaah-Harrison, former president, Association of Ghana Industries, advisor on industrial and vocational training (Accra, September 18, 2006).

78. See sources in note 77.

79. James K. Glover, director, National Coordinating Committee for Technical and Vocational Education and Training (NACVET), Accra, September 4, 2006. (Interview also included and Edwin Billy Akorli, assistant director).

80. Interviews: Ivan Addae-Mensah (Legon, October 5, 2006), J. S. Djangmah (September 20, 2006), Nancy Keteku (Accra, August 17, 2006), and Henrietta Mensah-Bonsu (Legon, November 25, 2005).

81. As noted in Chapters 1 and 2, this wisdom was based on rate-of-return studies showing that primary education was more beneficial in poorer economies (Psacharopoulos 1973, 1981, 1994). But see also Blaug (1976) and Birdsall (1996).

Chapter 6

1. High and inflexible skilled wages also led Brazilian industrialists to prefer machinery to workers. Industry in Brazil is thus tremendously capital-intensive (Birdsall, Bruns, and Sabot 1996).

2. Brazilian economist Ricardo Barros described the worker-training system to me as adjusting to fix "bottlenecks to economic growth," rather than educating workers with a coherent vision for economic development. He himself attended a specialized engineering school that graduated only a few dozen students a year, but with whose graduates the Brazilian government developed a world-class aviation industry (interview, Rio de Janeiro, June 1, 2006).

3. This section draws heavily on Pereira (1984); Evans (1979); Skidmore and Smith (1997); Schwartzman (2003); and Castro (1973).

4. From Pereira: "the Revolution of 1930 was above all a revolution of the middle class" (1984, 16).

5. An 1877 account of Escada, a town near the prosperous northeastern city of Recife, gives a very rough sense of just how tiny:

> To the twenty thousand heads of the population in the district, this city contributes three thousand, more or less. In relation to these three thousand souls, or, to put it a better way, in relation to these three thousand bellies, the following calculation is probable:

90 percent are needy, almost indigent;

8 percent live tolerably;

1.5 percent live well;

0.5 percent are relatively rich.

(From Tobias Barreto, "Discourse in Shirt Sleeves," quoted in Pereira (1984, 55)).

6. Elites and the parasitical middle class generally were educated while the remainder of the population was not (see below); thus, with illiteracy at 85 percent and most of the remaining population not able to write (Castro 1973), this vital constituency probably accounted, at most, for between 5 and 10 percent of the population. During the First Republic (1889–1930), literacy increased but probably never topped 25 percent of the population (Schwartzman 2003).

7. Prior to 1891, the country was an empire, which gained its independence from Portugal in 1822.

8. Because one of the states, Minas Gerais, had a large ranching sector, this arrangement was also called *Café com Leite*—coffee with milk.

9. To encourage investment in railroads, British railroad manufacturers were initially guaranteed 5, and later 7, percent profit. This guarantee eventually cost the government 6 percent of the value of imports, but with agricultural profits high, the burden was easy to meet (Evans 1979).

10. Pereira (1984, 15) writes that immigrants came with "great ambition."

11. There is some debate about why the federal government failed to intervene. Some scholars have suggested that the agrarian-elite dominated governments had an ideological objection to such heavy government intervention in the economy (see the discussion in Evans 1979), though this seems somewhat implausible given the existence, since 1906, of a government policy of buying excess coffee and destroying it to prop up the price. Others contend that the government resisted spending too much money, which would have led to high inflation, because of its need to maintain the convertability of the currency, the real, to satiate foreign creditors (Skidmore and Smith 1997). The failure could also have been related to infighting among agrarian elites, which certainly hampered their ability to agree on other policies— most importantly who would be the next president—and opened the door to the middle class's revolt (Pereira 1984).

12. This was not the first time they had tried: in 1922, in the aftermath of another fraudulent election, the junior officers staged the *tenente* (lieutenant) rebellion, which failed but forced the federal government to rule in a state of near siege. By 1930, conditions were so ripe for political change that the "revolution" was in fact a bloodless coup.

13. In the 1930 election Vargas was the candidate of the "Liberal Alliance," which included the emerging urban middle and industrial class. Vargas was himself a wealthy *gaúcho* (cattle rancher) and governor of the southern state of Rio Grande do Sul. In the 1920s and 1930s, Rio Grande do Sul, like many states, was also growing discontented with the dominance of São Paulo and Minas Gerais.

14. This figure is illustrative but may not be completely accurate: it uses spending on primary students in Rio de Janeiro as representative of spending on primary students across Brazil, and does not include per-student spending on academic secondary education, which was heavily geared toward elites and was probably much higher than spending on any other level.

15. Schwartzman (1989). However, the church was only a supporter as long as it seemed as though Vargas was democratizing the country. It withdrew its support when his government turned autocratic.

16. The centrality of unions to political entrepreneurship in Brazil differs from Ghana and Taiwan, in which organizational help was usually delivered through the party, which may or may not have been affiliated with unions. Unlike in Ghana and Taiwan, in which political entrepreneurs organized both the agricultural and the industrial poor, the citizens in Vargas's vital constituency who needed help organizing were all industrial workers.

17. Vargas's corporatist mediation of worker and industry conflicts was reputedly modeled on Mussolini's.

18. See, e.g., Evans (1979); Pereira (1984); or Birdsall, Bruns, and Sabot (1996).

19. Pereira (1984) surveyed industrial entrepreneurs in São Paulo. He found that half were immigrants or the children of immigrants; only 16 percent were of Brazilian origin. Only 4 percent were from the aristocracy.

20. The preceding discussion relies heavily on Pereira (1984, 14–19); and Skidmore and Smith (1997, 167–73).

21. Ashworth-Gorden (1980) describes two periods in the regulation of coffee: to raise the international price, the government destroyed excess production prior to the *Estado Novo* in 1937; thereafter, it tried to increase Brazil's market share by encouraging greater production.

22. In presenting this table, Pereira notes that the top category probably vastly overstated the true upper class, since many of those classified by the census as owners owned businesses that were very small: the 1950 Census also reported that 80 percent of Brazilian industrial firms employed fewer than 10 people. Instead, Pereira estimates that the upper class—the very rich and a few remaining members of the old agrarian aristocracy—probably constituted 1 percent of the population.

23. The first was the Pact of Union Unity (*Pacto de Unidade Sindical*).

24. Enrollment rate of children aged 5–14, from the 1960 Demographic Census, taken from Plank (1996, table 3.5).

25. The ideas for this pattern of expansion were developed in a 1932 manifesto by a group of left-leaning intellectuals calling themselves the Pioneers of the New Education (*Pioneiros da Educação Nova*). On the *Pioneiros da Educação Nova* and their influence on Vargas and the 1934 Constitution, see Plank, Sobrinho, and Xavier (1996); Romanelli (1978, 146–49); and Plank (1996).

26. The ministry was very nearly the first federal agency in charge of education in Brazil's history; the only exception is a Ministry of Education, Post, and Telegraphs, which was set up in the early days of the First Republic but disbanded shortly thereafter.

27. The constitution also gave each citizen a right to basic education—a right that, unsurprisingly, was never realized.

28. Enrollment rate of children aged 5–14, from the 1940 and 1950 Demographic Censuses, taken from Plank (1996, table 3.5).

29. In general, under Malthusian assumptions, wealthier families have fewer children than poorer families (see, e.g., Becker 1988).

30. More discussion of this is below. Particularly on the lack of a system for training teachers, see Schwartzman (1998). But Schwartzman notes that, in the 1930s and 40s, major urban areas did develop institutions to train qualified teachers.

31. Interviews with Ruben Klein, Eraldo Tinoco, and Katia Siqueira de Freitas.

32. In this era, some pedagogic schools still trained at the elementary level, but most were at the secondary (*médio*) level: over three-quarters, on average, from 1932 to 1945.

33. Maria Helena Guimarães de Castro, the São Paulo state secretary of science and technology and an expert on education, told me that scholars who examine education in this period have a difficult time identifying any substantial changes (interview, São Paulo, April 28, 2006).

34. Gustavo Capanema was by far the longest-serving minister of education in Brazilian history. He was minister from 1934 to 1945.

35. The educational provisions of the constitution were the subject of heated debate, and the constitution therefore left the specifics to a new Basic Education Law, which it directed the government to draft. Such a bill was not passed until 1962.

36. It is, of course, impossible from only these numbers to know what proportion of this spending actually went to private schools; but there is no doubt that the 1950s ushered in the pattern of channeling ever-larger sums of public money to private schools.

37. This is a key feature of Selective Worker Training, as defined in Chapter 2 (see Figure 2.4): Selective Worker Training draws students from inside the vital constituency. The inflexibility of the labor market that causes employers to demand Selective Worker Training is the result of workers being inside the vital constituency. (In contrast, Broad Worker Training, which requires a flexible labor market, draws its students from outside the vital constituency.)

38. In Taiwan, worker training was "vocational education"; in Ghana it was "technical education." In Brazil, this education is known as "professional." Rather than decide on a common name, I am simply using the name each country uses.

39. A World Bank report noted that SENAI, in particular, provided workers well-trained to industry needs: "SENAI, in particular, has developed some of the most successful schemes for training highly skilled workers since its creation some 30 years ago. In sharp contrast with the erratic attempts of the formal system, SENAI has closely monitored labor market demand and responded with creative and sound programs" (World Bank 1979, 40).

40. The University of Brazil, today the Federal University of Rio de Janeiro, was formed from a reorganization of the first University of Rio de Janeiro, founded in 1920.

41. As with secondary education, there is no telling how much additional public money went to private institutions (Plank, Sobrinho, and Xavier 1996).

42. Pereira quotes elitist leaders making "alarmist" statements, such as: "communist revolution is knocking at our door"; "I don't think a year will pass before there is a communist revolution in Brazil"; and "Let's take advantage of the last days of bourgeois comfort" (quoted in Pereira 1984, 83).

43. Source: Federation of Industries of the State of São Paulo (FIESP) in Pereira (1984, 86).

44. This coup is a notable example of the institutional fluidity that prevents democratically-elected pro-poor governments from ignoring elite demands when there is no political entrepreneur of the poor: elites can simply step in and change the institutions when the institutions don't produce results they like. (See Chapters 1 and 3.)

45. The Guidelines and Bases for National Education (*Lei de Diretrizes e Bases da Educação Nacional*).

46. Maria Helena Guimarães de Castro, the São Paulo state secretary of science and technology and an education scholar, told me that, while the only major educational policy change from 1961 to 1964 was the new basic education law, there was a great deal of discussion of education during the period: new social movements prompted a fierce debate about educational priorities (interview, São Paulo, April 28, 2006).

47. Much of the controversy was about public financing of private education. "Subventions" to private schools had increased throughout the 1950s, prompting concern among those who thought public money should go solely to public education. The LDB tried to resolve this question by, on the one hand, formally giving priority to financing public education, but also allowing private schools to receive public funds in cases where public educational provision was judged to be insufficient (Plank, Sobrinho, and Xavier 1996).

48. The 1964 coup ended implementation of the law (Sobrinho 1985).

49. Evans (1979) cites a survey by *Visão* in the mid-1970s that showed most SOEs were not inherited by the military, but were created by it.

50. For the federal Senate, ARENA had 44 percent of the vote to MDB's 29 percent; in the Chamber of Deputies, the lower house, ARENA had 48 percent to MDB's 21 percent (Brown 1995). However, blank ballots—a protest vote against both parties—were 22 percent in the Senate and 21 percent in the Chamber of Deputies (Skidmore 1988).

51. Mainwaring (1986) identifies four strains on the military government: it had a difficult time constructing legitimacy, as the regime's *raison d'être* was negative—it was anti-corruption, anti-chaos, anti-communist; there were ongoing tensions within the military between its role as a military and its role as a government; by 1974, the military had decimated the left, controlled the popular movements, and faced a weak opposition, weakening the rationale for its repression; and Brazil's stunning economic miracle made it think it could afford to liberalize.

52. Among other things, the package provided: that future constitutional amendments required only a congressional majority; that state governors would be elected indirectly and a third of state senators would be elected through state electoral colleges; that federal deputies would be allocated by population, rather than by registered voters (which made the Northeast, where the government had virtually unchallenged support, more important); and for severe censorship of radio and television (Brown 1995).

53. The electoral college was both houses of Congress plus six representatives from each state.

54. Mainwaring (1986, 160) writes: "never before in Brazilian history had so many people demonstrated for anything."

55. This section relies on Souza (1997) and on interviews with Celina Souza, professor of political science, Universidade Federal da Bahia, (Salvador, June 8, 2006), and Bob Verhine, professor of economics and education and director, Centro de Estudos Interdisciplinares para o Setor Público, Universidade Federal da Bahia (Salvador, June 5, 2006).

56. The military needed the agrarian elites because they generally decided who became mayor, governor, or state legislator, and the military's system of indirect elections relied increasingly on those mayors, governors, and state legislatures to elect supportive representatives to the federal Congress.

57. This section draws on the two sections above—on the federal government before and after 1974—and on interviews with Rose Neubauer, former São Paulo state secretary of education (São Paulo, May 29, 2006), Guimar Namo de Mello, former São Paulo municipal secretary of education (1981) (São Paulo, June 19, 2006), and Bernadette Gatti, coordinator of the Department for Education Research, Fundação Carlos Chagas (São Paulo, May 19. 2006).

58. In Brazil, private universities (*universidades*) are distinct from private institutions of higher education (*faculdades*), which generally concentrate on low-cost education that can be taught by a part-time teacher and that requires only a room and a chalkboard. The expansion I am referring to here is of these *faculdades*, not *universidades*. I am grateful to Robert Verhine for urging me to clarify this point.

59. Among the many who have detailed the difference between the actual and ostensible purposes of the expansion of primary education, see, e.g., Harbison and Hanushek (1992); Plank (1996); and Plank, Sobrinho, and Xavier (1996).

60. De Mello e Souza (1989) estimated that the awarding of school contracts to political supporters increased their construction costs by as much as 40 percent. The schools frequently appeared and disappeared according to the politics (Harbison and Hanushek 1992).

61. I asked Paulo Renato de Souza, the powerful and widely respected Minister of Education from 1995 to 2002, "Is it fair to say that for most of recent Brazilian history the purpose of the public education system was not to educate students, but to provide jobs?" He answered, "Yes." (Interview, Paulo Renato de Souza, São Paulo, April 12, 2006.)

62. Some examples (taken from Plank, Sobrinho, and Xavier 1996): The secretary of education of the northeastern state of Ceará has discretion over 19 percent of all the functionaries in the state government (Leite and de Anchieta Esmeraldo Barreto 1983). In the state of Rio de Janeiro, each new secretary of education makes around 4,000 political appointments (Leal 1990).

63. Alberto Rodriguez, the World Bank's Lead Education Specialist in Brazil, told me that teaching jobs are highly prized in Brazilian villages: the hours are short and the work is easy, teachers are difficult to fire, and while the salary is low, it is guaranteed monthly and goes up with seniority. (Interview, Alberto Rodriguez, Brasília, May 16, 2006.)

64. Hanushek, Gomes-Neto, and Harbison (1996) found that mean teacher salary in the Northeast was less than 60 percent of the minimum wage.

65. Source: 1960, 1970, and 1980 demographic censuses, cited in Plank (1990, 88).

66. There is some disagreement about how much of underperformance in Brazilian basic education is due to dropping out and how much is due to endless repetition, after which the student drops out. The evolving consensus is that repetition is the much more serious problem. Fletcher and Ribeiro (1989), for example, estimated that at the time, while 54 percent of Brazilian first graders repeated first grade, only 2 percent actually dropped out. (In the rural Northeast, 73 percent repeated first grade; five percent dropped out.) However, the dropout rate got higher with higher grades: in fourth grade, only 20 percent repeated; 18 percent dropped out. (In the rural northeast, 44 percent repeated and 29 percent dropped out.)

67. Birdsall, Bruns, and Sabot (1996) surveyed several developing countries on the proportion of students who began school in 1987 who reached the final grade without repeating or dropping out. Brazil's was the most inefficient system they surveyed, worse than that of Costa Rica, Venezuela, Mexico, Colombia, Thailand, Korea, Malaysia, Indonesia, or Turkey.

68. In the late 1980s, fees were even kept explicitly in line with the (also regulated) salaries of the middle class—much to the annoyance of private school directors, who would have liked to charge more (Plank, Sobrinho, and Xavier 1996).
69. The World Bank (1979) reported tax deduction records that show that 75 percent of deductions went to groups with incomes between 8 and 44 times the minimum wage. This is not surprising, since higher income families spent vastly more on education: in Rio de Janeiro, spending on education by the two highest income categories was 57 times the spending of the lowest two categories; in São Paulo, they spent 66 times more; in Recife, 55 times more; and in Porte Alegre, 58 times more.
70. Plank, Sobrinho, and Xavier (1996) note four ways in which governments assist private schools: providing space in public buildings for private schools; paying public-school teachers to teach in private schools; providing scholarships to private-school students; and providing direct assistance ("subventions") to private schools that accept public-school students.
71. Interview, Alberto de Mello e Souza, director of the School of Economics, UERJ, Rio de Janeiro, May 4, 2006.
72. Businesses used this provision very liberally: for example, a report by Cunha and Góes (1985) suggested that in three northeastern states the number of places bought using money withheld from the *salário educação* was more than the total number of spots available in all private schools in those states.
73. I did hear one estimate just for Bahia: that total World Bank assistance was $600 million, of which $216 million was for education (Interview, Jansen Teixeira, Lider do Projeto, Educar para Vencer, Bahia State Education Secretariat, Salvador, June 7, 2006).
74. Interview, Alberto Rodriguez, lead education specialist, World Bank, Brasília, May 16, 2006.
75. See also Gomes-Neto and Hanushek (1996).
76. Elsewhere I explore the effectiveness of aid to basic education (Kosack 2009).
77. Pastore and Zylberstajn find that "intergenerational upward mobility became more difficult in 1982 as compared to 1973. Downward mobility became more prevalent" (1996, 296).
78. For a company to qualify for the tax breaks, the Ministry of Labor had to approve its training program.
79. This example is from an interview with Ricardo Barros, an IPEA economist, who went to the school (interview, Rio de Janeiro, June 1, 2006).
80. Interviews, Alberto de Mello e Souza, director of the School of Economics, UERJ, Rio de Janeiro, May 4, 2006, and Ricardo Barros, economist at IPEA, Rio de Janeiro, June 1, 2006.
81. Birdsall, Bruns, and Sabot (1996) note that what I am calling Brazil's elite track—its exceptional private primary and secondary schools—created a severe economic inefficiency in Brazilian higher education: most of the money spent on public universities helped wealthy students who would probably have been willing to pay the costs themselves.
82. In other faculties the numbers were lower but still large. Even at the less-prestigious state university, more than two-thirds of students had been to private secondary school (Plank, Sobrinho, and Xavier 1996).
83. As I noted earlier in note 58, not all private institutions are inferior: older private universities like the Pontifícia Universidade Católica and the Fundação Getúlio Vargas offered, and continue to offer, excellent education. But unlike most private institutions, these private universities received a great deal of public funding, starting in the 1960s (Interview, Creso Franco, professor of economics, PUC-Rio, Rio de Janeiro, May 4, 2006).
84. Eraldo Tinoco, the vice governor of Bahia and a former Bahian secretary of education and federal minister of education, told me that he himself attended public schools from 1955 to 1963, and that his education was excellent. Today he sends his grandchildren to private schools and would not think of putting them in the public system (interview, Salvador, June 8, 2006). Katia Siqueira de Freitas, a professor of education at the Federal University of Bahia, echoed these sentiments (interview, Salvador, Bahia, June 5, 2006).
85. Interview, Eraldo Tinoco, Salvador, June 8, 2006.

86. Interviews, Renata Procerpio, former Bahian secretary of education, Salvador, Bahia, June 6, 2006; Bob Verhine, professor of economics and education and director, Centro de Estudos Interdisciplinares para o Setor Público, Universidade Federal da Bahia, June 5, 2006; and Eraldo Tinoco, Salvador, June 8, 2006.

87. Interview, Katia Siqueira de Freitas, Salvador, June 5, 2006.

88. Source: 1960, 1970, 1980 demographic censuses, cited in Plank (1990, 88).

89. Interviews, Eraldo Tinoco, Salvador, June 8, 2006; Renata Procerpio, former Bahian secretary of education, Salvador, Bahia, June 6, 2006; and Bob Verhine, professor of economics and education and director, Centro de Estudos Interdisciplinares para o Setor Público, Universidade Federal da Bahia, June 5, 2006.

90. Interview, Renata Procerpio, former Bahian secretary of education, Salvador, Bahia, June 6, 2006.

91. Interview, Bob Verhine, Salvador, June 8, 2006.

92. Edivaldo Boaventura, who was secretary of education during the creation of this university, told me that the university was also created partly at the request of mayors and municipal councilors (interview, Salvador, June 9, 2006).

93. Interviews, Bernadette Gatti, coordinator of the Department for Education Research, Fundação Carlos Chagas, São Paulo, May 19, 2006; and Rose Neubauer, former São Paulo state secretary of education, São Paulo, May 29, 2006.

94. Source: 1960 and 1970 demographic censuses, cited in Plank (1990, 88). The two states with enrollment rates higher than São Paulo's were Rio Grande do Sul and Rio de Janeiro.

95. In Bahia I often heard complaints about São Paulo's dominance of federal R&D funding (Interview, Alexandre Paupério, president of FAPESB, the Bahian state research foundation, Salvador, June 8, 2006).

96. Source: 1970 and 1980 demographic censuses, cited in Plank (1990, 88).

97. Rose Neubauer, a former São Paulo state secretary of education, told me that in the 1980s she was involved in World Bank projects all over Brazil. The World Bank was reluctant to loan any money for school improvements to São Paulo, thinking that the state was rich and that it should concentrate its money on the poorer states in the Northeast. She and her team were able to show them that schools in São Paulo were nearly as bad as in the Northeast, and they eventually offered São Paulo an educational improvement loan (interview, São Paulo, May 29, 2006).

98. Interview, Rose Neubauer, São Paulo, May 29, 2006.

99. Alberto Rodriguez, the World Bank's Lead Education Specialist in Brazil, told me that because teachers were one of the few villagers with guaranteed salaries, they often even functioned as small banks, because they could issue credit in exchange for goods (interview, Brasília, May 16, 2006).

100. The size of the Chamber increased to 513 seats in 1994. The PT also won 1 senate seat in 1990, 4 in 1994, and 3 in 1998; the Senate had 31 seats in 1990, 54 in 1994, and 27 in 1998.

101. Cardoso's coalition also included two other parties: the Brazilian Labor Party (PTB), which supported him in the election, and the Brazilian Progressive Party (PPB), which joined in 1996. Both, despite their names, were right-wing. Before the 1998 election, the five-party coalition held 66 percent of the seats in the Chamber of Deputies; after 1998 it held 74 percent.

102. This section relies on Souza (1997) and on interviews with Celina Souza, professor of political science, Universidade Federal da Bahia, (Salvador, June 8, 2006), and Bob Verhine, professor of economics and education and director, Centro de Estudos Interdisciplinares para o Setor Público, Universidade Federal da Bahia (Salvador, June 5, 2006).

103. This section draws on interviews with Celina Souza, professor of political science, Universidade Federal da Bahia, (Salvador, June 8, 2006); Rose Neubauer, former São Paulo state secretary of education (São Paulo, May 29, 2006); Guimar Namo de Mello, former São Paulo municipal secretary of education (1981) (São Paulo, June 19, 2006); and Bernadette Gatti, coordinator of the Department for Education Research, Fundação Carlos Chagas (São Paulo, May 19, 2006).

104. State and municipal governments were required to spend 25 percent of their revenues on education, but enforcement of this requirement was very poor (Plank and Verhine 1995). The provision most widely discussed was the "actionable" right: while a right to education has long been a feature of Brazilian constitutions, the 1988 Constitution was the first to give citizens the right to sue the government if it did not provide them with education (Plank, Sobrinho, and Xavier 1996).

105. Paulo Renato told me that he knew the inertia in Brazilian basic education and did not really want the ministry: he knew any changes would come only after difficult struggles (interview, São Paulo, April 12, 2006).

106. The SAEB was actually created under the Collor administration, but was refined under Cardoso to make it more useful in judging student performance.

107. On the political process behind the FUNDEF amendment, see Brown (2002).

108. Only two states ended up net gainers from FUNDEF relative to their municipalities; in all others, the fund shifted resources to municipalities (Verhine and Rosa 2002; World Bank 2002a).

109. Schwartzman (2003) quotes "qualified state administrators" who claim that it is impossible to provide quality basic education for less than R$1,000 per student. At the time the floor had been raised to R$446 per year for grades 1–4 and R$468.3 for grades 5–8.

110. On the political logic behind the FUNDEF, see Brown (2002).

111. Some have alleged that the government did not release the results because the study showed that the costs per student were higher than the FUNDEF floor (World Bank 2002a). Paulo Renato de Souza told me that R$315 number came from an ECLAC study offering $300 as the minimum required amount per-student (interview, São Paulo, April 12, 2006).

112. There are exceptions: in São Paulo, for example, municipal schools are better than state schools. But the vast majority of municipal schools, which were built under the military to provide construction contracts and jobs (see Section 6), are today of very poor quality.

113. Examining specifically Bahia, Verhine and Rosa (2002) find a much smaller increase in teacher salaries—around 7 percent—in municipal schools, and a decline of 21 percent in teacher salaries in state schools.

114. World Bank and IDB (2000) found that teacher quality was relatively impervious to efforts to improve it: a teacher's salary, education, and pedagogical style significantly improved student learning. The World Bank (2004b) found that in 1998, 34 percent of teachers were still extremely under-qualified—lacking at least a secondary education. Ruben Klein, of Cesgranrio, and Sergei Soares, an education economist at IPEA, told me that the problem was that even after pedagogy training and higher salaries, teachers still didn't know their subjects (interviews, Ruben Klein, Rio de Janeiro, May 5, 2006; and Sergei Soares, Brasília, May 15, 2006).

115. Schwartzman (2003) observes that "secondary education, which has expanded enormously in recent years, is by most accounts a disaster area." Because of the poor quality of and repetition in basic education, most of the students are older than they should be. Courses are poorly run and irrelevant, but students go largely for a credential that they can use in the job market. Sixty percent of students go to school at night, because a majority of them must work full-time (World Bank and IDB 2000).

116. To provide private education to their children, families in the top income decile spend more than 20 times the median value for all families (World Bank and IDB 2000). Wealthy families continue to enjoy generous tax breaks on the money they spend: José Marcelino Pinto, an education professor at the University of São Paulo, told me that families are still able to deduct R$2,000 from their income taxes for every child they have in private school (interview, São Paulo, May 26, 2006).

117. On the connection between achievement and wealth, see also Barros et al. (2001); Barros, Henriques, and Mendonça (2000); and the edited volume by Birdsall, Bruns, and Sabot (1996).

118. In late 2006 the exchange rate was about R$2.13 to a dollar.

119. Results of the 2005 *Exame Nacional do Ensino Médio*.

120. Not coincidentally, companies in the 1990s began to contest *salário educação* payments in court. Schwartzman (1998) cites a 1998 statement by Paulo Renato in which he says that there were at the time 10,600 such legal actions pending, because of which states were receiving R$158 million less than they should have.

121. Interviews, Denisard Alves, professor of economics, USP, São Paulo, April 12, 2006; and Alberto de Mello e Souza, director of the school of economics, UERJ, Rio de Janeiro, May 4, 2006. Alberto de Mello e Souza told me about a World Bank study showing that the price of a SENAI education is ten times the cost of a public school secondary education.

122. Schwartzman (2003) notes that many observers saw far less coherency in the federal government's higher-education policies.

123. These students were overwhelmingly from private schools: even as late as 2005, only 35 percent of the student body in federal universities was from public secondary schools. Reynaldo Fernandez, president of the Ministry of Education's National Institute of Educational Research, told me that the 35 percent were overwhelmingly in the lower quality federal universities (interview, Reynaldo Fernandez, president of INEP (Instituto Nacional de Estudos e Pesquisas Educacionais), MEC, Brasília, May 16, 2006).

124. Schwartzman (2003) observes that "the persistence and improvement of good quality professional education in many institutions can be explained by the early policy of not opening the public universities to unlimited admissions, as it happened in countries like Argentina, Uruguay or Mexico."

125. Schwartzman (1998; 2003). Schwartzman provides a description of typical teachers in a private higher education institution: they are "persons with little qualification or too young to have gotten a position in a public university when it was easier, compelled to teach in different places many hours a week to make ends meet. They have no career perspectives, no long-term contracts with their employers, no common identity, and very little bargaining power" (1998, 15).

126. Isaura Belloni, legislative counsel to the Comissão de Educação e Cultura, Câmara dos Deputados, told me that the original argument for the Provão was that it would reveal how bad the public universities were, and would therefore be an argument for privatization (interview, Brasília, May 18, 2006).

127. Interview, Eunice Ribeiro Durham, former secretary of higher education in the Ministry of Education in the Cardoso administration, São Paulo, April 13, 2006.

128. The private sector also offers a limited range of options: outside of a few older private universities, the private sector generally offers courses that required few resources, like law and business administration.

129. Interviews, Maurício Campos, superintendent of development, science and technology, secretary of science, technology, and innovation, State of Bahia, Salvador, June 7, 2006; Renata Procerpio, Salvador, June 6, 2006; and Edilson Freire, Salvador, June 9, 2006.

130. Interviews, Eraldo Tinoco, vice governor of Bahia and a former Bahian secretary of education and federal minister of education, Salvador, June 8, 2006; Renata Procerpio, former Bahian secretary of education, Salvador, Bahia, June 6, 2006; and Bob Verhine, professor of economics and education and director, Centro de Estudos Interdisciplinares para o Setor Público, Universidade Federal da Bahia, June 5, 2006.

131. The secretary was Renata Procerpio (interview, Salvador, June 6, 2006).

132. Interview, Edilson Freire, ombudsman of Bahia (Ouvidor Geral do Estado) and former secretary of education from 1995 to 1998, Salvador, June 9, 2006. The name of this program was "*Aquisiçons de Vagas*." I asked how it was consistent with constitutional provisions that that tried to prevent public money from going to private institutions, and he responded that the government can give money to students, just not to institutions. When Freire became secretary of education in 1995, he ended the program.

133. Interviews, Bernadette Gatti, coordinator of the Department for Education Research, Fundação Carlos Chagas, São Paulo, May 19, 2006; Rose Neubauer, former São Paulo state secretary of education, São Paulo, May 29, 2006; and Guimar Namo de Mello, former São Paulo municipal secretary of education (1981), São Paulo, June 19, 2006.

134. The phrase was Ricardo Barros's (interview, Rio de Janeiro, June 1, 2006). See note 2.
135. Indeed this work was foundational to my own thinking about the politics of education policy.
136. For this reason, as I noted in Section 3, note 33, Maria Helena Guimarães de Castro, the São Paulo state secretary of science and technology and an expert on education, told me that scholars who examine education in this period have a difficult time identifying any substantial changes (interview, São Paulo, April 28, 2006).

Chapter 7

1. In Kosack (2009), I examine the success of aid for primary education in more depth.
2. For example, Waldner (1989) and Huntington (1968).
3. See, for example, Gurr (1970).
4. In the other two—Taiwan and Ghana in the 1960s—the end of the political entrepreneurship came with the end of the elite split. In Taiwan, the elite split ended when the incumbent elites won and did not need the poor on their side anymore. The autocratic government of Kwame Nkrumah, Ghana's founding father, fell in 1966 to hostile elites, and when these elites retook the government, the poor lost their political entrepreneur.

Appendix A

1. "If two or more instances of the phenomenon under investigation have only one circumstance in common, the circumstance in which alone all the instances agree, is the cause (or effect) of the given phenomenon" (Mill 1973 [1843]).
2. This actually is the weaker version of the "unit homogeneity" assumption, which the authors call the "constant effect" version (King, Keohane, and Verba 1994).
3. I relied for Gini coefficients on the World Bank's *World Development Indicators* and on the United Nation's *World Income Inequality Database*, v. 2.0a.
4. In fact, though my findings eventually disagreed somewhat with his, my thinking was heavily influenced by David Brown's (1995; 2002) studies of education policy and spending in Brazil.

REFERENCES

Abrahão, Jorge. 2001. "Relatório do Grupo de Trabalho sobre Financiamento da Educação." *Revista Brasileira de Estudos Pedagógicos* 82 (200/201/202): 117–136.

Acemoglu, Daren, Simon Johnson, James A. Robinson, and Pierre Yared. 2004. "From Education to Democracy?" *American Economic Review* 95(2): 44–49.

Acemoglu, Daren, and James Robinson. 2005. *Economic Origins of Dictatorship and Democracy*. New York: Cambridge University Press.

Acemoglu, Daren, James A. Robinson, and Simon Johnson. 2002. "Reversal of Fortune: Geography and Institutions in the Making of the Modern World." *Quarterly Journal of Economics* 117: 1231–1294.

Addae-Mensah, Ivan. 2000. *Education in Ghana: A Tool for Social Mobility or Social Stratification?, The J.B. Danquah Memorial Lectures*. Accra: Ghana Academy of Arts and Sciences.

Addae-Mensah, Ivan, J. S. Djangmah, and C. O. Agbenyega. 1981. *Family Background and Educational Opportunities in Ghana: A Critical Look at the Secondary School Selection Mechanism—the Common Entrance Examination*. Cape Coast, Ghana: Ghana Universities Press.

Adelman, I., and C. T. Morris. 1973. *Economic Growth and Social Equity in Developing Countries*. Stanford, CA: Stanford University Press.

Adelman, Irma, Samuel Morley, Christoph Schenzler, and Stephen Vogel. 1996. "Education, Mobility, and Growth." In *Opportunity Foregone: Education in Brazil*. Edited by Nancy Birdsall and Richard H. Sabot, 319–336. Washington, DC: Johns Hopkins University Press.

Ahmed, B., and L. M. Blaug. 1973. *The Practice of Manpower Forecasting*. San Francisco: Jossey-Bass.

Altbach, P., R. Hopper, G. Psacharopoulos, D. Bloom, and H. Rosovsky. 2004. "The Task Force on Higher Education and Society." *Comparative Education Review* 48(1): 70–88.

Amankrah, J. Y., Bema Wadieh, A. Amuzu, and N. Kristensen. 1999. "Evidence from Survey on the Street Youth in Accra: Education does not matter on the Streets." *Labor Market Skills Newsletter* 2 (January): 2–5.

Amaral, Nelson C. 2003. *Financiamento da Educação Superior: Estado X Mercado*. São Paulo e Piracicaba: Cortez Editora e Editora UNIMEP.

Ames, Barry. 1994. "The Reverse Coattails Effect: Local Party Organization in the 1989 Brazilian Presidential Election." *American Political Science Review* 88(1): 95–111.

Ansell, Ben. 2005. *From the Ballot to the Blackboard? Partisan and Institutional Effects on Human Capital Policy in the OECD*. Paper prepared for the Annual Meeting of the American Political Science Association, Washington, DC.

———. 2006. *From the Ballot to the Blackboard: The Redistributive Political Economy of Education*. PhD Dissertation, Department of Government, Harvard University, Cambridge, MA.

Aryeetey, Ernest, Jane Harrigan, and Machiko Nissanke. 2000. *Economic reforms in Ghana: the miracle and the mirage*. Trenton, NJ: Africa World Press.

Ashworth-Gorden, Fiona. 1980. "Agricultural Commodity Control under Vargas in Brazil, 1930–1945." *Journal of Latin American Studies* 12(1): 87–105.

Ayisi, Gabriel A. 2001. Economic Growth and the Need for an Expanded Tertiary Education in Ghana. PhD Dissertation, Teachers College, Columbia University, New York.

Baer, Werner. 1979. *The Brazilian Economy: Its Growth and Development*. Columbus, Ohio: Grid Inc.

Baeta, C. G., J. C. Caldwell, G. E. Hurd, N. A. Ollennu, and P. A. Tetteh. 1967. *Some Aspects of Social Structure*. Edited by Walter Birmingham, I. Neustadt and E. N. Omaboe. 2 vols. Vol. 2, *A Study of Contemporary Ghana*. London: George Allen & Unwin Ltd.

Banks, Olive. 1976. *The Sociology of Education*. New York: Schocken Books.

Barro, Robert J. 1991. "Economic Growth in a Cross-Section of Countries." *Quarterly Journal of Economics* 106(2): 407–443.

———. 1999. "The Determinants of Democracy." *Journal of Political Economy* 107: S158–S183.

Barro, Robert J., and Jong-Wha Lee. 1993. "International Comparisons of Educational Attainment." *Journal of Monetary Economics* 32(3): 363–394.

———. 1994. "Losers and Winners in Economic Growth." In *Proceedings of the World Bank Annual Conference on Development Economics, 1993*. Washington, DC: World Bank.

Barros, Ricardo, R. Henriques, and R. Mendonça. 2000. "Education and Equitable Economic Development." *Economia* 1(1): 111–144.

Barros, Ricardo, Rosane Mendonça, Daniel Santos, and Giovani Quintaes. 2001. *Determinants of Educational Performance in Brazil*. Working Paper No. 834, IPEA, Rio de Janeiro, Brasil.

Bartels, Larry. 2010. *Unequal Democracy: The Political Economy of the New Gilded Age*. Princeton, NJ: Princeton University Press.

Bates, Robert. 1981. *Markets and States in Tropical Africa: The Political Basis of Agricultural Policies*. Berkeley: University of California Press.

———. 1995. "Social Dilemmas and Rational Individuals: An Assessment of the New Institutionalism." In *The New Institutional Economics and Third World Development*. Edited by John Harriss, Janet Hunter and Colin M. Lewis, 27–48. London: Routledge.

Baum, Matthew A., and David Lake. 2003. "The *Political* Economy of Growth: Democracy and Human Capital." *American Journal of Political Science* 47(2): 333–347.

Becker, Gary. 1964. *Human Capital: A Theoretical and Empirical Analysis, with Special Reference to Education*. New York: National Bureau of Economic Research (distributed by Columbia University Press).

Becker, Gary S. 1983. "A Theory of Competition Among Pressure Groups for Political Influence." *Quarterly Journal of Economics* 98: 371–400.

———. 1988. "Family Economics and Macro Behavior." *American Economic Review* 78(1): 1–13.

Becker, Gary S., and Barry R. Chiswick. 1966. "Education and the Distribution of Earnings." *American Economic Review* 56: 358–369.

Behrman, Jere R., Robert A. Pollak, and Paul Taubman. 1989. "Family Resources, Family Size, and Access to Financing for College Education." *Journal of Political Economy* 97(2): 398–419.

Bergstrom, T., D. Rubinfeld, and P. Shapiro. 1982. "Micro-Based Estimates of Demand Functions for Local School Expenditures." *Econometrica* 50: 1183–1205.

Berlin, Isaiah. 1975. "General Education." *Oxford Review of Education* 1(3): 287–292.

Bils, Mark, and Peter J. Klenow. 2000. "Does Schooling Cause Growth?" *American Economic Review* 90(5): 1160–1183.

Birdsall, Nancy. 1993. *Social Development Is Economic Development*. Policy Research Working Paper 1123, World Bank, Washington, DC.

———. 1996. "Public Spending on Higher Education in Developing Countries: Too Much or Too Little?" *Economics of Education Review* 15(4): 407–419.

Birdsall, Nancy, Barbara Bruns, and Richard H. Sabot. 1996. "Education in Brazil: Playing a Bad Hand Badly." In *Opportunity Foregone: Education in Brazil*. Edited by Nancy Birdsall and Richard H. Sabot, 7–47. Washington, DC: Johns Hopkins University Press.

Blaug, Mark. 1976. "The Empirical Status of Human Capital Theory: A Slightly Jaundiced Survey." *Journal of Economic Literature* 14(4): 827–855.

Boix, Carlos. 2003. *Democracy and Redistribution*. New York: Cambridge University Press.

Boix, Carlos, and Susan Stokes. 2003. "Endogenous Democratization." *World Politics* 55: 517–549.

Boone, Peter. 1996. "Politics and the Effectiveness of Foreign Aid." *European Economic Review* 40(2): 289–329.

Bourguignon, François, Francisco H. G. Ferreira, and Marta Menéndez. 2003. *Inequality of Outcomes and Inequality of Opportunities in Brazil.* Policy research paper 3174, World Bank, Washington, DC.

Brazil. 1927. *Annuario Estatistico do Brasil, 1912.* Rio de Janeiro: Directoria Geral de Estatistica.

Brazil, Ministério do Planejamento e Coordenação Econômica. 1965. *Programa de Ação Econômica do Governo 1964–1966.* Rio de Janeiro: IBGE.

Brown, D.S. 1999. "Reading, Writing, and Regime Type: Democracy's Impact on Primary School Enrollment." *Political Research Quarterly* 52(4): 681–707.

———. 2002. "Democracy, Authoritarianism and Education Finance in Brazil." *Journal of Latin American Studies* 34: 115–141.

Brown, D. S., and W. Hunter. 1999. "Democracy and Social Spending in Latin America, 1980–92." *American Political Science Review* 93(4): 779–790.

Brown, D. S. 1995. *Democracy, Human Capital, and Economic Growth.* PhD Dissertation, Department of Political Science, University of California, Los Angeles, Los Angeles, CA.

Bueno de Mesquita, Bruce, James Morrow, Randolph Siverson, and Alastair Smith. 2002. "Political Institutions, Policy Choice and the Survival of Leaders." *British Journal of Political Science* 32(4): 559–590.

Bueno de Mesquita, Bruce, Alastair Smith, Randolph Siverson, and James Morrow. 2003. *The Logic of Political Survival.* Cambridge, MA: MIT Press.

Busia, K. A. 1971. *The Students' Loans Scheme. Parliamentary Address,* June 7, 1971, Public Relations Department, Government of Ghana, Accra.

Calvo, Guillermo A. 1978. "Urban Unemployment and Wage Determination in LDCs: Trade Unions in the Harris-Todaro Model." *International Economic Review* 19(1): 65–81.

Card, David, and Alan B. Krueger. 1996a. "Labor Market Effects of Schooling Quality: Theory and Evidence." In *Does Money Matter? The Effect of School Resources on Student Achievement and Adult Success.* Edited by Gary Burtless, 97–140. Washington, DC: Brookings Institution.

———. 1996b. "School Resources and Student Outcomes: An Overview of the Literature and New Evidence from North and South Carolina." *Journal of Economic Perspectives* 10(4): 31–50.

Castro, Cláudio de Mauro. 1973. *Investimento em educação no Brasil: um estudo sócio-econômico de duas comunidades industriais.* Rio de Janeiro: IPEA/INPES.

———. 1975. "Academic Education Versus Technical Education." In *Education Alternatives in Latin America.* Edited by T. J. LaBelle. Los Angeles: University of California, Los Angeles, Latin American Center.

CEC/IPEA. 1987. *Relatório Anual de Acompanhamento—1987: Educação.* Brasília, Brasil: Coordenação de Educação e Cultura, Instituto de Planejamento Econômico e Social.

Chen, Jyh Jia. 2003. State Formation, Pedagogic Reform, and Textbook (De)Regulation in Taiwan, 1945–2000. PhD Dissertation, Curriculum and Instruction, University of Wisconsin, Madison, WI.

Chen, Vivien Wen Chun, and Evelyn Yu Ling Lin. 2004. *Political Exclusion of Socioeconomic Reproduction? Ethnic Educational Stratification in Taiwan.* Working Paper, Institute of European and American Studies, Academia Sinica, Taipei.

Chen, Wan Chi. 2005. "Ethnicity, Gender, and Class: Ethnic Difference in Taiwan's Educational Attainment Revisited (in Chinese)." *Taiwanese Sociology* 10 (December 2005): 1–40.

Chu, Yun Han, and Jih Wen Lin. 2001. "Political Development in 20th-Century Taiwan: State-Building, Regime Transformation and the Construction of National Identity." *The China Quarterly*: 102–129.

Coleman, James Samuel. 1966. *Equality of Educational Opportunity.* Washington, DC: U.S. Department of Health, Education, and Welfare, Office of Education.

Colonial Secretary. 2007. *Secret Memorandum on Gold Coast Independence.* Secretary of State for the Colonies 19562007. Available from http://www.learningcurve.gov.uk/empire/transcript/g3cs2s3t.htm.

Cox, Gary W. 2004. "Lies, Damned Lies, and Rational Choice Analyses." In *Problems and Methods in the Study of Politics*. Edited by Ian Shapiro, Rogers M. Smith and Tarek E. Masoud. New York: Cambridge University Press.

Cox, Gary W., and Mathew D. McCubbins. 1993. *Legislative Leviathan: Party Government in the House*. Berkeley: University of California Press.

Culpepper, Pepper. 2010. *Quiet Politics and Business Power*. New York: Cambridge University Press.

Cunha, Luiz António. 1991. *Educação, estado e democracia no Brasil*. São Paulo, Brasil: Cortez Editoria.

Cunha, Luiz António, and M. Góes. 1985. *O Golpe na Educação*. Rio de Janeiro: Zahar.

Dai, Hongchao. 1989. *Confucianism and economic development: an oriental alternative?* Washington, DC: Washington Institute Press.

Darden, Keith. Forthcoming. *Resisting Occupation: Mass Literacy and the Creation of Durable National Loyalties*. New York: Cambridge University Press.

Davenport, Christian. 2007. "State Repression and the Tyrannical Peace." *Journal of Peace Research* 44(4): 485–504.

Davies, Scott. 1995. "Leaps of Faith: Shifting Currents in Critical Sociology of Education." *American Journal of Sociology* 100(6): 1448–1478.

De Gregorio, J., and Jong-Wha Lee. 2002. "Education and Income Distribution: New Evidence from Cross-Country Data." *Review of Income and Wealth* 48: 395–416.

de Mello e Souza, Alberto. 1989. "Considerações sobre a Distribuição dos Recursos Educacionais." *Em Aberto* 42 (April/June): 31–33.

de Mello e Souza, Alberto, and Nelson do Valle Silva. 1996. "Family Background, Quality of Education and Public and Private Schools: Effects on School Transitions." In *Opportunity Foregone: Education in Brazil*. Edited by Nancy Birdsall and Richard H. Sabot, 367–384. Washington, DC: Johns Hopkins University Press.

de Oliveira Romanelli, Otaiza. 1978. *História da Educação no Brasil*. Petrópolis: Editora Vozes.

Deininger, K., L. Squire, and World Bank. 2004. Unpublished Data Provided by World Bank Based on Unit Record Data. World Bank, Washington, DC.

Denison, E.F. 1962. "Education, Economic Growth and Gaps in Information." *Journal of Political Economy* 70(5): 124–128.

Deraniyagala, S. 1995. Technical Change and Efficiency in Sri Lanka's Manufacturing Industry. PhD Dissertation, University of Oxford, Oxford, UK.

Dewey, John. 1916. *Democracy and Education*. New York: MacMillan.

Djang, T. K. 1977. *Industry and Labor in Taiwan, Monograph Series No. 10*. Nankang, Taipei, Taiwan (ROC): The Institute of Economics, Academia Sinica.

Djangmah, J. S. 2005. *Introducing Competency-Based Training (CBT) in Ghana's Technical and Vocational Education and Training (TVET) System: Issues, Challenges and Prospects*, Ministry of Education and Sports and Ministry of Manpower, Youth, and Employment, Accra.

Doner, Richard F., Bryan K. Ritchie, and Dan Slater. 2005. "Systemic Vulnerability and the Origins of Developmental States: Northeast and Southeast Asia in Comparative Perspective." *International Organization* 59: 327–361.

Downs, Anthony. 1957. *An Economic Theory of Democracy*. New York: Harper.

Estevez-Abe, Margarita, Torben Iverson, and David Soskice. 2001. "Social Protection and the Formation of Skills: A Reinterpretation of the Welfare State." In *Varieties of Capitalism: The Institutional Foundations of Comparative Advantage*. Edited by Peter Hall and David Soskice, 145–183. New York: Oxford University Press.

Evans, Peter. 1979. *Dependent Development: The Alliance of Multinational, State, and Local Capital in Brazil*. Princeton, NJ: Princeton University Press.

Ewusi, Kodwo. 1986. *Statistical Tables of the Republic of Ghana, 1950–1985, Institute of Statistical, Social, and Economic Research*. University of Ghana, Legon, Ghana.

Fei, John C. H., Gustav Ranis, and Shirley W. Y. Kuo. 1979. *Growth with Equity: The Taiwan Case*. New York: Oxford University Press.

Findlay, Ronald, and Henryk Kierzkowski. 1983. "International Trade and Human Capital: A Simple General Equilibrium Model." *Journal of Political Economy* 91(6): 957–978.

Fleischer, David V., and Robert Wesson. 1983. *Brazil in Transition*. New York: Praeger.

Fletcher, P. R., and S. C. Ribeiro. 1989. *Modeling Education System Performance with Demographic Data: An Introduction to the PROFLUXO Model*. Brasília, Brasil: Mimeo.

Flug, K., A. Spilimbergo, and E. Wachtenheim. 1998. "Investment in Education: Do Economic Volatility and Credit Constraints Matter?" *Journal of Development Economics* 55: 465–481.

FNDE. 1990. *Salário-Educação: Séries Históricas*. Brasília, Brasil: Fundo Nacional de Desenvolvimento da Educação, Ministério da Educação e Cultura.

Foster, P. J. 1963. "Secondary Schooling and Social Mobility in a West African Nation." *Sociology of Education* 37(2): 150–171.

Frey, R. Scott. 1984. "Does n-Achievement Cause Economic Development? A Cross-Lagged Panel Analysis of the McClelland Thesis." *Journal of Social Psychology* 122(1): 67–70.

Friedman, Milton. 1953. *Essays in Positive Economics*. Chicago, IL: University of Chicago Press.

———. 1962. *Capitalism and Freedom*. Chicago, IL: University of Chicago Press.

Frohlich, Norman, Joe A. Oppenheimer, and Oran A. Young. 1971. *Political Leadership and Collective Goods*. Princeton, NJ: Princeton University Press.

Gandhi, Jennifer. 2008. *Political Institutions under Dictatorship*. New York: Cambridge University Press.

Gandhi, Jennifer, and Adam Przeworski. 2007. "Authoritarian Institutions and the Survival of Autocrats." *Comparative Political Studies* 40(11): 1279–1301.

Gannicott, K. 1973. *Rates of Return to Education in Taiwan, Republic of China*. Taipei: Executive Yuan, Council for International Economic Cooperation and Development, Manpower Development Working Group.

Geddes, Barbara. 1994. *Politician's Dilemma: Building State Capacity in Latin America*. Berkeley, CA: University of California Press.

———. 1999. *The Effect of Regime Type on Authoritarian Breakdown: Empirical Test of a Game Theoretic Argument*. Paper presented at the Annual Meeting of the American Political Science Association, Atlanta, GA.

Ghana, Government of. 1962. *Ministry of Education Report for the Years 1958–1960*. Accra: Government Printing Department.

———. 1968. *The Annual Estimates for 1968–69*. Vol. VIII. Accra: Government of Ghana.

———. 1969. *The Annual Estimates for 1969–70*. Vol. XIII. Accra: Government of Ghana.

———. 1970. *The Annual Estimates for 1970–71*. Vol. VIII. Accra: Government of Ghana.

———. 1971. *Educational Statistics, 1968–69*. Accra: Ministry of Education.

———. 1973. *Educational Statistics, 1970–71*. Accra: Ministry of Education.

———. 1997. *Quarterly Digest of Statistics*. Accra, Ghana: Statistical Service, Republic of Ghana.

———. 1999. *The Annual Estimates for 1999*. Vol. X. Accra: Government of Ghana.

———. 2005a. *2003 Core Welfare Indicators Questionnaire*. Accra, Ghana: Ghana Statistical Service.

———. 2005b. *2003 Core Welfare Indicators Questionnaire (CWIQ II) Survey Report: Statistical Abstract*. Accra: Ghana Statistical Service.

Ghana Manpower Projects. 1964. *Seven-Year Development Plan*. Accra: Government of Ghana.

Gilleard, Christopher J. 1989. "The Achieving Society Revisited: A Further Analysis of the Relation Between National Economic Growth and Need Achievement." *Journal of Economic Psychology* 10(1): 21–34.

Glick, Peter, and David E. Sahn. 2006. "The demand for primary schooling in Madagascar: Price, quality, and the choice between public and private providers." *Journal of Development Economics* 79: 118–145.

Gomes-Neto, João Batista, and Eric A. Hanushek. 1996. "The Causes and Effects of Grade Repetition." In *Opportunity Foregone: Education in Brazil*. Edited by Nancy Birdsall and Richard H. Sabot, 425–460. Washington, DC: Johns Hopkins University Press.

Gradstein, Mark, Moshe Justman, and Volker Meier. 2004. *The Political Economy of Education: Implications for Growth and Inequality*. Cambridge, MA: MIT Press.

Graetz, Michael J., and Ian Shapiro. 2006. *Death by a Thousand Cuts: The Fight over Taxing Inherited Wealth*. Princeton, NJ: Princeton University Press.

Green, Donald P., and Ian Shapiro. 2004. *Pathologies of Rational Choice Theory: A Critique of Applications in Political Science*. New Haven, CT: Yale University Press.

Groseclose, Tim, and James M. Snyder, Jr. 1996. "Buying Supermajorities." *American Political Science Review* 90(2): 303–315.

Grossman, Gene M., and Elhanan Helpman. 1994. "Protection for Sale." *American Economic Review* 84(4): 833–850.

———. 2001. *Special Interest Politics.* Cambridge, MA: MIT Press.

Gurr, Ted Robert. 1970. *Why Men Rebel.* Princeton, NJ: Princeton University Press.

Gyimah-Boadi, E. 2001. "A Peaceful Turnover in Ghana." *Journal of Democracy* 12(2): 103–117.

Hacker, Jacob S., and Paul Pierson. 2010. *Winner-Take-All Politics: How Washington Made the Rich Richer—and Turned Its Back on the Middle Class.* New York: Simon and Schuster.

Hall, Peter, and David Soskice. 2001. *Varieties of Capitalism: The Institutional Foundations of Comparative Advantage.* New York: Oxford University Press.

Hanushek, Eric A. 2003. "The Failure of Input-Based Schooling Policies." *Economic Journal* 113: F64–F98.

Hanushek, Eric A., João Batista Gomes-Neto, and Ralph W. Harbison. 1996. "Efficiency-Enhancing Investments in School Quality." In *Opportunity Foregone: Education in Brazil.* Edited by Nancy Birdsall and Richard H. Sabot, 385–424. Washington, DC: Johns Hopkins University Press.

Harbison, F., and C. A. Myers. 1964. *Education, Manpower, and Economic Growth.* New York: McGraw-Hill.

Harbison, Ralph W., and Eric A. Hanushek. 1992. *Educational Performance of the Poor: Lessons from Rural Northeastern Brazil.* New York: Oxford University Press.

Harris, John R., and Michael P. Todaro. 1970. "Migration, Unemployment and Development: A Two-Sector Analysis." *American Economic Review* 60(1): 126–142.

Hou, Chi-ming. 1978. "Manpower Planning and Development in Taiwan." *Industry of Free China* (August and September): 8–22.

Hsiao, Hsin Huang, and Alvin Y. So. 1996. "The Taiwan-Mainland Economic Nexus: Sociopolitical Origins, State-Society Impacts, and Future Prospects." *Bulletin of Concerned Asian Scholars* 28(1): 3–12.

Huntington, Samuel P. 1968. *Political Order in Changing Societies.* New Haven: Yale University Press.

Hurd, G. E., and T. J. Johnson. 1966. Preliminary, unpublished study of VI formers and university students, University of Ghana, Legon-Accra.

Hyman, Herbert. 1953. "The Value Systems of Different Classes: A Social Psychological Contribution to the Analysis of Stratification." In *Class Status and Power.* Edited by Reinhard Bendix and Seymour Martin Lipset, 426–442. Glencoe, IL: Free Press.

IBGE. 1972. *Anuário Estatístico do Brasil.* Rio de Janeiro, Brasil: Instituto Brasileiro de Geografia e Estatística.

IPEA. 2006. *Dados Macroeconômicos e Regionais,* Instituto de Pesquisa Econômica Aplicada, Brasília, http://www.ipeadata.gov.br.

Iverson, Torben, and David Soskice. 2006. *Distribution and Redistribution: The Shadow of the Nineteenth Century.* Paper presented to the 2006 Annual Meeting of the American Political Science Association, Philadelphia, PA.

Jacoby, Neil H. 1967. *U.S. Aid to Taiwan: A Study of Foreign Aid, Self-help, and Development.* New York: F. A. Praeger.

Jamison, D., and P. Moock. 1984. "Farmer Education and Farm Efficiency in Nepal: The Role of Schooling, Extension Services, and Cognitive Skills." *World Development* 12(1): 67–86.

Jensen, Aurthur R. 1981. "Raising the IQ: The Ramey and Haskins Study." *Intelligence* 5: 29–40.

Jones, Philip. 1978. "The Appeal of the Political Entrepreneur." *British Journal of Political Science* 8(4): 498–504.

Kanbur, Ravi. 1994. *Welfare Economics, Political Economy, and Policy Reform in Ghana.* Policy Research Working Paper 1381, World Bank, Accra.

Kao, Charles H. C., Y. C. Hsu, and Ming-Chung Lee. 1976. "An Empirical Analysis of Manpower Utilization of Recent College Graduates: A Case Study of Taiwan." *Industry of Free China:* 8–29.

Keck, Margaret E. 1992. *The Workers' Party and Democratization in Brazil.* New Haven: Yale Univ. Press.

Keteku, Nancy. 2005. *AACRAO EDGE Profile: Ghana,* U.S. State Department, Accra.

Killick, Tony. 1966. "The Economics of Cocoa." In *A Study of Contemporary Ghana*. Edited by Walter Birmingham, I. Neustadt and E. N. Omaboe, 365–390. London: George Allen & Unwin Ltd.

Killick, Tony, E. N. Omaboe, and Robert Szereszewski. 1966. *The Economy of Ghana*. Edited by Walter Birmingham, I. Neustadt and E. N. Omaboe. 2 vols. Vol. 1, *A Study of Contemporary Ghana*. London: George Allen & Unwin Ltd.

Kimble, D. 1963. *A Political History of Ghana, 1850–1928*. Oxford: Clarendon Press.

King, Gary, Robert O. Keohane, and Sidney Verba. 1994. *Designing Social Inquiry: Scientific Inference in Qualitative Research*. Princeton, NJ: Princeton University Press.

Knight, Jack. 1992. *Institutions and Social Conflict*. Cambridge, UK: Cambridge University Press.

Kosack, Stephen. 2009. "Realizing Education For All: Defining and Using the Political Will to Invest in Primary Education." *Comparative Education* 45(4): 495–523.

Kraus, J. 1979. "Strikes and Labor Power in Ghana." *Development and Change* 10(2): 259–286.

Krishna, Anirudh. 2009. "Why Don't 'the Poor' Make Common Cause? The Importance of Subgroups." *Journal of Development Studies* 45(6): 947–965.

Kuo, Shirley W. Y., Gustav Ranis, and John C. H. Fei. 1981. *The Taiwan Success Story: Rapid Growth with Improved Distribution in the Republic of China, 1952–1979*. Boulder, CO: Westview Press.

Kuznets, Simon. 1955. "Economic Growth and Income Inequality." *American Economic Review* 45: 1–28.

Kwakwa, Margaret. 1973. *Ghanaian Times*, March 14.

Lake, David, and Matthew A. Baum. 2001. "The Invisible Hand of Democracy: Political Control and the Provision of Public Services." *Comparative Political Studies* 34(6): 587–621.

Lam, David, and Deborah Levinson. 1991. "Declining Inequality in Schooling in Brazil and its Effects on Inequality in Earnings." *Journal of Development Economics* 37: 199–226.

Landry, Pierre F. 2008. *Decentralized Authoritarianism in China: The Communist Party's Control of Local Elites in the Post-Mao Era*. New York: Cambridge University Press.

Leal, Maria Cristina. 1990. *Os Des (mandos) do Clientelismo de Estado sobre os Recursos Públicos da Educação de 1° e 2° Graus*. PhD Dissertation, Universidade Federal do Rio de Janeiro, Rio de Janeiro, Brasil.

Leite, Raimundo Hélio, and José de Anchieta Esmeraldo Barreto. 1983. "O Comportamento Institucional da Secretaria de Educação do Ceará." *Revista Brasileira de Administração da Educação* 1 (January/June): 90–119.

Lerner, Abba P. 1952. "Factor Prices and International Trade." *Economica* 19: 1–15.

Levitsky, Steven, and Lucan A. Way. 2002. "The Rise of Competitive Authoritarianism." *Journal of Democracy* 13(2): 51–65.

———. 2010. *Competitive Authoritarianism: Hybrid Regimes After the Cold War*. New York: Cambridge University Press.

Levy, Gilat. 2005. "The Politics of Public Provision of Education." *Quarterly Journal of Economics* 120(4): 1507–1534.

———. 2004. "A Model of Political Parties." *Journal of Economic Theory* 115(2): 250–277.

Levy, Gilat, and Raquel Fernández. 2007. Diversity and Redistribution. Working paper, London School of Economics, London.

Lewis, W. Arthur. 1953. *Report on Industrialization and the Gold Coast*. Accra, Gold Coast: Government Printing Department.

———. 1954. "Economic Development with Unlimited Supplies of Labour." *Manchester School of Economic and Social Studies* 22(2): 139–191.

Li, K. T. 1981. *The Evolution of Policy Behind Taiwan's Development Success*. New Haven, CT: Yale University Press.

Library of Congress. 1994. *Ghana: A Country Study*. Washington, DC: Department of the Army.

Lindblom, Charles Edward. 1977. *Politics and Markets: The World's Political Economic Systems*. New York: Basic Books.

Lipset, Seymour Martin. 1959. "Some Social Requisites of Democracy: Economic Development and Political Legitimacy." *American Political Science Review* 53: 69–105.

Ljungqvist, Lars. 1993. "Economic Underdevelopment: The Case of a Missing Market for Human Capital." *Journal of Development Economics* 40: 219–239.

Lohmann, Susanne. 1994. "The Dynamics of Informational Cascades: The Monday Demonstrations in Leipzig, East Germany, 1989–91." *World Politics* 47(1): 42–101.

Lucas, Robert E. 1988. "On the Mechanics of Economic Development." *Journal of Monetary Economics* 21: 3–42.

Luoh, Ming-Ching. 2001. "Differences in Educational Attainment across Ethnic and Gender Groups in Taiwan." *Taiwan Economic Review* 29(2): 117–152.

———. 2003. "The Ethnic Bias in Recruitment Examinations for the Civil Service in Taiwan." *Taiwan Economic Review* 31(1): 87–106.

Lust-Okar, Ellen. 2005. *Structuring Conflict in the Arab World: Incumbents, Opponents, and Institutions*. New York: Cambridge University Press.

Mainwaring, Scott. 1986. "The Transition to Democracy in Brazil." *Journal of Interamerican Studies and World Affairs* 28(1): 149–179.

Mankiw, Gregory D., D. Romer, and D. N. Weil. 1992. "A Contribution to the Empirics of Economic Growth." *Quarterly Journal of Economics* 107: 407–437.

Manu, Emmanuel Osei. 1998. "Problems of Higher Education." *Daily Graphic*, July 25.

Marshall, M. G., and K. Jaggers. 2000. *Polity IV Project*. College Park, MD: University of Maryland Press.

Mayda, Anna Marie. 2006. "Who is Against Immmigration? A Cross-Country Investigation of Individual Attitudes toward Immigrants." *The Review of Economics and Statistics* 88(3): 510–530.

Mayhew, David R. 1974. *Congress: The Electoral Connection*. New Haven: Yale University Press.

Mazur, Allan, and Eugene Rosa. 1977. "An Empirical Test of McClelland's 'Achieving Society' Theory." *Social Forces* 55(3): 769–774.

McClelland, David C. 1961. *The Achieving Society*. Princeton, NJ: Van Nostrand.

McPheeters, Alphonso A. 1957. "The Gold Coast Begins Self-Government." *The Phylon Quarterly* 18(1): 35–41.

McWilliam, H.O.A. 1959. *The Development of Education in Ghana: An Outline*. London: Longmans Green and Co Ltd.

Meltzer, Allan H., and Scott F. Richard. 1981. "A Rational Theory of the Size of Government." *Journal of Political Economy* 89(5): 914–927.

Mill, J. S. 1973 [1843]. "A System of Logic, Book III, Chapter viii." In *Collected Works of J. S. Mill*. Edited by J. M. Robson. Toronto: University of Toronto Press.

Mincer, Jacob. 1974. *Schooling, Experience, and Earnings*. New York: Columbia University Press.

Moe, Terry M. 1988. *The Organization of Interests: Incentives and the Internal Dynamics of Political Interest Groups*. Chicago: University of Chicago Press.

Moore, Barrington. 1966. *Social Origins of Dictatorship and Democracy: Lord and Peasant in the Making of the Modern World*. Boston: Beacon Press.

Mosley, Paul, J. Hudson, and S. Horrel. 1987. "Aid, the Public Sector and the Market in Less Developed Countries." *Economic Journal* 97(387): 616–641.

Mulligan, Casey B., Ricard Gil, and Xavier Sala-i-Martin. 2004. "Do Democracies Have Different Public Policies than Nondemocracies?" *Journal of Economic Perspectives* 18(1): 51–74.

Nimako, Kwame. 1991. *Economic Change and Political Conflict in Ghana, 1600–1990*. Amsterdam: Tinbergen Institute.

Noll, Roger. 1989. "Economic Perspectives on the Politics of Regulation." In *Handbook of Industrial Organization*. Edited by R. Schmalensee and R. Willig, 1253–1287. New York: Elsevier Science Publishers.

Nooruddin, Irfan. 2011. *Coalition Politics and Economic Development: Credibility and the Strength of Weak Governments*. New York: Cambridge University Press.

North, Douglass Cecil. 1990. *Institutions, Institutional Change, and Economic Performance: The Political Economy of Institutions and Decisions*. Cambridge, UK and New York: Cambridge University Press.

O'Neil, Kevin. 2003. *Brain Drain and Gain: The Case of Taiwan* 2003 [cited September 2003]. Available from http://www.migrationinformation.org.

OECD. 2003. *Literacy Skills for the World of Tomorrow: Further Results from PISA 2000*. Paris: Organization for Economic Cooperation and Development.

Olson, Mancur. 1965. *The Logic of Collective Action: Public Goods and the Theory of Groups*. Cambridge, MA: Harvard University Press.

———. 1984. *The Rise and Decline of Nations: Economic Growth, Stagflation, and Social Rigidities*. New Haven: Yale University Press.

Paiva, Ruy Millar. 1961. "The Development of Brazilian Agriculture, 1945–1960." *Journal of Farm Economics* 43(5): 1092–1100.

Pastore, José, and Hélio Zylberstajn. 1996. "Social Mobility: The Role of Education in Determining Social Class." In *Opportunity Foregone: Education in Brazil*. Edited by Nancy Birdsall and Richard H. Sabot, 289–318. Washington, DC: Johns Hopkins University Press.

Peltzman, Samuel. 1976. "Toward a General Theory of Regulation." *Journal of Law and Economics* 19(2): 211–248.

Pepinsky, Thomas. 2009. *Economic Crises and the Breakdown of Authoritarian Regimes: Indonesia and Malaysia in Comparative Perspective*. New York: Cambridge University Press.

Pereira, Luiz Bresser. 1984. *Development and Crisis in Brazil, 1930–1983*. Boulder, CO: Westview Press.

Perotti, R. 1996. "Growth, Income Distribution, and Democracy: What the Data Say." *Journal of Economic Growth* 1: 149–187.

Pierson, Paul. 2000. "Increasing Returns, Path Dependence, and the Study of Politics." *American Political Science Review* 94(2): 251–267.

———. 2004. *Politics in Time: History, Institutions, and Social Analysis*. Princeton, NJ: Princeton University Press.

Plank, David N. 1990. "The Politics of Basic Education Reform in Brazil." *Comparative Education Review* 34(4): 538–559.

———. 1996. *The Means of Our Salvation: Public Education in Brazil, 1930–1995*. Boulder, CO: Westview Press.

Plank, David N., José Amaral Sobrinho, and Antonio Carlos da Ressurreição Xavier. 1996. "Why Brazil Lags Behind in Educational Development." In *Opportunity Foregone: Education in Brazil*. Edited by Nancy Birdsall and Richard H. Sabot, 117–146. Washington, DC: Johns Hopkins University Press.

Plank, David N., and Robert E. Verhine. 1995. "Schooling for Some: Local Finance Commitment to Basic Education in Bahia, Brazil." *Education Economics* 3(1): 43–60.

Pritchett, Lant. 2001. *Ought Ain't Is: An Economist's Midnight Thoughts on Education*. Working Paper, Kennedy School of Government, Harvard University, Cambridge, MA.

———. 2006. *Let Their People Come: Breaking the Gridlock on Global Labor Mobility*. Washington, DC: Center for Global Development.

———. 2009. "The Policy Irrelevance of the Economics of Education: Is 'Normative as Positive' Useless, or Worse?" In *What Works in Development? Thinking Big and Thinking Small*. Edited by William Easterly and Jessica Cohen, 130–164. Washington, DC: Brookings Institution Press.

Przeworski, Adam. 1991. *Democracy and the Market: Political and Economic Reforms in Eastern Europe and Latin America*. Cambridge, UK: Cambridge University Press.

———. 2004. "Institutions Matter?" *Government and Opposition* 39(2): 527–540.

Przeworski, Adam, Michael Alvarez, José Antonio Cheibub, and Fernando Limongi. 2000. *Democracy and Development: Political Institutions and Material Well-being in the World, 1950–1990*. Cambridge, UK: Cambridge University Press.

Przeworski, Adam, and Michael Wallerstein. 1988. "Structural Dependence of the State on Capital." *American Political Science Review* 82(1): 11–29.

Psacharopoulos, George. 1973. *Returns to Education*. New York: American Elsevier.

———. 1981. "Returns to Education: An Updated International Comparison." *Comparative Education* 17(3): 321–341.

———. 1994. "Returns to Investment in Education: A Global Update." *World Development* 22(9): 1325–1343.

Ranis, Gustav. 1979. "Industrial Development." In *Economic Growth and Structural Change in Taiwan: The Postwar Experience of the Republic of China*. Edited by Walter Galenson, 519. Ithaca, NY: Cornell University Press.

Ranis, Gustav, Frances Stewart, and Alejandro Ramirez. 2000. "Economic Growth and Human Development." *World Development* 28(2): 197–219.

Republic of China. 1965. *Taiwan Statistical Data Book*. Taipei: Council for International Economic Cooperation and Development, Executive Yuan, Republic of China.

———. 1974. *Analysis of Rates of Return to Education in Taiwan (in Chinese)*, Committee on Educational Planning, Taipei.

———. 1977. *Analysis of Rates of Return to Education in Taiwan (in Chinese)*, Committee on Educational Planning, Taipei.

———. 1982. *Taiwan Statistical Data Book*. Taipei: Council for Economic Planning and Development, Executive Yuan, Republic of China.

———. 1988. *Education Statistics of the Republic of China*. Taipei: Ministry of Education, Republic of China.

———. 2005a. *Consumer Price Index*. Taipei: Directorate-General of Budget, Accounting, and Statistics, Executive Yuan, Republic of China.

———. 2005b. *Education Statistics of the Republic of China*. Taipei: Ministry of Education, Republic of China.

———. 2007. *Figures of Interest (93SNA)*, Directorate-General of Budget, Accounting, and Statistics, Executive Yuan, Republic of China, Taipei.

Rigger, Shelley. 1999. *Politics in Taiwan: Voting for Democracy*. New York: Routledge.

Riker, William H. 1962. *The Theory of Political Coalitions*. New Haven: Yale University Press.

———. 1986. *The Art of Political Manipulation*. New Haven: Yale University Press.

Rodrik, Dani. 1999. "Democracies Pay Higher Wages." *Quarterly Journal of Economics* 114: 707–738.

Rogowski, Ronald. 1989. *Commerce and Coalitions: How Trade Affects Domestic Political Alignments*. Princeton, NJ: Princeton University Press.

Romer, Paul. 1986. "Increasing Returns and Long-Run Growth." *Journal of Political Economy* 94(5): 1002–1036.

Rosovsky, Henry, David Bloom, and David Steven. 2000. *Higher Education and Developing Countries: Peril and Promise*, World Bank, Washington, DC.

———. 2002. "We must make efforts to level the playing field." *Times Higher Education Supplement*, www.timeshighereducation.co.uk/story.asp?storyCode=167947&sectioncode=26.

Ross, Michael. 2006. "Is Democracy Good for the Poor?" *American Journal of Political Science* 50(4): 860–874.

Rostow, W. W. 1961. *The Stages of Economic Growth, a Non-Communist Manifesto*. Cambridge, UK: Cambridge University Press.

Rozman, Gilbert. 1991. *The East Asian Region: Confucian Heritage and Its Modern Adaptation*. Princeton, NJ: Princeton University Press.

Rubinfeld, D., and P. Shapiro. 1989. "Micro-Estimation of the Demand for Schooling." *Regional Science and Urban Economics* 19: 381–398.

Rubinfeld, D., P. Shapiro, and J. Roberts. 1987. "Tiebout Bias and the Demand for Local Public Schooling." *Review of Economics and Statistics* 69: 426–437.

Rudra, N. 2002. "Globalization and the decline of the welfare state in less-developed countries." *International Organization* 56(2): 411–445.

———. 2008. *Globalization And The Race To The Bottom In Developing Countries: Who Really Gets Hurt?* New York: Cambridge University Press.

Samuels, David. 2004. "From Socialism to Social Democracy: Party Organization and the Transformation of the Workers' Party in Brazil." *Comparative Political Studies* 37: 999–1024.

Samuelson, Paul A. 1948. "International Trade and the Equalisation of Factor Prices." *Economic Journal* 58: 163–184.

———. 1949. "International Factor-Price Equalisation Once Again." *Economic Journal* 59: 181–197.

Schneider, Mark, and Paul Teske. 1992. "Toward A Theory of the Political Entrepreneur: Evidence from Local Government." *American Political Science Review* 86(3): 737–747.

Schultz, T. Paul. 1988. "Education Investments and Returns." In *Handbook of Development Economics*. Edited by H. Chenery and T. N. Srinivasan, 543–630. Amsterdam: North Holland.

Schultz, Theodore W. 1961. "Investment in Human Capital." *American Economic Review* 51(1): 1–17.
———. 1963. *The Economic Value of Education*. New York: Columbia University Press.
Schwartzman, Simon. 1989. *Education in Latin America: A Perspective From Brazil*. Lecture, School of Education, University of California, Los Angeles, CA.
———. 1991. *The Future of Higher Education in Brazil*. Paper presented to the XVI International Congress, April 4–6, 1991, Latin American Studies Association, Washington, DC.
———. 1998. *Higher Education in Brazil: The Stakeholders*. LCSHD Paper Series 28, Human Resources Department, World Bank, Washington, DC.
———. 2003. *The Challenges of Education in Brazil*. Working paper, Centre for Brazilian Studies, University of Oxford, Oxford, UK.
———. 2004. *The National Assessment of Courses in Brazil, Policy Analysis series, Public Policy for Academic Quality Research Program*, University of North Carolina, Chapel Hill, NC.
Schwartzman, Simon, and L. Klein. 1993. "Higher Education Policies in Brazil: 1970–90." *Higher Education* 25(1): 21–34.
Sen, Amartya. 1999. *Development as Freedom*. New York: Alfred A. Knopf.
Shapiro, Ian. 2002. "Why the Poor don't Soak the Rich." *Daedalus* 131(1): 118–128.
Shiman, D. A. 1971. "Selection for Secondary School in Ghana: The Problem of Choosing the Most Capable." *West African Journal of Education* 15(3): 173.
Skidmore, Thomas E. 1988. *The Politics of Military Rule in Brazil, 1964–85*. New York: Oxford University Press.
Skidmore, Thomas E., and Peter H. Smith. 1997. *Modern Latin America*. 4th ed. New York: Oxford University Press.
Skocpol, Theda. 1995. *Protecting Soldiers and Mothers: The Political Origins of Social Policy in United States*. Cambridge, MA: Belnap Press.
Sobrinho, José Amaral. 1985. *The Economic and the Political in the Brazilian Education System, 1956–1982*. PhD Dissertation, School of Education, Stanford University, Stanford, CA.
Solow, Robert M. 1957. "Technical Change and the Aggregate Production Function." *Review of Economics and Statistics* 39: 312–320.
Souza, Celina. 1997. *Constitutional Engineering in Brazil: The Politics of Federalism and Decentralization*. New York: St. Martin's Press.
Stasavage, David. 2005. "Democracy and Education Spending in Africa." *American Journal of Political Science* 49(2): 343–358.
Stepan, Alfred. 1971. *The Military in Politics: Changing Patterns in Brazil*. Princeton, NJ: Princeton University Press.
———. 1978. "Political Leadership and Regime Breakdown: Brazil." In *The Breakdown of Democratic Regimes: Latin America*. Edited by Juan Linz and Alfred Stepan, 110–137. Baltimore, MD: Johns Hopkins University Press.
Stigler, G. 1971. "The Theory of Economic Regulation." *Bell Journal of Economics and Management Science* 2: 137–146.
Stolper, Wolfgang F., and Paul A. Samuelson. 1941. "Protection and Real Wages." *Review of Economic Studies* 9: 58–73.
Sylwester, K. 2000. "Income Inequality, Education Expenditures, and Growth." *Journal of Development Economics* 63: 379–398.
Telles, Jover. 1962. *O Movimento Sindical no Brasil*. Rio de Janeiro: Editoria Vitória.
Tignor, Robert L. 2006. *W. Arthur Lewis and the Birth of Development Economics*. Princeton, NJ: Princeton University Press.
Tsurumi, E. Patricia. 1977. *Japanese Colonial Education in Taiwan, 1895–1945*. Cambridge, MA: Harvard University Press.
Tullock, Gordon. 1971. "The Charity of the Uncharitable." *Western Economic Journal* 9: 379–392.
Turkheimer, Eric, Andreana Haley, Mary Waldron, Brian D'Onofrio, and Irving I. Gottesman. 2003. "Socioeconomic Status Modifies Heritability of IQ in Young Children." *Pcychological Science* 14(6): 623–628.
Turkheimer, Eric, and Mary Waldron. 2000. "Nonshared Environment: A Theoretical, Methodological, and Quantitative Review." *Psychological Bulletin* 126: 78–108.

UNDP. 1990. *Human Development Report*. New York: Oxford University Press for the United Nations Development Program.

United Nations. 1968. *Demographic Yearbook*. New York: United Nations.

Vahl, Teodoro Rogério. 1980. *A privatização do ensino superior no Brasil: causas e conseqüências*. Editora Lundardelli, Co-Edição UFSC.

Velloso, Jacques. 1988. "A Nova Lei de Diretrizes e Bases de Educação e o Financiamento do Ensino: Pontos de Partida." *Educação e Sociedade* 30 (August): 5–42.

Verhine, Robert E. 1993. *Educational Alternatives and the Determination of Earnings in Brazilian Industry*. Frankfurt: Peter Lang.

Verhine, Robert E., and Dora Leal Rosa. 2002. *Desempenho e Impacto do Fundef no Estado da Bahia*. Working paper, Universidade Federal da Bahia, Salvador, Bahia.

Vreeland, James Raymond. 2003. *The IMF and Economic Development*. New York: Cambridge University Press.

———. 2008. "Political Institutions and Human Rights: Why Dictatorships Enter into the United Nations Convention Against Torture." *International Organization* 62(1): 65–101.

Wade, Robert. 1990. *Governing the Market: Economic Theory and the Role of Government in East Asian Industrialization*. Princeton, NJ: Princeton University Press.

Waldner, David. 1999. *State Building and Late Development*. Ithaca, NY: Cornell University Press.

Wan, H. Y. 1972. *An Economic Analysis of Technical and Vocational Education in Taiwan*. Paper presented at the Sino-American Conference on Manpower, Taiwan, Taipei.

Weber, Max. 1952 [1904]. *The Protestant Ethic and the Spirit of Capitalism*. New York: Scribner.

Weiss, Harry. 1964. "Manpower Problems and Programs on Taiwan." *Industry of Free China* (March 1964): 9–18.

Wereko-Brobby, C. 1998. "Capacity Wastage." *The Crusading Guide* 25 (July 21–27).

Wiseman, J. 1987. "Public Finance in Education." In *Economics of Education: Research and Studies*. Edited by George Psacharopoulos, 436–439. Oxford: Pergamon Press.

Woo, Jennie Hay. 1991. "Education and Economic Growth in Taiwan: A Case of Successful Planning." *World Development* 19(8): 1029–1044.

World Bank. 1979. *Brazil: Human Resources Special Report, A World Bank Country Study*. Washington, DC: World Bank.

———. 1993. *The East Asian Miracle: Economic Growth and Public Policy*. New York: Published for the World Bank by Oxford University Press.

———. 1995. *Priorities and Strategies for Education. A World Bank Review, Development in Practice Series*. Washington, DC: World Bank.

———. 2002a. *Brazil: Municipal Education: Resources, Incentives, and Results*. Vol. II, Research Report 24413-BR. Washington, DC: World Bank.

———. 2002b. *Constructing Knowledge Societies: New Challenges for Tertiary Education*. Washington, DC: World Bank.

———. 2004a. *Books, Buildings, and Learning Outcomes: An Impact Evaluation of World Bank Support to Basic Education in Ghana*. Washington, DC: World Bank Operations Evaluation Department.

———. 2004b. *Brazil: Equitable, Competitive, Sustainable: Contributions for Debate*. Washington, DC: World Bank.

———. 2007. *World Development Indicators*. World Bank, Washington, DC.

World Bank, and IDB. 2000. *Secondary Education in Brazil: Time to Move Forward*. Report No. 19409-BR. Washington, DC: World Bank.

Wu, Chung-li. 2003. "Local Factions and the Kuomintang in Taiwan's Electoral Politics." *International Relations of the Asia-Pacific* 3: 89–111.

Xavier, Antonio Carlos da Ressurreição, and Antonio Emílio Sendim Marques. 1987. *Quanto Custa um Aluno nas Escolas que os Brasileiros Freqüentam*. Brasília, Brasil: IPEA.

Young, Yi Rong. 1995. "Taiwan." In *Education and Development in East Asia*. Edited by Paul Morris and Anthony Sweeting, 105–124. New York: Garland Pub.

Zweifel, T. D., and P. Navia. 2000. "Democracy, Dictatorship, and Infant Mortality." *Journal of Democracy* 11: 99–114.

INDEX